TOGARI

TOGARI

TOGARI
VOL. 1

STORY AND ART BY NATSUME YOSHINORI

TRANSLATION/HIROKO YODA AND MATT ALT
TOUCH-UP ART & LETTERING/STEVE DUTRO
DESIGN/SAM ELZWAY
EDITOR/ANDY NAKATANI

EDITOR IN CHIEF, BOOKS/ALVIN LU
EDITOR IN CHIEF, MAGAZINES/MARC WEIDENBAUM
VP OF PUBLISHING LICENSING/RIKA INOUYE
VP OF SALES/GONZALO FERREYRA
SR. VP OF MARKETING/LIZA COPPOLA
PUBLISHER/HYOE NARITA

PRINTED IN THE U.S.A.

PUBLISHED BY VIZ MEDIA, LLC
P.O. BOX 77010
SAN FRANCISCO, CA 94107

10 9 8 7 6 5 4 3 2 1
FIRST PRINTING, JULY 2007

store.viz.com   www.viz.com

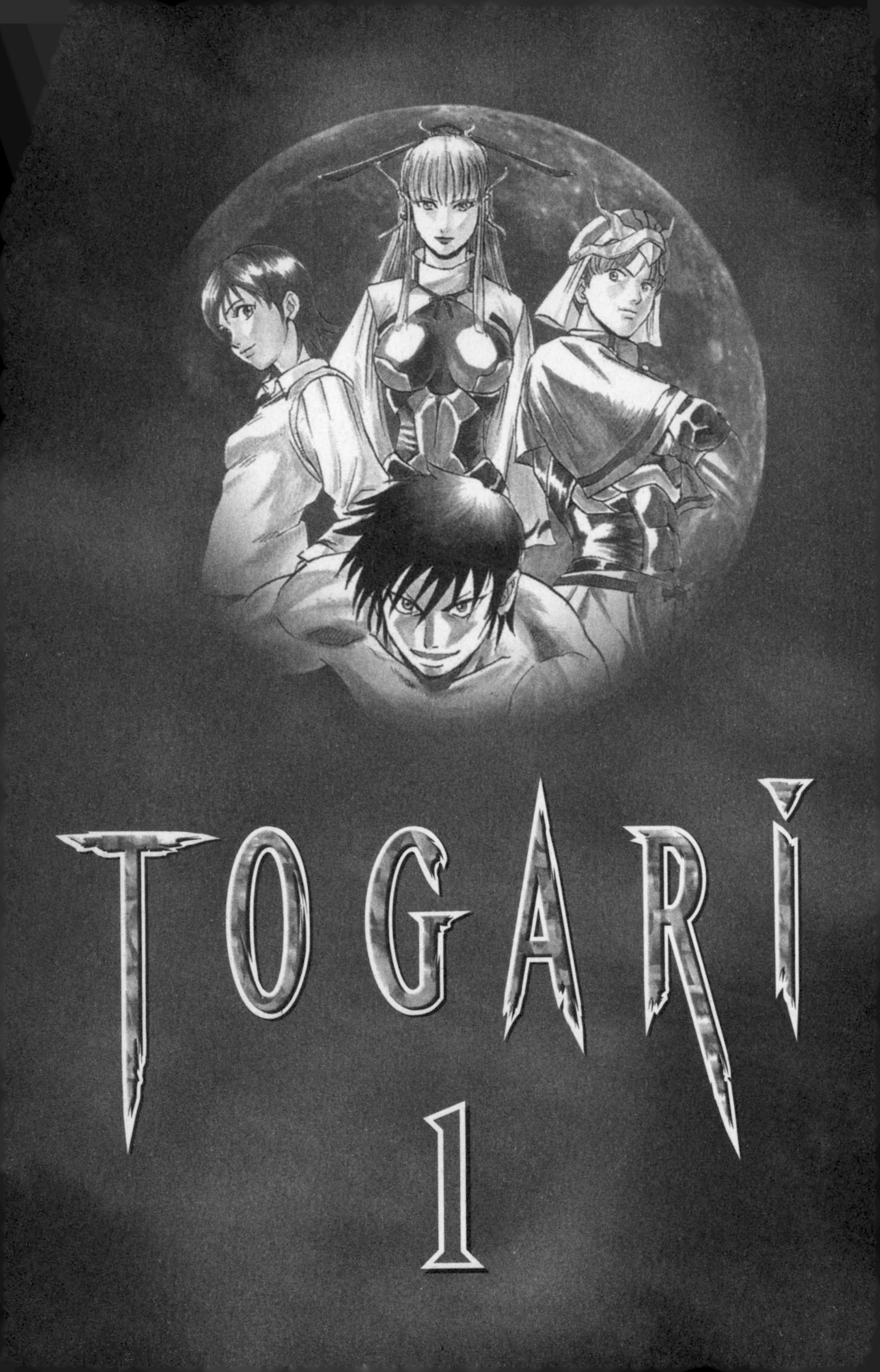
TOGARI
1

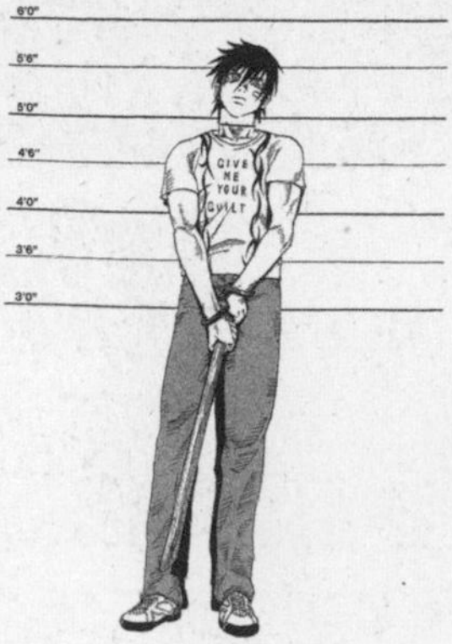
6'0"
5'6"
5'0"
4'6"
4'0"
3'6"
3'0"
GIVE ME YOUR GUILT

TOGARI Vol. 1

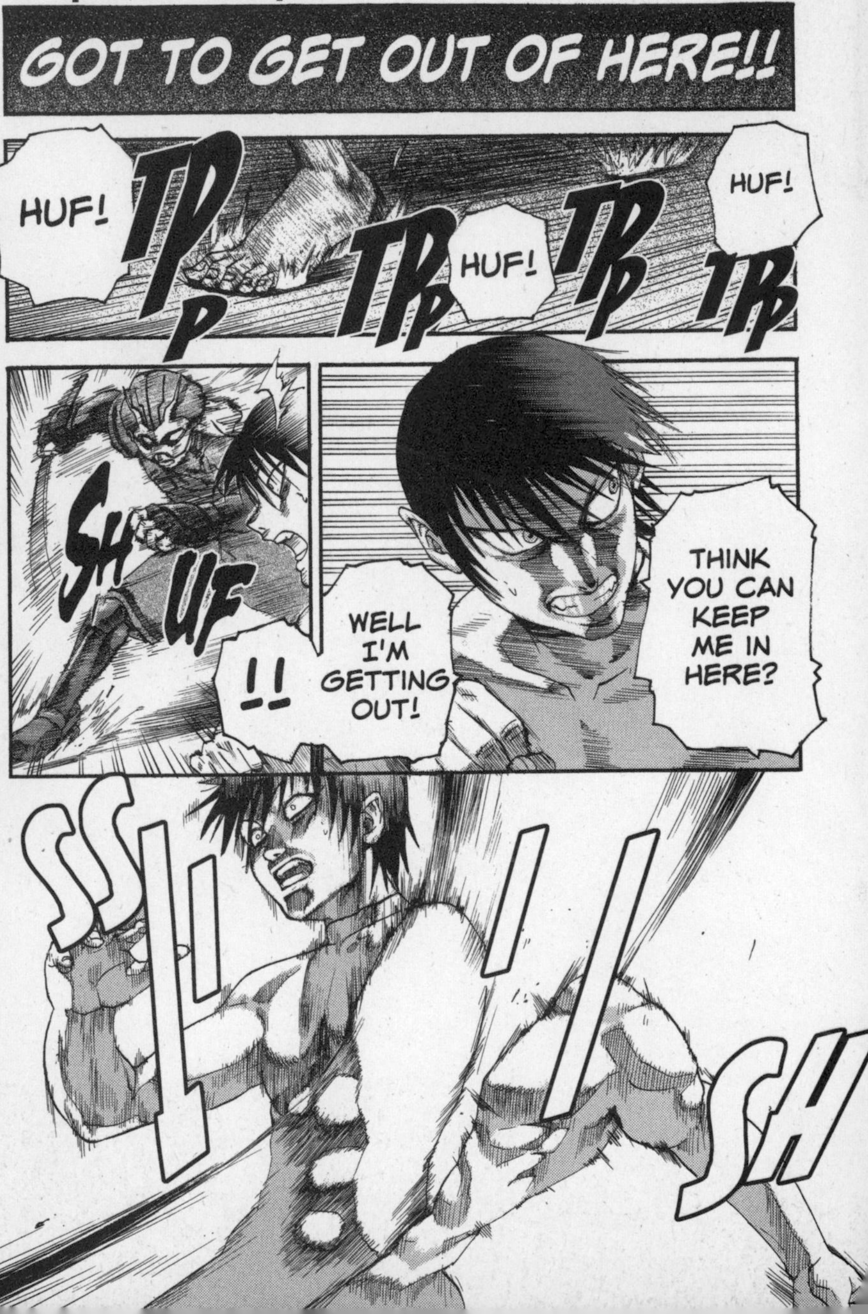
GOT TO GET OUT OF HERE!!
HUF!
TR
TP
HUF!
TP
TP
HUF!
THINK YOU CAN KEEP ME IN HERE?
WELL I'M GETTING OUT!
!!
SHUF
SH
SSH

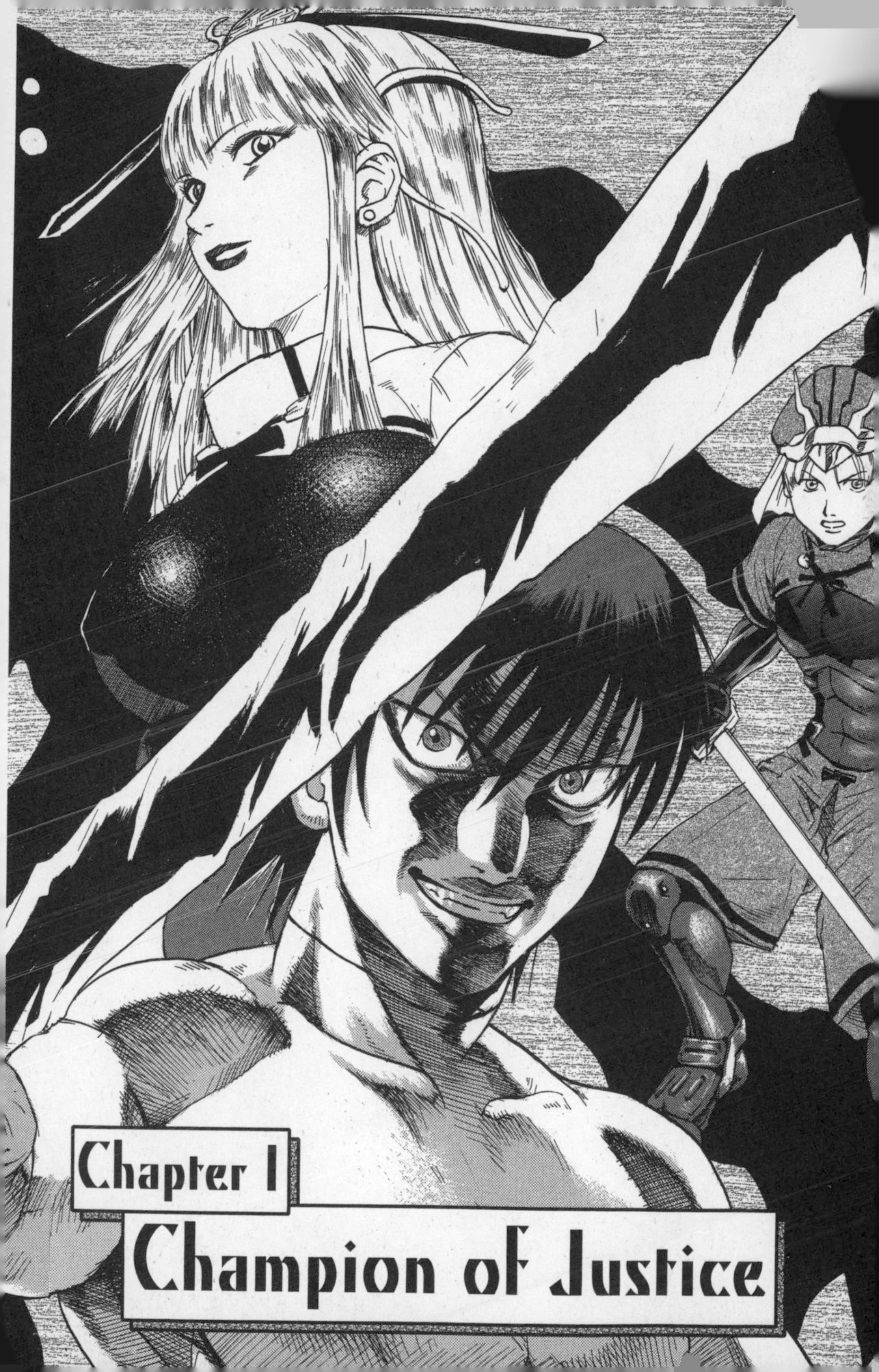
Chapter 1
Champion of Justice

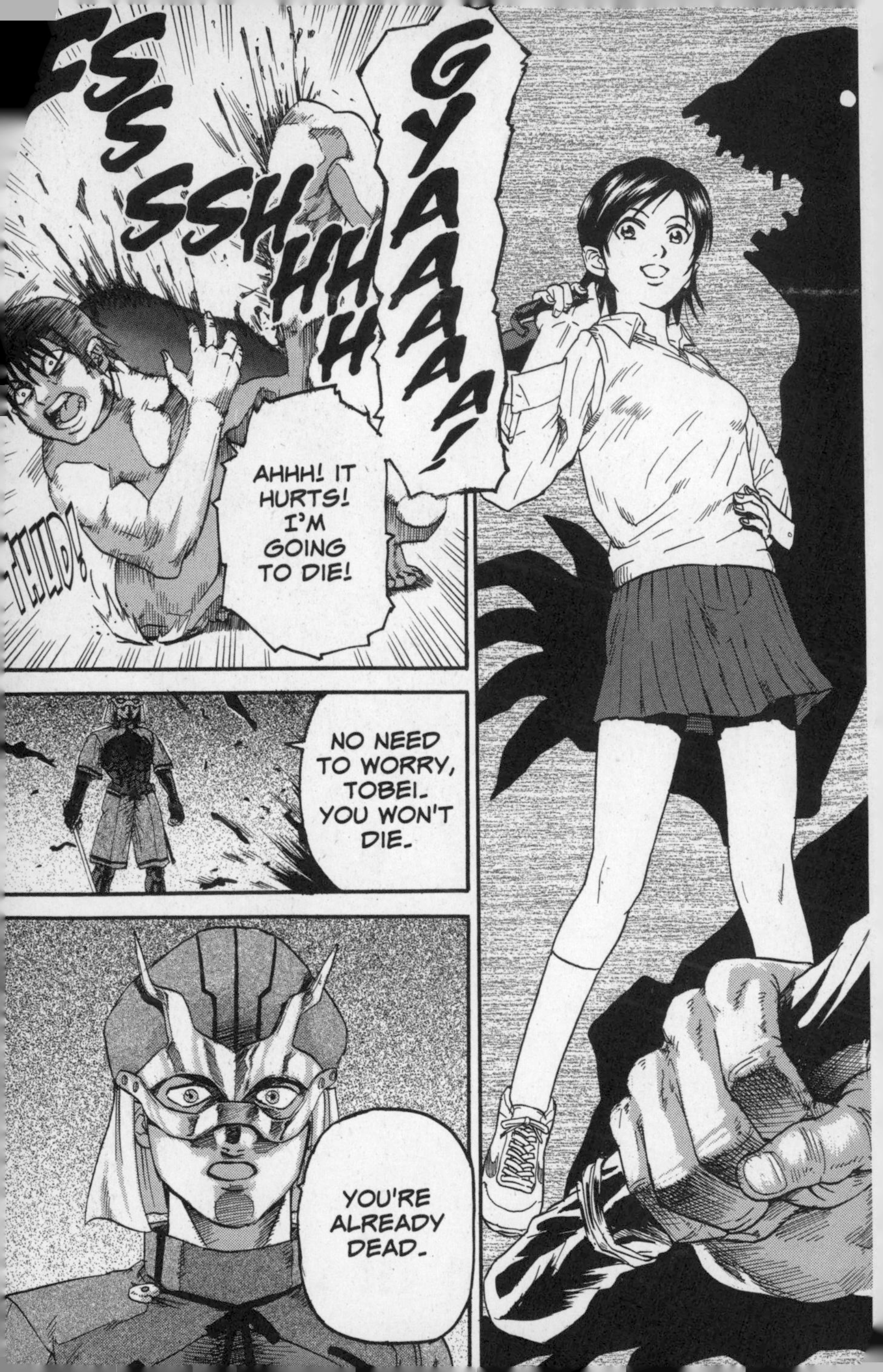
GYAAAAA!
SSSSHHHHH
AHHH! IT HURTS! I'M GOING TO DIE!
THUD!
NO NEED TO WORRY, TOBEI. YOU WON'T DIE.
YOU'RE ALREADY DEAD.

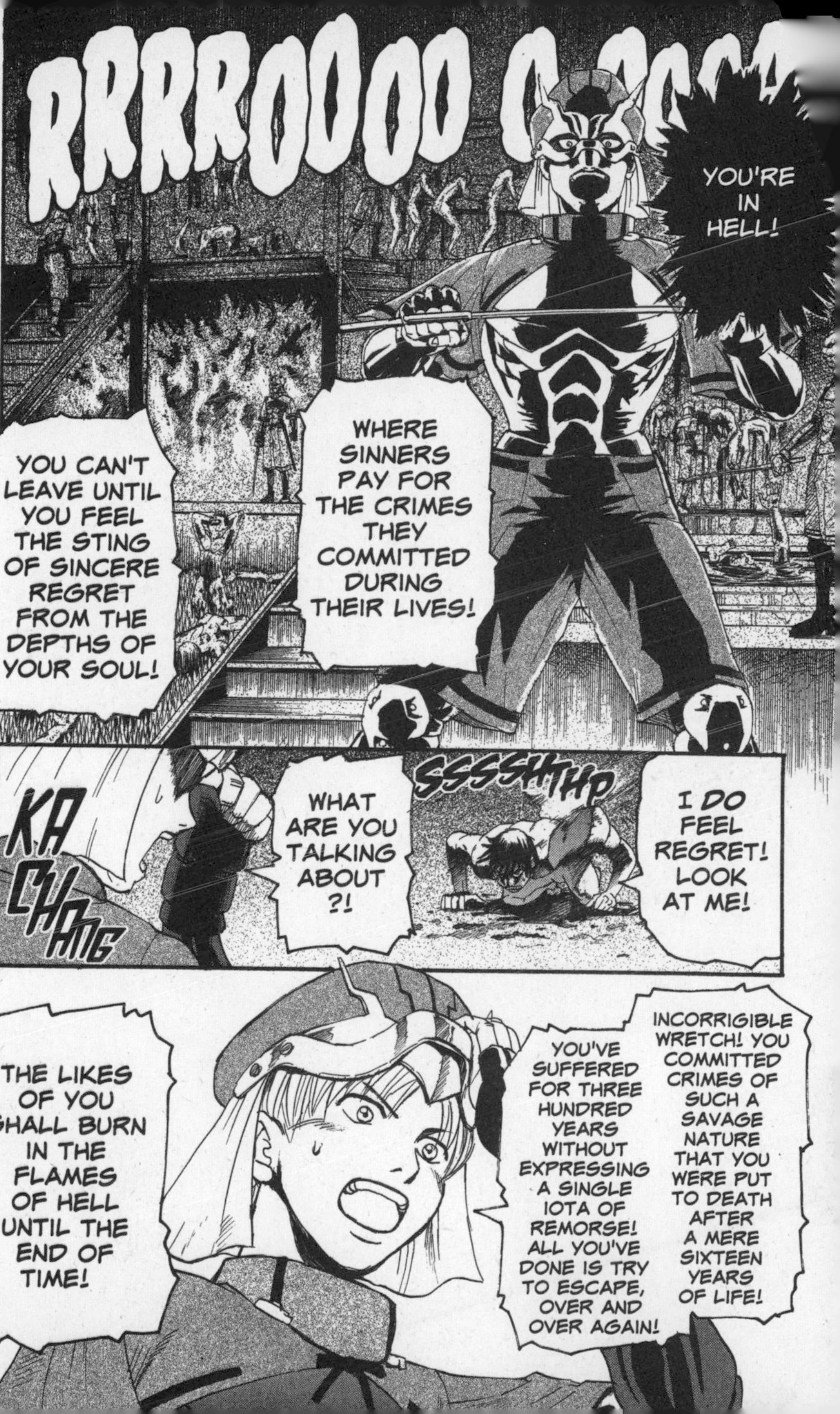
RRRROOOO
YOU'RE IN HELL!
WHERE SINNERS PAY FOR THE CRIMES THEY COMMITTED DURING THEIR LIVES!
YOU CAN'T LEAVE UNTIL YOU FEEL THE STING OF SINCERE REGRET FROM THE DEPTHS OF YOUR SOUL!
I DO FEEL REGRET! LOOK AT ME!
SSSSHTHP
WHAT ARE YOU TALKING ABOUT ?!
KA CHANG
INCORRIGIBLE WRETCH! YOU COMMITTED CRIMES OF SUCH A SAVAGE NATURE THAT YOU WERE PUT TO DEATH AFTER A MERE SIXTEEN YEARS OF LIFE!
YOU'VE SUFFERED FOR THREE HUNDRED YEARS WITHOUT EXPRESSING A SINGLE IOTA OF REMORSE! ALL YOU'VE DONE IS TRY TO ESCAPE, OVER AND OVER AGAIN!
THE LIKES OF YOU SHALL BURN IN THE FLAMES OF HELL UNTIL THE END OF TIME!

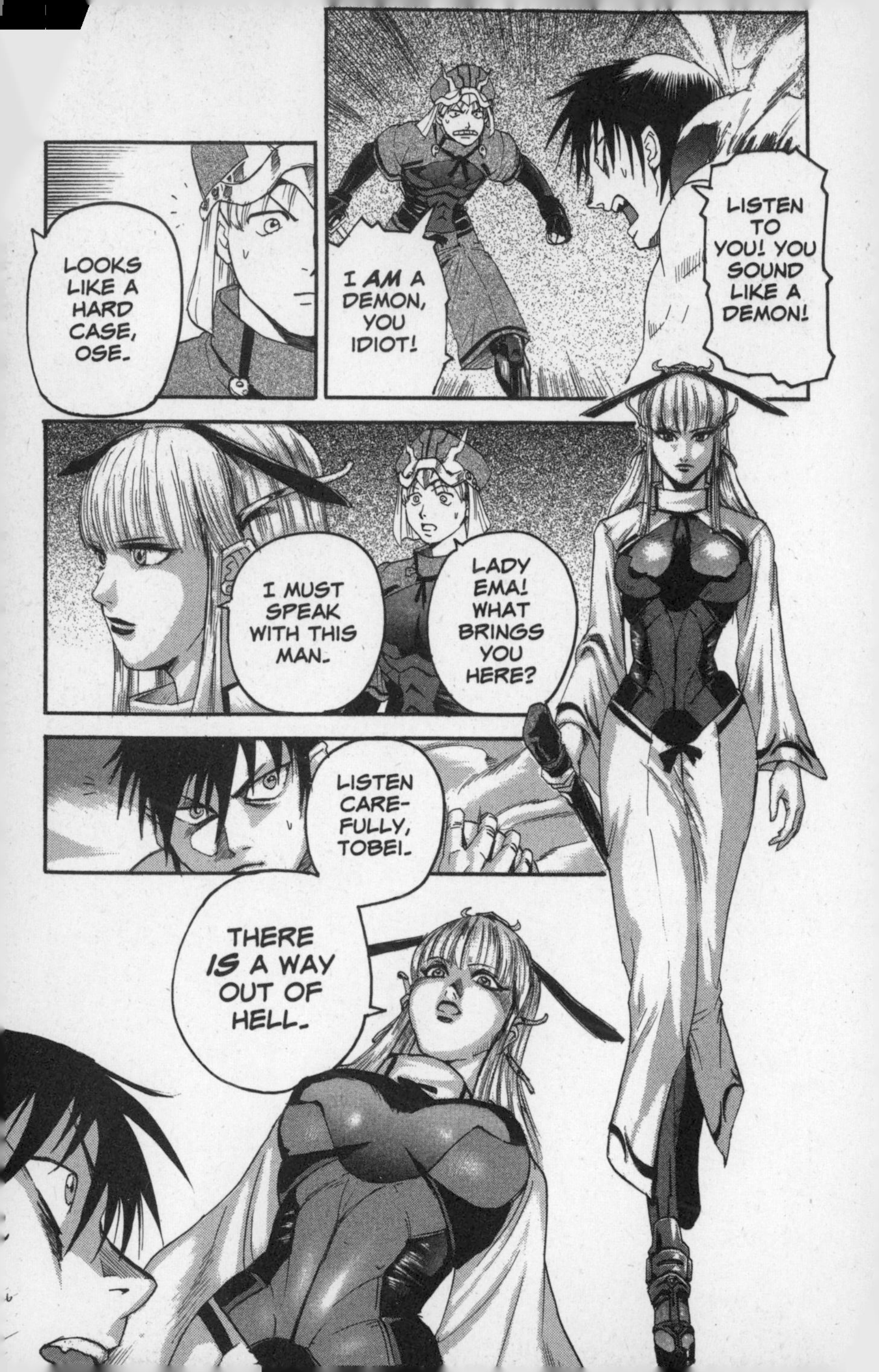
LISTEN TO YOU! YOU SOUND LIKE A DEMON!
I *AM* A DEMON, YOU IDIOT!
LOOKS LIKE A HARD CASE, OSE.
LADY EMA! WHAT BRINGS YOU HERE?
I MUST SPEAK WITH THIS MAN.
LISTEN CARE-FULLY, TOBEI.
THERE *IS* A WAY OUT OF HELL.

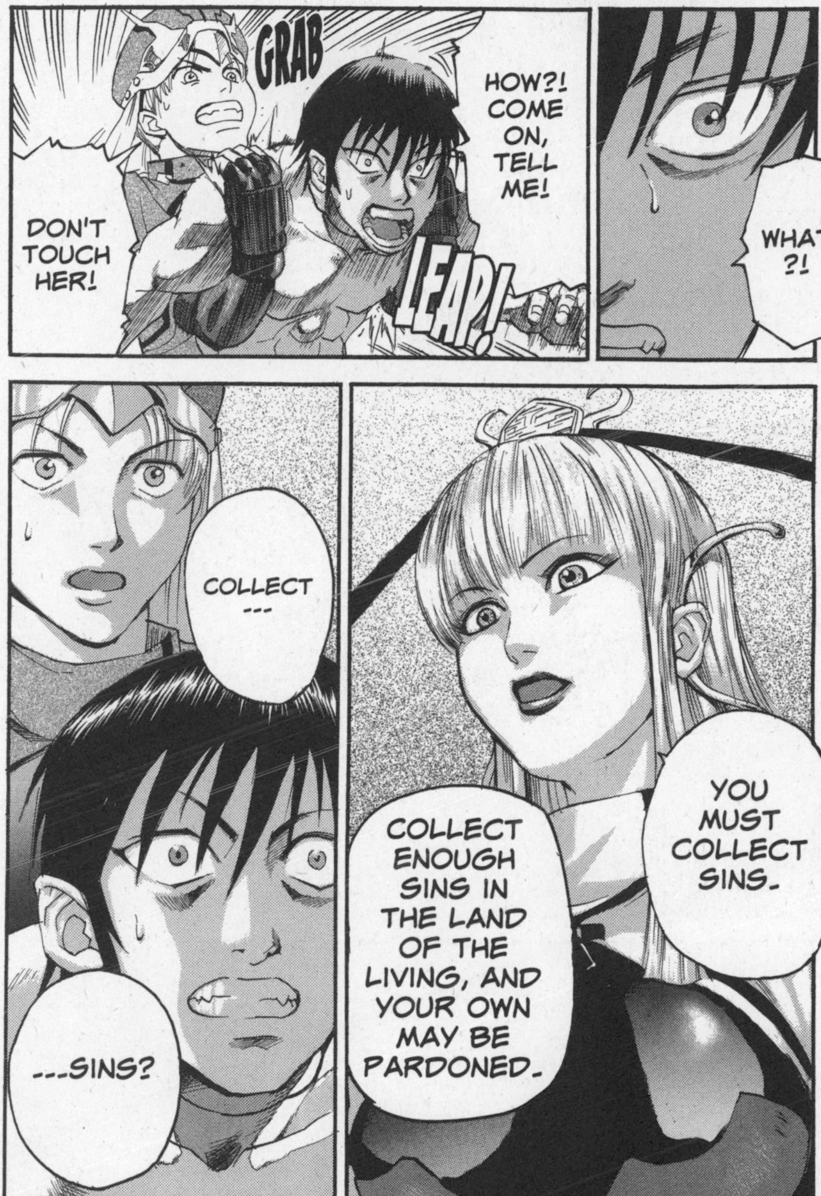
WHAT?!
HOW?! COME ON, TELL ME!
GRAB
LEAP!
DON'T TOUCH HER!
YOU MUST COLLECT SINS.
COLLECT ENOUGH SINS IN THE LAND OF THE LIVING, AND YOUR OWN MAY BE PARDONED.
COLLECT---
---SINS?

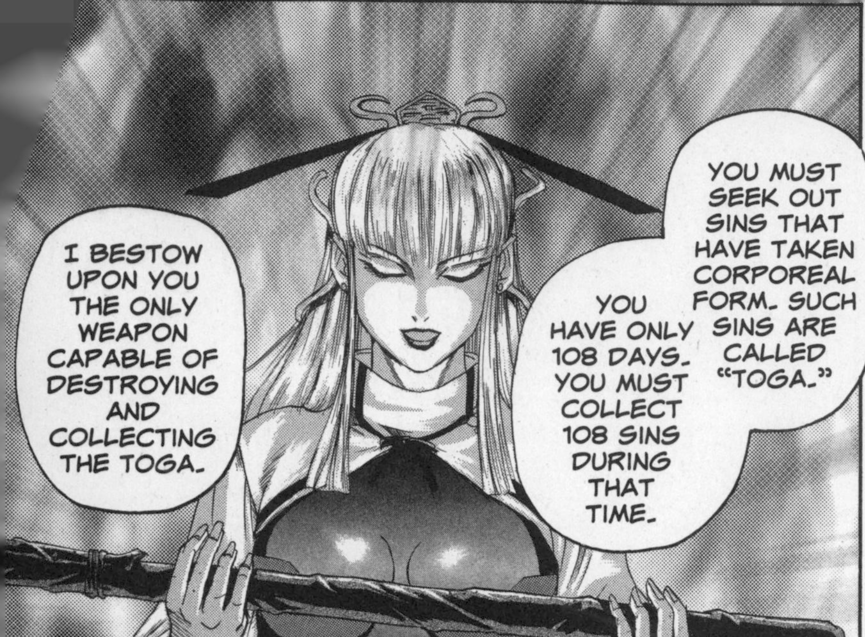
YOU MUST SEEK OUT SINS THAT HAVE TAKEN CORPOREAL FORM. SUCH SINS ARE CALLED "TOGA."
YOU HAVE ONLY 108 DAYS. YOU MUST COLLECT 108 SINS DURING THAT TIME.
I BESTOW UPON YOU THE ONLY WEAPON CAPABLE OF DESTROYING AND COLLECTING THE TOGA.
IT IS CALLED "TOGARI"--THE TOGA HUNTER.

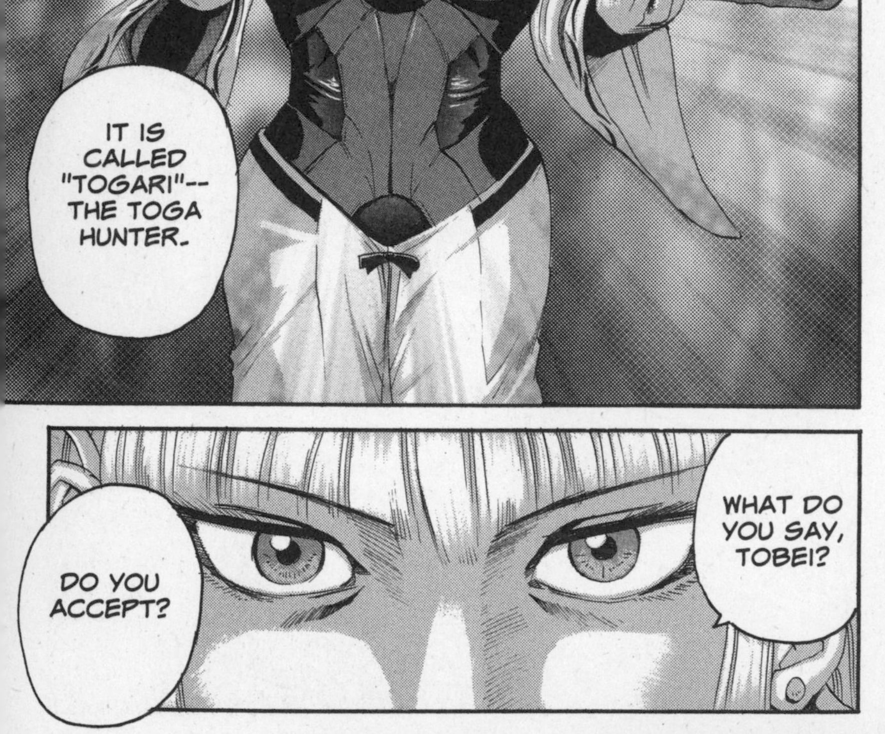
WHAT DO YOU SAY, TOBEI?
DO YOU ACCEPT?

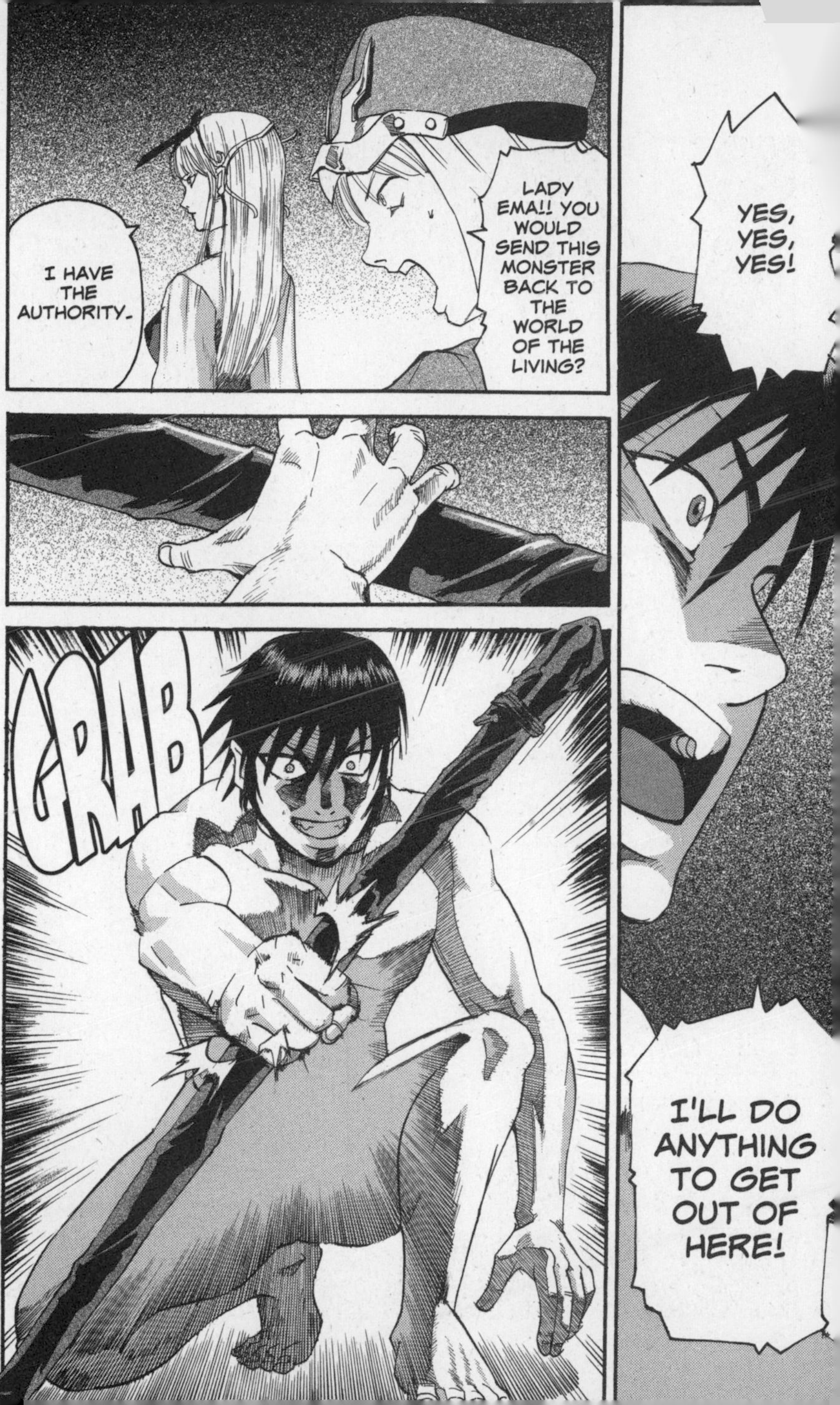
YES, YES, YES!
I'LL DO ANYTHING TO GET OUT OF HERE!
LADY EMA!! YOU WOULD SEND THIS MONSTER BACK TO THE WORLD OF THE LIVING?
I HAVE THE AUTHORITY...
GRAB

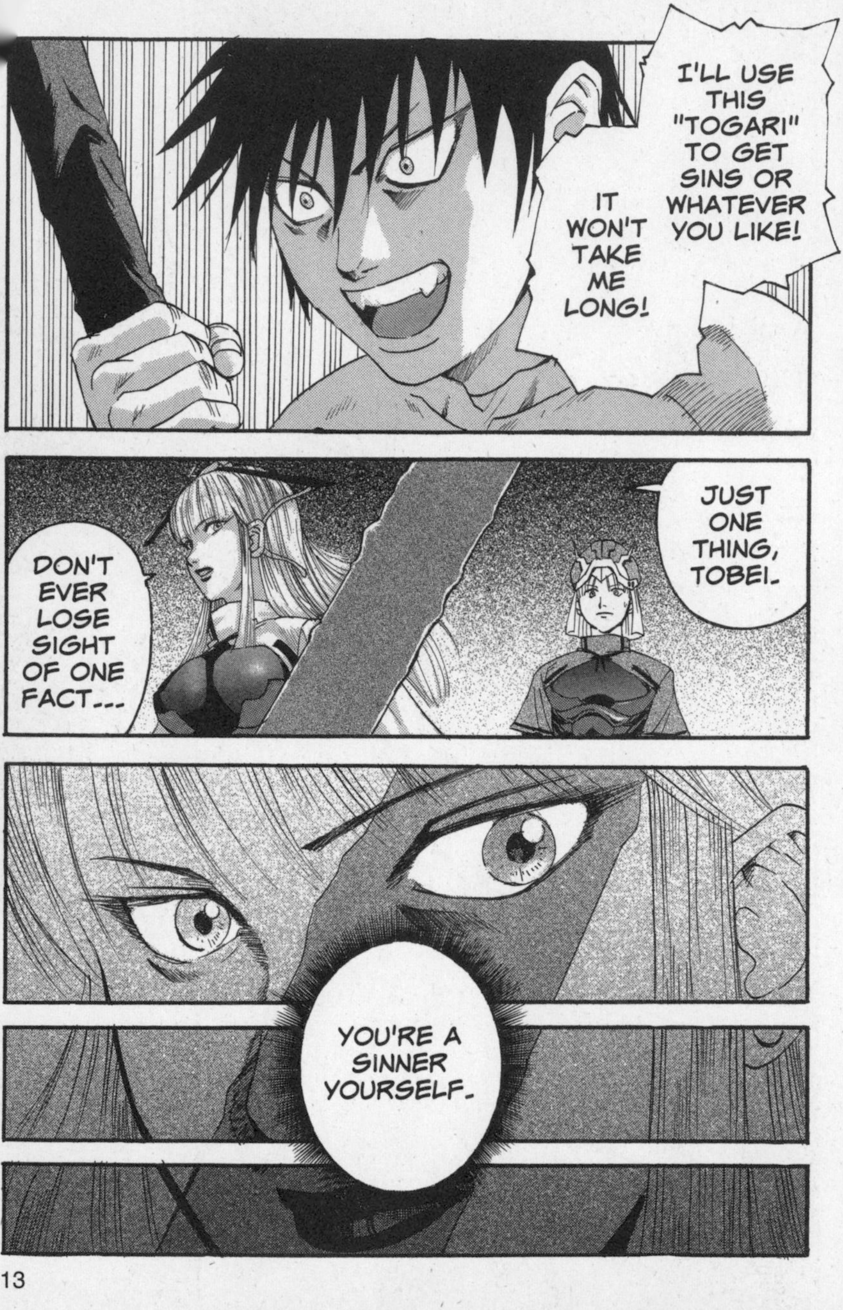
I'LL USE THIS "TOGARI" TO GET SINS OR WHATEVER YOU LIKE!
IT WON'T TAKE ME LONG!
JUST ONE THING, TOBEI.
DON'T EVER LOSE SIGHT OF ONE FACT...
YOU'RE A SINNER YOURSELF.

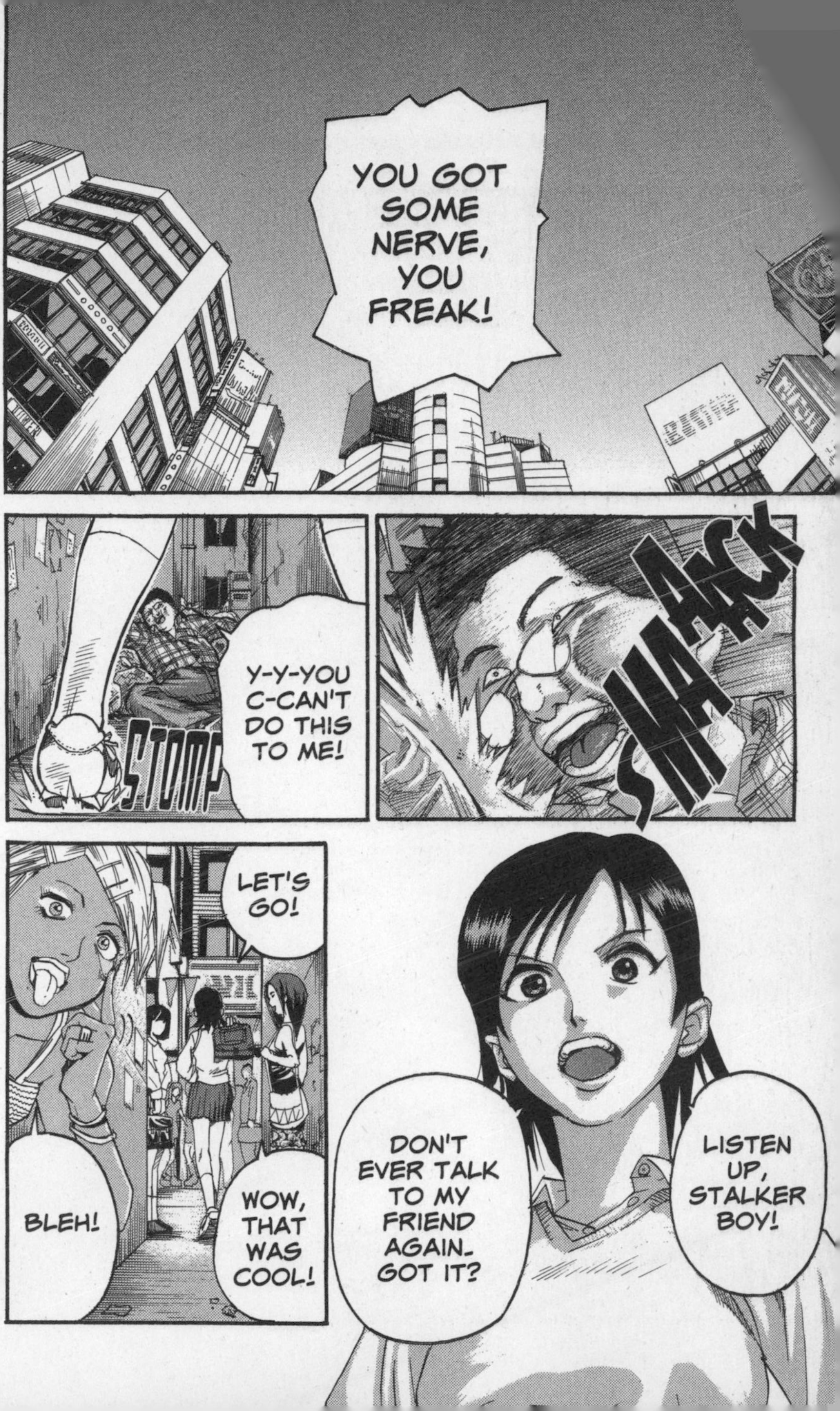
YOU GOT SOME NERVE, YOU FREAK!
SMACK
Y-Y-YOU C-CAN'T DO THIS TO ME!
STOMP
LISTEN UP, STALKER BOY!
DON'T EVER TALK TO MY FRIEND AGAIN. GOT IT?
LET'S GO!
WOW, THAT WAS COOL!
BLEH!

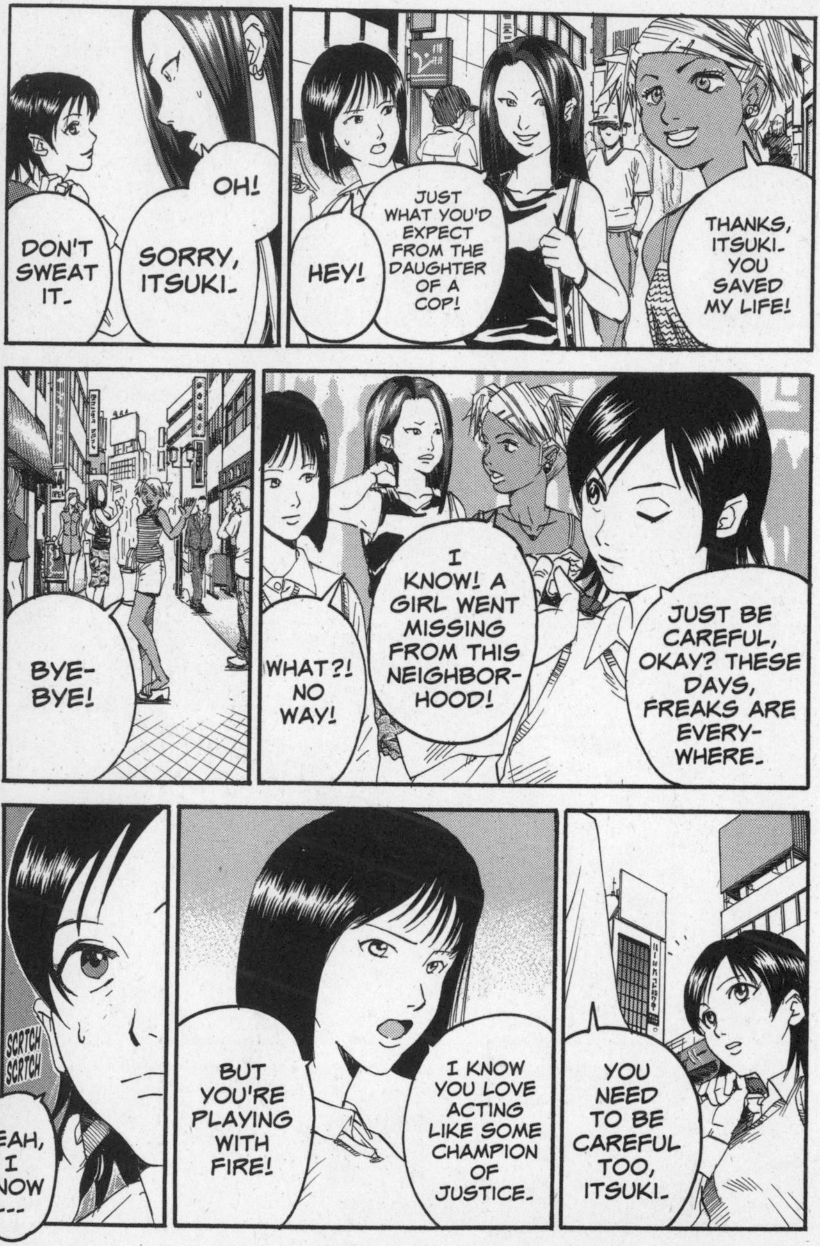
THANKS, ITSUKI. YOU SAVED MY LIFE!
JUST WHAT YOU'D EXPECT FROM THE DAUGHTER OF A COP!
HEY!
OH!
SORRY, ITSUKI.
DON'T SWEAT IT.
JUST BE CAREFUL, OKAY? THESE DAYS, FREAKS ARE EVERYWHERE.
I KNOW! A GIRL WENT MISSING FROM THIS NEIGHBORHOOD!
WHAT?! NO WAY!
BYE-BYE!
YOU NEED TO BE CAREFUL TOO, ITSUKI.
I KNOW YOU LOVE ACTING LIKE SOME CHAMPION OF JUSTICE.
BUT YOU'RE PLAYING WITH FIRE!
SCRTCH SCRTCH
YEAH, I KNOW...

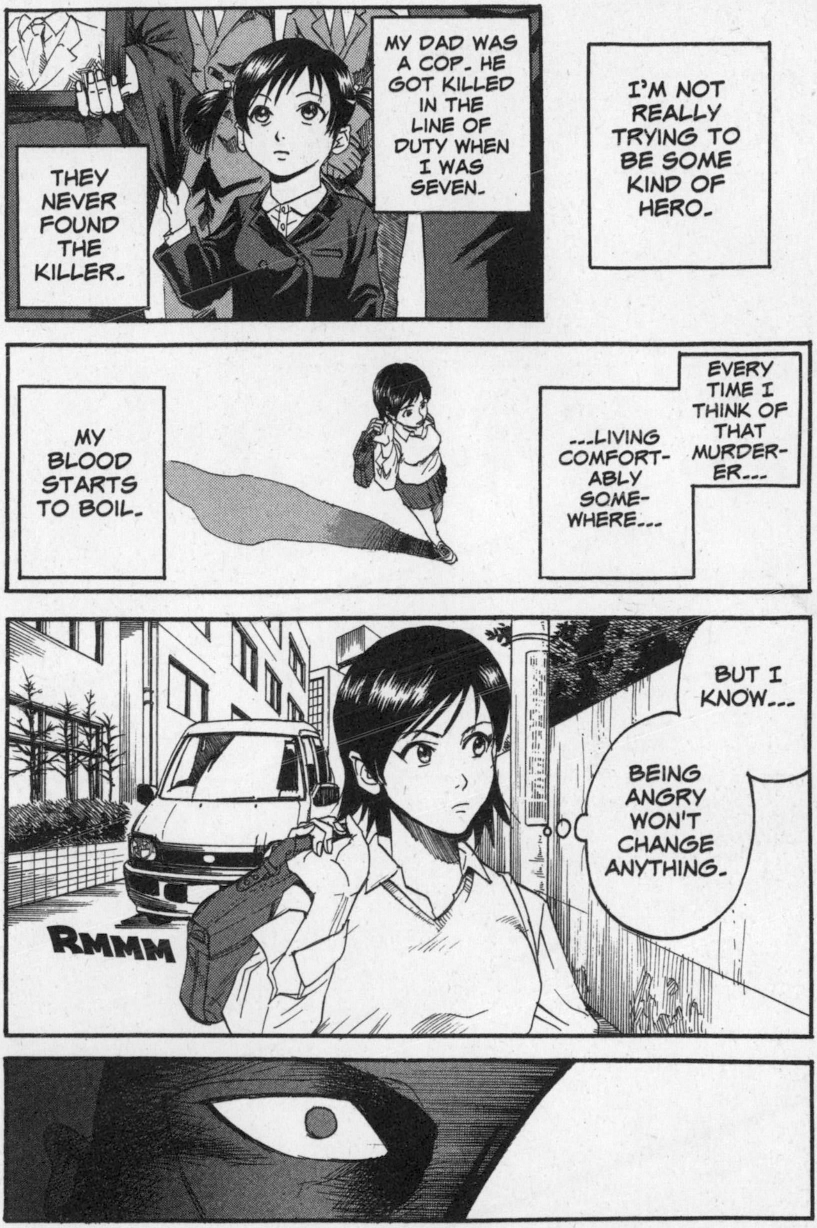
I'M NOT REALLY TRYING TO BE SOME KIND OF HERO.
MY DAD WAS A COP. HE GOT KILLED IN THE LINE OF DUTY WHEN I WAS SEVEN.
THEY NEVER FOUND THE KILLER.
EVERY TIME I THINK OF THAT MURDERER...
...LIVING COMFORTABLY SOMEWHERE...
MY BLOOD STARTS TO BOIL.
BUT I KNOW...
BEING ANGRY WON'T CHANGE ANYTHING.
RMMM

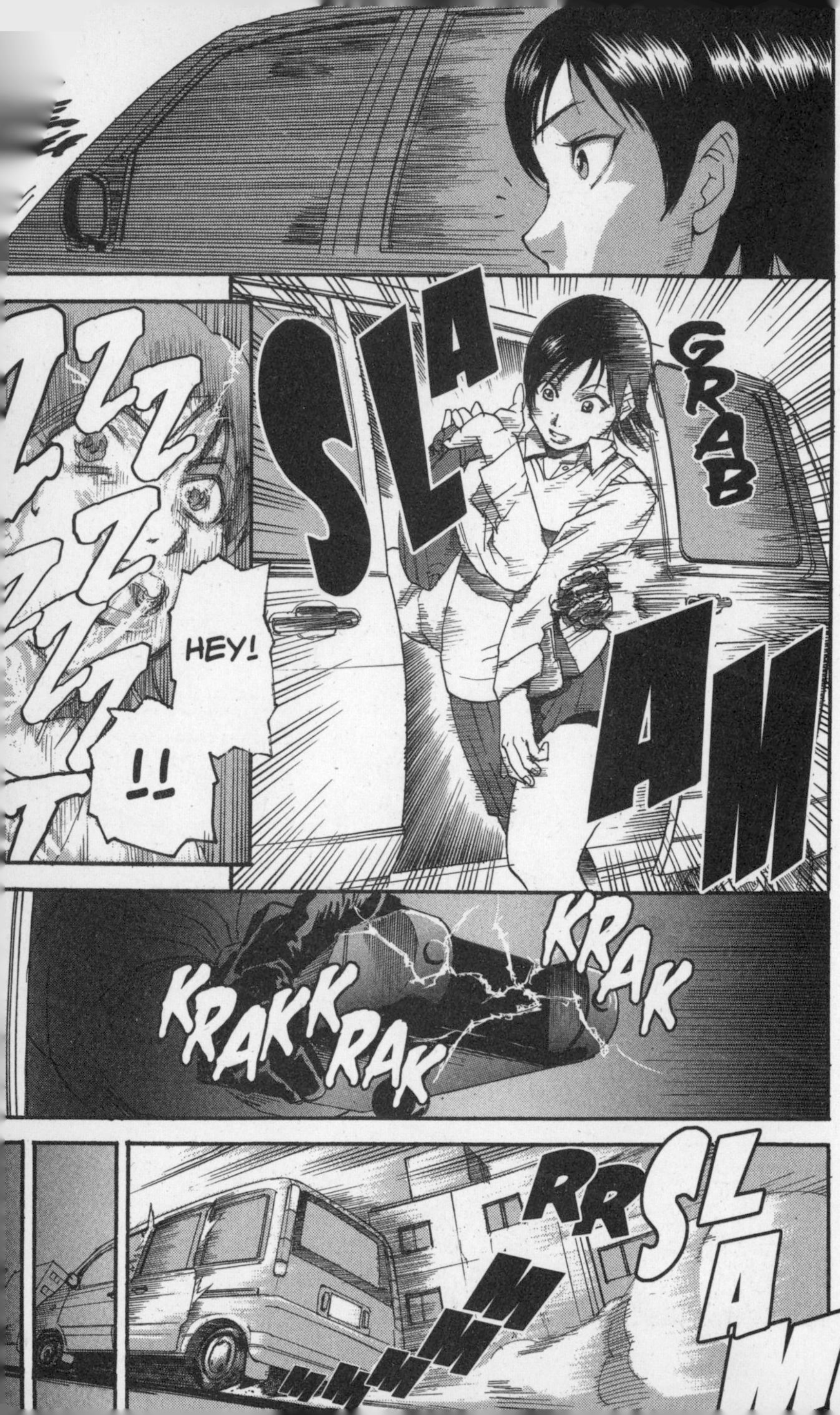
GRAB
SLA
AM
HEY!
!!
KRAK
KRAKK RAK
RR SLAM
MMMMMMMM

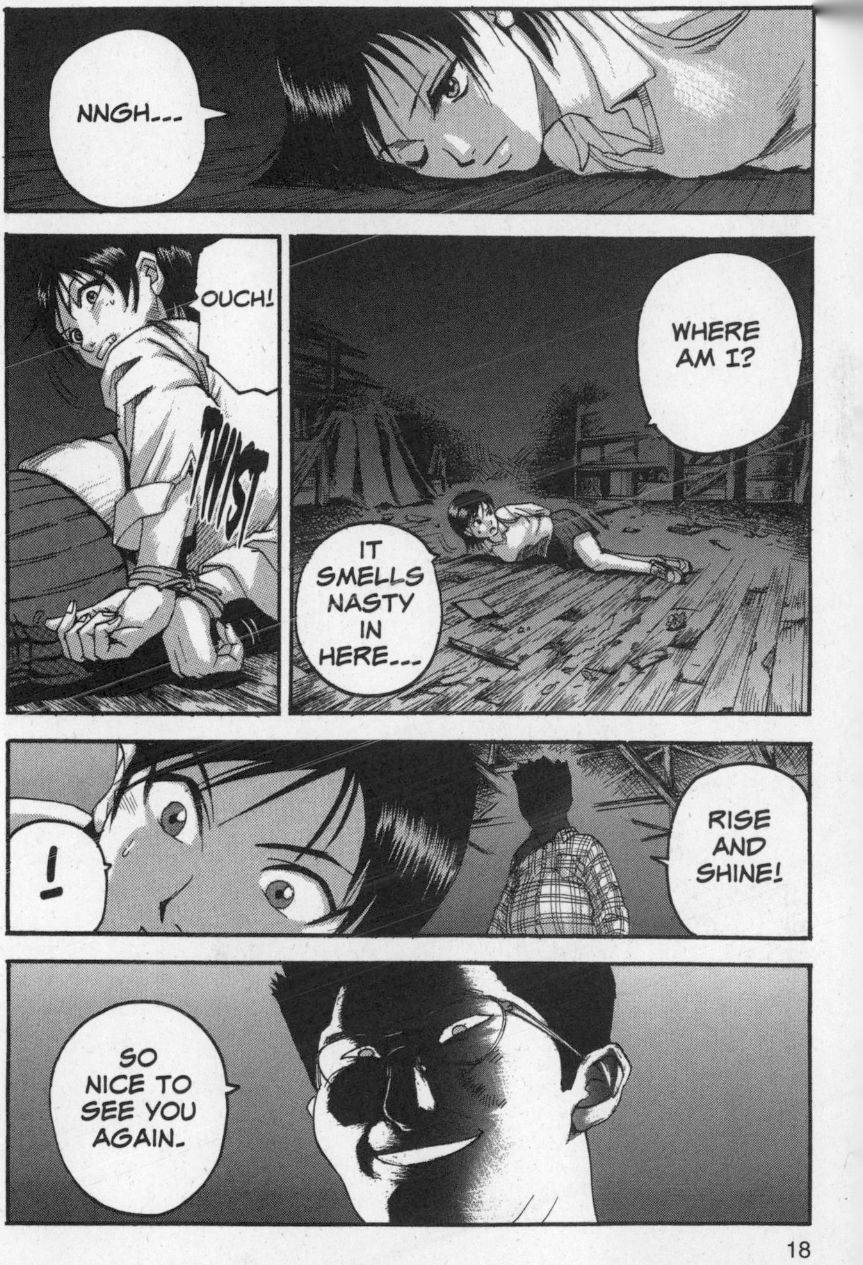
NNGH...
WHERE AM I?
IT SMELLS NASTY IN HERE...
OUCH!
TWIST
RISE AND SHINE!
!
SO NICE TO SEE YOU AGAIN.

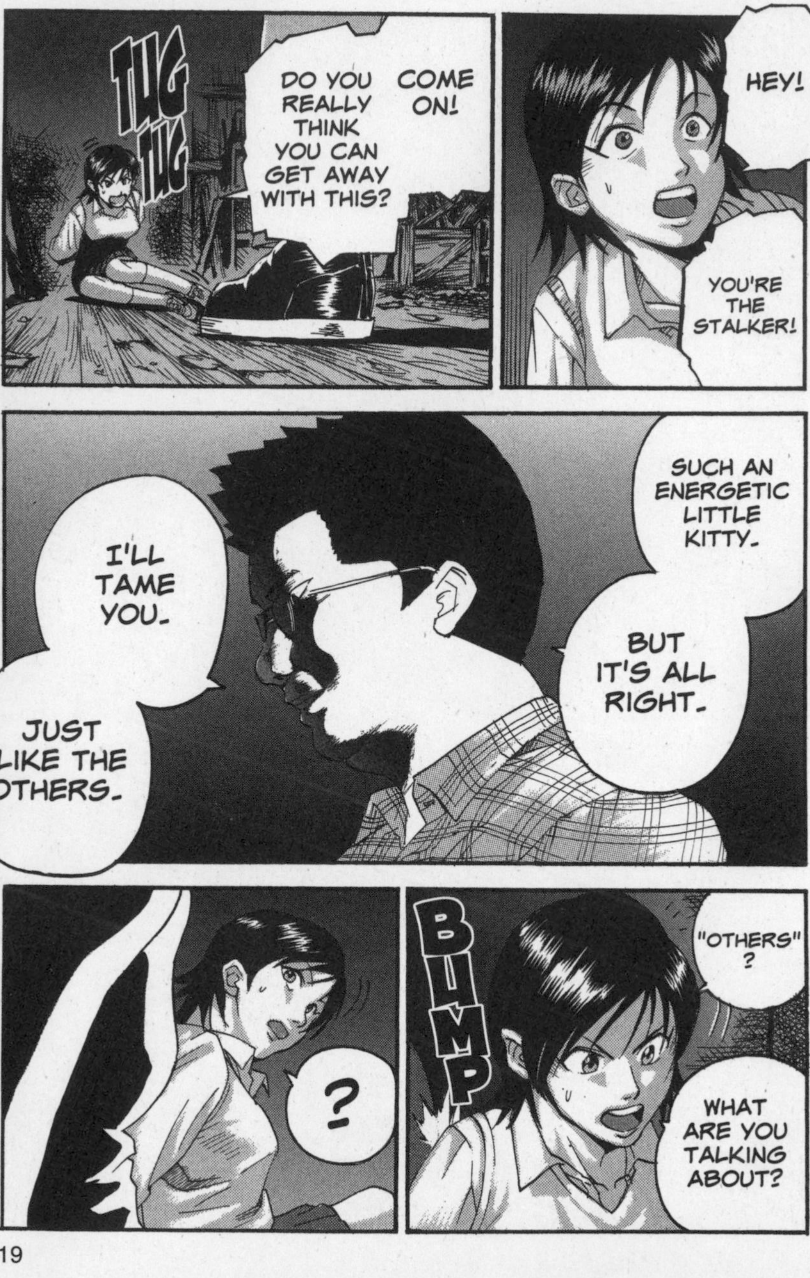
HEY!
YOU'RE THE STALKER!
COME ON!
DO YOU REALLY THINK YOU CAN GET AWAY WITH THIS?
TUG TUG
SUCH AN ENERGETIC LITTLE KITTY...
BUT IT'S ALL RIGHT...
I'LL TAME YOU...
JUST LIKE THE OTHERS...
"OTHERS"?
WHAT ARE YOU TALKING ABOUT?
BUMP
?

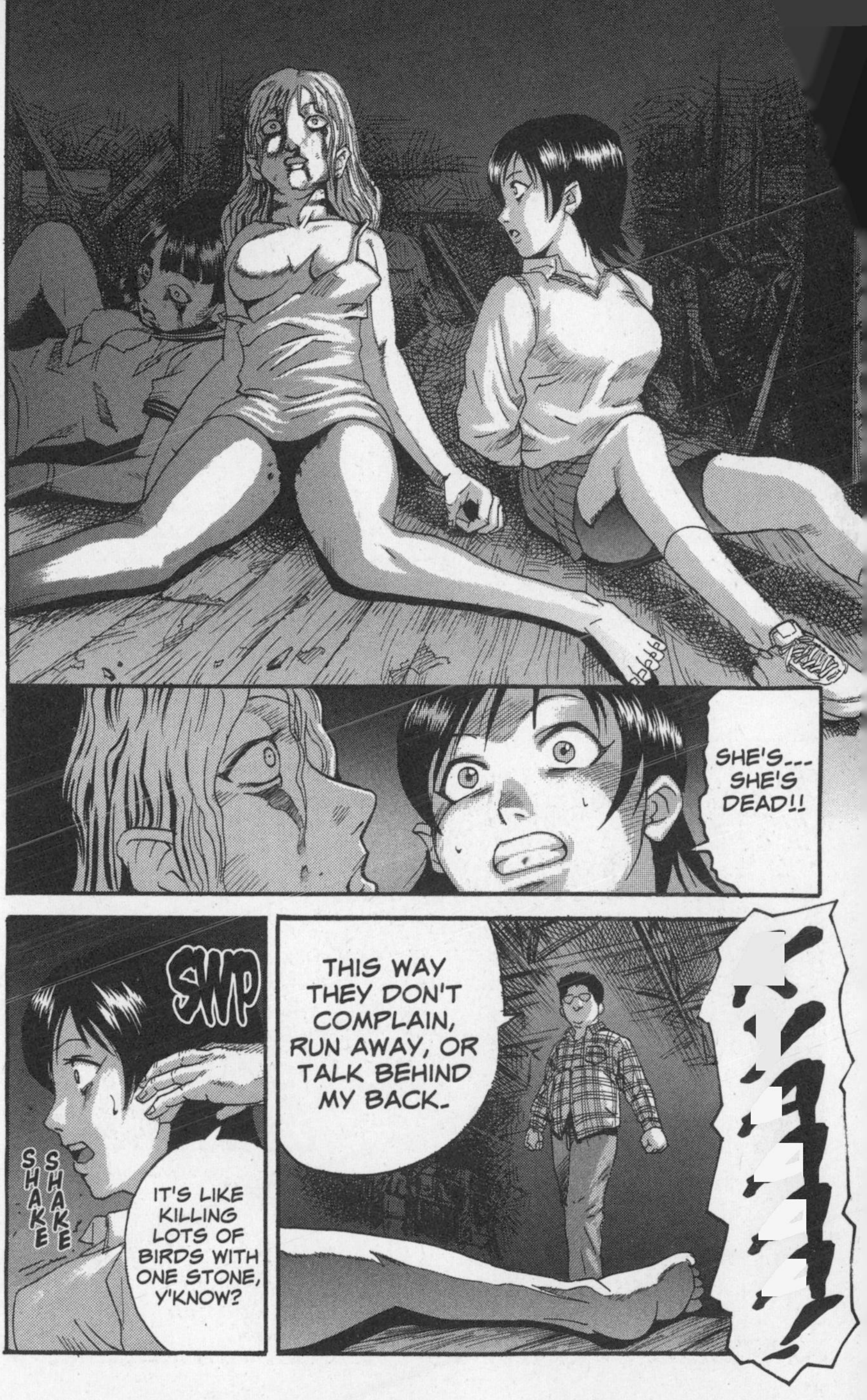
SHE'S... SHE'S DEAD!!
THIS WAY THEY DON'T COMPLAIN, RUN AWAY, OR TALK BEHIND MY BACK.
SWP
IT'S LIKE KILLING LOTS OF BIRDS WITH ONE STONE, Y'KNOW?
SHAKE SHAKE

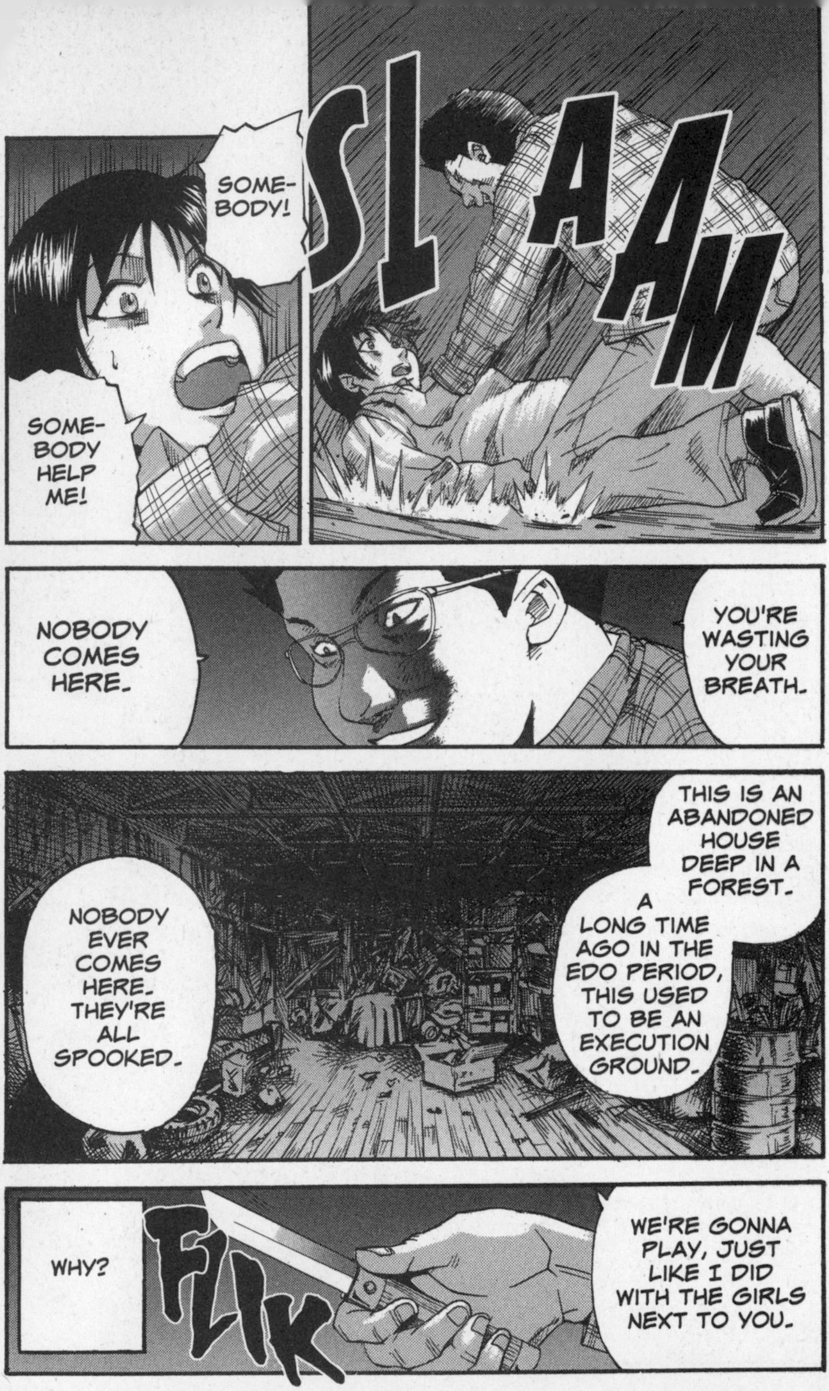
SLAAAM
SOME-BODY!
SOME-BODY HELP ME!
YOU'RE WASTING YOUR BREATH.
NOBODY COMES HERE.
THIS IS AN ABANDONED HOUSE DEEP IN A FOREST.
A LONG TIME AGO IN THE EDO PERIOD, THIS USED TO BE AN EXECUTION GROUND.
NOBODY EVER COMES HERE. THEY'RE ALL SPOOKED.
WE'RE GONNA PLAY, JUST LIKE I DID WITH THE GIRLS NEXT TO YOU.
FLIK
WHY?

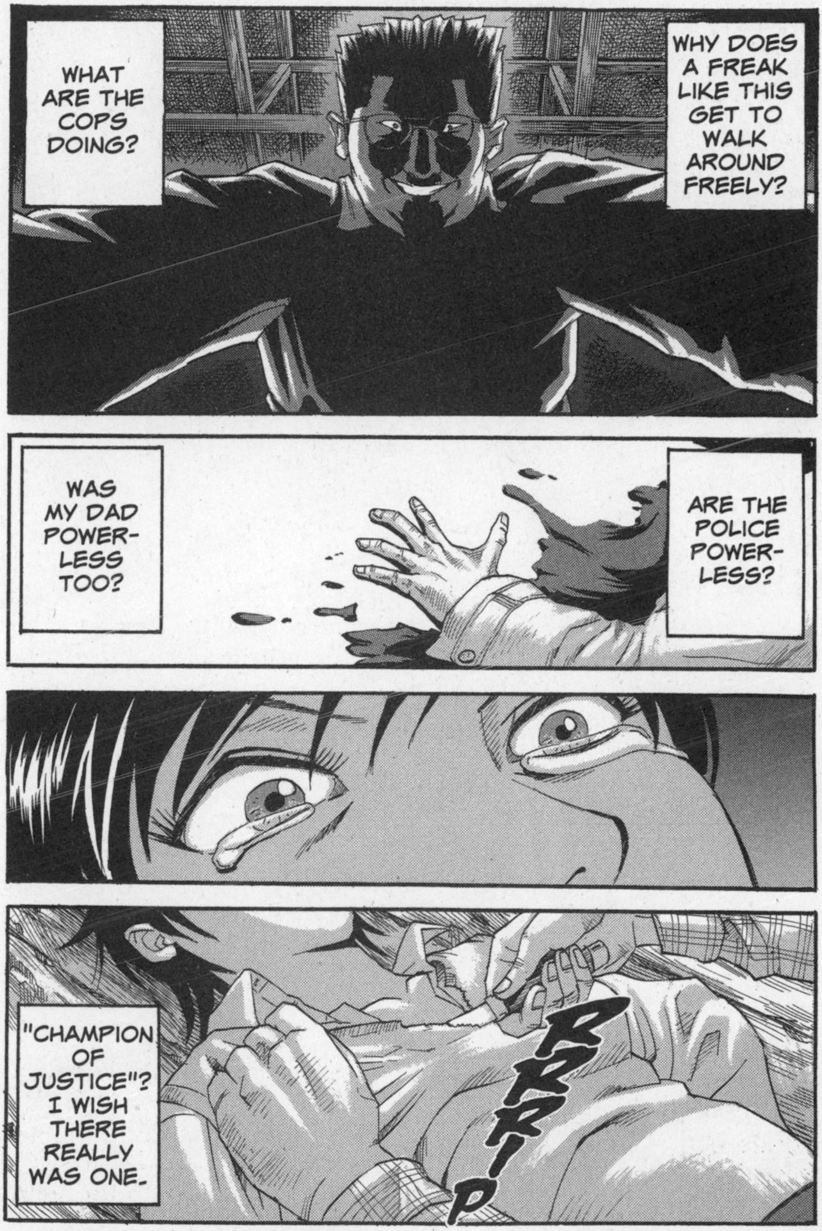
WHY DOES A FREAK LIKE THIS GET TO WALK AROUND FREELY?
WHAT ARE THE COPS DOING?
ARE THE POLICE POWER-LESS?
WAS MY DAD POWER-LESS TOO?
RRRIP
"CHAMPION OF JUSTICE"? I WISH THERE REALLY WAS ONE.

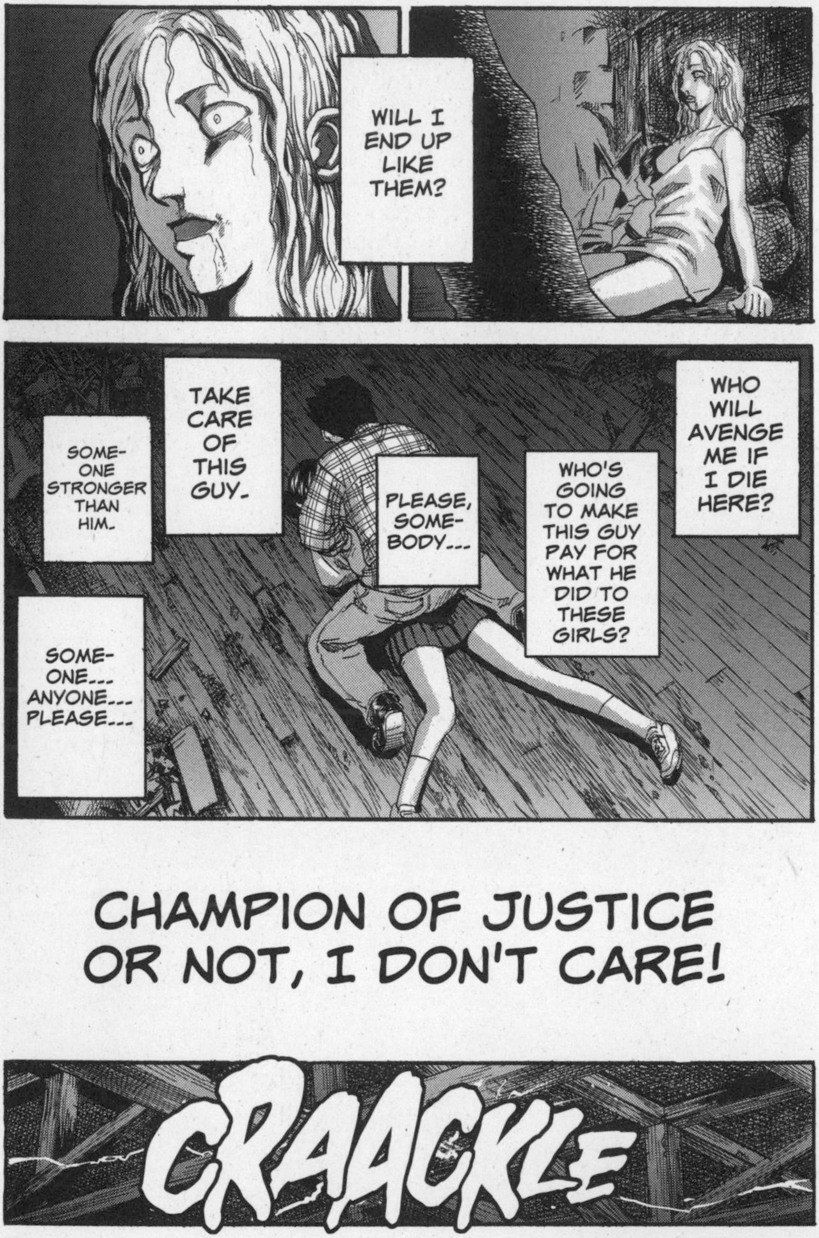
WILL I END UP LIKE THEM?
WHO WILL AVENGE ME IF I DIE HERE?
WHO'S GOING TO MAKE THIS GUY PAY FOR WHAT HE DID TO THESE GIRLS?
PLEASE, SOMEBODY...
TAKE CARE OF THIS GUY.
SOMEONE STRONGER THAN HIM.
SOMEONE... ANYONE... PLEASE...
CHAMPION OF JUSTICE OR NOT, I DON'T CARE!
CRAACKLE

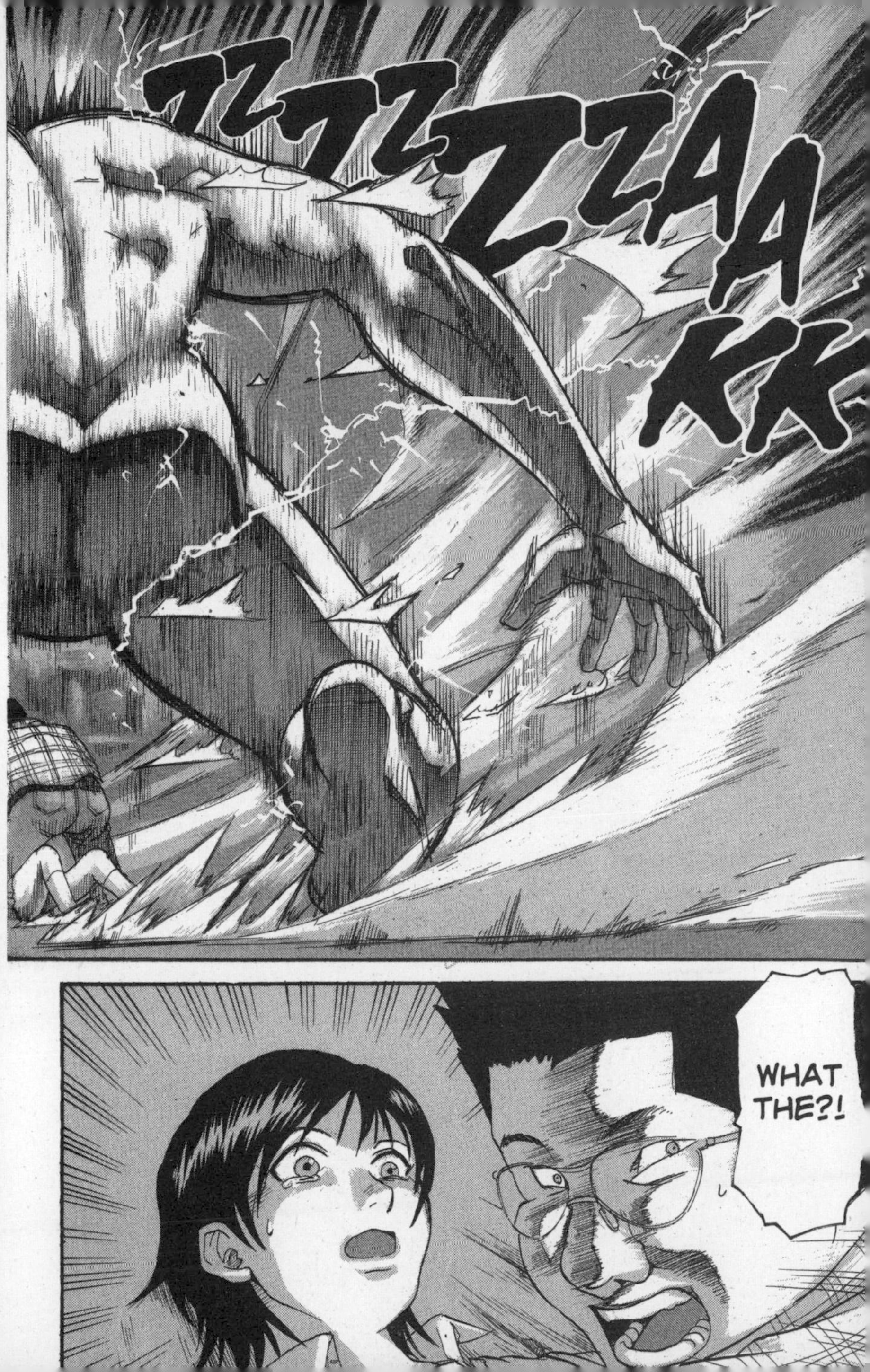
ZZZZZZAAKK
WHAT THE?!

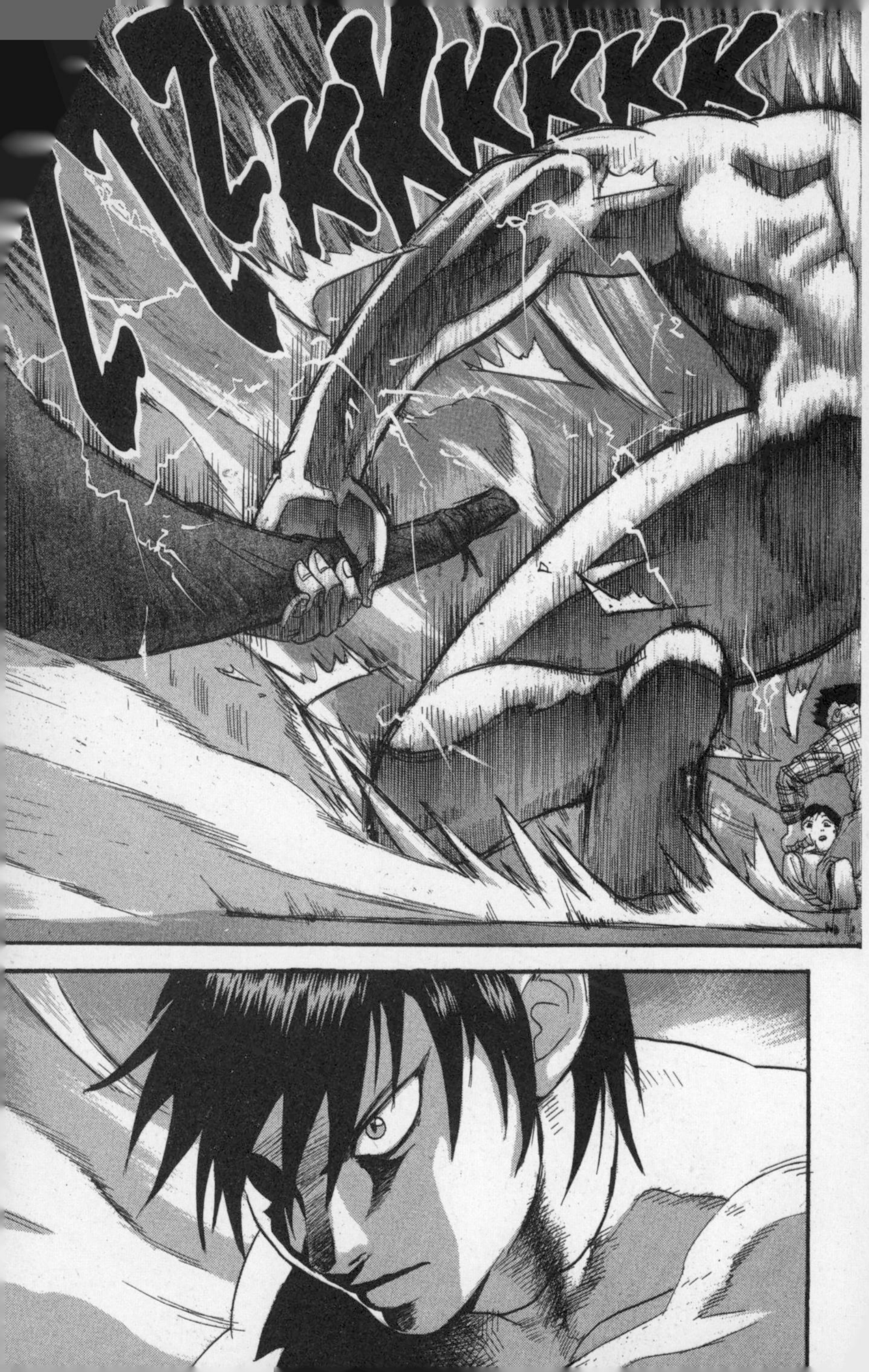

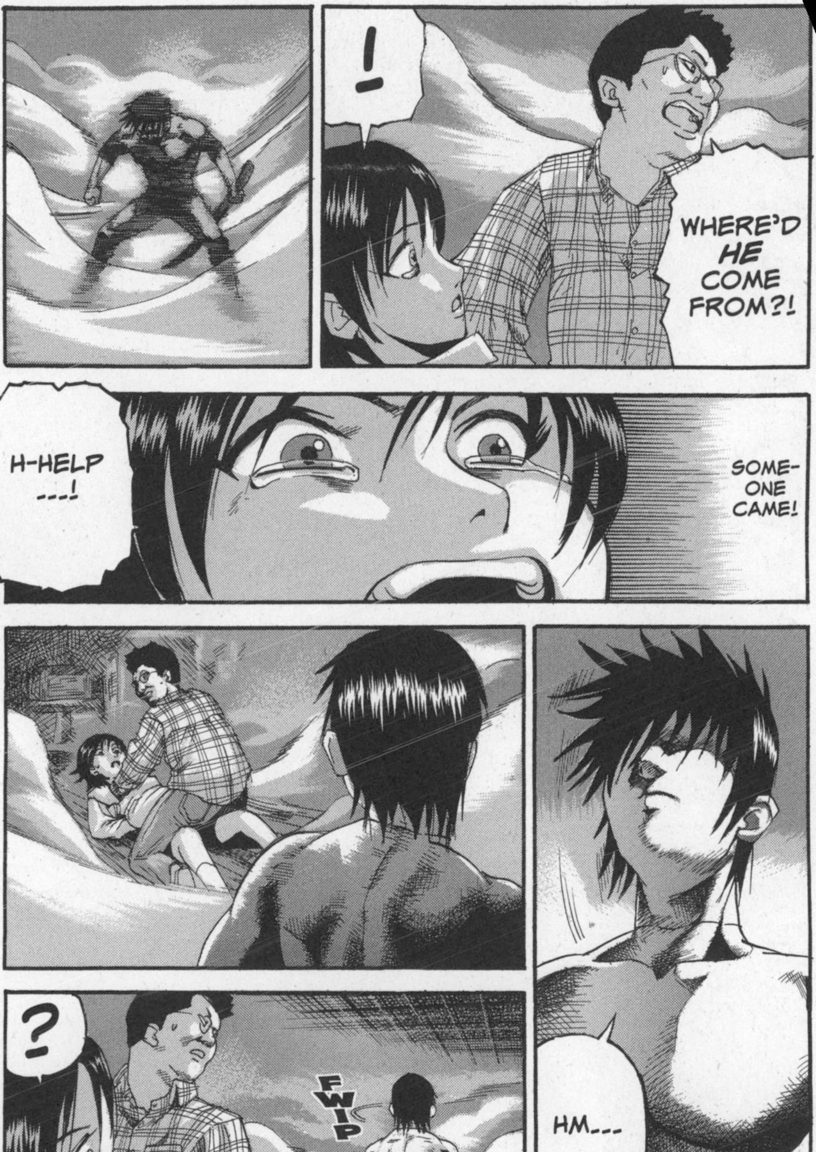
!
WHERE'D HE COME FROM?!
SOME-ONE CAME!
H-HELP ---!
HM---
?
FWIP

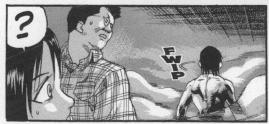

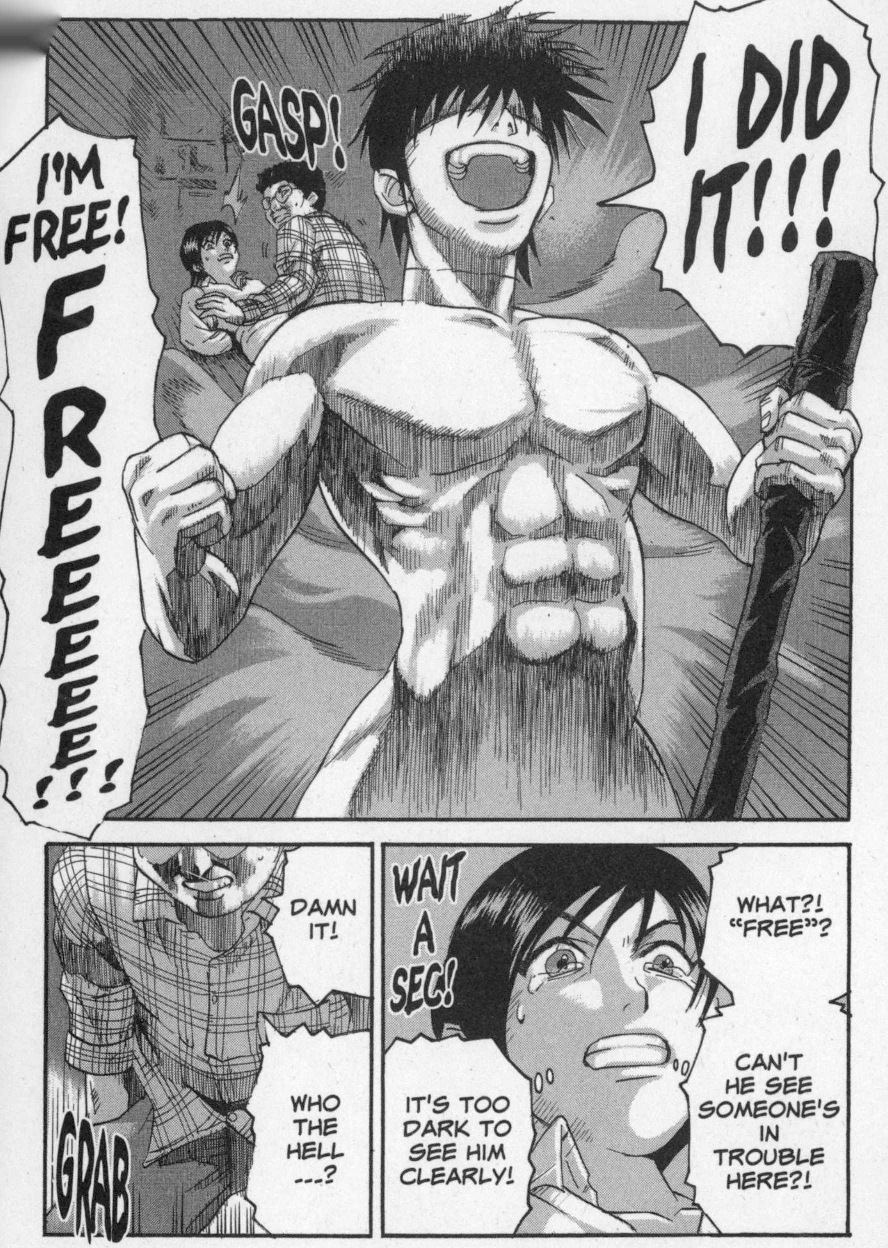
I DID IT!!!
GASP!
I'M FREE! FREEEEEE!!!
WHAT?! "FREE"?
WAIT A SEC!
CAN'T HE SEE SOMEONE'S IN TROUBLE HERE?!
IT'S TOO DARK TO SEE HIM CLEARLY!
DAMN IT!
WHO THE HELL---?
GRAB

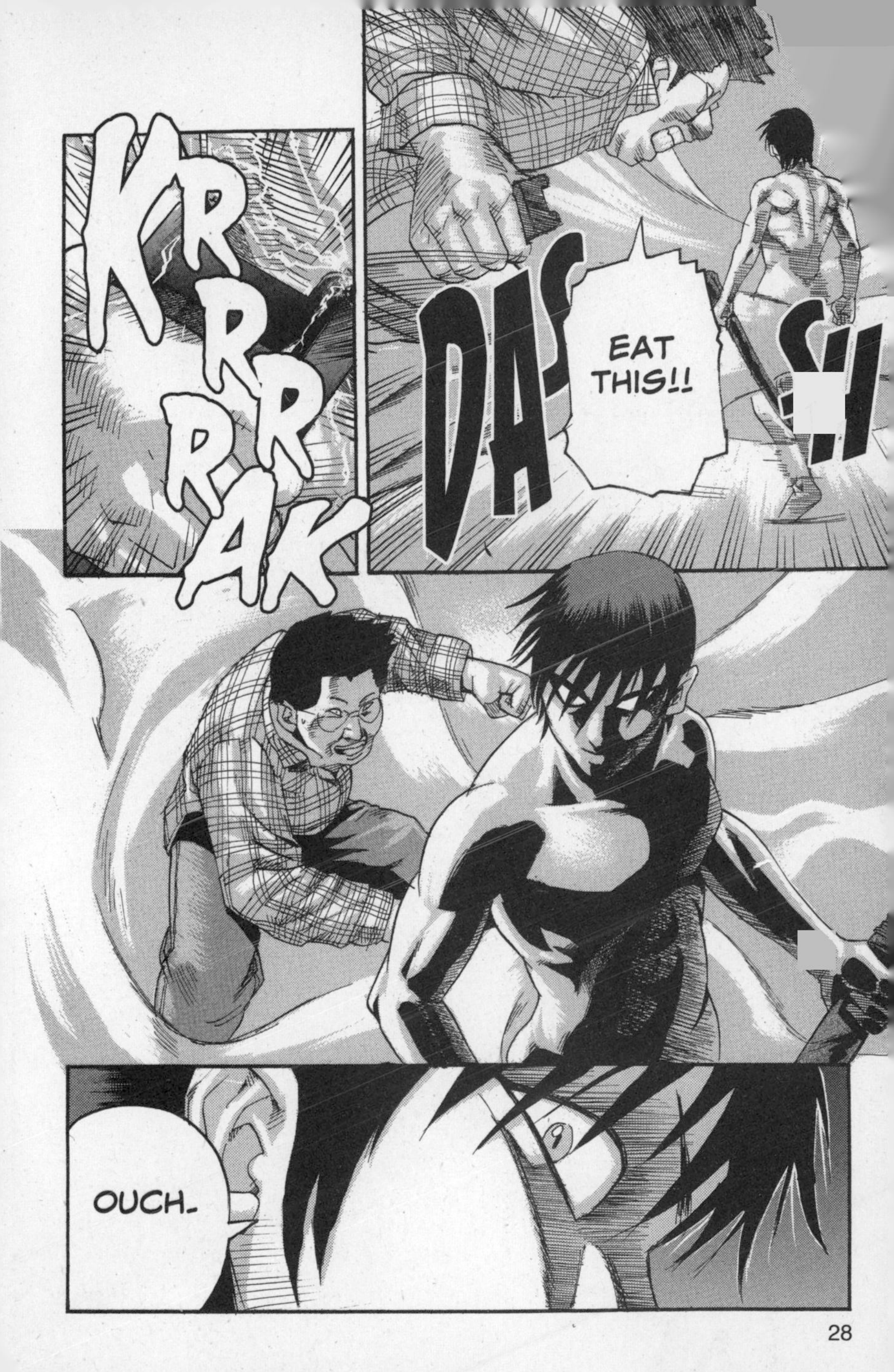
EAT THIS!!
DASH
KRRRAK
OUCH-

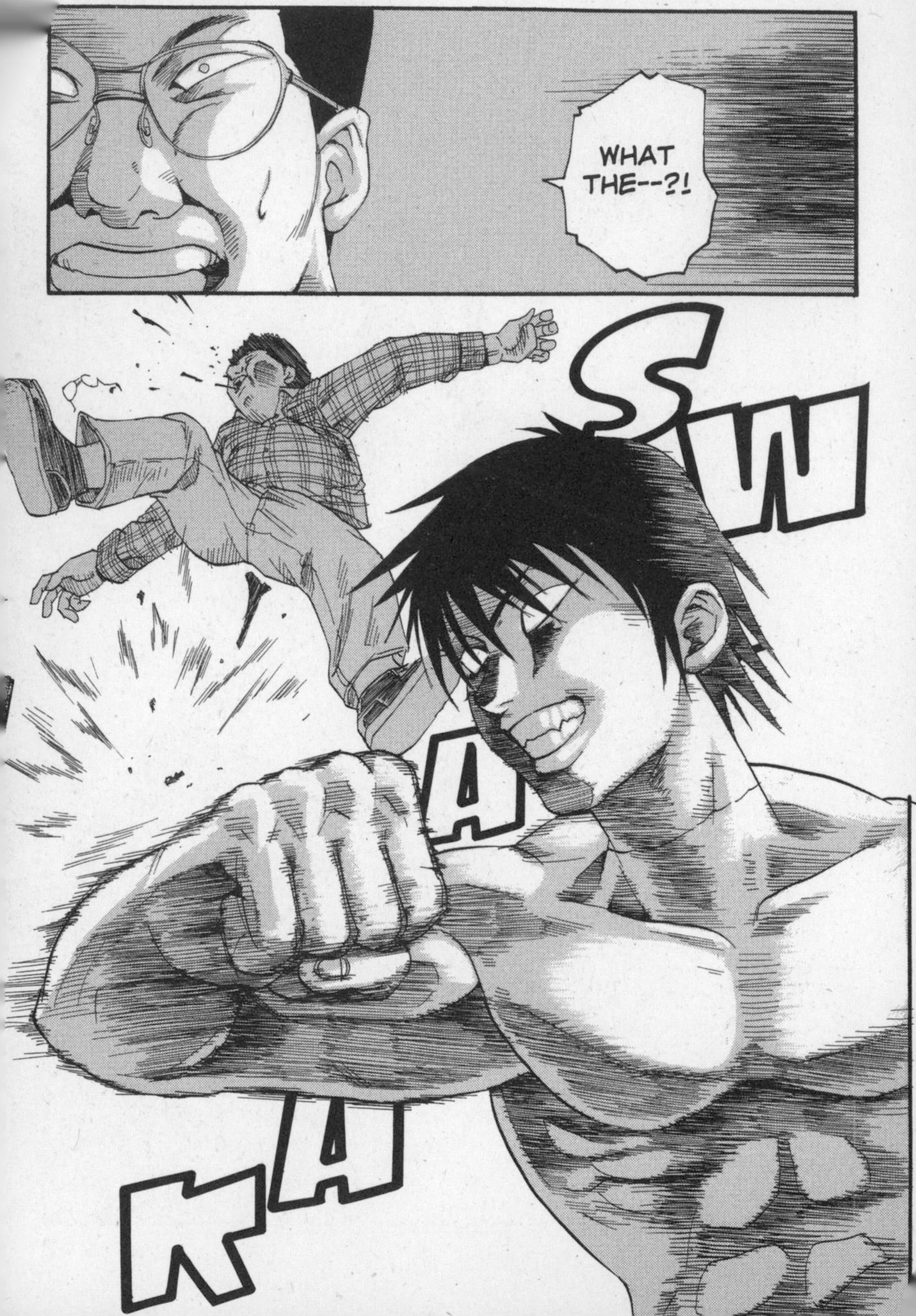
WHAT THE--?!
SW
A
KA

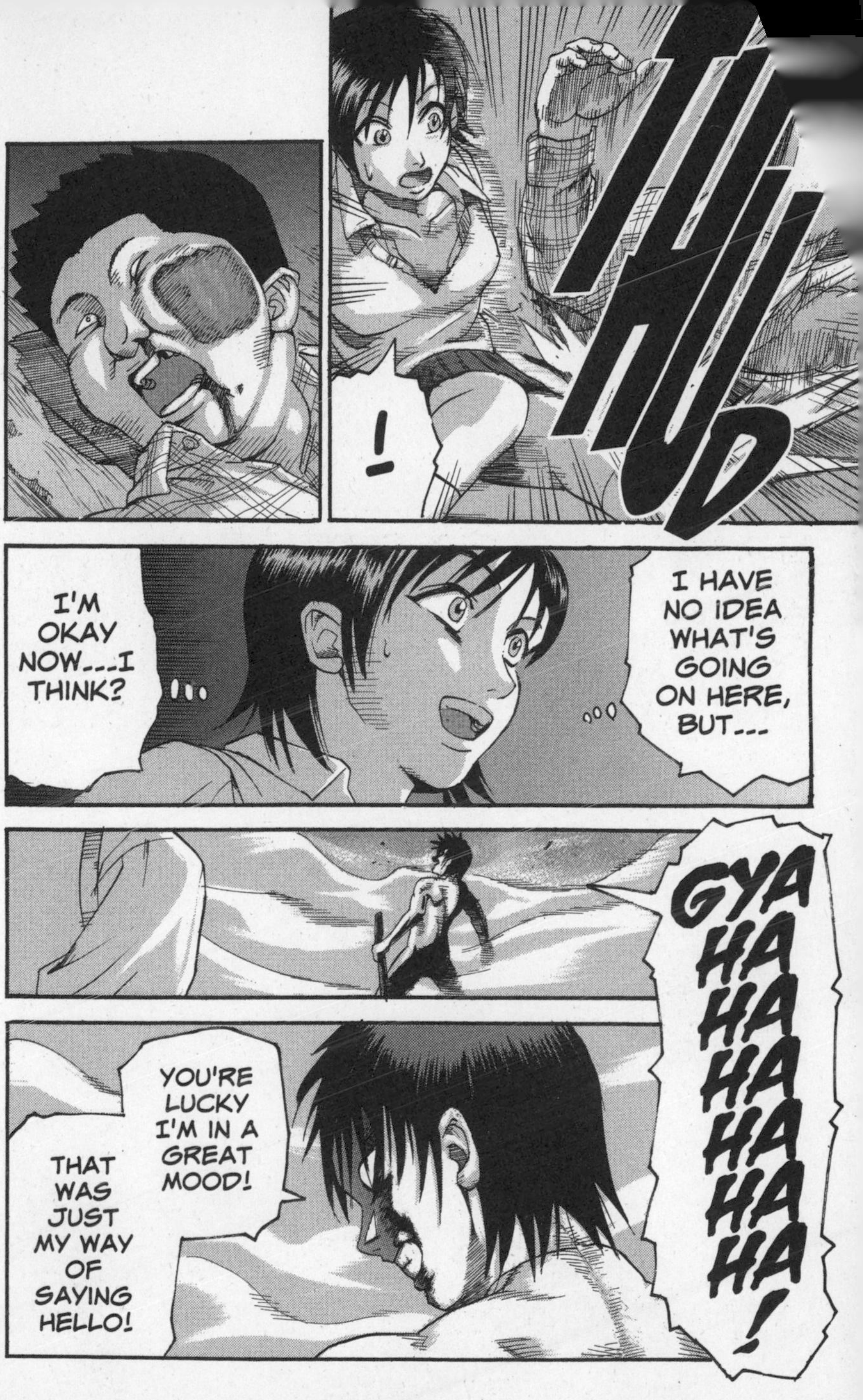
THUD
!
I HAVE NO IDEA WHAT'S GOING ON HERE, BUT...
I'M OKAY NOW...I THINK?
GYAHAHAHAHAHAHAHAHA!
YOU'RE LUCKY I'M IN A GREAT MOOD!
THAT WAS JUST MY WAY OF SAYING HELLO!

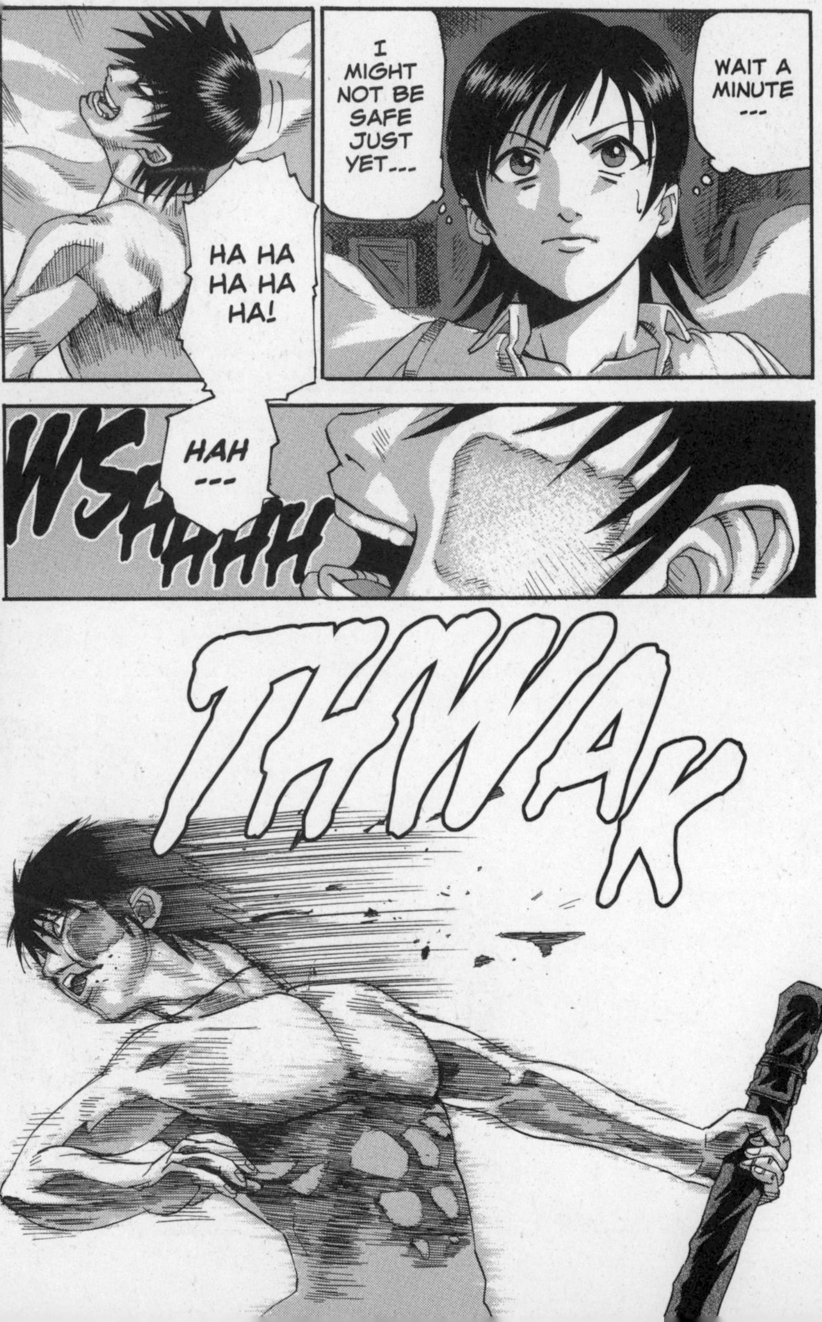
WAIT A MINUTE ---
I MIGHT NOT BE SAFE JUST YET---
HA HA HA HA HA!
HAH ---
WSHHHHH
THWAK

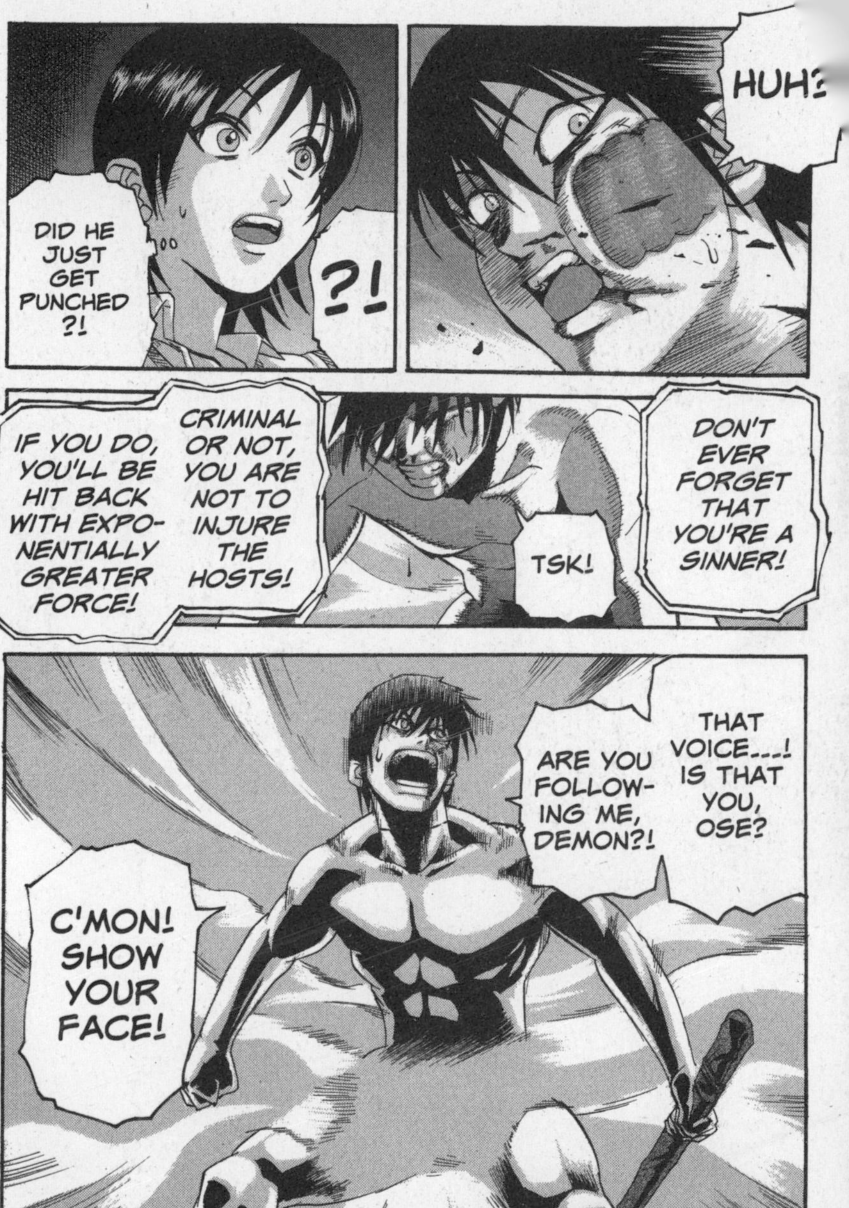
HUH?
?!
DID HE JUST GET PUNCHED?!
DON'T EVER FORGET THAT YOU'RE A SINNER!
TSK!
CRIMINAL OR NOT, YOU ARE NOT TO INJURE THE HOSTS!
IF YOU DO, YOU'LL BE HIT BACK WITH EXPONENTIALLY GREATER FORCE!
THAT VOICE...! IS THAT YOU, OSE?
ARE YOU FOLLOWING ME, DEMON?!
C'MON! SHOW YOUR FACE!

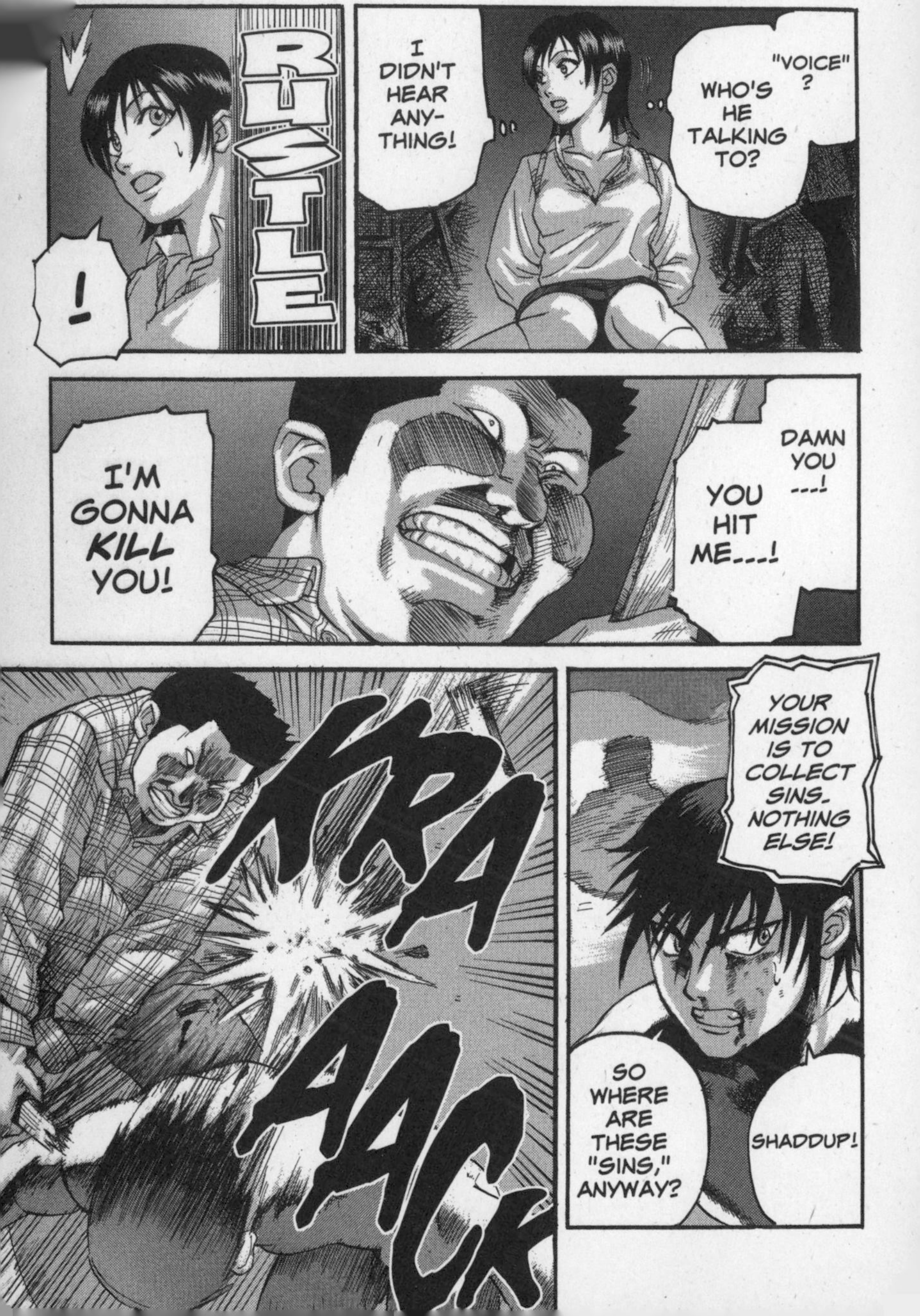
"VOICE"?
WHO'S HE TALKING TO?
I DIDN'T HEAR ANY-THING!
RUSTLE
!
DAMN YOU---!
YOU HIT ME---!
I'M GONNA KILL YOU!
YOUR MISSION IS TO COLLECT SINS. NOTHING ELSE!
SHADDUP!
SO WHERE ARE THESE "SINS," ANYWAY?
KRAAACK

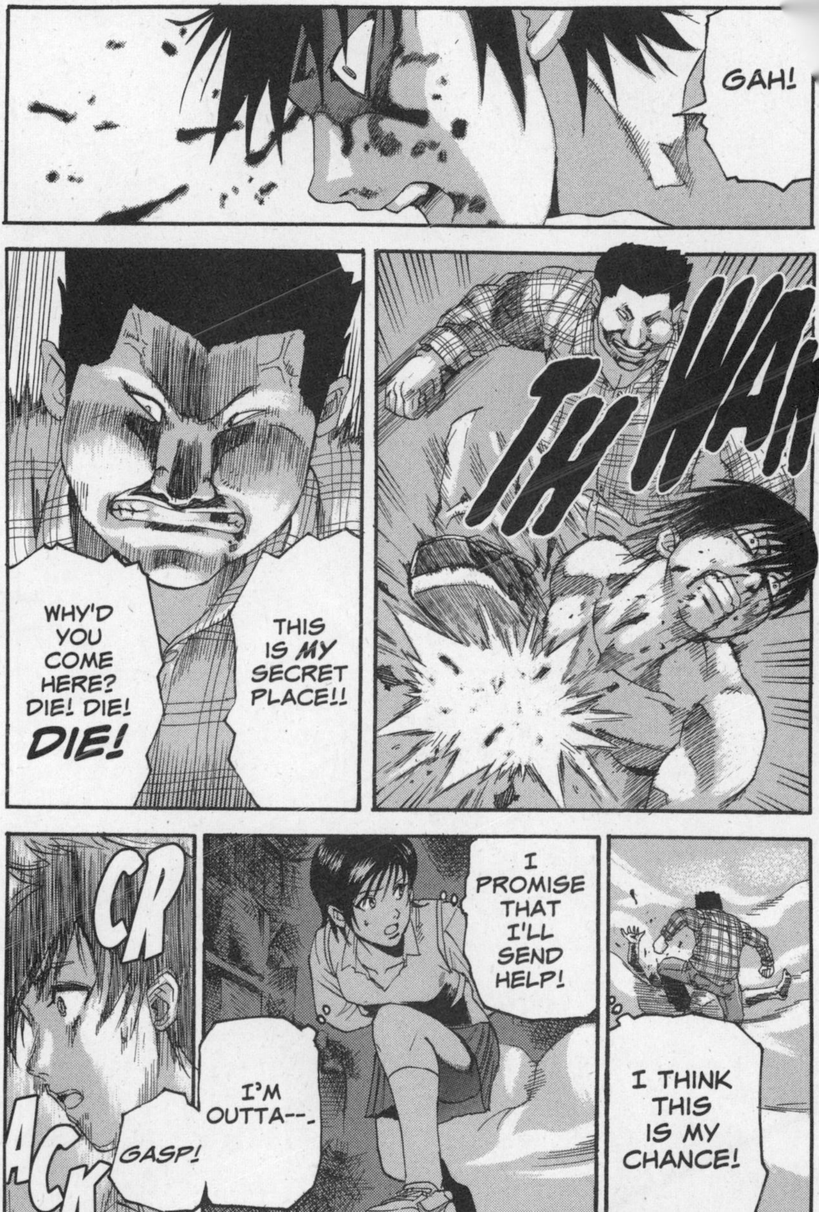
GAH!
THWA
THIS IS MY SECRET PLACE!!
WHY'D YOU COME HERE? DIE! DIE! DIE!
I THINK THIS IS MY CHANCE!
I PROMISE THAT I'LL SEND HELP!
I'M OUTTA--.
CR
ACK
GASP!

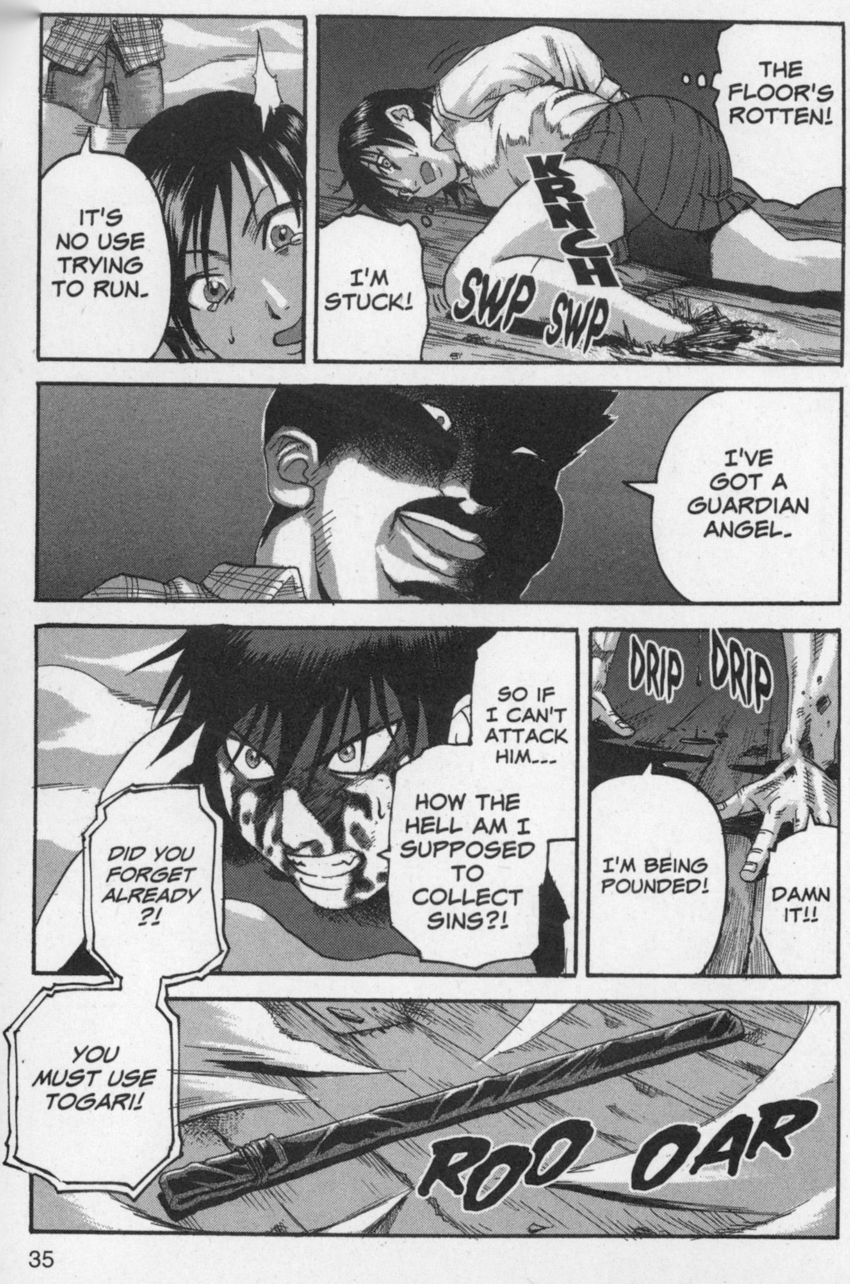
THE FLOOR'S ROTTEN!
I'M STUCK!
KRNCH
SWP SWP
IT'S NO USE TRYING TO RUN.
I'VE GOT A GUARDIAN ANGEL.
DRIP DRIP
I'M BEING POUNDED!
DAMN IT!!
SO IF I CAN'T ATTACK HIM...
HOW THE HELL AM I SUPPOSED TO COLLECT SINS?!
DID YOU FORGET ALREADY ?!
YOU MUST USE TOGARI!
ROO OAR

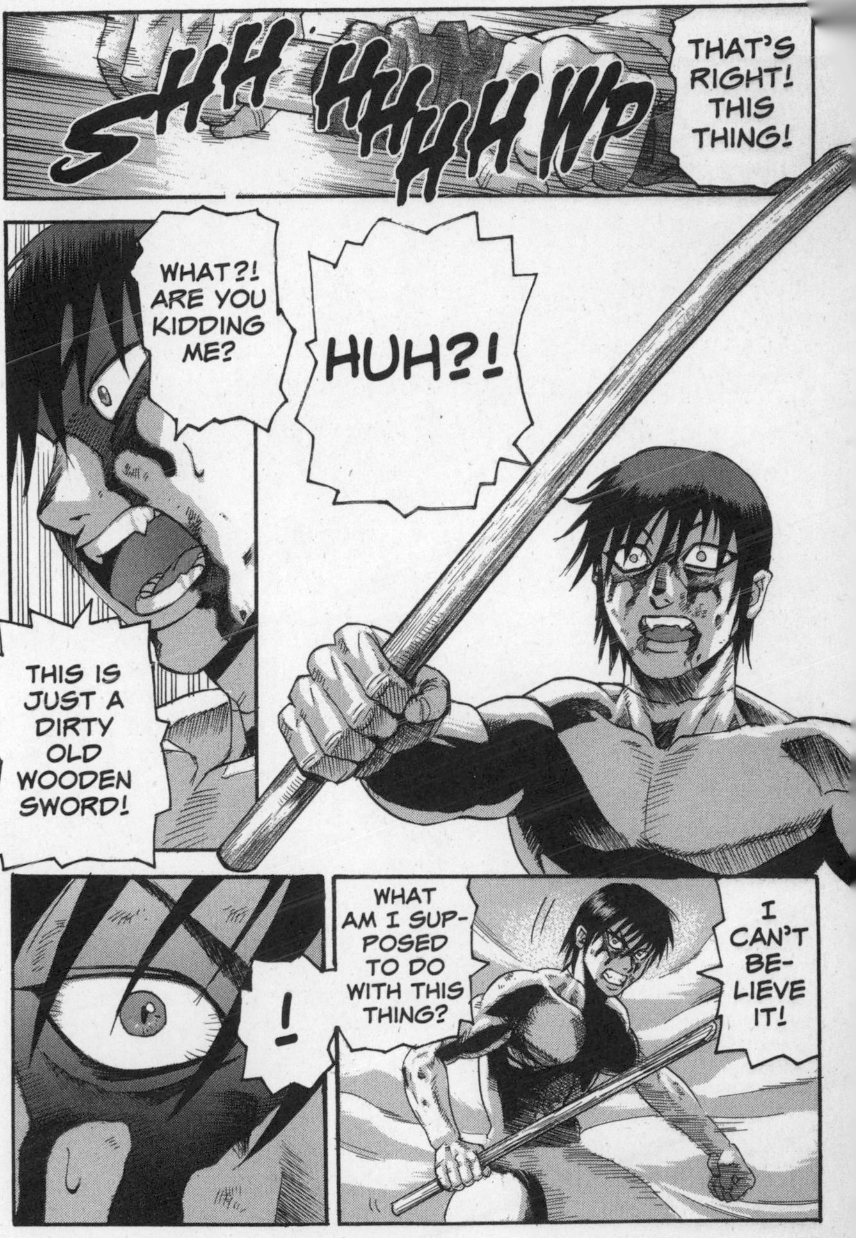
THAT'S RIGHT! THIS THING!
SHHHHHHHWP
HUH?!
WHAT?! ARE YOU KIDDING ME?
THIS IS JUST A DIRTY OLD WOODEN SWORD!
I CAN'T BE-LIEVE IT!
WHAT AM I SUP-POSED TO DO WITH THIS THING?
!

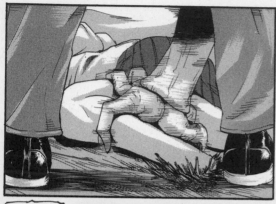

WHAT *IS* THAT?

WHAT?!

ONLY THOSE WHO WIELD TOGARI CAN SEE THE TOGA!

TOGA ARE SINS THAT HAVE TAKEN MATERIAL FORM. THEY SUBSIST ON A SINNER'S MALICE AND PROTECT THEIR HOST IN A SYMBIOTIC EXCHANGE. LIKE A DEMONIC GUARDIAN ANGEL.

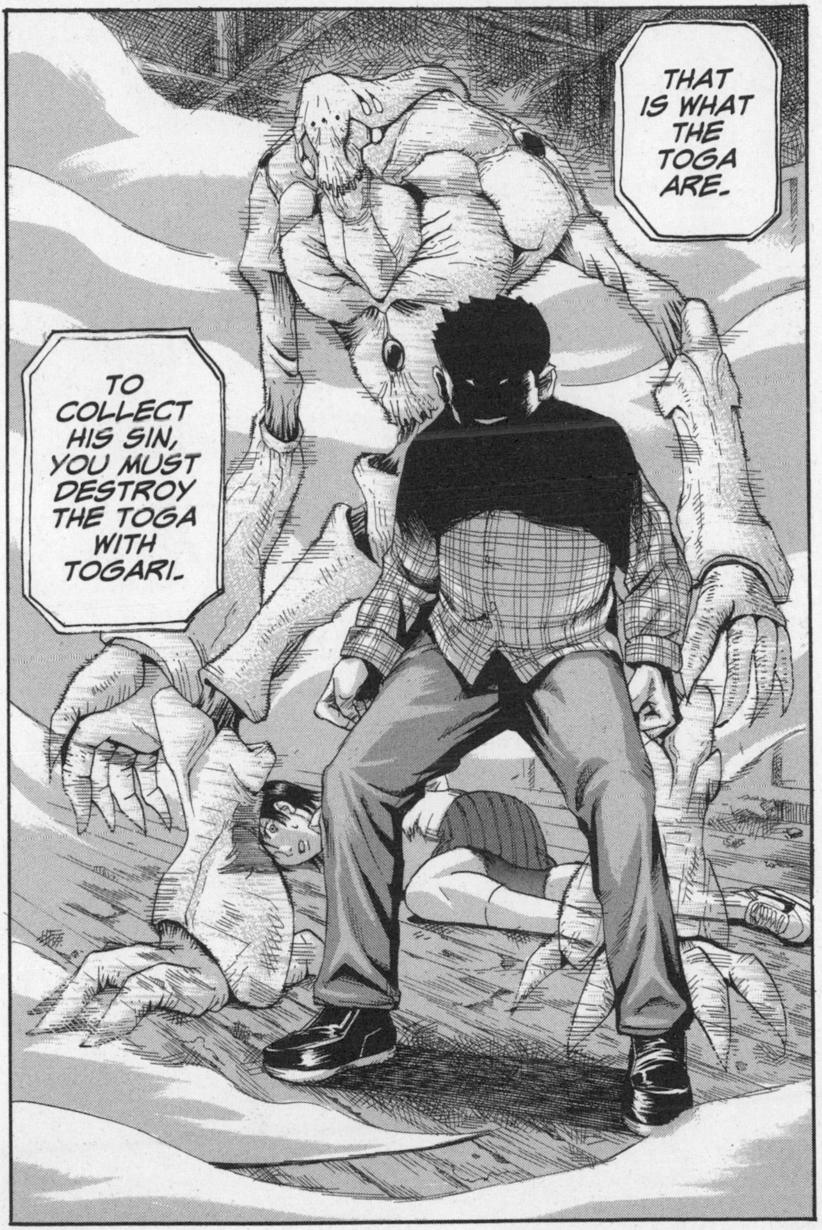
THAT IS WHAT THE TOGA ARE...
TO COLLECT HIS SIN, YOU MUST DESTROY THE TOGA WITH TOGARI...

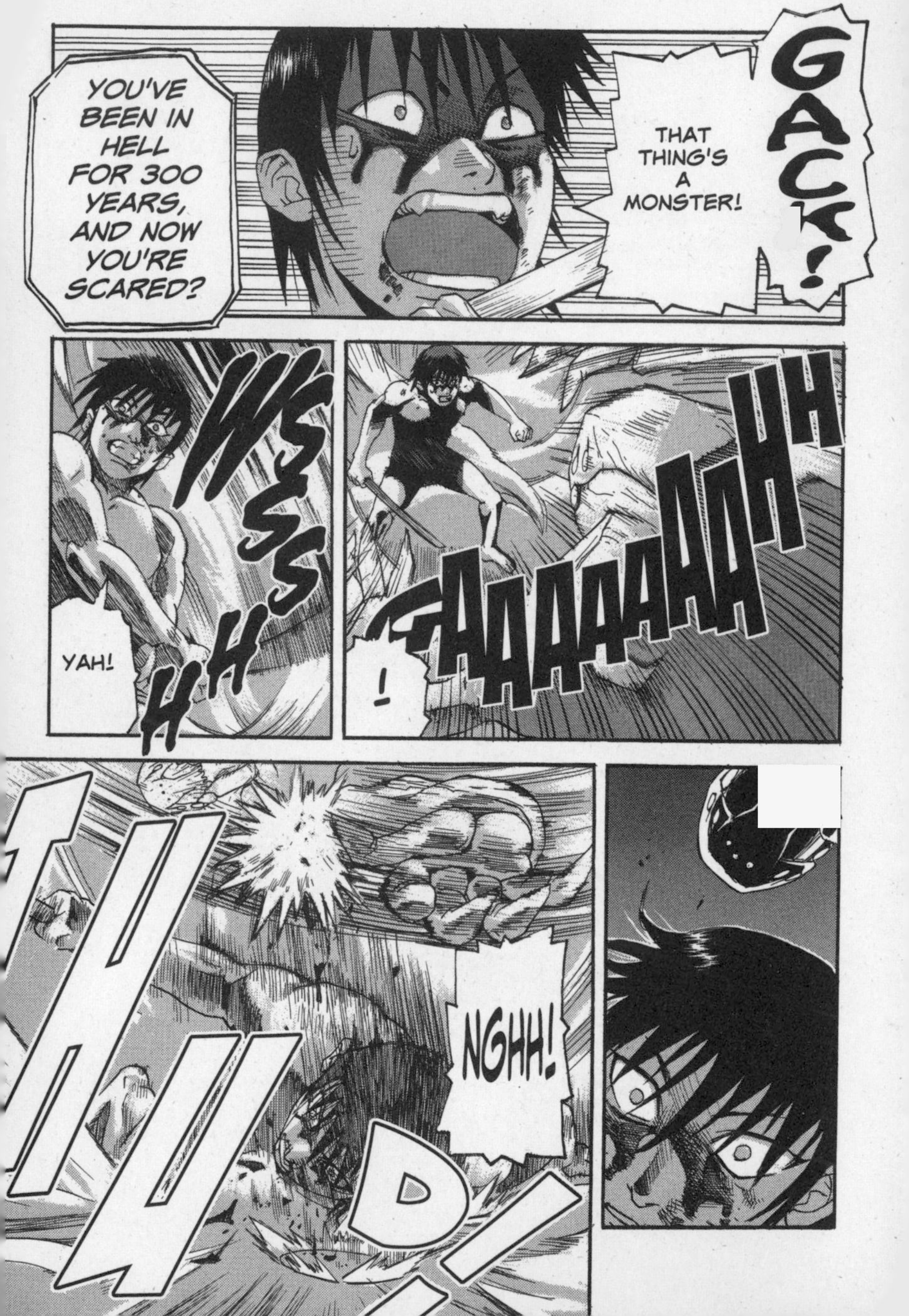
GACK!
THAT THING'S A MONSTER!
YOU'VE BEEN IN HELL FOR 300 YEARS, AND NOW YOU'RE SCARED?
AAAAAAAHHH
!
WSSSHHH
YAH!
NGHH!

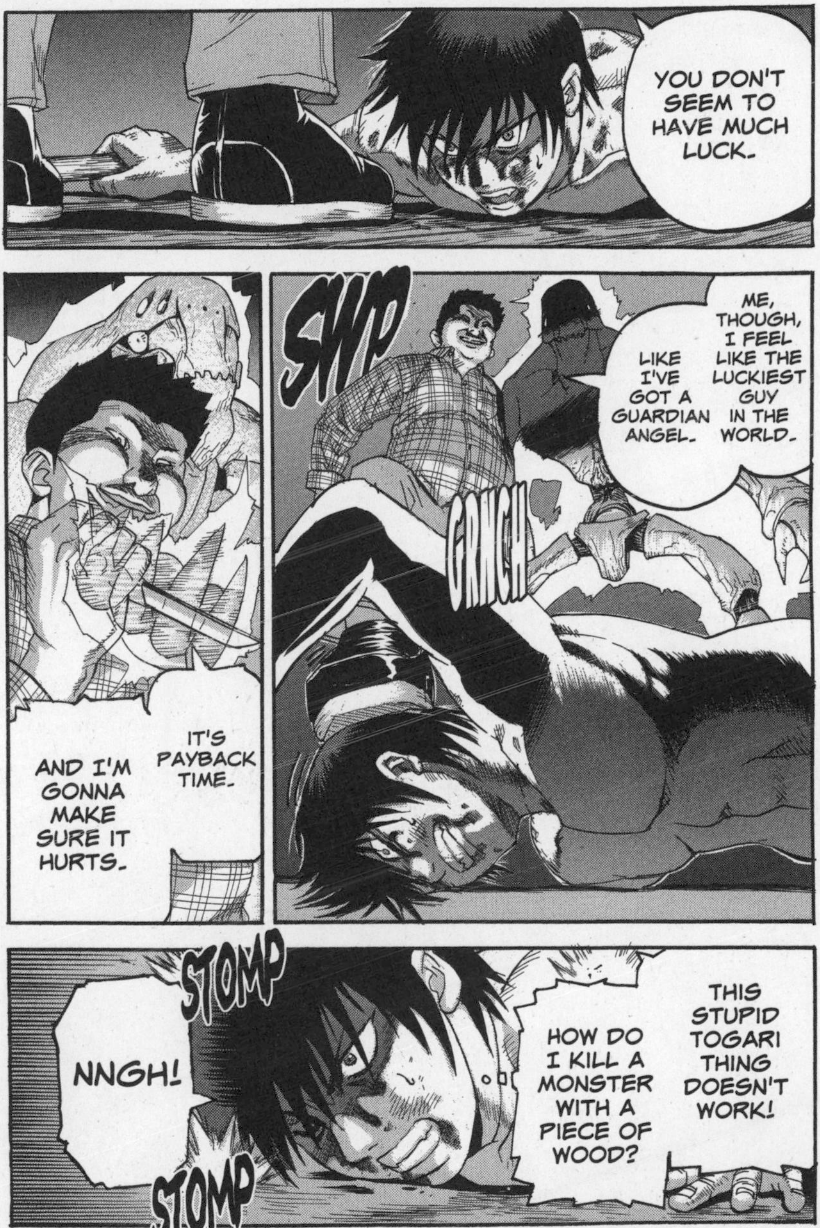
YOU DON'T SEEM TO HAVE MUCH LUCK.
ME, THOUGH, I FEEL LIKE THE LUCKIEST GUY IN THE WORLD.
LIKE I'VE GOT A GUARDIAN ANGEL.
SWIP
GRNCH
IT'S PAYBACK TIME.
AND I'M GONNA MAKE SURE IT HURTS.
THIS STUPID TOGARI THING DOESN'T WORK!
HOW DO I KILL A MONSTER WITH A PIECE OF WOOD?
STOMP
NNGH!
STOMP

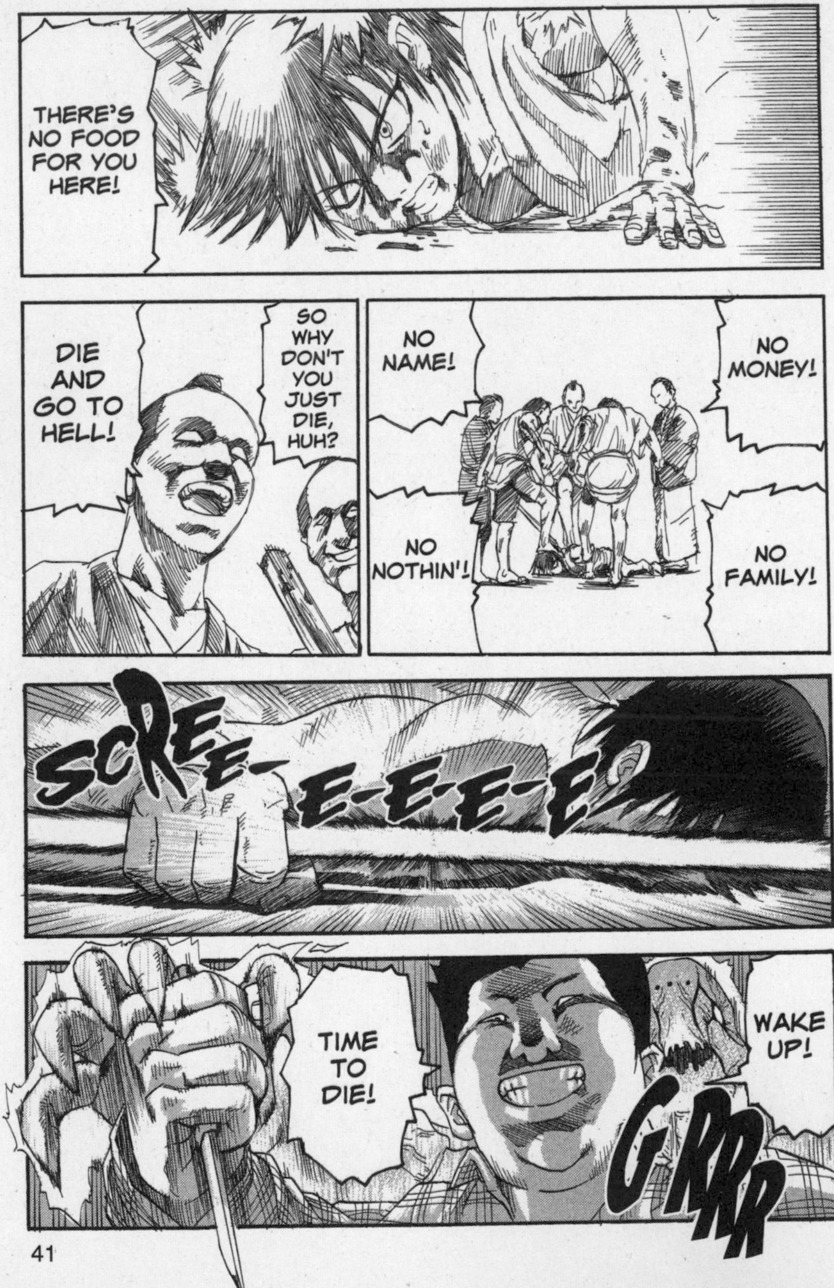
THERE'S NO FOOD FOR YOU HERE!
NO MONEY!
NO NAME!
NO FAMILY!
NO NOTHIN'!
SO WHY DON'T YOU JUST DIE, HUH?
DIE AND GO TO HELL!
SCREE-E-E-E-E-E
WAKE UP!
GRRR
TIME TO DIE!

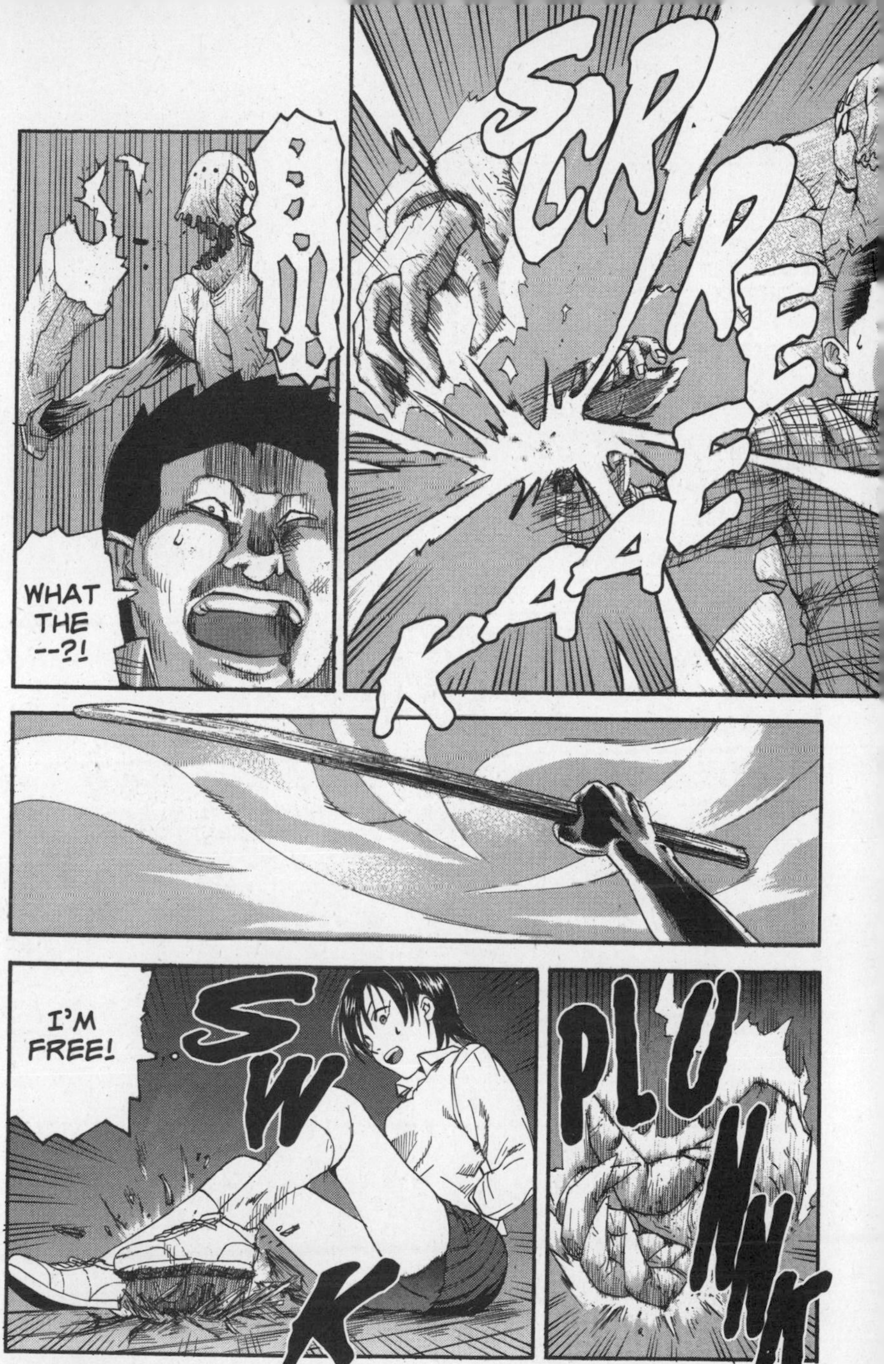
SCRREEAAK
!!
WHAT THE --?!
PLUNNK
SWK
I'M FREE!

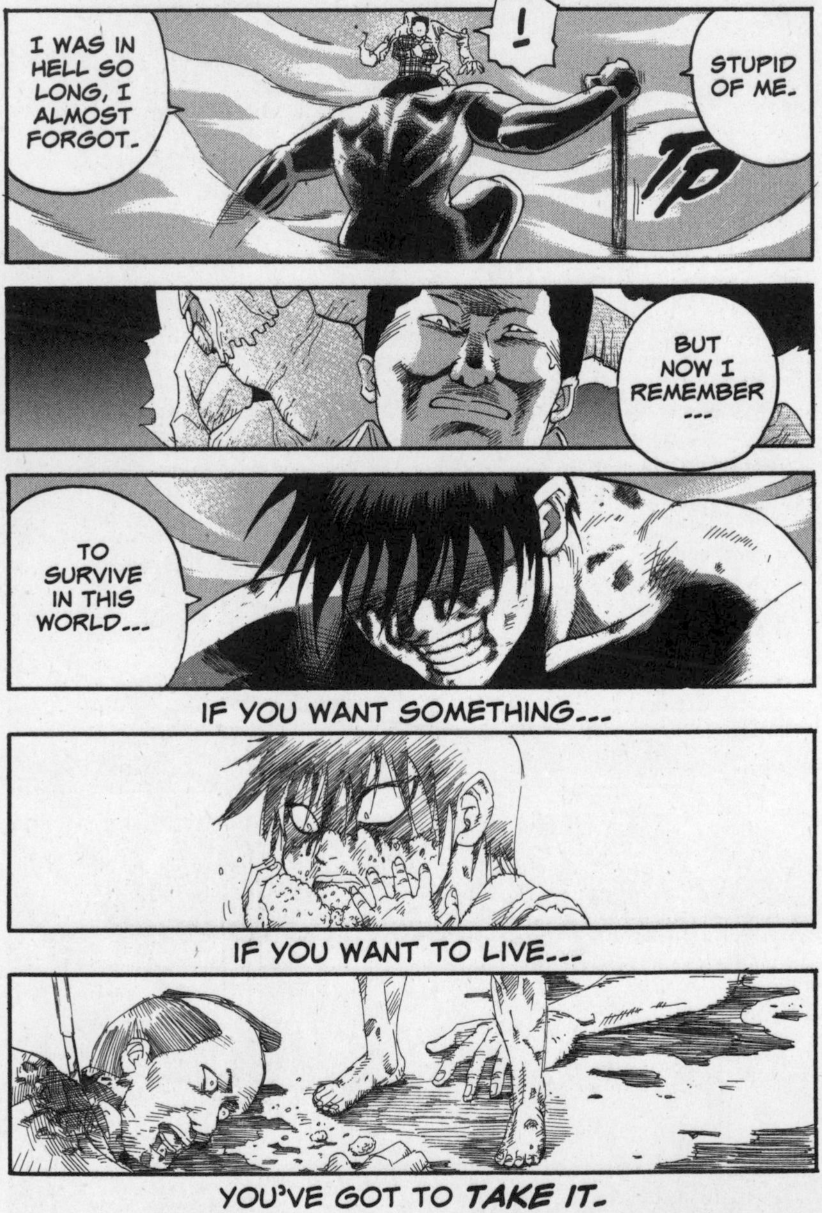
STUPID OF ME.
TP
!
I WAS IN HELL SO LONG, I ALMOST FORGOT.
BUT NOW I REMEMBER...
TO SURVIVE IN THIS WORLD...
IF YOU WANT SOMETHING...
IF YOU WANT TO LIVE...
YOU'VE GOT TO *TAKE IT*.

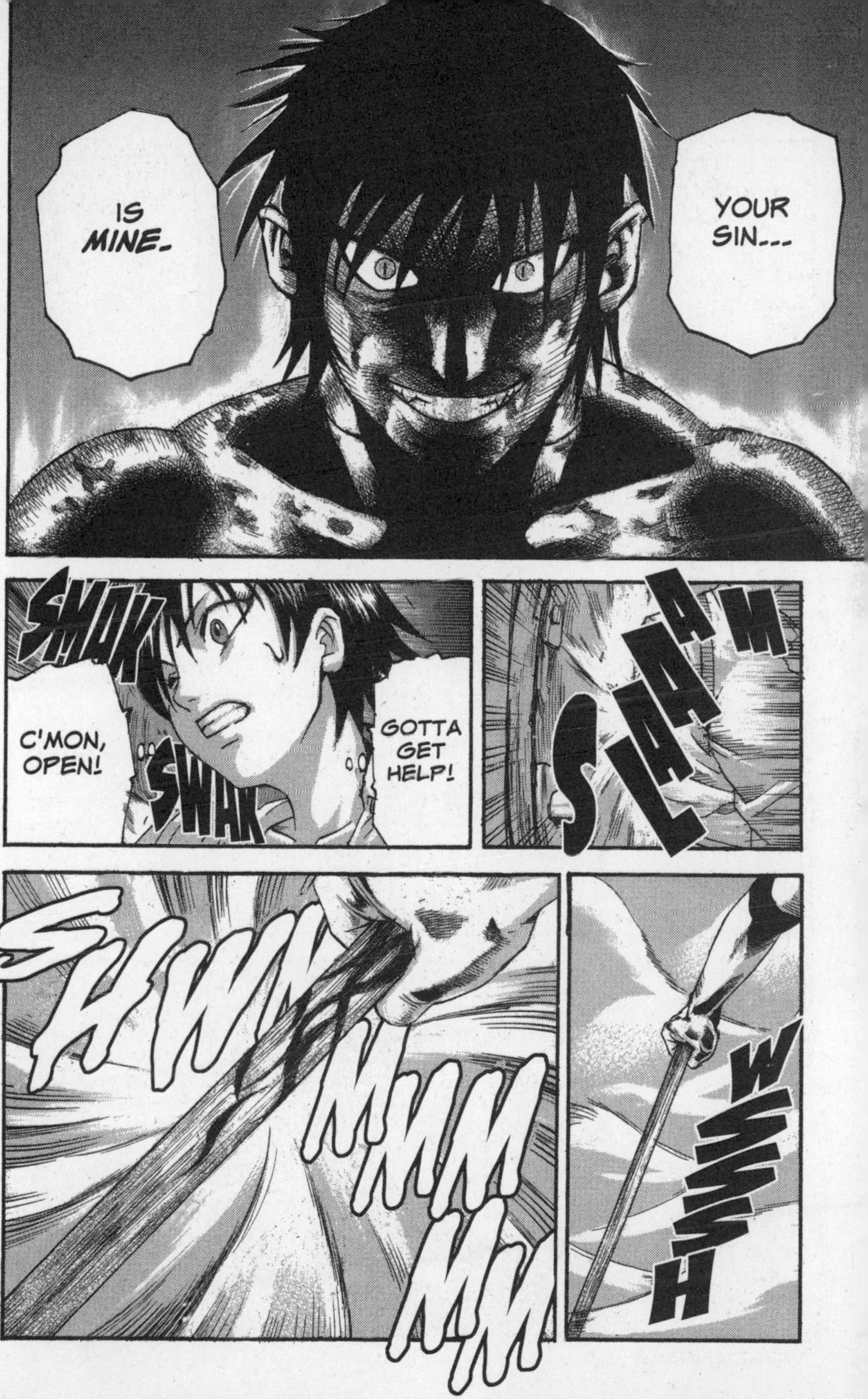
YOUR SIN...
IS MINE.
SLAAAM
SMAK
GOTTA GET HELP!
C'MON, OPEN!
SWAK
WHSSSH
SHWMMMMMM

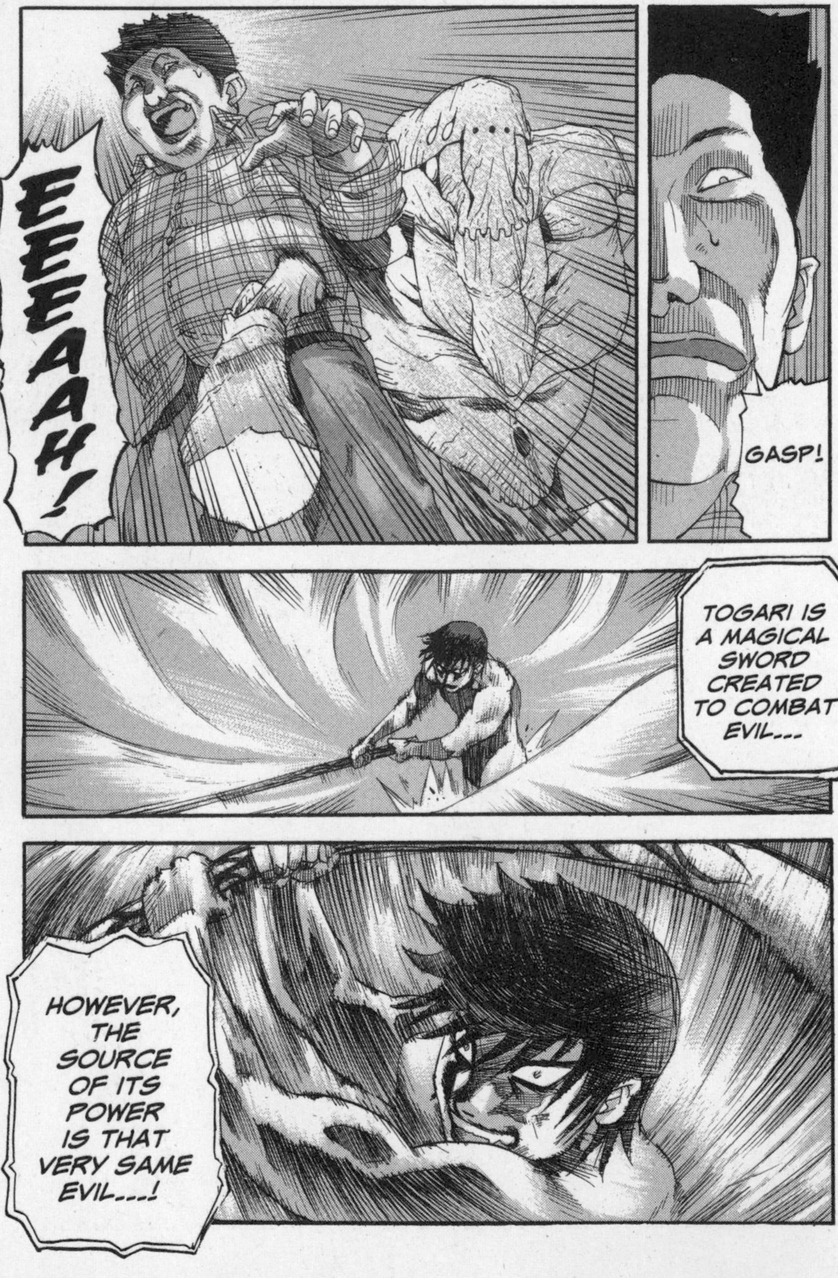
GASP!
EEEAAAH!
TOGARI IS A MAGICAL SWORD CREATED TO COMBAT EVIL...
HOWEVER, THE SOURCE OF ITS POWER IS THAT VERY SAME EVIL...!

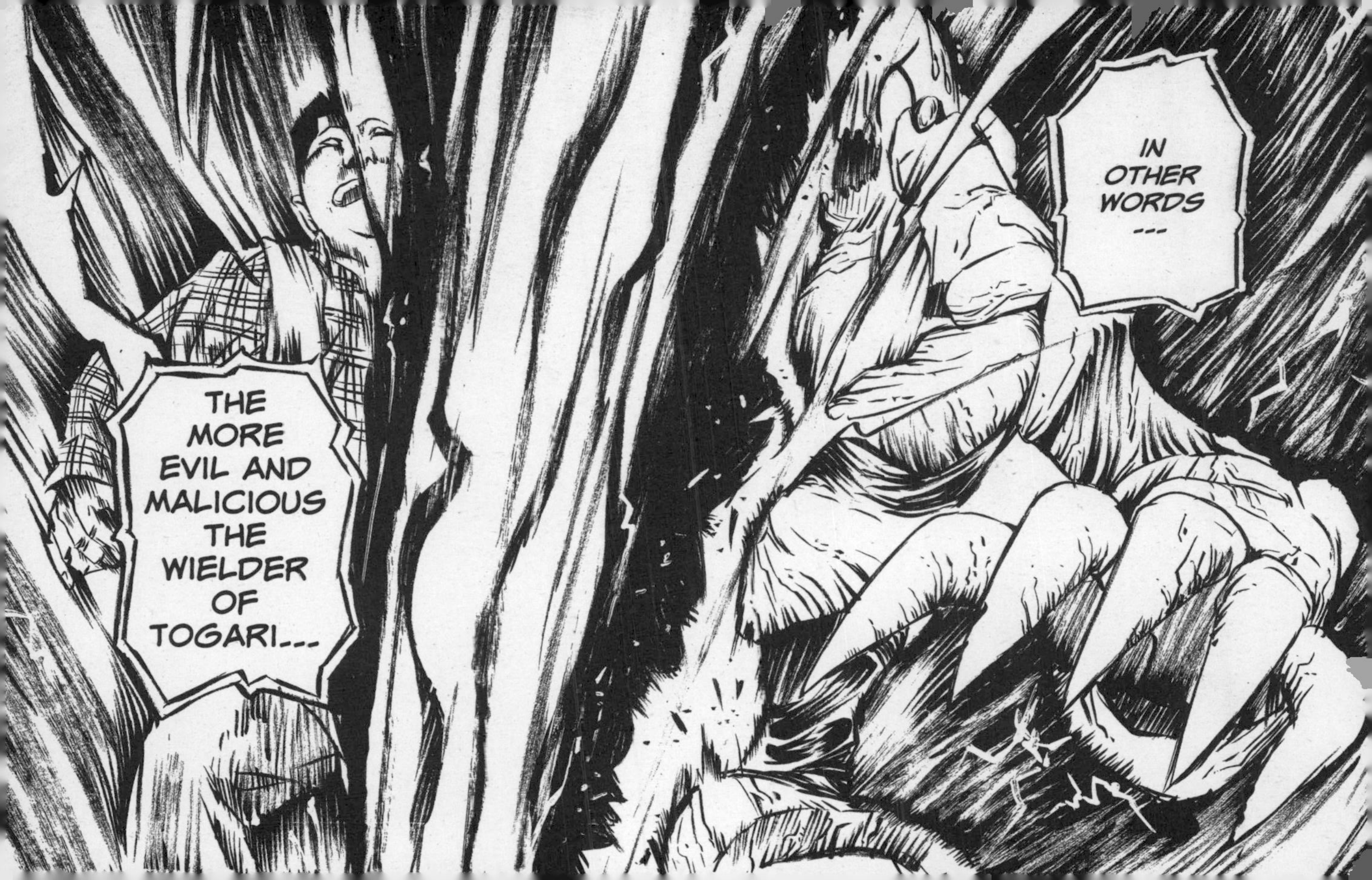
IN OTHER WORDS ---
THE MORE EVIL AND MALICIOUS THE WIELDER OF TOGARI...

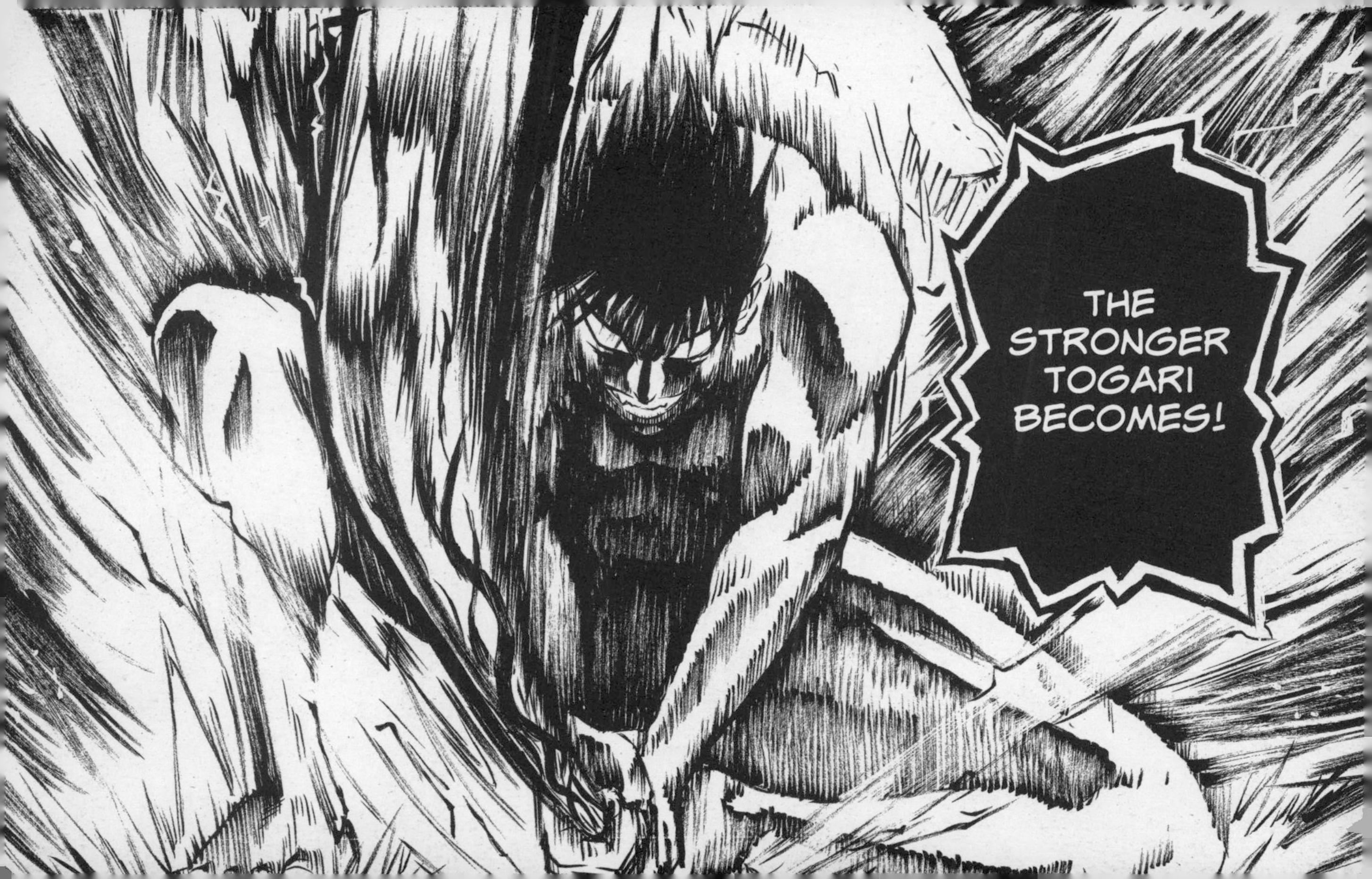
THE STRONGER TOGARI BECOMES!

BAMM
AHH!
SWMP
OUCH!
IT'S OPEN! I DID IT!
CRACK
CRICK
GRROAAR
WSSSS
SHHH

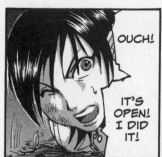

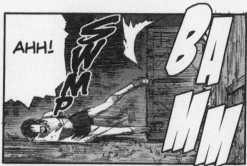

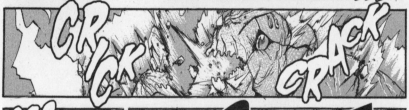

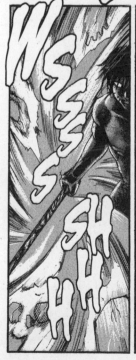

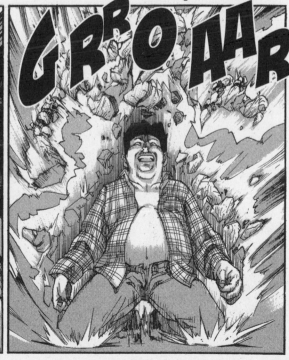

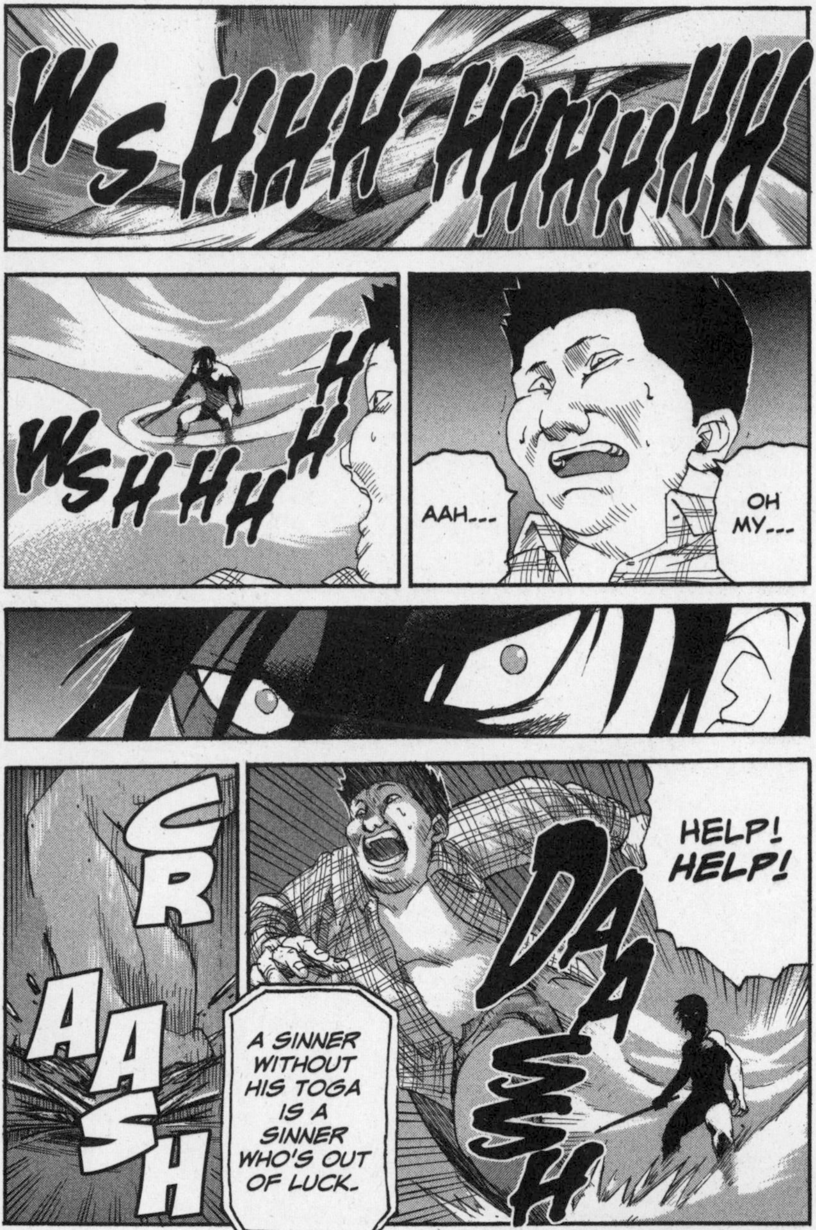
WSHHH HHHHHH
OH MY...
AAH...
WSHHHHHHH
HELP! HELP!
DAASH
A SINNER WITHOUT HIS TOGA IS A SINNER WHO'S OUT OF LUCK.
CRAASH

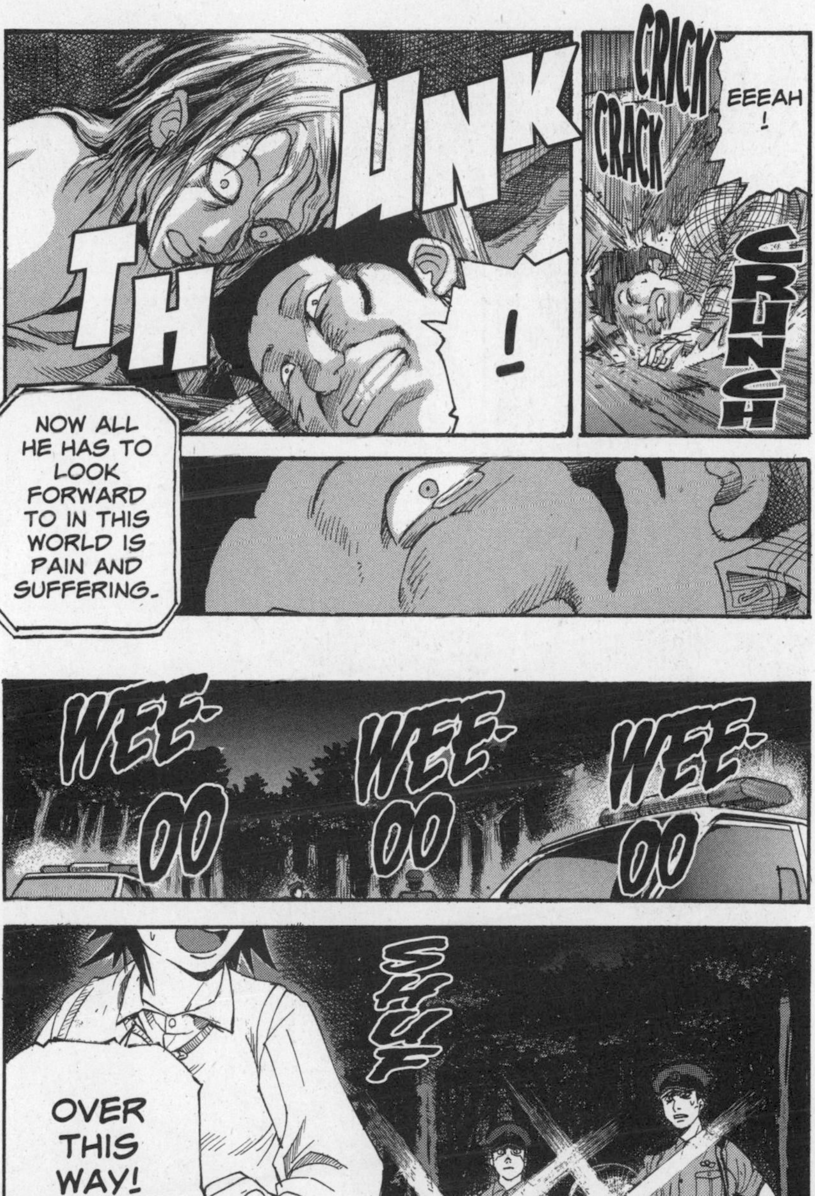
EEEAH!
CRICK
CRACK
CRUNCH
THUNK
!
NOW ALL HE HAS TO LOOK FORWARD TO IN THIS WORLD IS PAIN AND SUFFERING...
WEE-OO
WEE-OO
WEE-OO
SHUF
OVER THIS WAY!

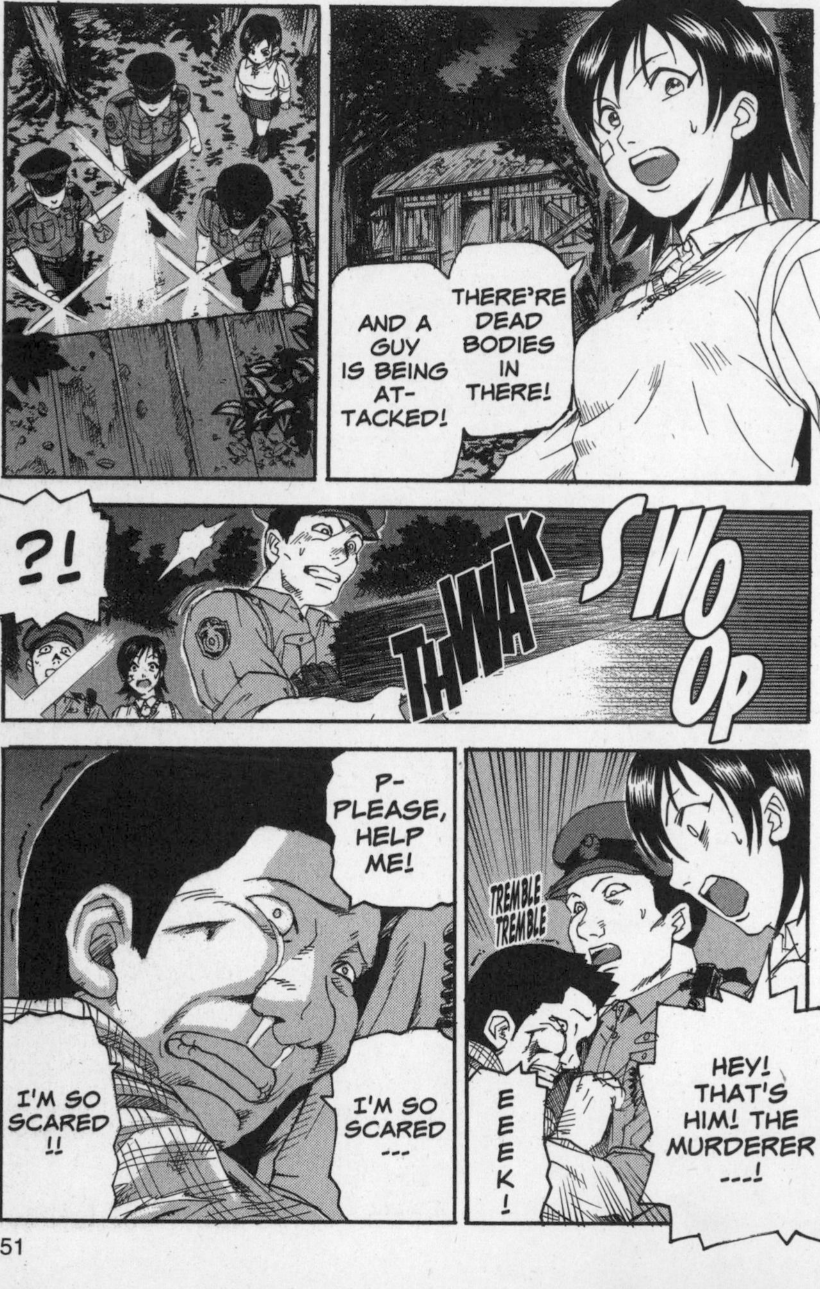
THERE'RE DEAD BODIES IN THERE!
AND A GUY IS BEING AT-TACKED!
SWOOP
THWAK
?!
TREMBLE TREMBLE
HEY! THAT'S HIM! THE MURDERER ---!
EEEK!
P-PLEASE, HELP ME!
I'M SO SCARED ---
I'M SO SCARED !!

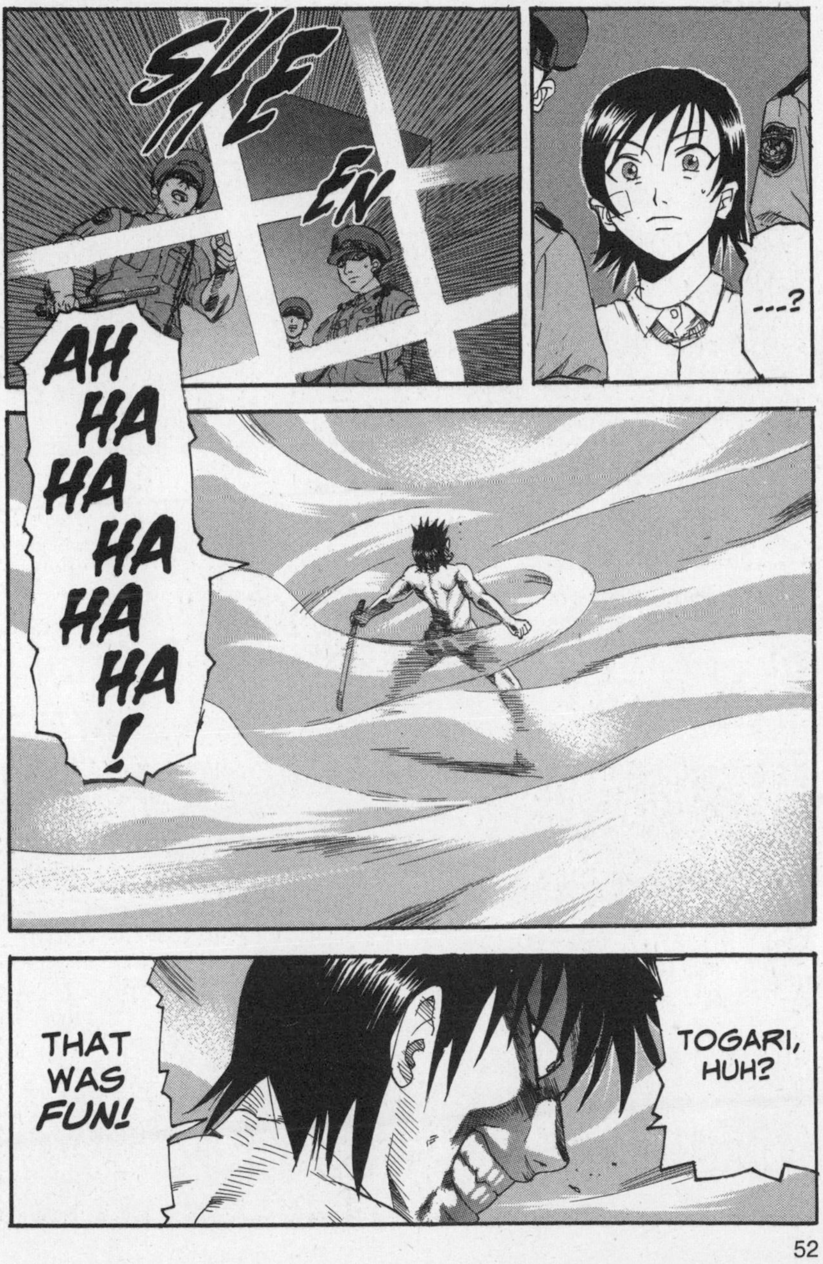
---?
SHEEN
AH HA HA HA HA HA HA HA!
TOGARI, HUH?
THAT WAS FUN!

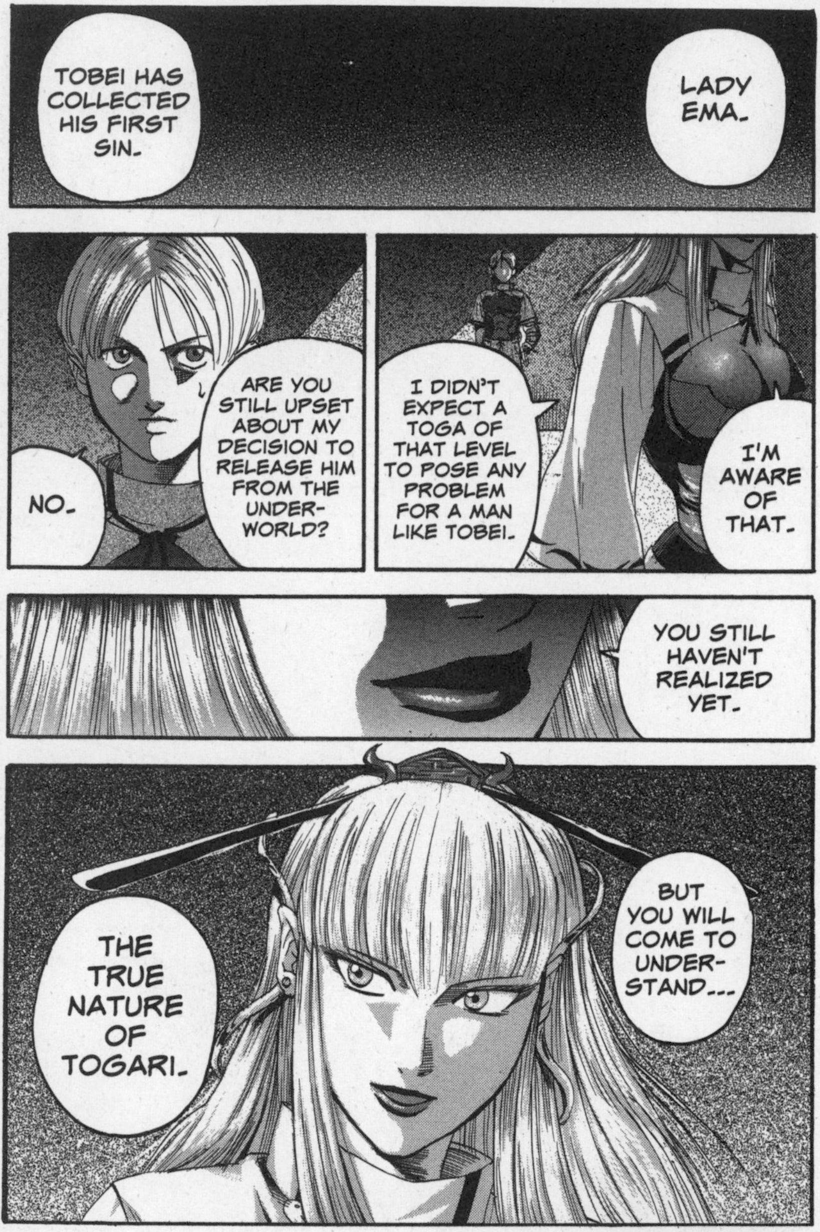
LADY EMA...
TOBEI HAS COLLECTED HIS FIRST SIN...
I DIDN'T EXPECT A TOGA OF THAT LEVEL TO POSE ANY PROBLEM FOR A MAN LIKE TOBEI...
I'M AWARE OF THAT...
ARE YOU STILL UPSET ABOUT MY DECISION TO RELEASE HIM FROM THE UNDER-WORLD?
NO...
YOU STILL HAVEN'T REALIZED YET...
BUT YOU WILL COME TO UNDER-STAND...
THE TRUE NATURE OF TOGARI...

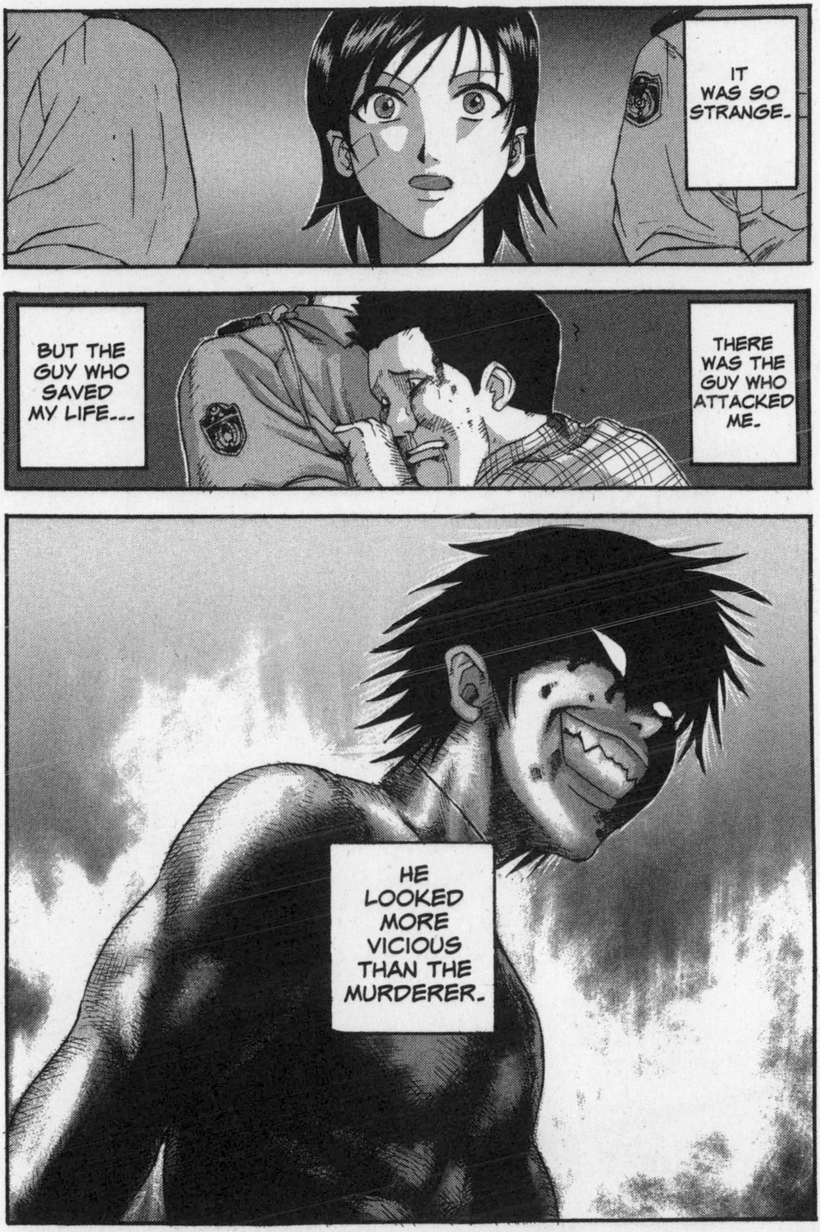
IT WAS SO STRANGE.
THERE WAS THE GUY WHO ATTACKED ME.
BUT THE GUY WHO SAVED MY LIFE...
HE LOOKED MORE VICIOUS THAN THE MURDERER.

Chapter 2 "Thank You"...?

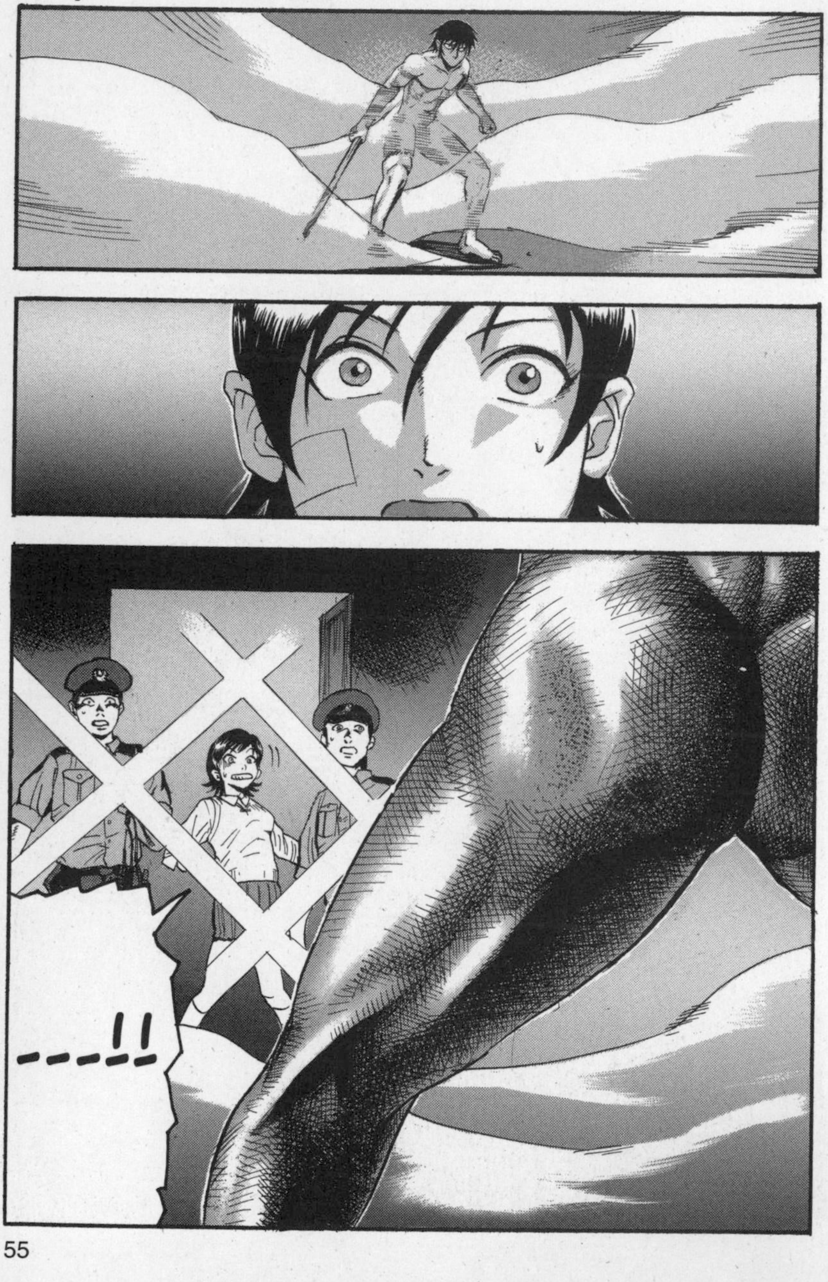
---!!

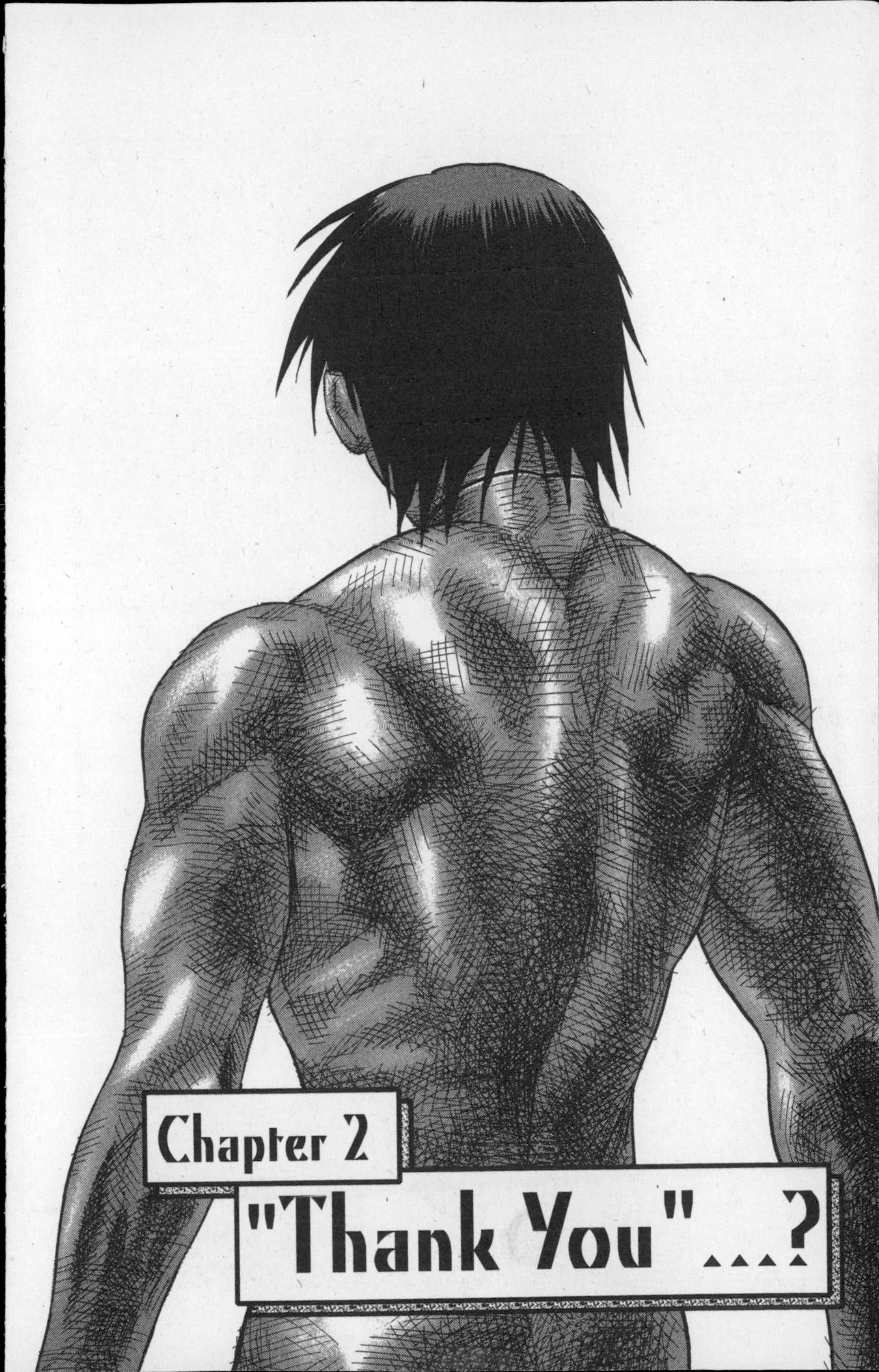
Chapter 2
"Thank You"...?

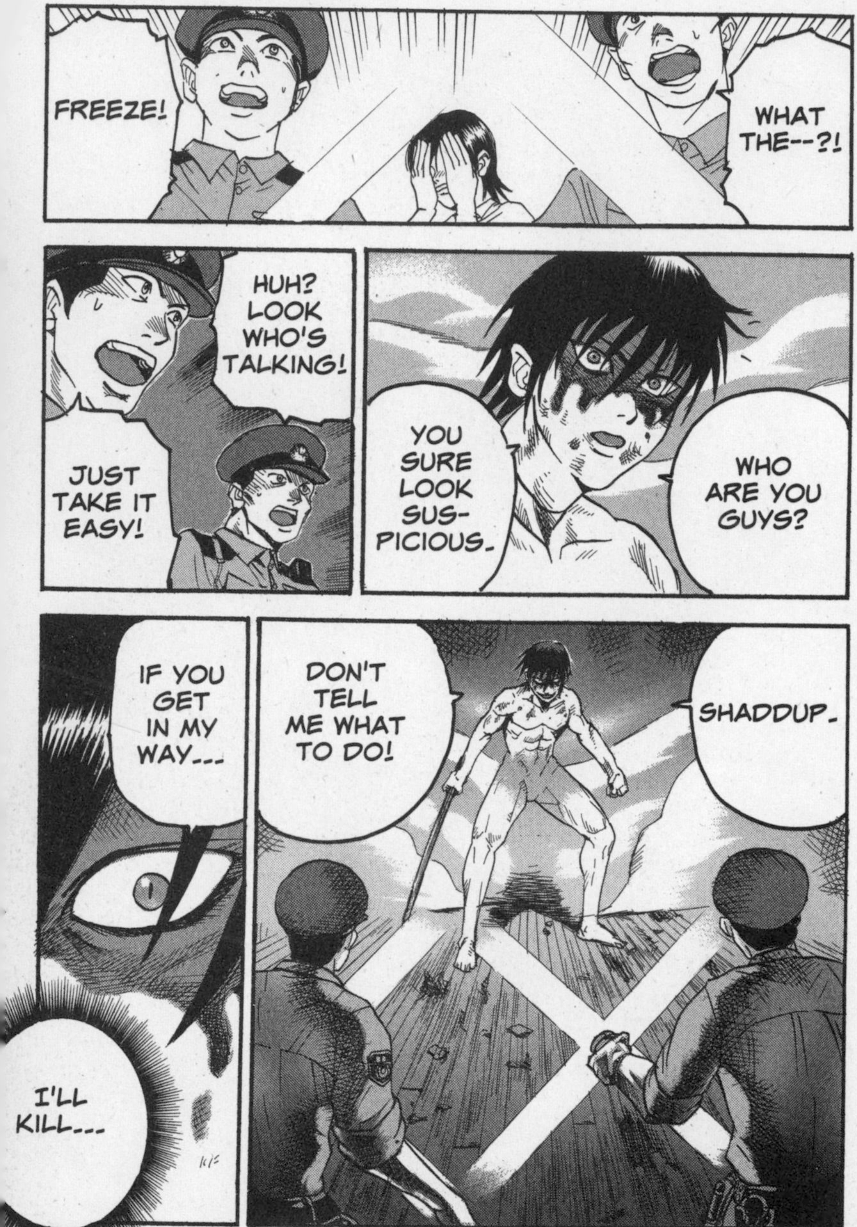
WHAT THE--?!
FREEZE!
WHO ARE YOU GUYS?
YOU SURE LOOK SUS-PICIOUS.
HUH? LOOK WHO'S TALKING!
JUST TAKE IT EASY!
SHADDUP.
DON'T TELL ME WHAT TO DO!
IF YOU GET IN MY WAY...
I'LL KILL...

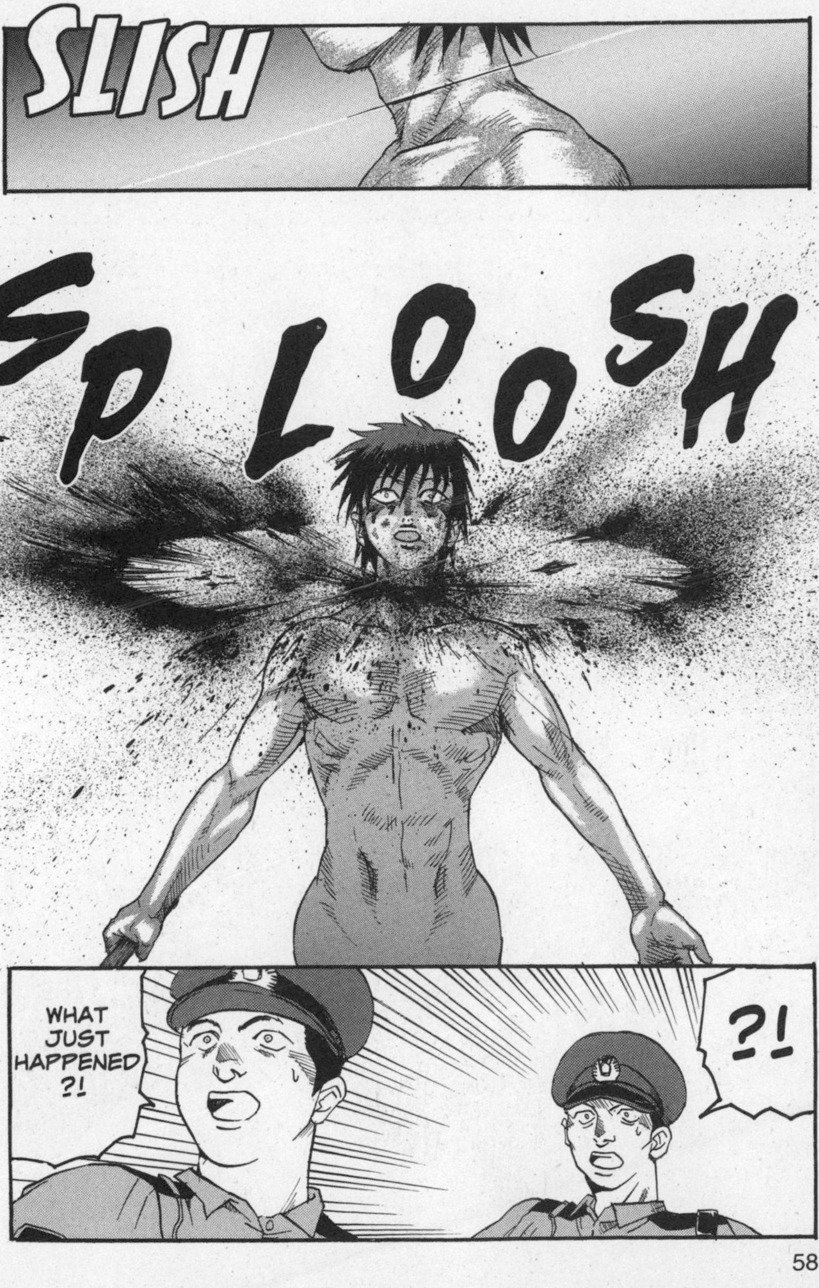
SLISH
SPLOOSH
?!
WHAT JUST HAPPENED ?!

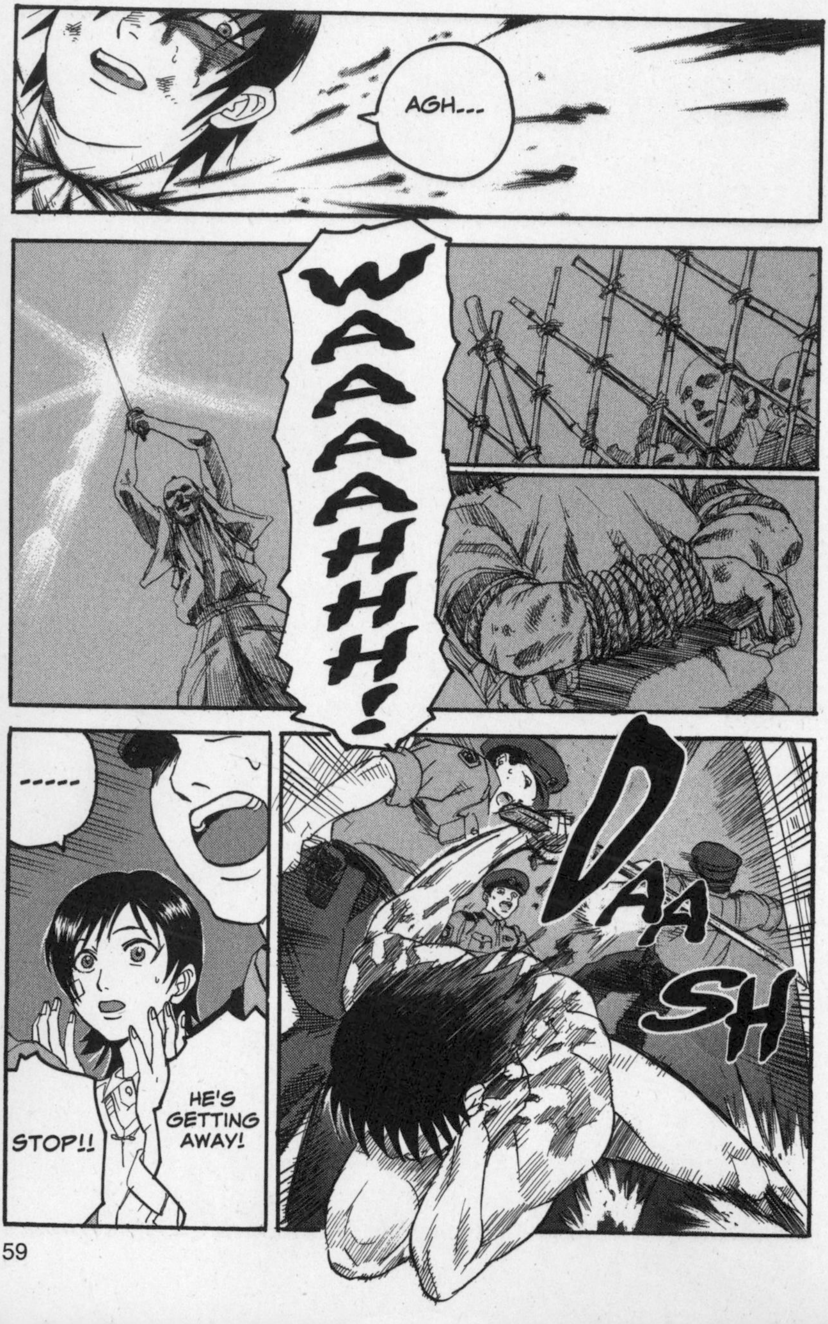
AGH...
WAAAAHHH!
DAASH

HE'S GETTING AWAY!
STOP!!

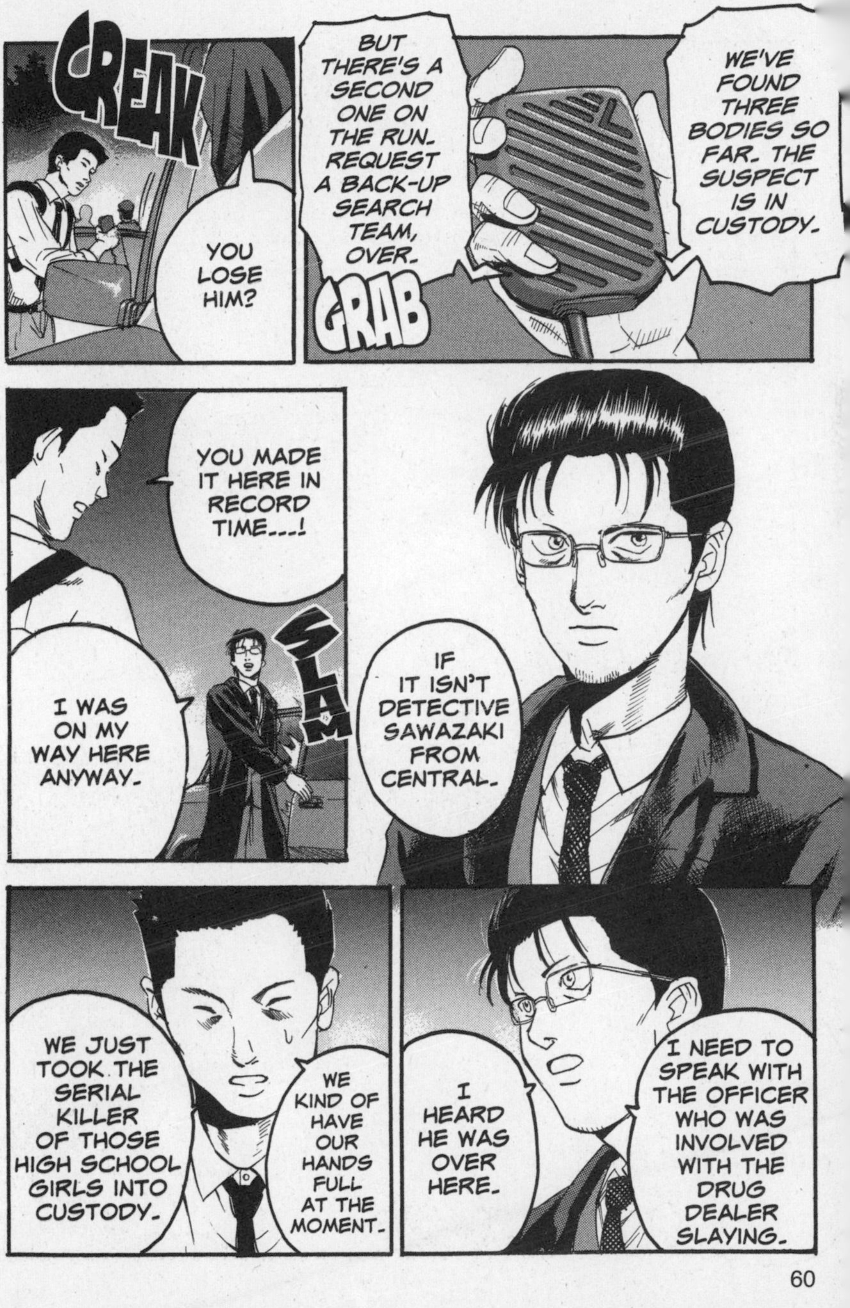
WE'VE FOUND THREE BODIES SO FAR. THE SUSPECT IS IN CUSTODY.
BUT THERE'S A SECOND ONE ON THE RUN. REQUEST A BACK-UP SEARCH TEAM, OVER.
GRAB
CREAK
YOU LOSE HIM?
IF IT ISN'T DETECTIVE SAWAZAKI FROM CENTRAL.
YOU MADE IT HERE IN RECORD TIME...!
SLAM
I WAS ON MY WAY HERE ANYWAY.
I NEED TO SPEAK WITH THE OFFICER WHO WAS INVOLVED WITH THE DRUG DEALER SLAYING.
I HEARD HE WAS OVER HERE.
WE KIND OF HAVE OUR HANDS FULL AT THE MOMENT.
WE JUST TOOK THE SERIAL KILLER OF THOSE HIGH SCHOOL GIRLS INTO CUSTODY.

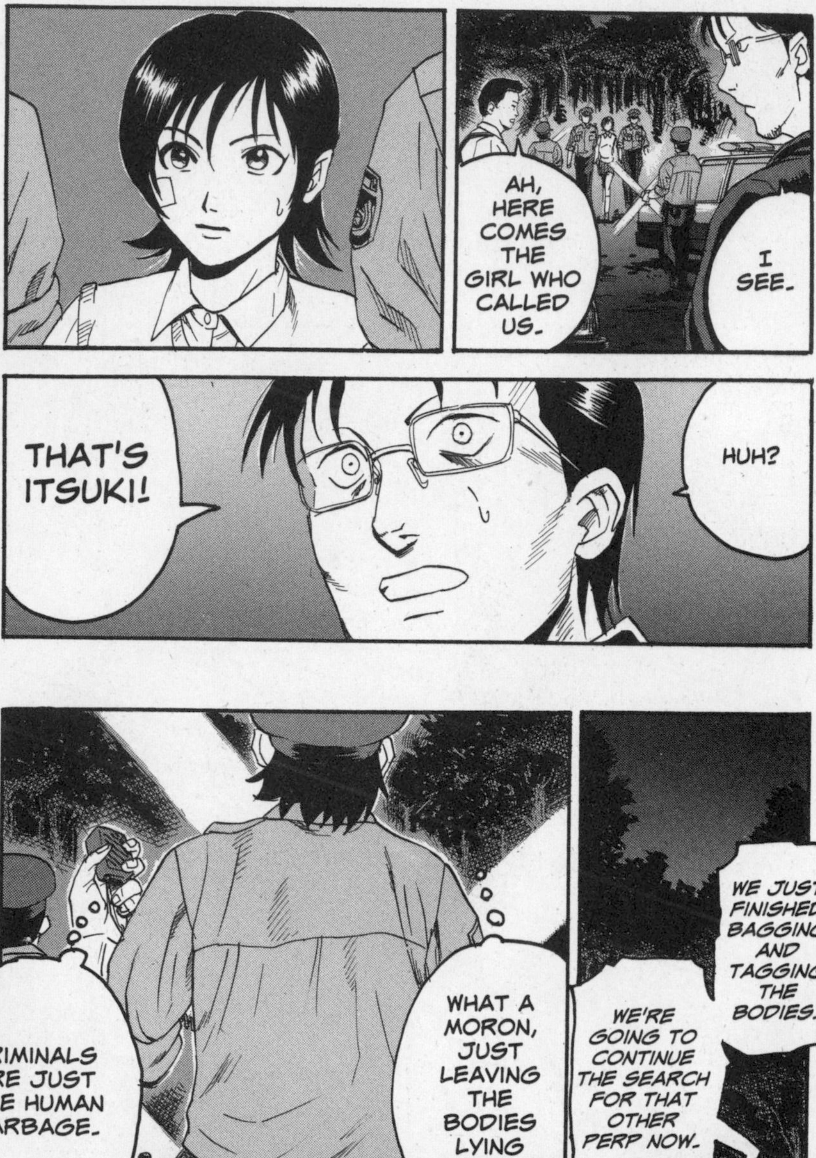
AH, HERE COMES THE GIRL WHO CALLED US.
I SEE.
HUH?
THAT'S ITSUKI!
WE JUST FINISHED BAGGING AND TAGGING THE BODIES.
WE'RE GOING TO CONTINUE THE SEARCH FOR THAT OTHER PERP NOW.
WHAT A MORON, JUST LEAVING THE BODIES LYING AROUND.
CRIMINALS ARE JUST LIKE HUMAN GARBAGE.

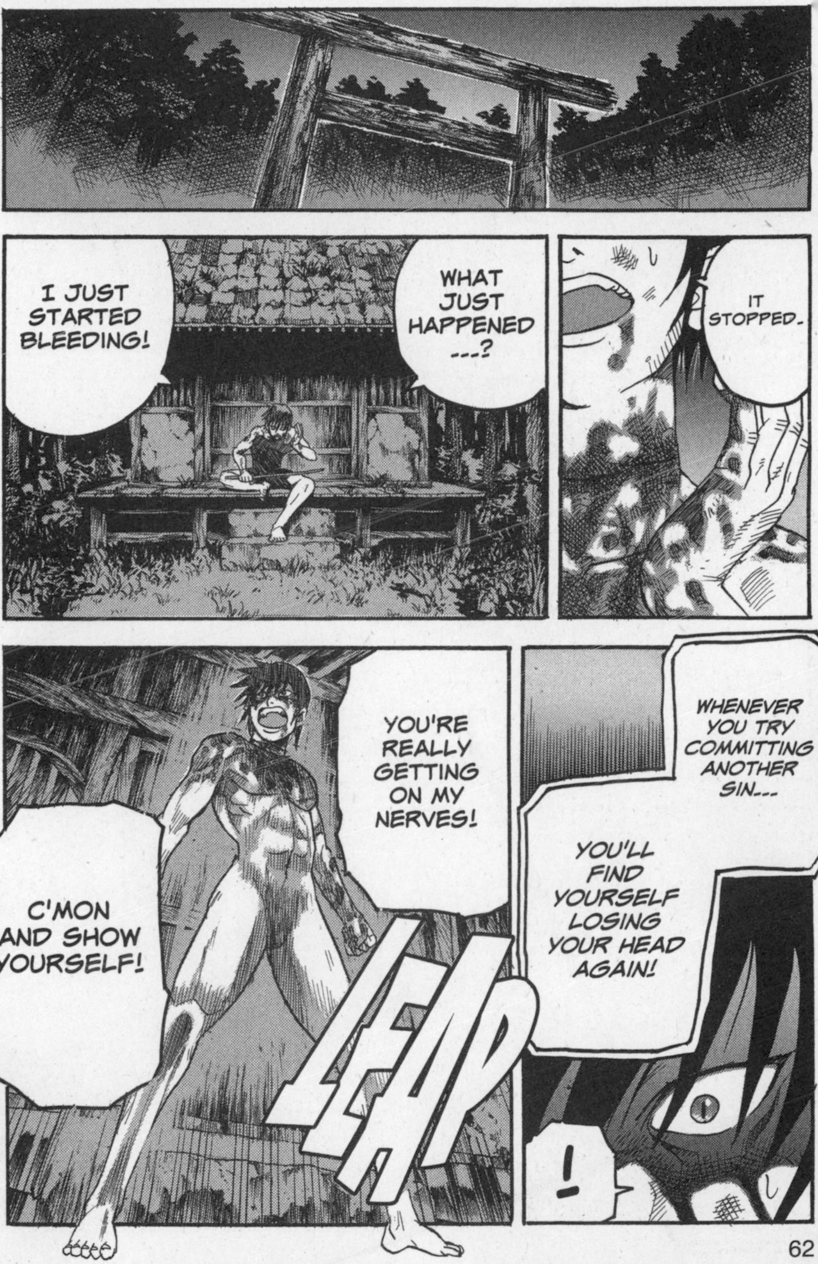
IT STOPPED...
WHAT JUST HAPPENED ...?
I JUST STARTED BLEEDING!
WHENEVER YOU TRY COMMITTING ANOTHER SIN...
YOU'LL FIND YOURSELF LOSING YOUR HEAD AGAIN!
!
YOU'RE REALLY GETTING ON MY NERVES!
LEAP
C'MON AND SHOW YOURSELF!

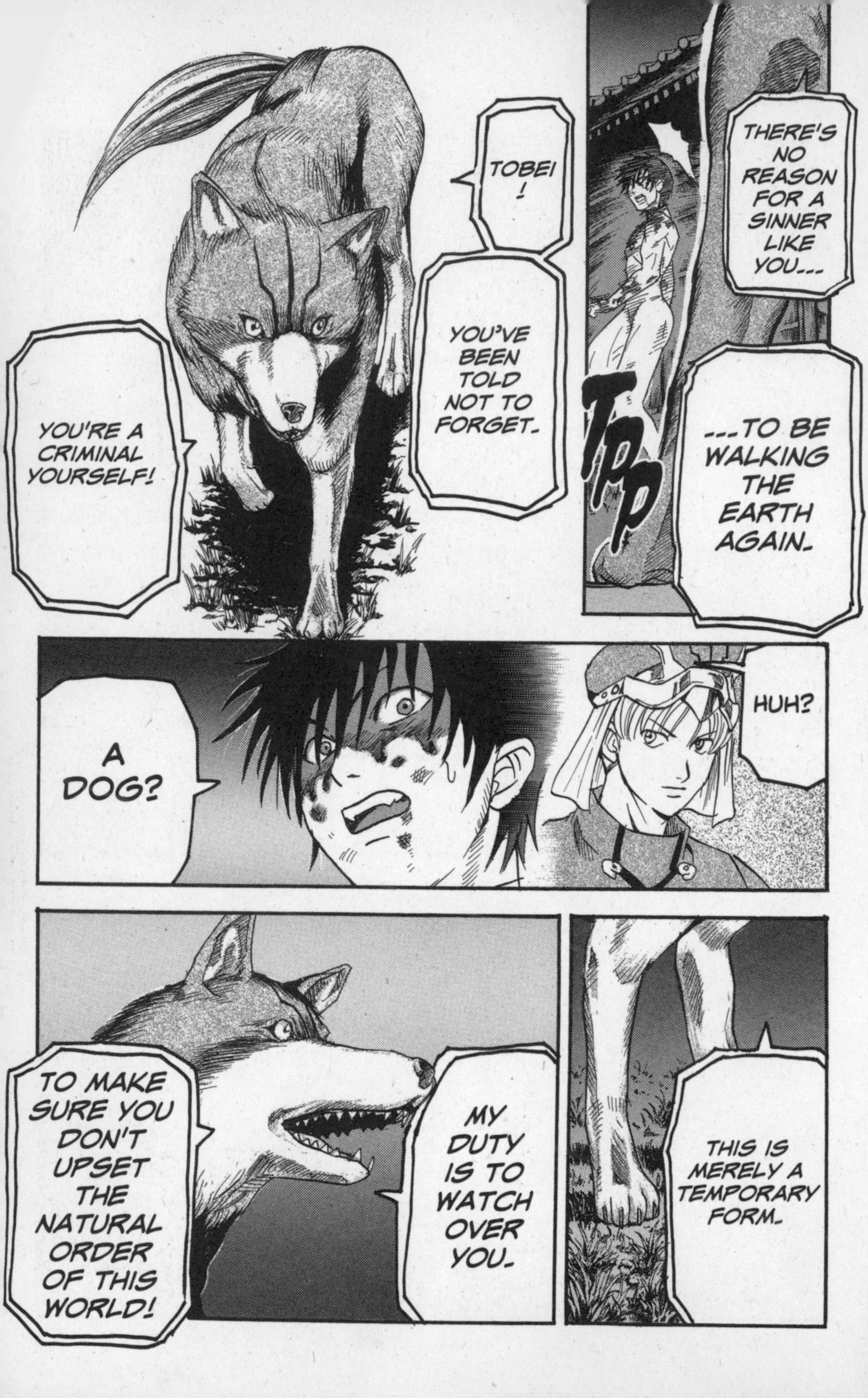
THERE'S NO REASON FOR A SINNER LIKE YOU...
...TO BE WALKING THE EARTH AGAIN.
TPP
TOBEI!
YOU'VE BEEN TOLD NOT TO FORGET.
YOU'RE A CRIMINAL YOURSELF!
HUH?
A DOG?
THIS IS MERELY A TEMPORARY FORM.
MY DUTY IS TO WATCH OVER YOU.
TO MAKE SURE YOU DON'T UPSET THE NATURAL ORDER OF THIS WORLD!

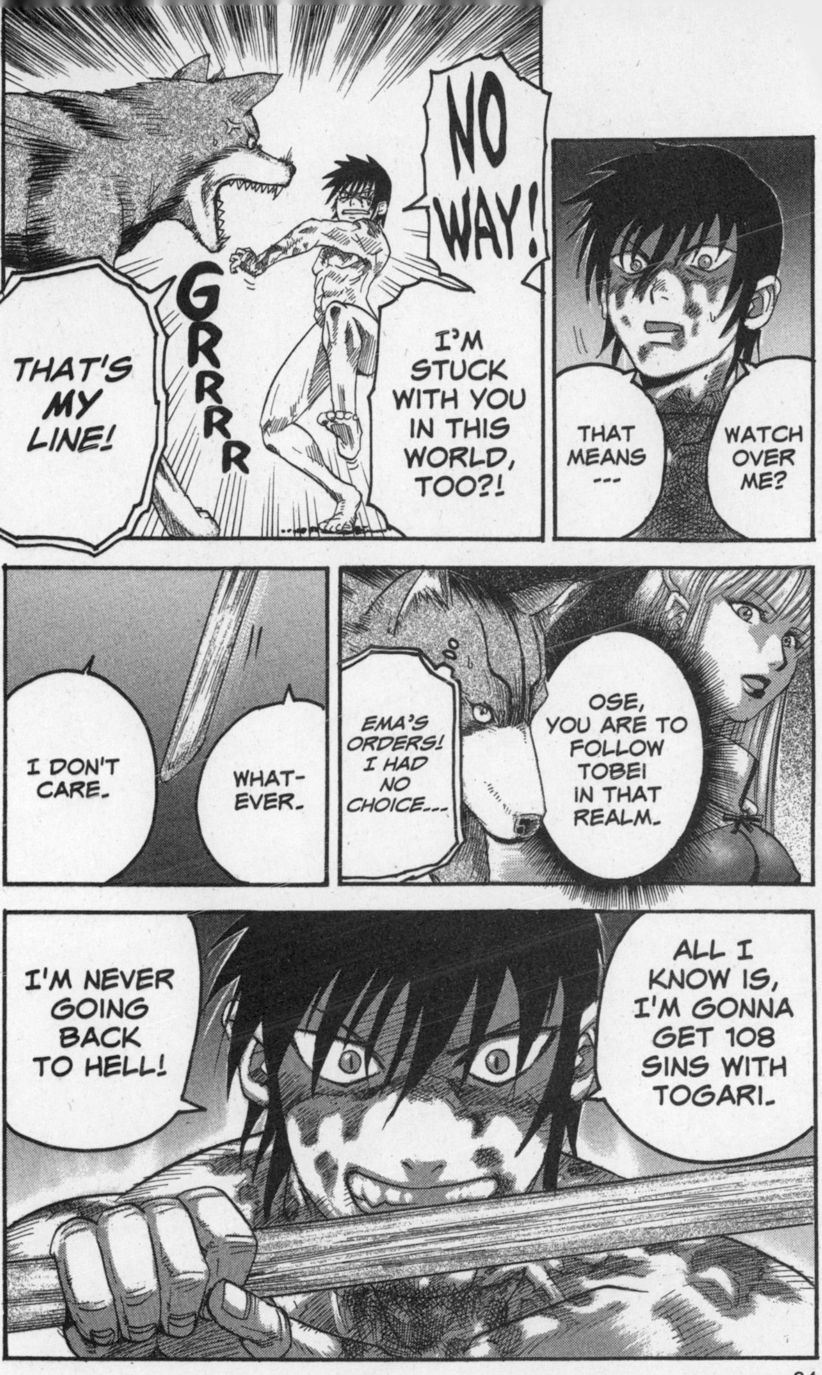
WATCH OVER ME?
THAT MEANS ---
NO WAY!
I'M STUCK WITH YOU IN THIS WORLD, TOO?!
GRRRR
THAT'S MY LINE!
OSE, YOU ARE TO FOLLOW TOBEI IN THAT REALM.
EMA'S ORDERS! I HAD NO CHOICE...
WHAT-EVER.
I DON'T CARE.
ALL I KNOW IS, I'M GONNA GET 108 SINS WITH TOGARI.
I'M NEVER GOING BACK TO HELL!

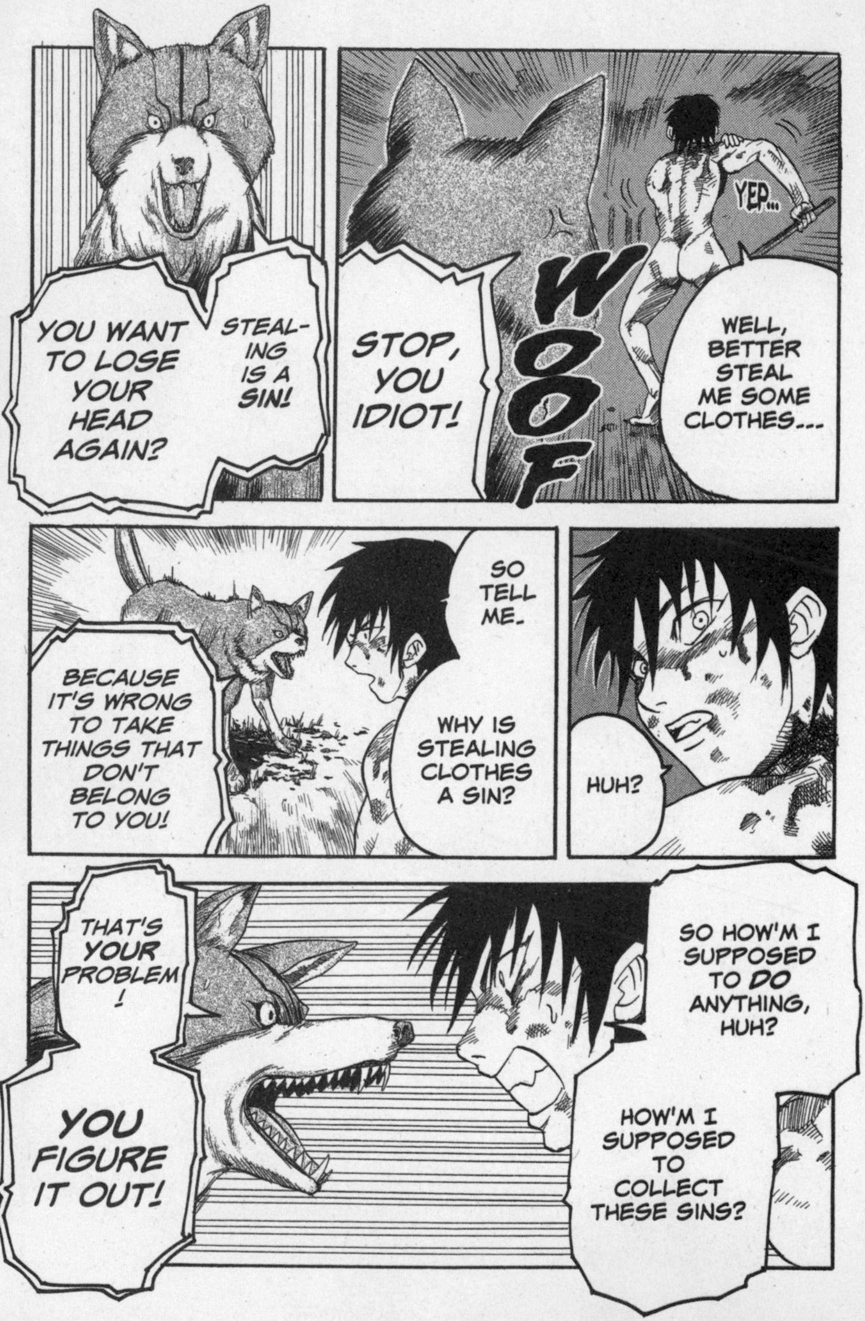
YEP...
WELL, BETTER STEAL ME SOME CLOTHES...
WOOF
STOP, YOU IDIOT!
STEAL-ING IS A SIN!
YOU WANT TO LOSE YOUR HEAD AGAIN?
HUH?
SO TELL ME.
WHY IS STEALING CLOTHES A SIN?
BECAUSE IT'S WRONG TO TAKE THINGS THAT DON'T BELONG TO YOU!
SO HOW'M I SUPPOSED TO *DO* ANYTHING, HUH?
HOW'M I SUPPOSED TO COLLECT THESE SINS?
THAT'S *YOUR* PROBLEM!
YOU FIGURE IT OUT!

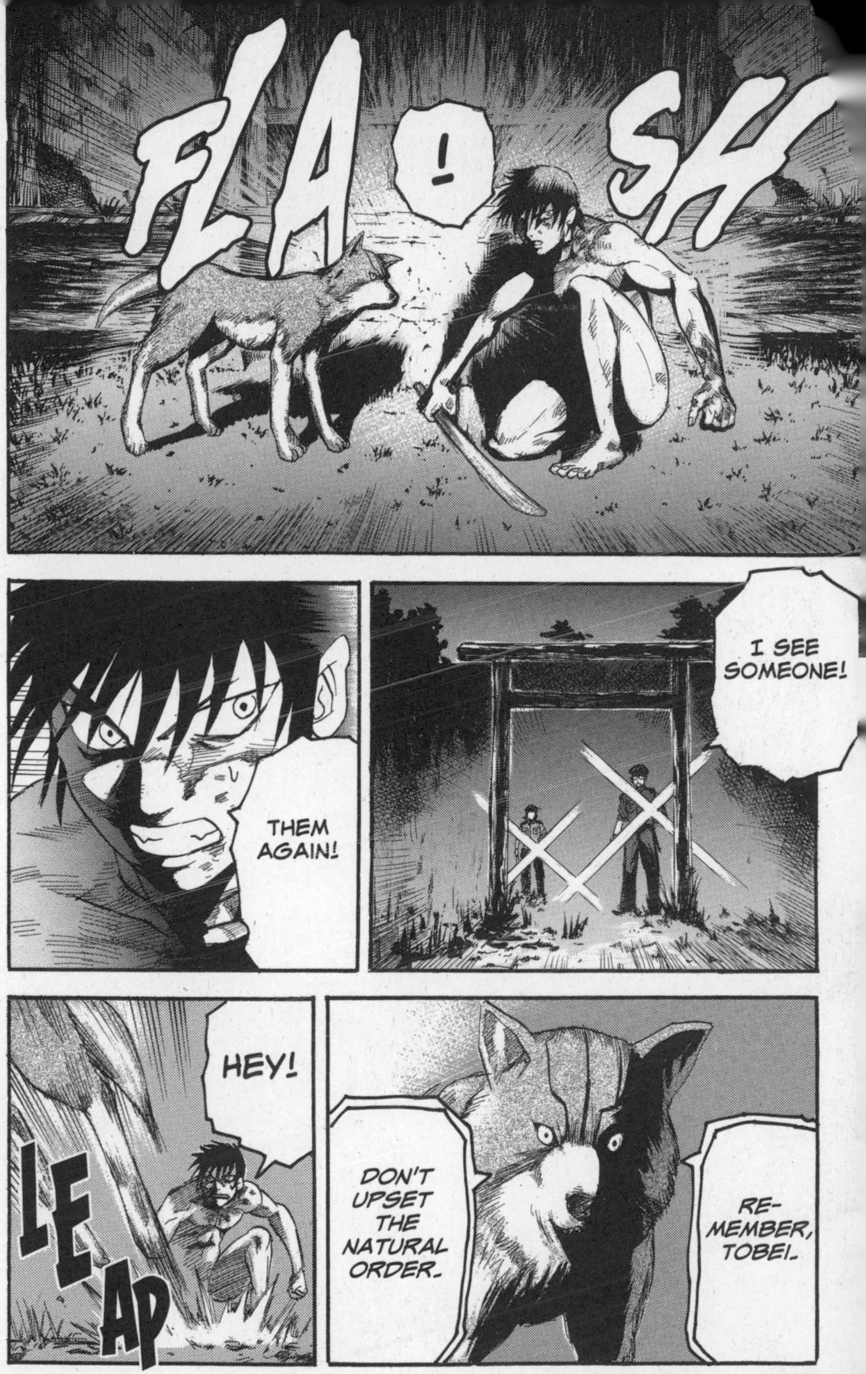

FLASH
!
I SEE SOMEONE!
THEM AGAIN!
RE-MEMBER, TOBEI...
DON'T UPSET THE NATURAL ORDER...
HEY!
LEAP

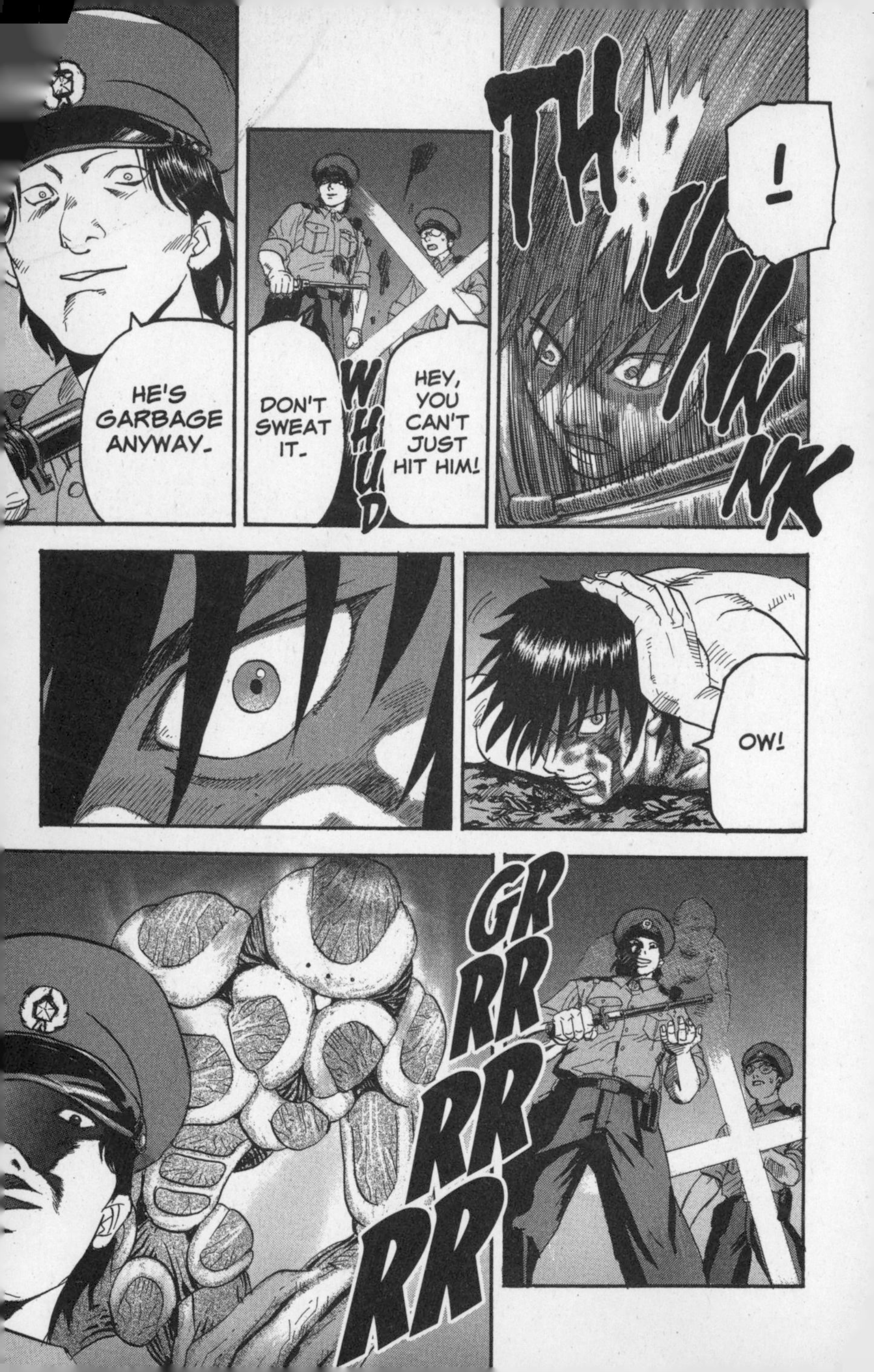
THUNNNNK
!
HEY, YOU CAN'T JUST HIT HIM!
WHUD
DON'T SWEAT IT.
HE'S GARBAGE ANYWAY.
OW!
GRRRRRRRRR

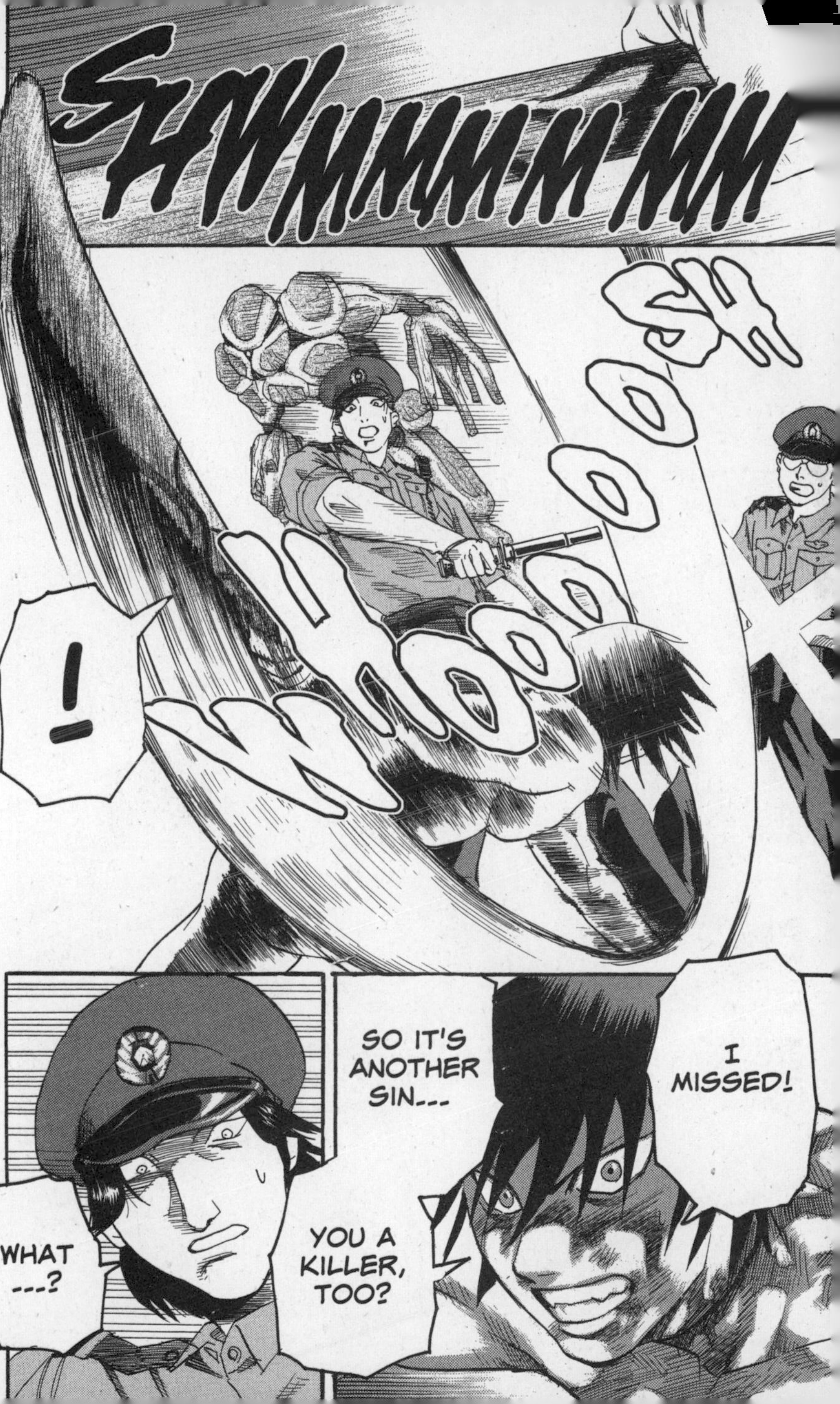
SHWMMMMMM MM
WHOOOOOOOSH
!
I MISSED!
SO IT'S ANOTHER SIN...
YOU A KILLER, TOO?
WHAT ---?

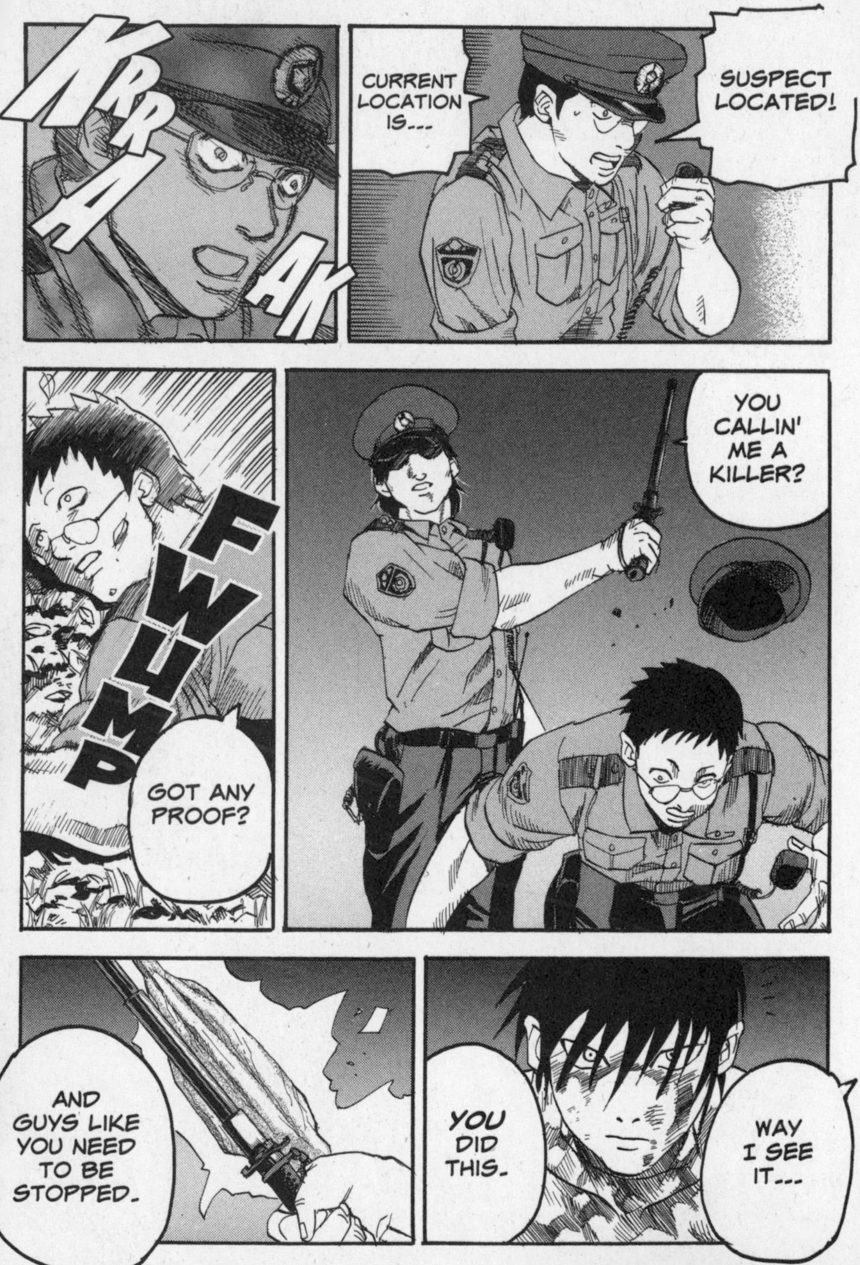
SUSPECT LOCATED!
CURRENT LOCATION IS...
KRRAAK
YOU CALLIN' ME A KILLER?
FWUMP
GOT ANY PROOF?
WAY I SEE IT...
YOU DID THIS.
AND GUYS LIKE YOU NEED TO BE STOPPED.

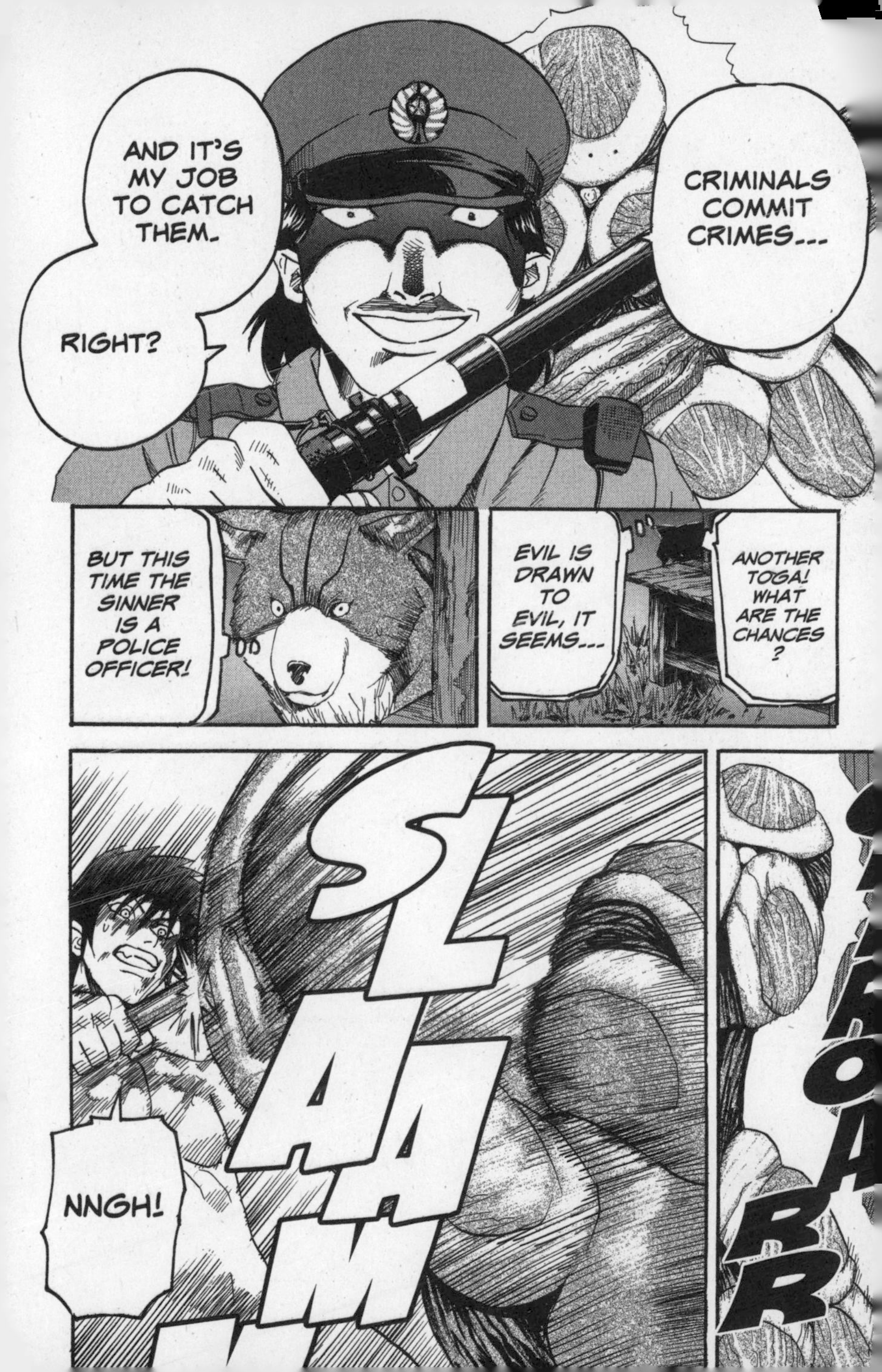
CRIMINALS COMMIT CRIMES...
AND IT'S MY JOB TO CATCH THEM.
RIGHT?
ANOTHER TOGA! WHAT ARE THE CHANCES?
EVIL IS DRAWN TO EVIL, IT SEEMS...
BUT THIS TIME THE SINNER IS A POLICE OFFICER!
SLAAM
NNGH!

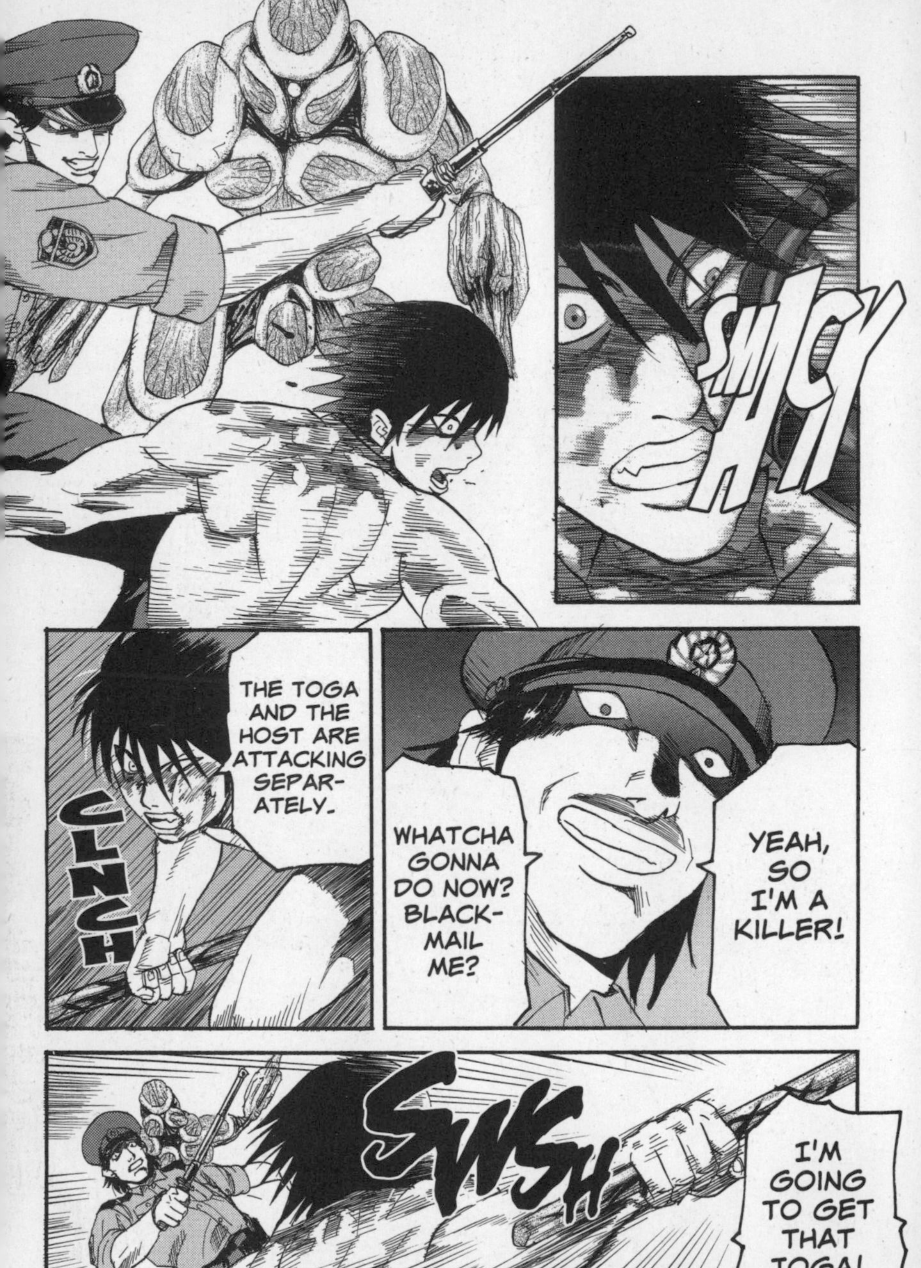
SMACK
YEAH, SO I'M A KILLER!
WHATCHA GONNA DO NOW? BLACK-MAIL ME?
THE TOGA AND THE HOST ARE ATTACKING SEPAR-ATELY...
CLNCH
I'M GOING TO GET THAT TOGA!
SWSH

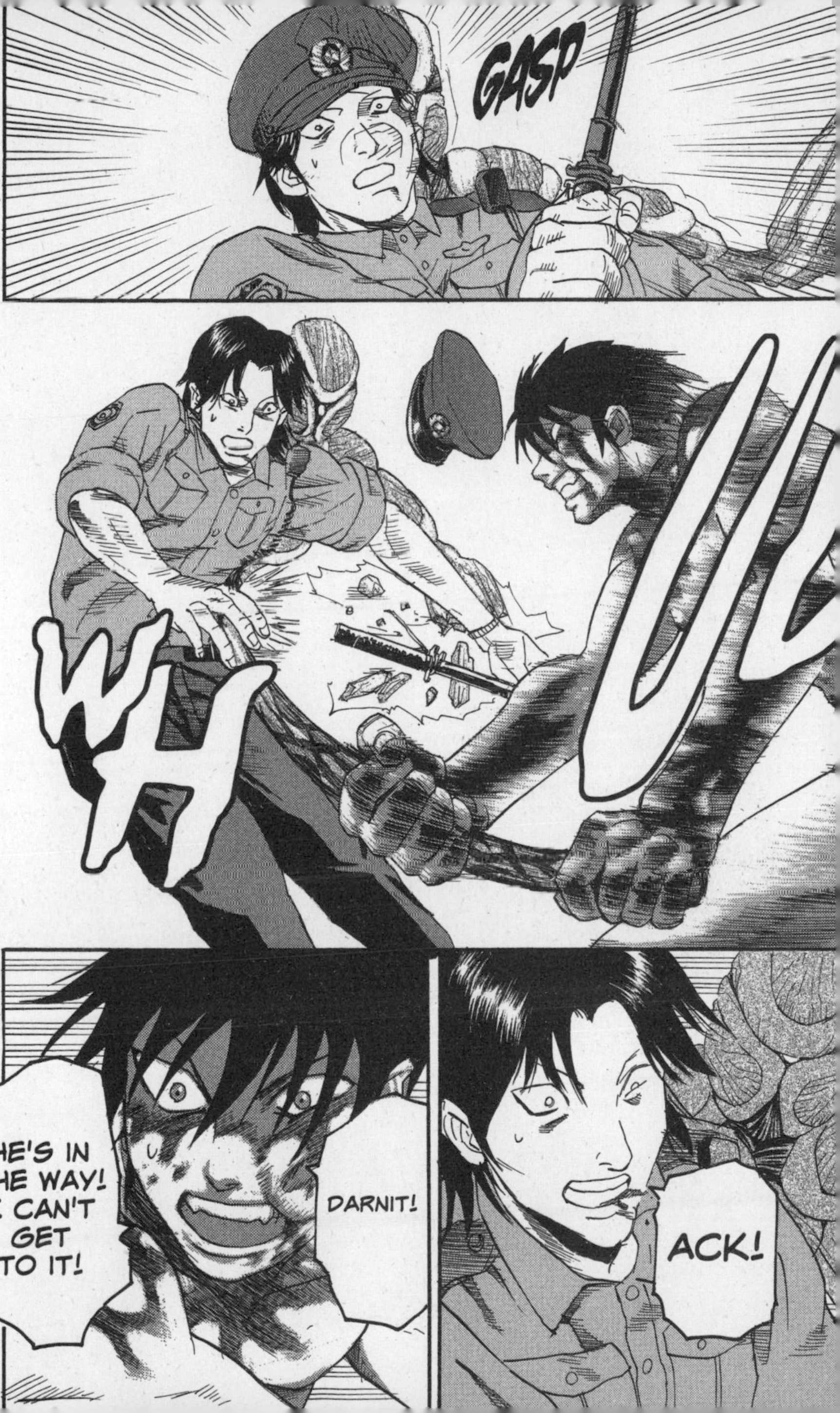
GASP
ACK!
DARNIT!
HE'S IN THE WAY! I CAN'T GET TO IT!

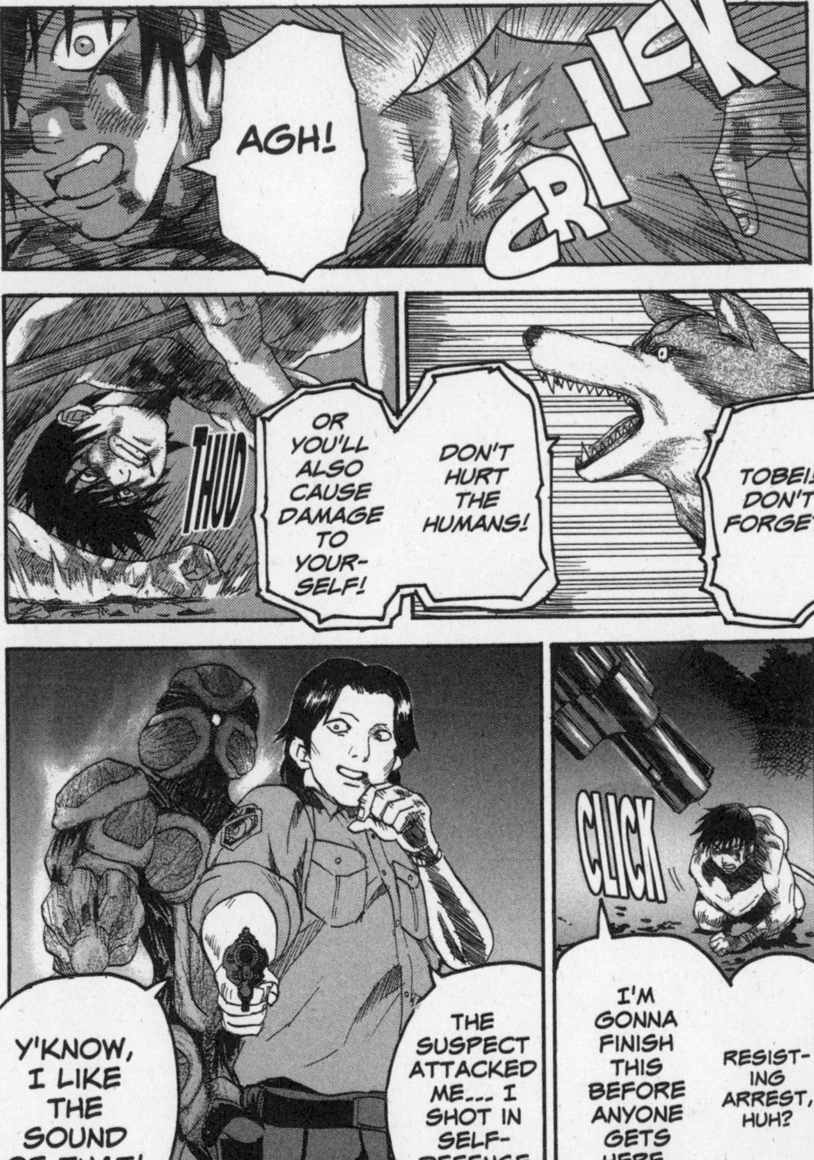
CRICK
AGH!
TOBEI! DON'T FORGET!
DON'T HURT THE HUMANS!
OR YOU'LL ALSO CAUSE DAMAGE TO YOURSELF!
THUD
CLICK
RESISTING ARREST, HUH?
I'M GONNA FINISH THIS BEFORE ANYONE GETS HERE.
THE SUSPECT ATTACKED ME... I SHOT IN SELF-DEFENSE...
Y'KNOW, I LIKE THE SOUND OF THAT!

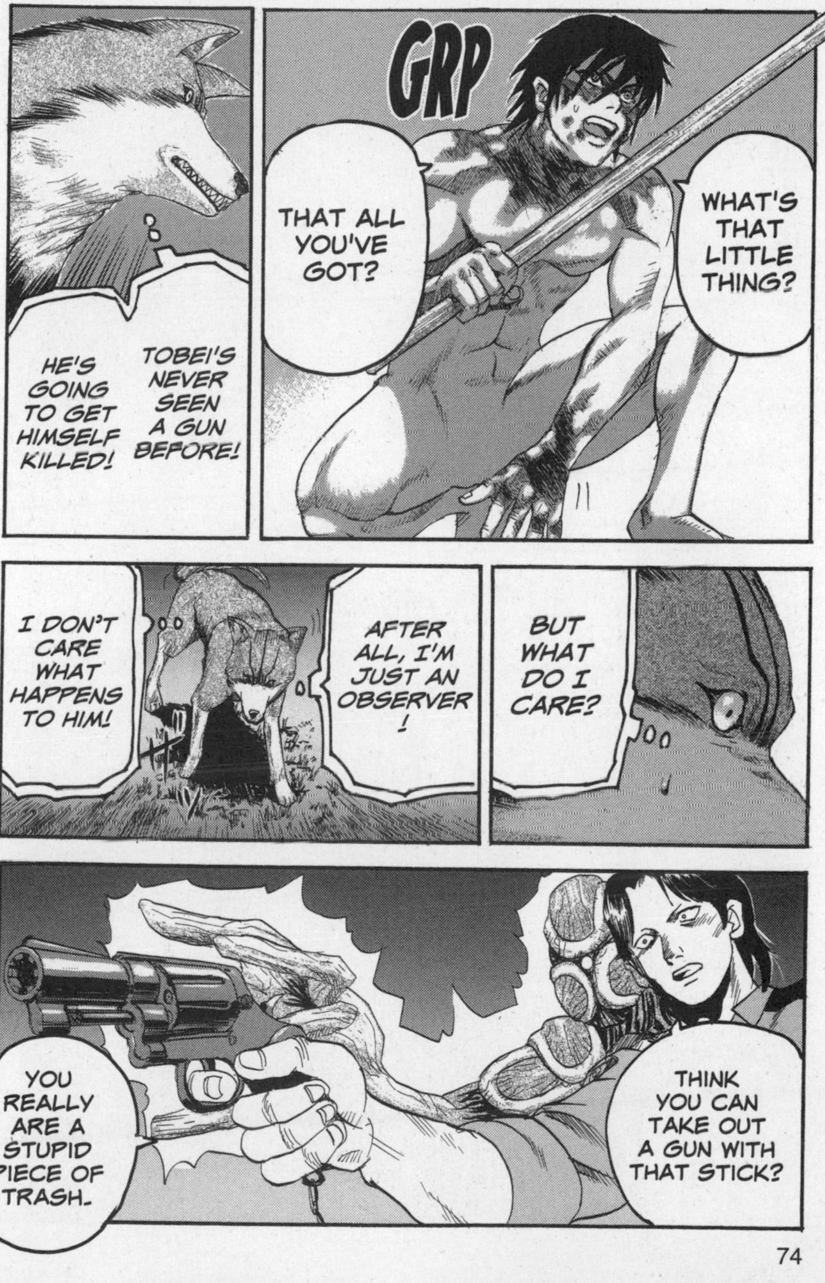
GRP
WHAT'S THAT LITTLE THING?
THAT ALL YOU'VE GOT?
TOBEI'S NEVER SEEN A GUN BEFORE!
HE'S GOING TO GET HIMSELF KILLED!
BUT WHAT DO I CARE?
AFTER ALL, I'M JUST AN OBSERVER!
I DON'T CARE WHAT HAPPENS TO HIM!
THINK YOU CAN TAKE OUT A GUN WITH THAT STICK?
YOU REALLY ARE A STUPID PIECE OF TRASH.

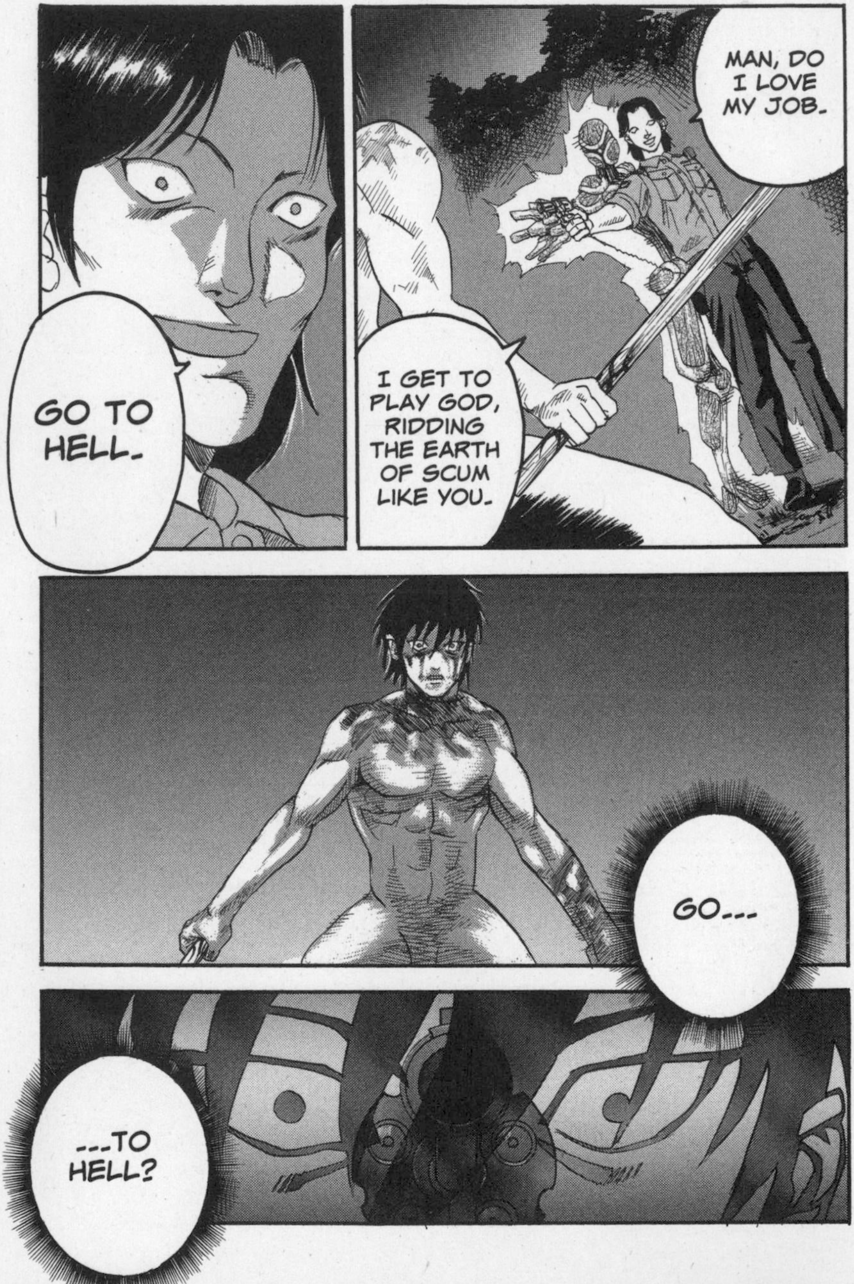
MAN, DO I LOVE MY JOB.
I GET TO PLAY GOD, RIDDING THE EARTH OF SCUM LIKE YOU.
GO TO HELL.
GO...
...TO HELL?

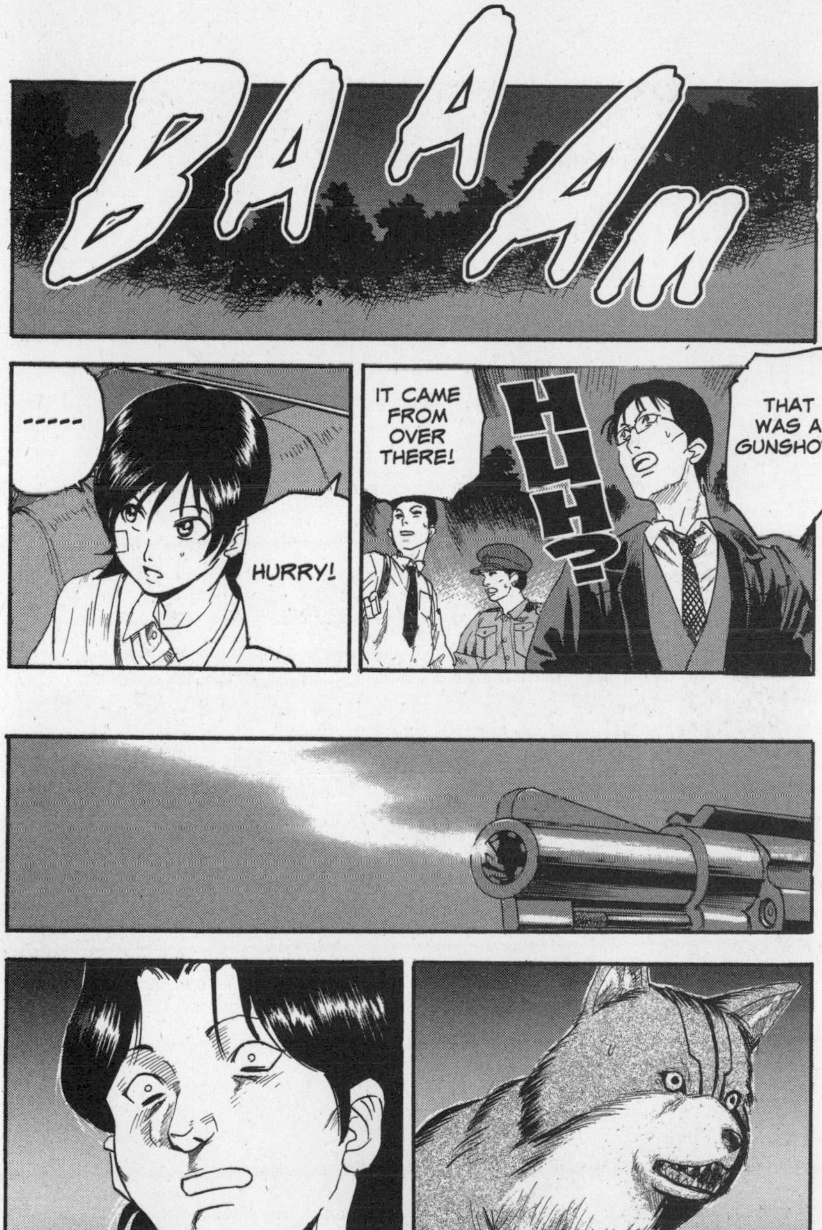
BAAAM
THAT WAS A GUNSHOT!
HUH?
IT CAME FROM OVER THERE!

HURRY!

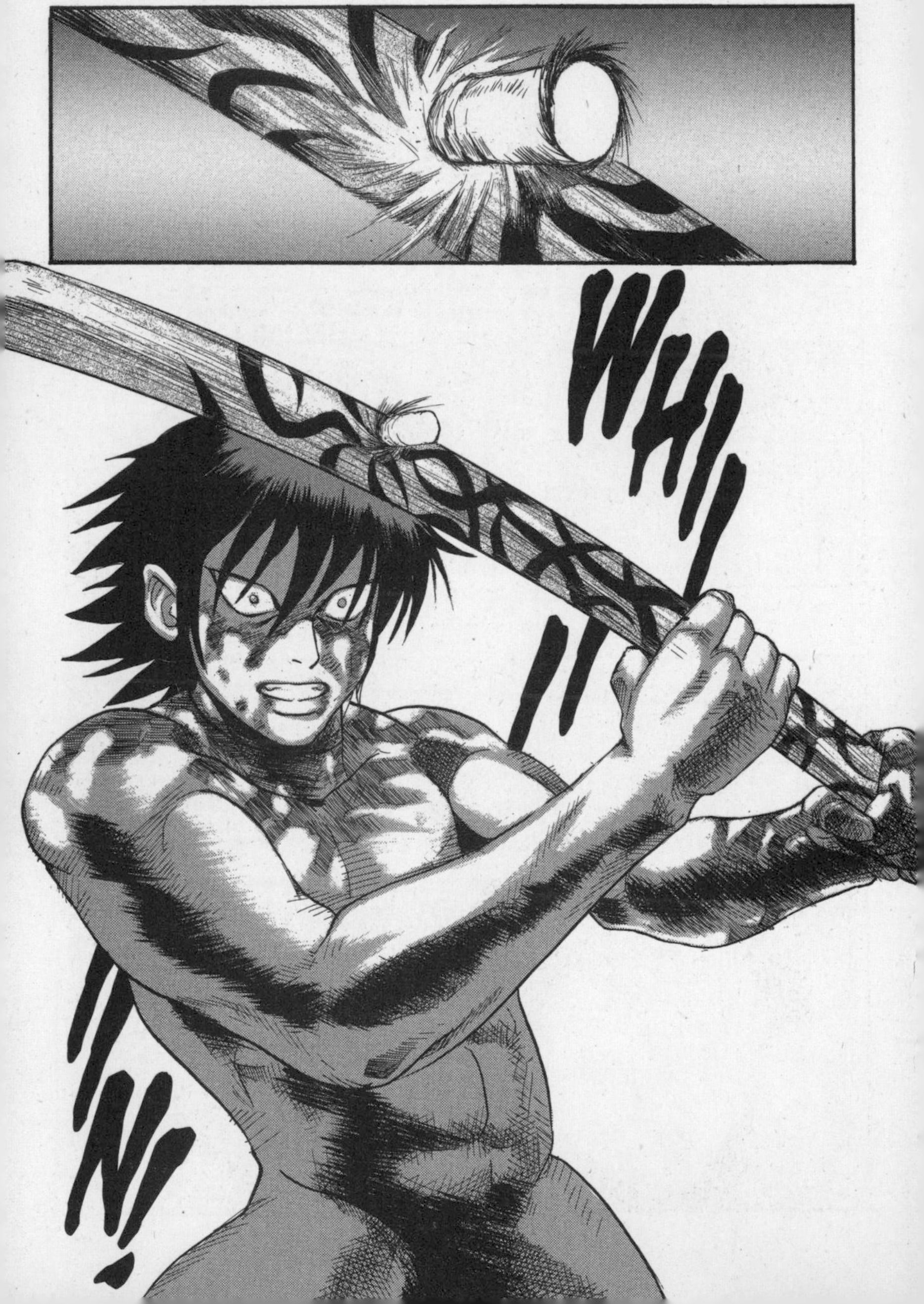
WHIIIIN!

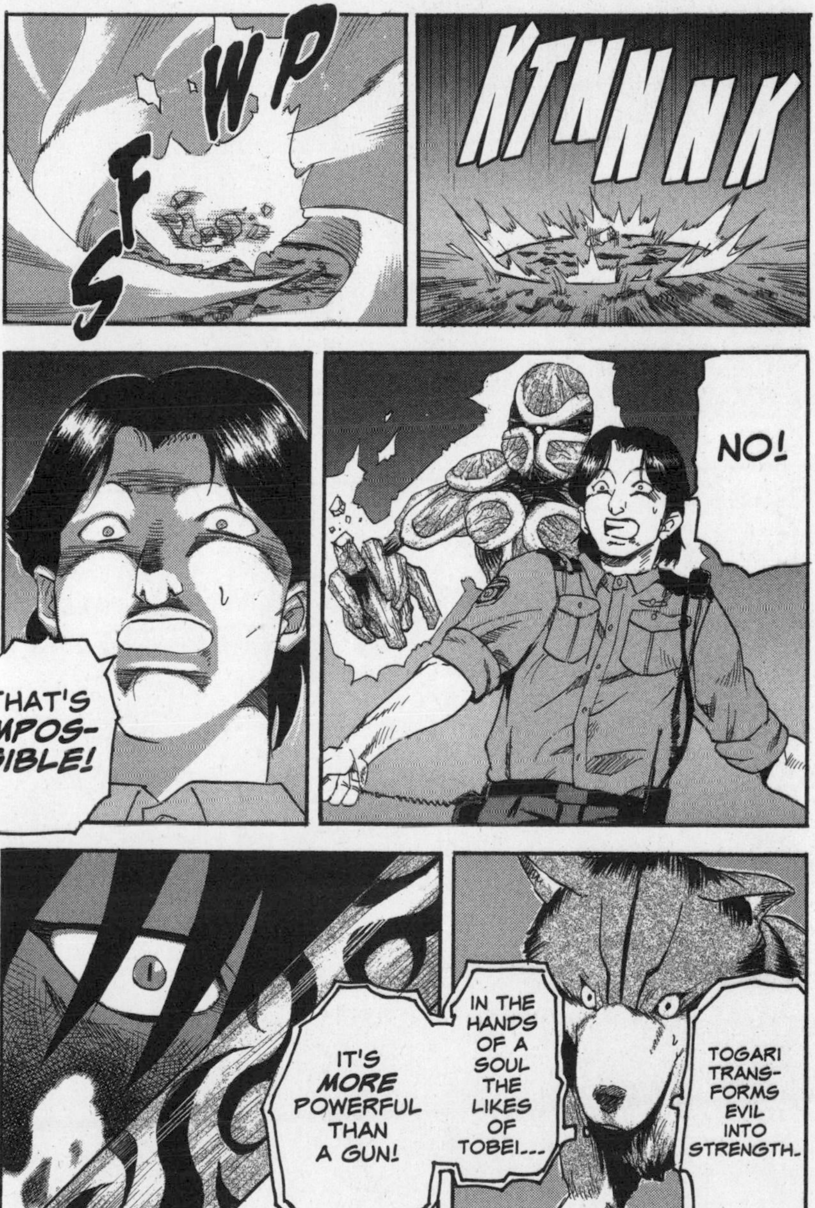
KTNNNK
SFWP
NO!
THAT'S *IMPOS-SIBLE!*
TOGARI TRANS-FORMS EVIL INTO STRENGTH.
IN THE HANDS OF A SOUL THE LIKES OF TOBEI...
IT'S *MORE* POWERFUL THAN A GUN!

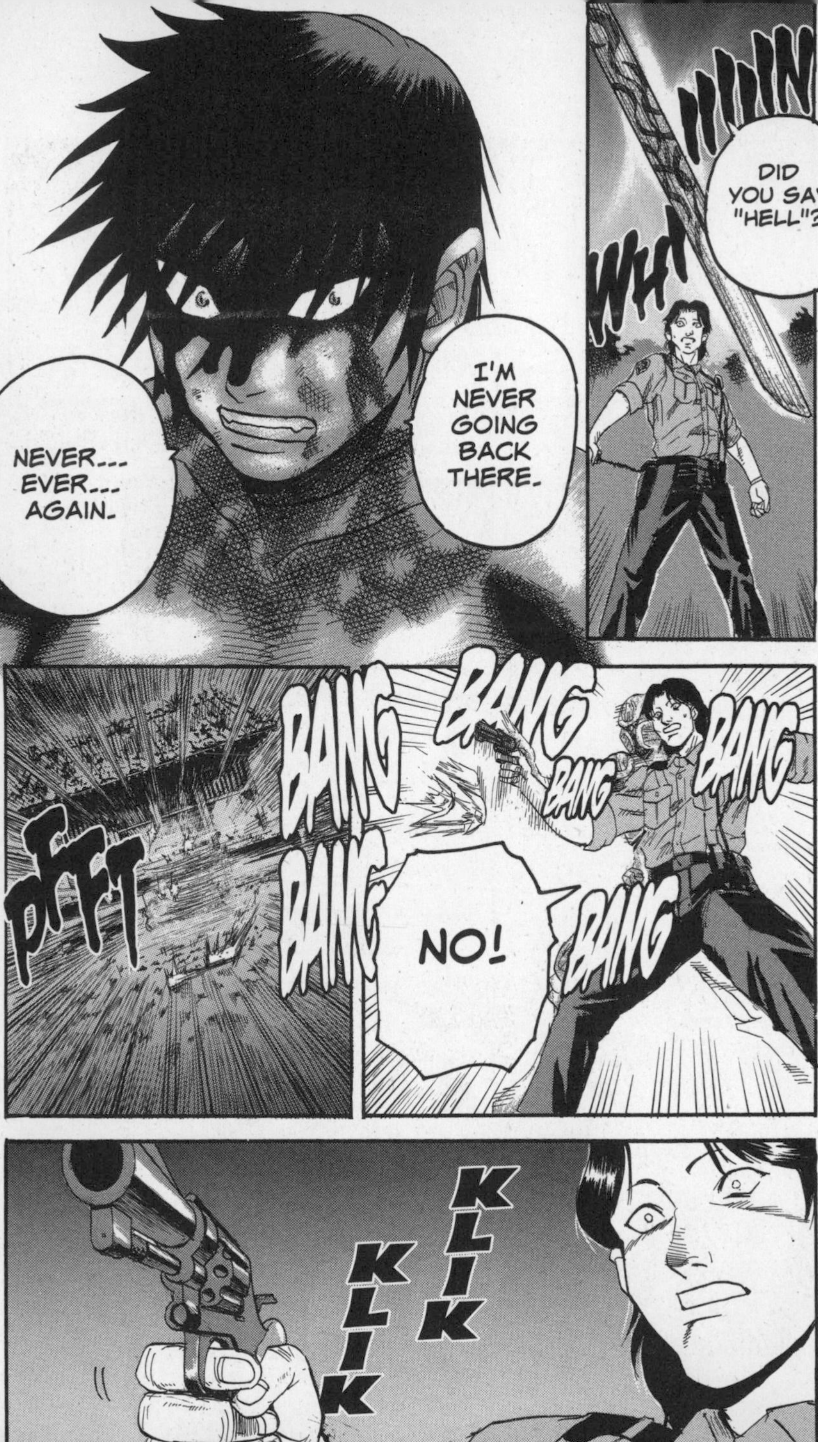
WHIIIIN
DID YOU SAY "HELL"?
I'M NEVER GOING BACK THERE.
NEVER... EVER... AGAIN.
BANG
BANG
BANG
BANG
BANG
BANG
NO!
PFFT
KLIK
KLIK
KLIK

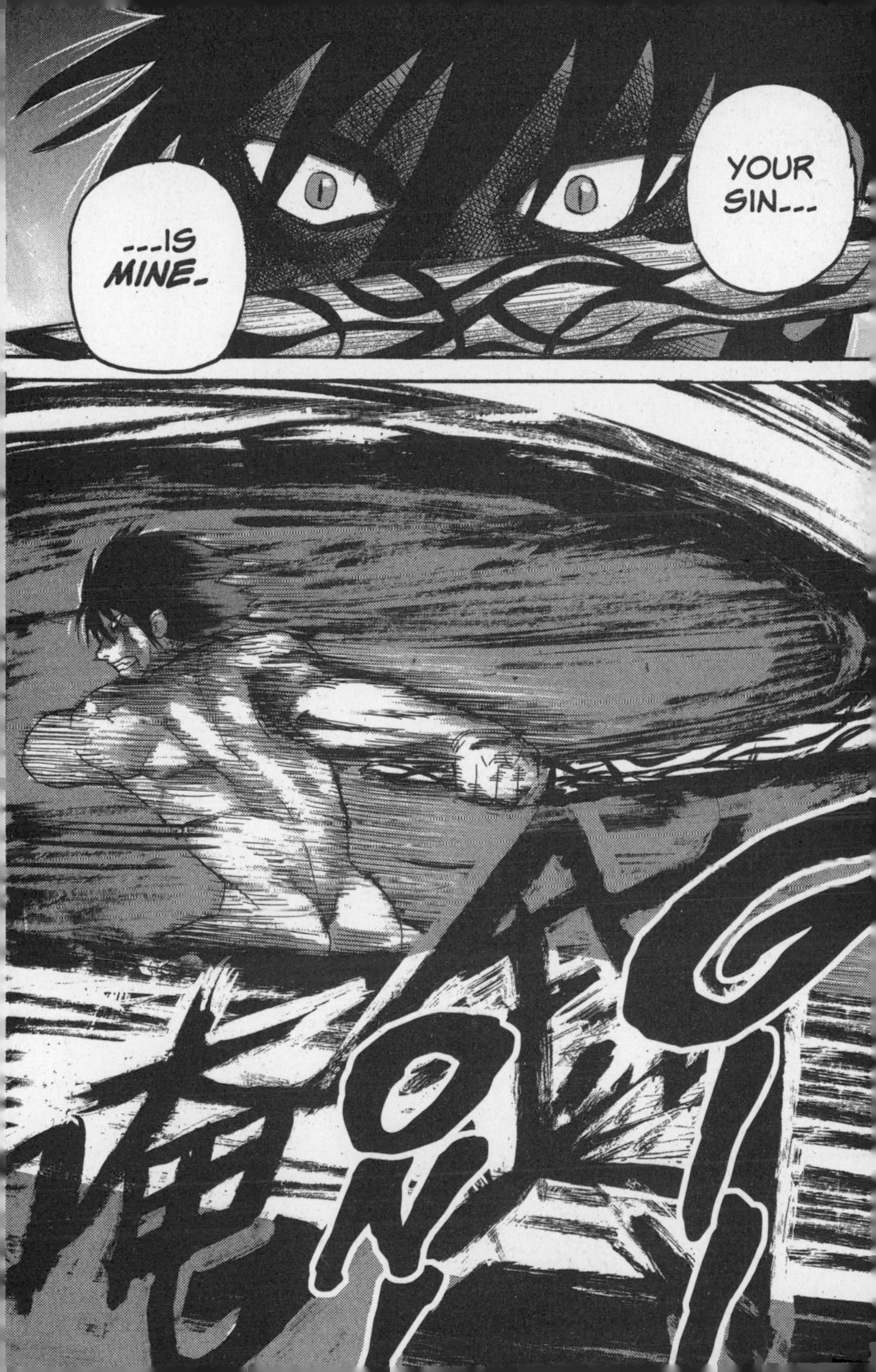
YOUR SIN...
...IS MINE.

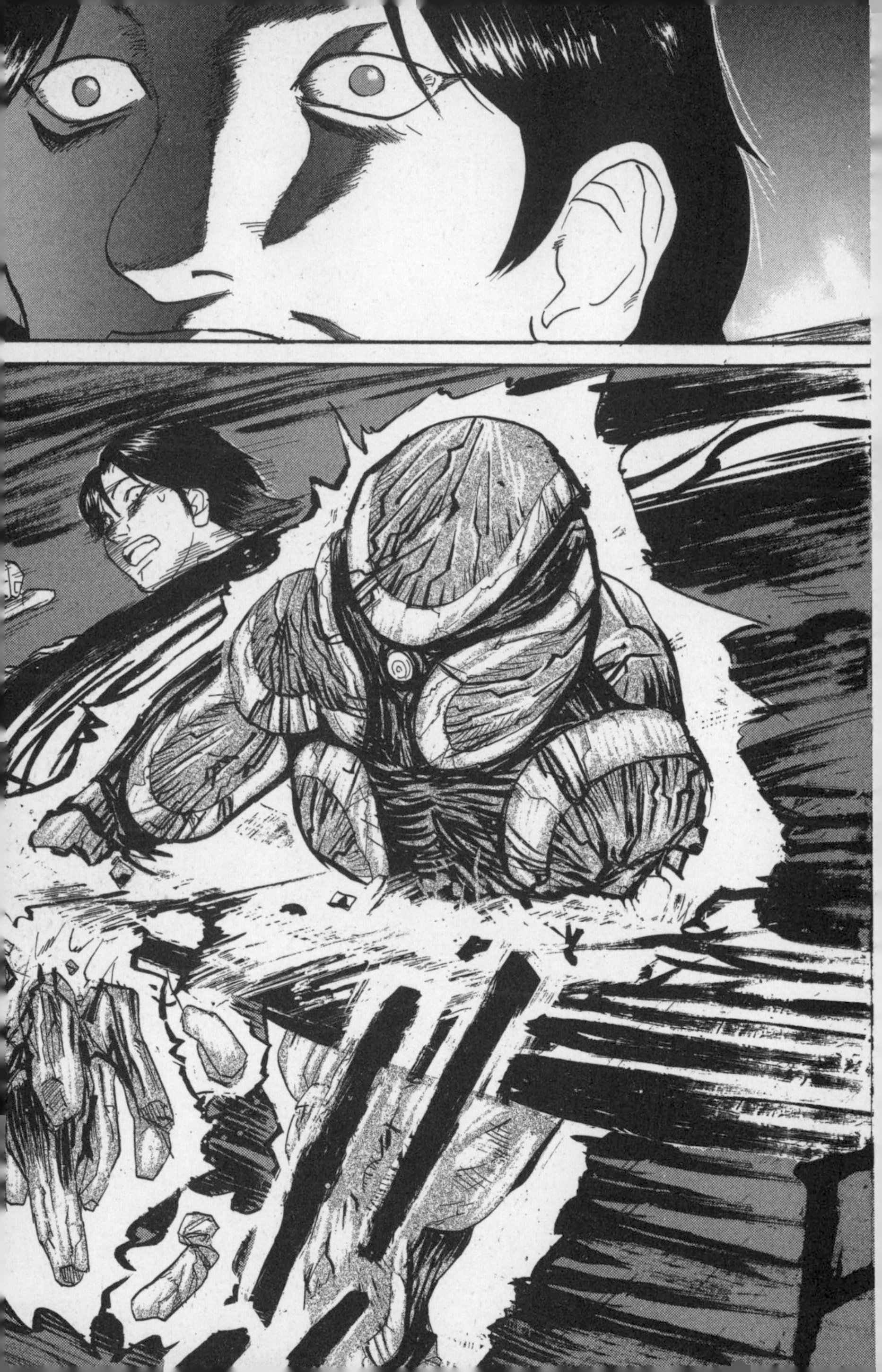

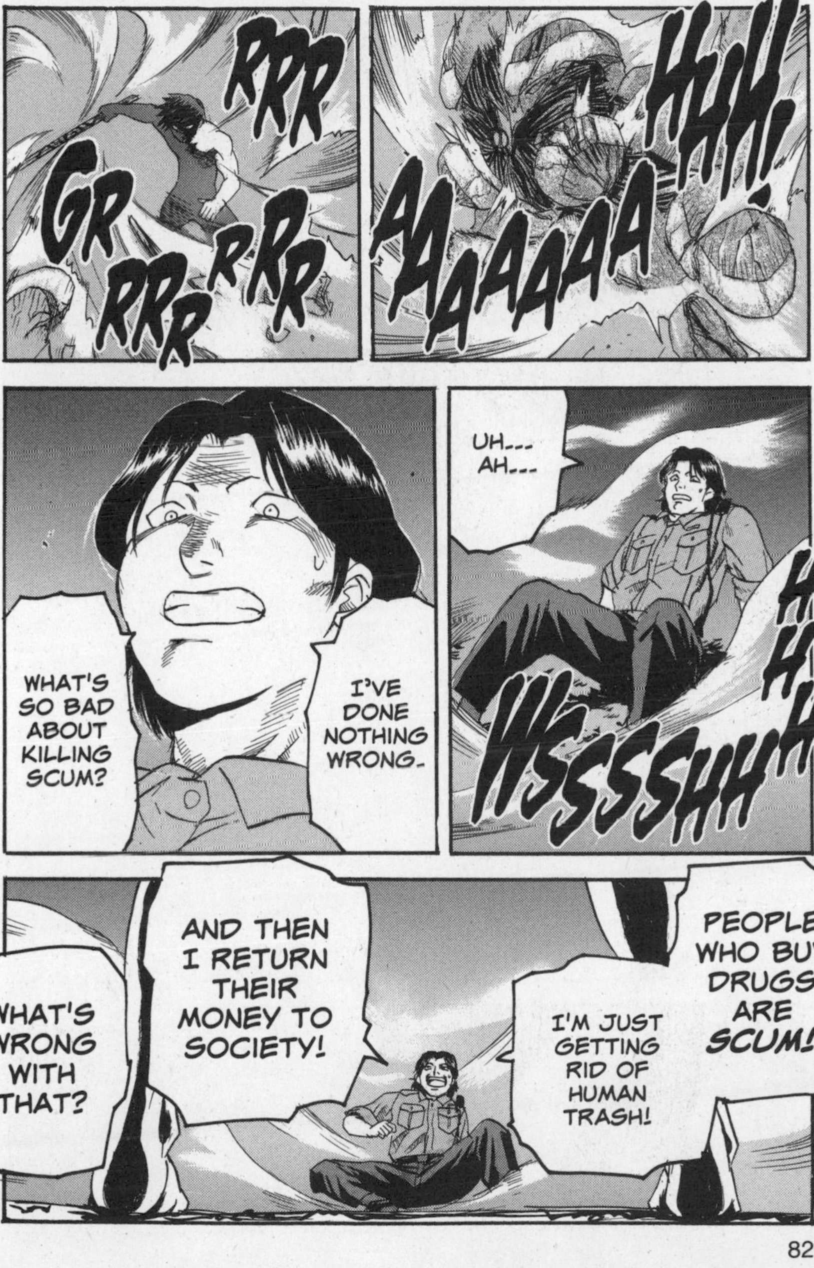
AAAAAAAAHHH!
GRRRRRRRRRRR
UH...
AH...
WSSSSHHHHHH
I'VE DONE NOTHING WRONG.
WHAT'S SO BAD ABOUT KILLING SCUM?
PEOPLE WHO BUY DRUGS ARE SCUM!
I'M JUST GETTING RID OF HUMAN TRASH!
AND THEN I RETURN THEIR MONEY TO SOCIETY!
WHAT'S WRONG WITH THAT?

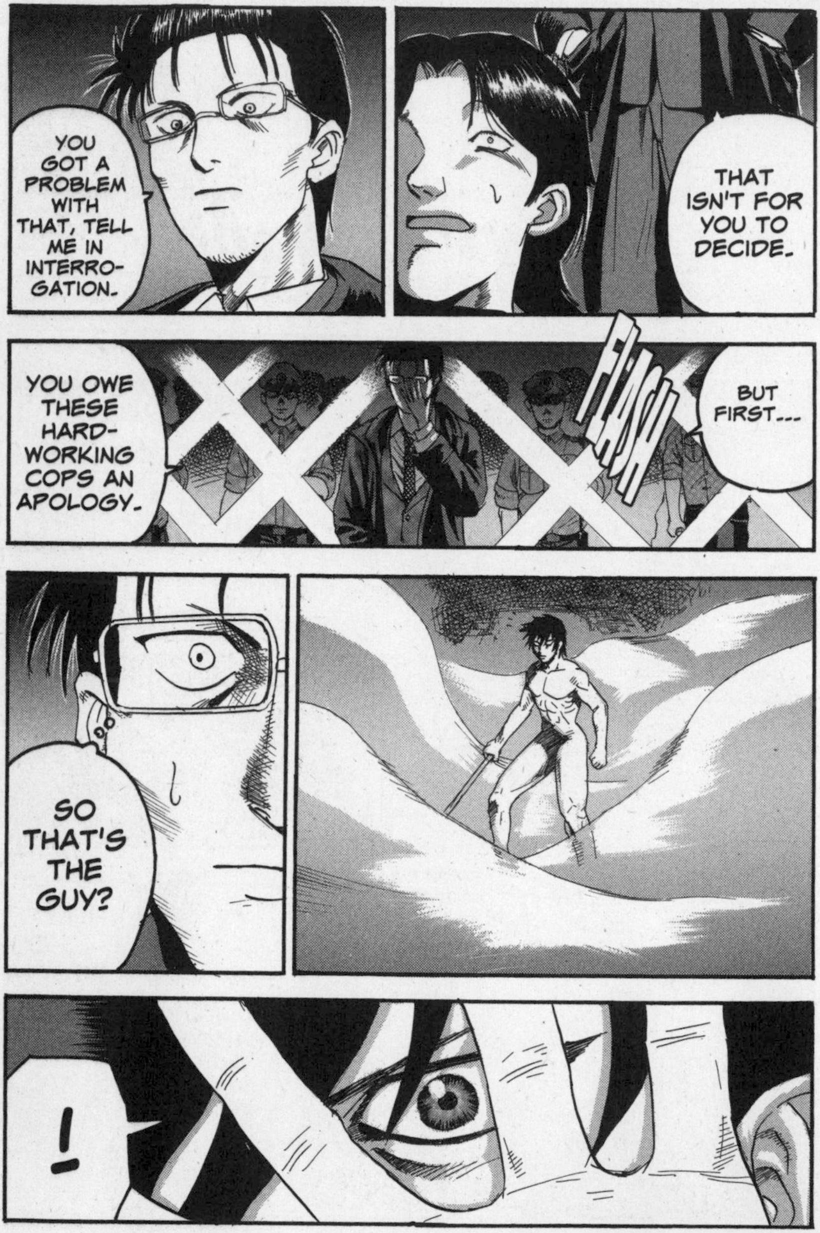
THAT ISN'T FOR YOU TO DECIDE...
YOU GOT A PROBLEM WITH THAT, TELL ME IN INTERRO-GATION...
BUT FIRST...
FLASH
YOU OWE THESE HARD-WORKING COPS AN APOLOGY...
SO THAT'S THE GUY?
!

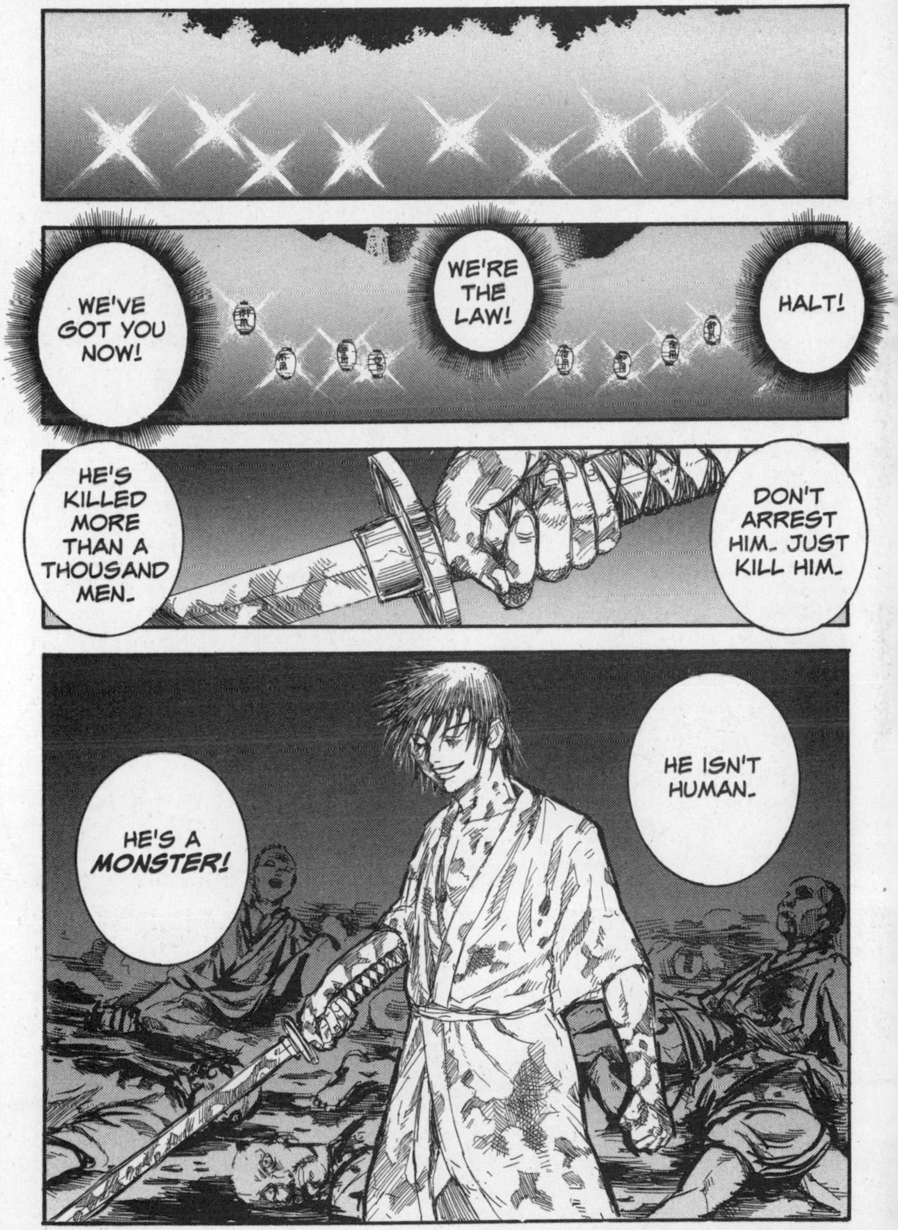
HALT!
WE'RE THE LAW!
WE'VE GOT YOU NOW!
DON'T ARREST HIM. JUST KILL HIM.
HE'S KILLED MORE THAN A THOUSAND MEN.
HE ISN'T HUMAN.
HE'S A *MONSTER!*

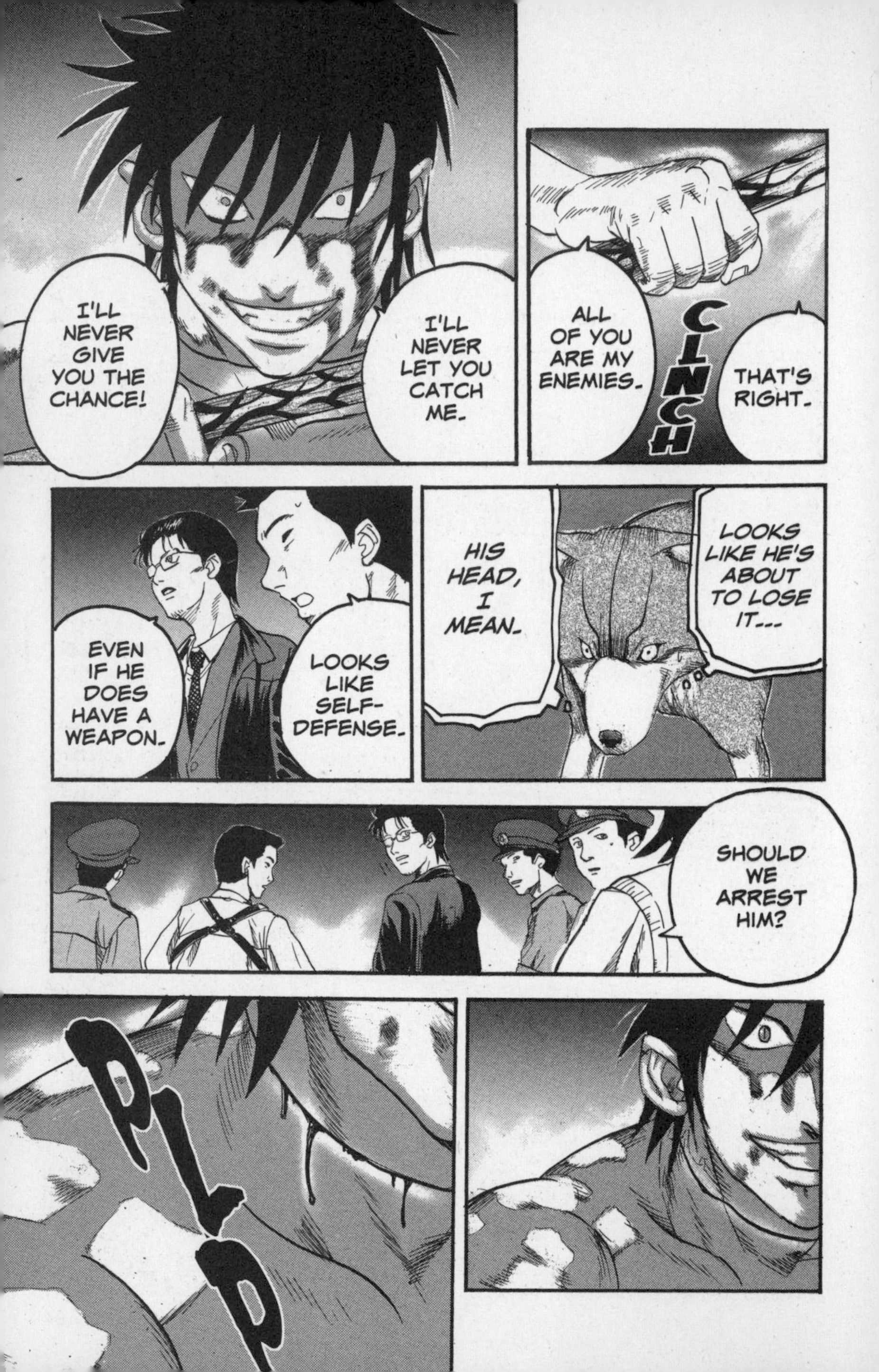
THAT'S RIGHT...
CINCH
ALL OF YOU ARE MY ENEMIES...
I'LL NEVER LET YOU CATCH ME...
I'LL NEVER GIVE YOU THE CHANCE!
LOOKS LIKE HE'S ABOUT TO LOSE IT...
HIS HEAD, I MEAN...
LOOKS LIKE SELF-DEFENSE...
EVEN IF HE DOES HAVE A WEAPON...
SHOULD WE ARREST HIM?
DRIP

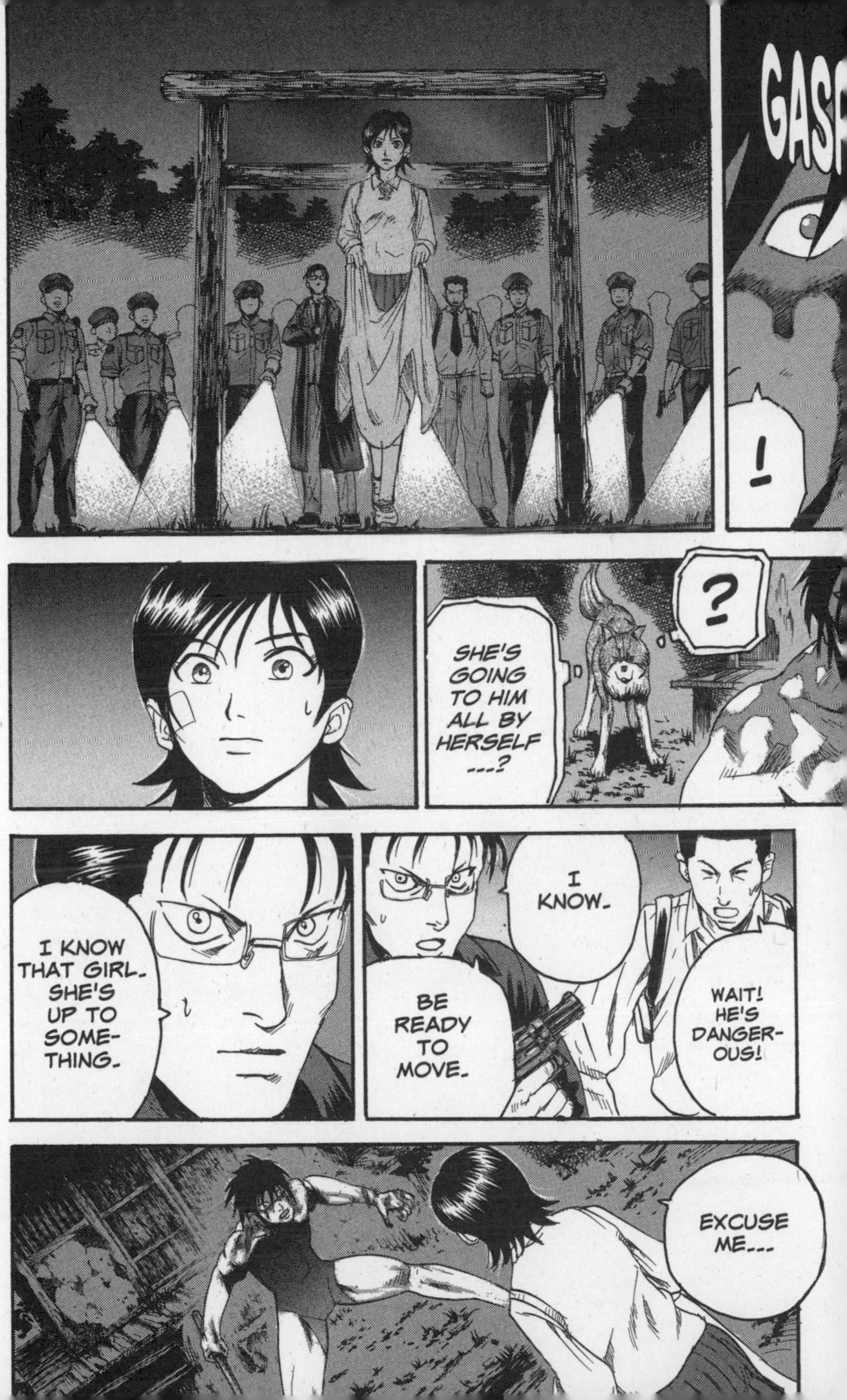
GASP
!
?
SHE'S GOING TO HIM ALL BY HERSELF ...?
I KNOW.
WAIT! HE'S DANGEROUS!
BE READY TO MOVE.
I KNOW THAT GIRL. SHE'S UP TO SOME-THING.
EXCUSE ME...

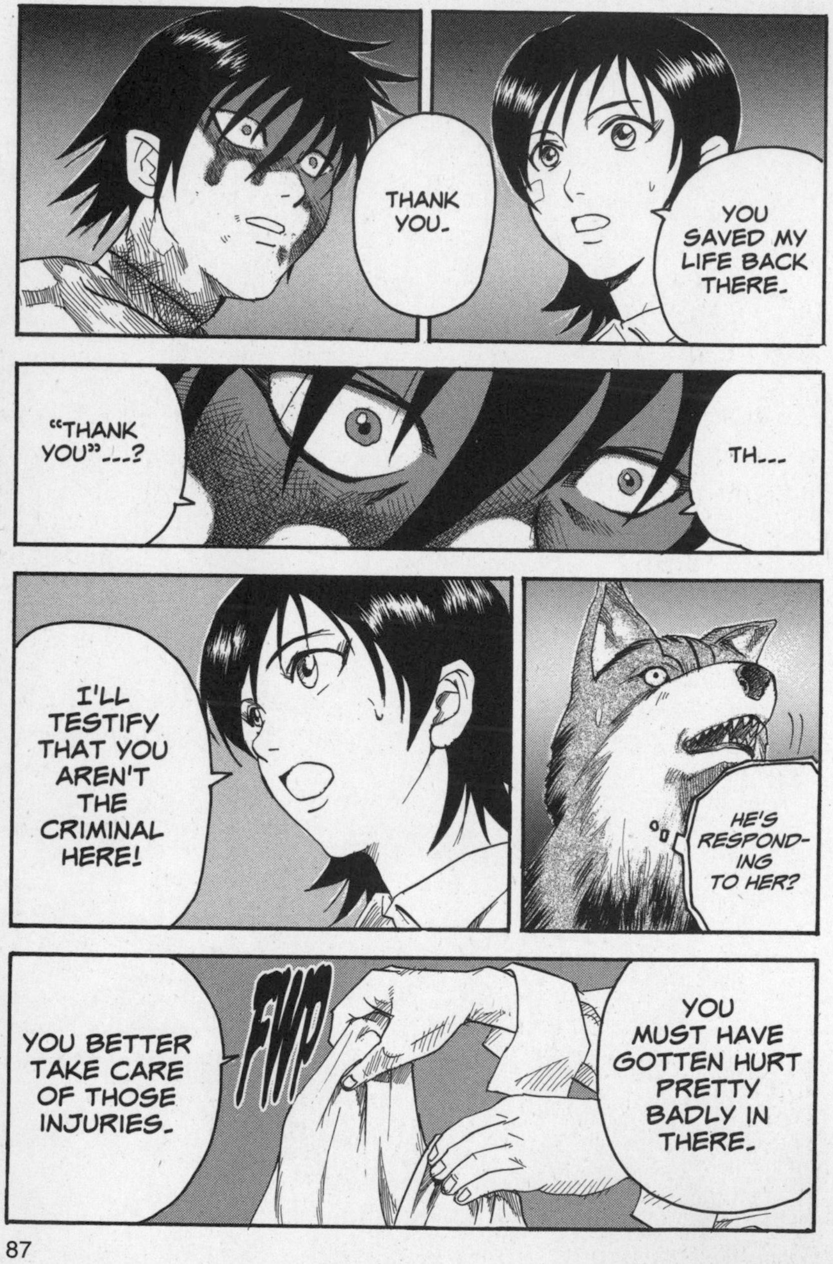
YOU SAVED MY LIFE BACK THERE.
THANK YOU.
TH...
“THANK YOU”...?
HE'S RESPONDING TO HER?
I'LL TESTIFY THAT YOU AREN'T THE CRIMINAL HERE!
YOU MUST HAVE GOTTEN HURT PRETTY BADLY IN THERE.
FWP
YOU BETTER TAKE CARE OF THOSE INJURIES.

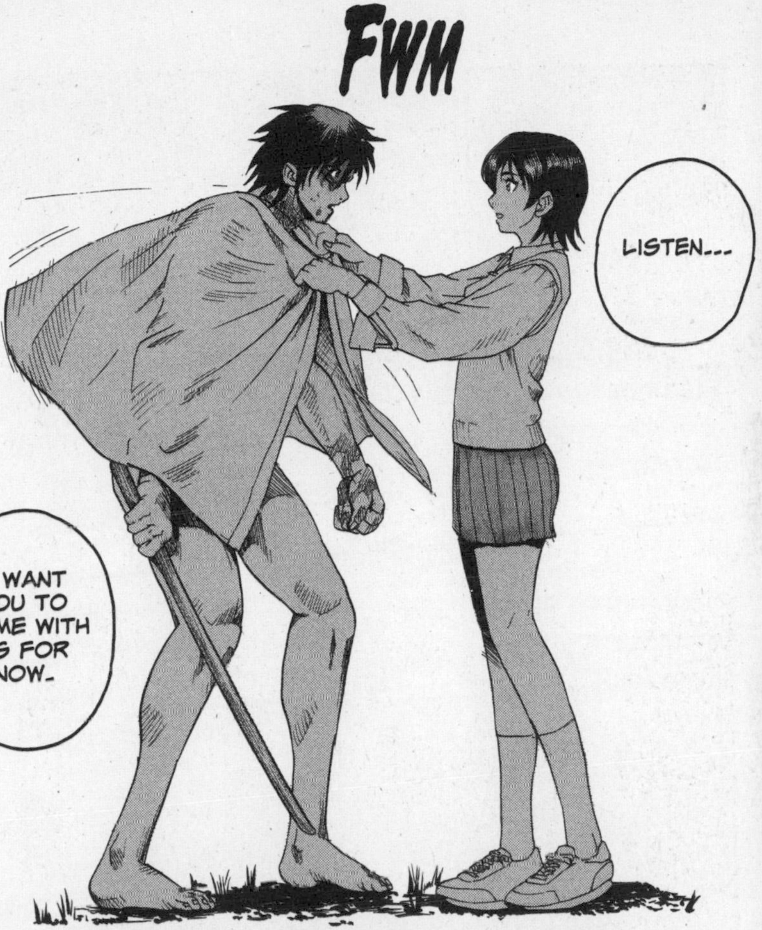
FWM
LISTEN...
I WANT YOU TO COME WITH US FOR NOW.

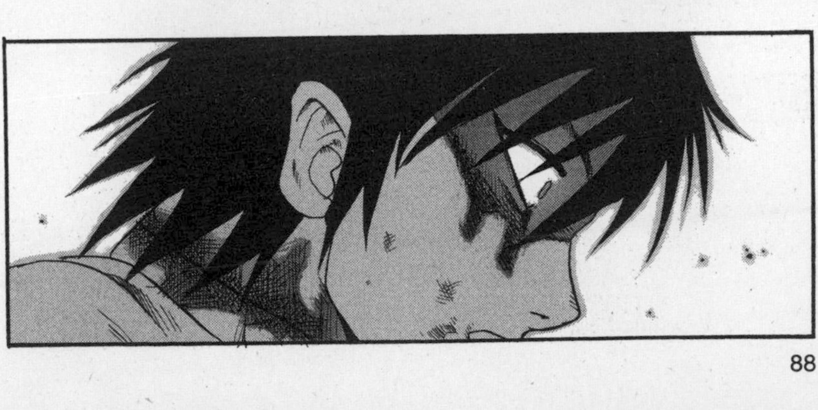

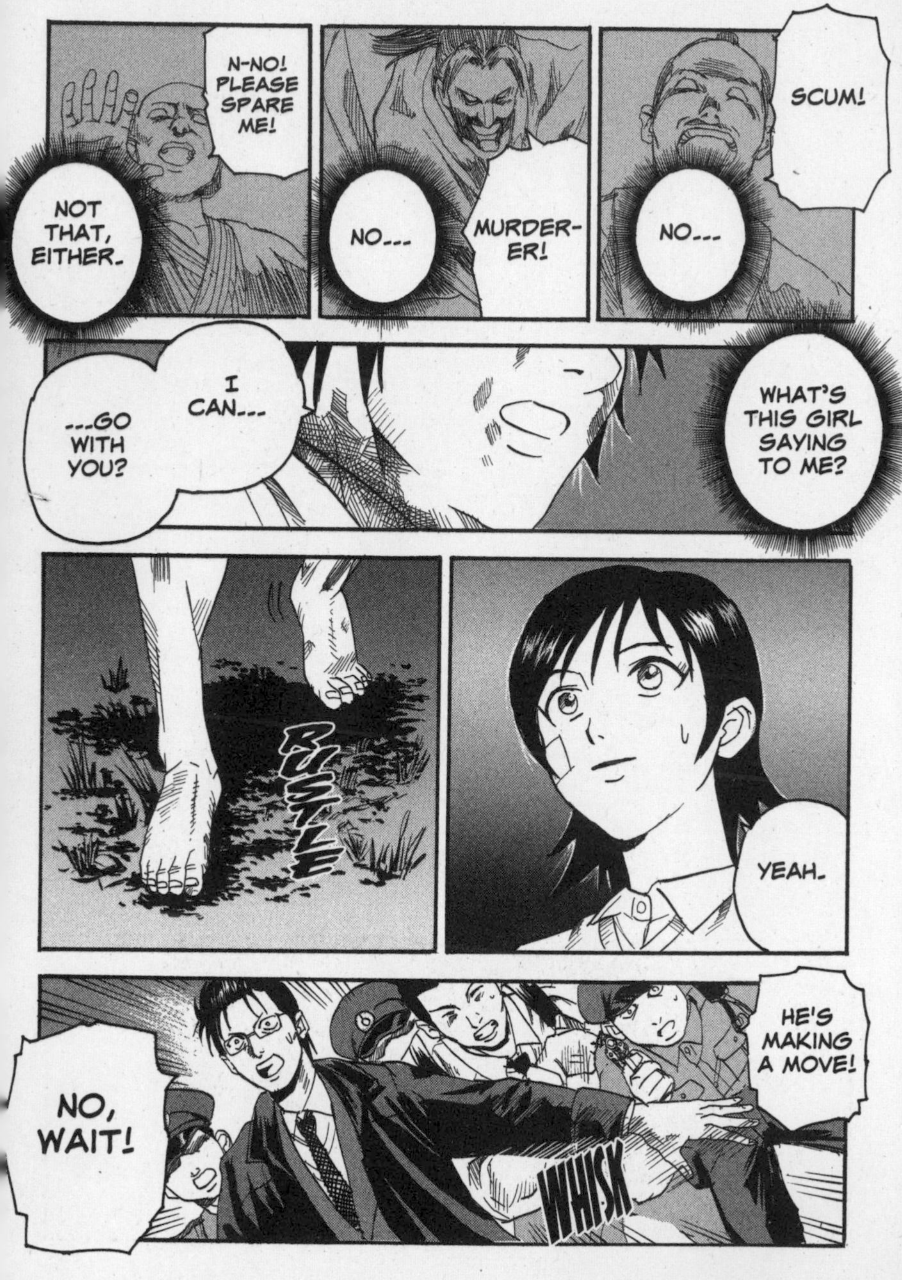
SCUM!
NO...
MURDER-ER!
NO...
N-NO! PLEASE SPARE ME!
NOT THAT, EITHER.
WHAT'S THIS GIRL SAYING TO ME?
I CAN...
...GO WITH YOU?
YEAH.
RUSTLE
HE'S MAKING A MOVE!
WHISK
NO, WAIT!

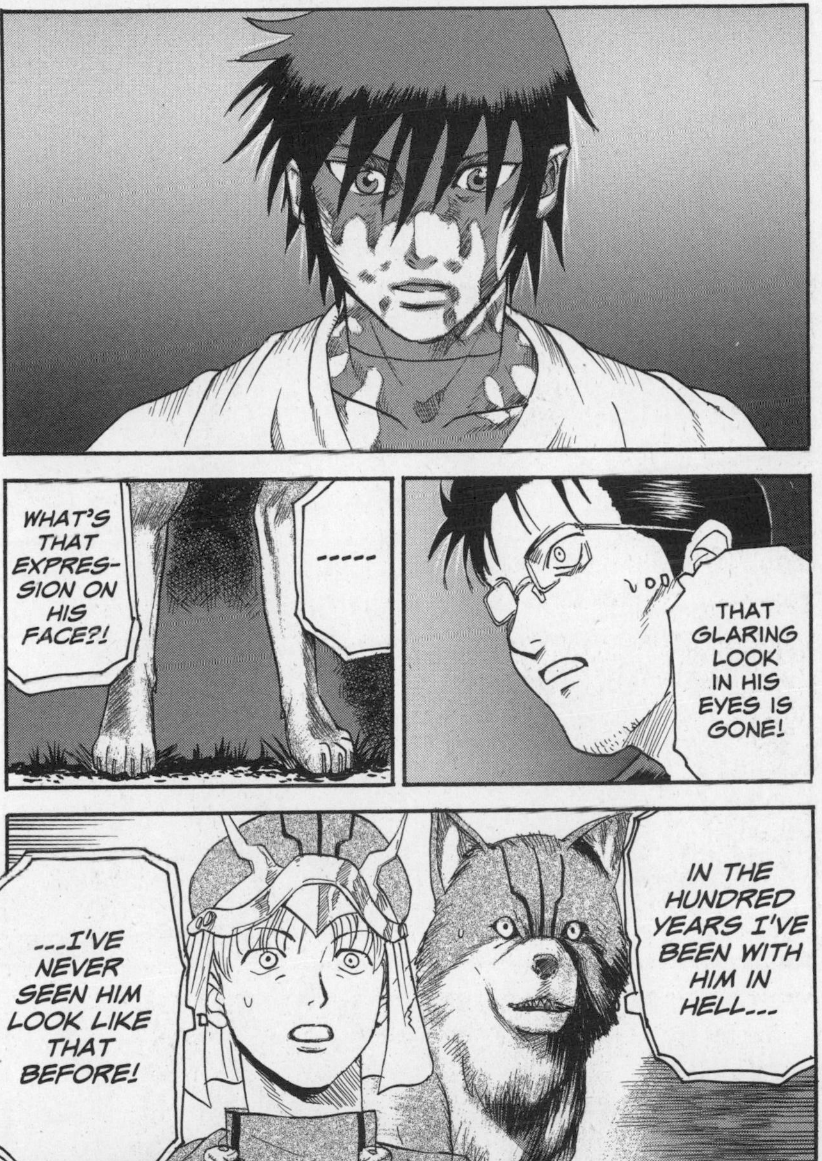
THAT GLARING LOOK IN HIS EYES IS GONE!

WHAT'S THAT EXPRES-SION ON HIS FACE?!
IN THE HUNDRED YEARS I'VE BEEN WITH HIM IN HELL...
...I'VE NEVER SEEN HIM LOOK LIKE THAT BEFORE!

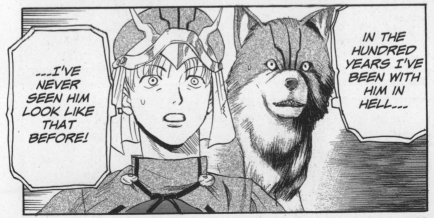

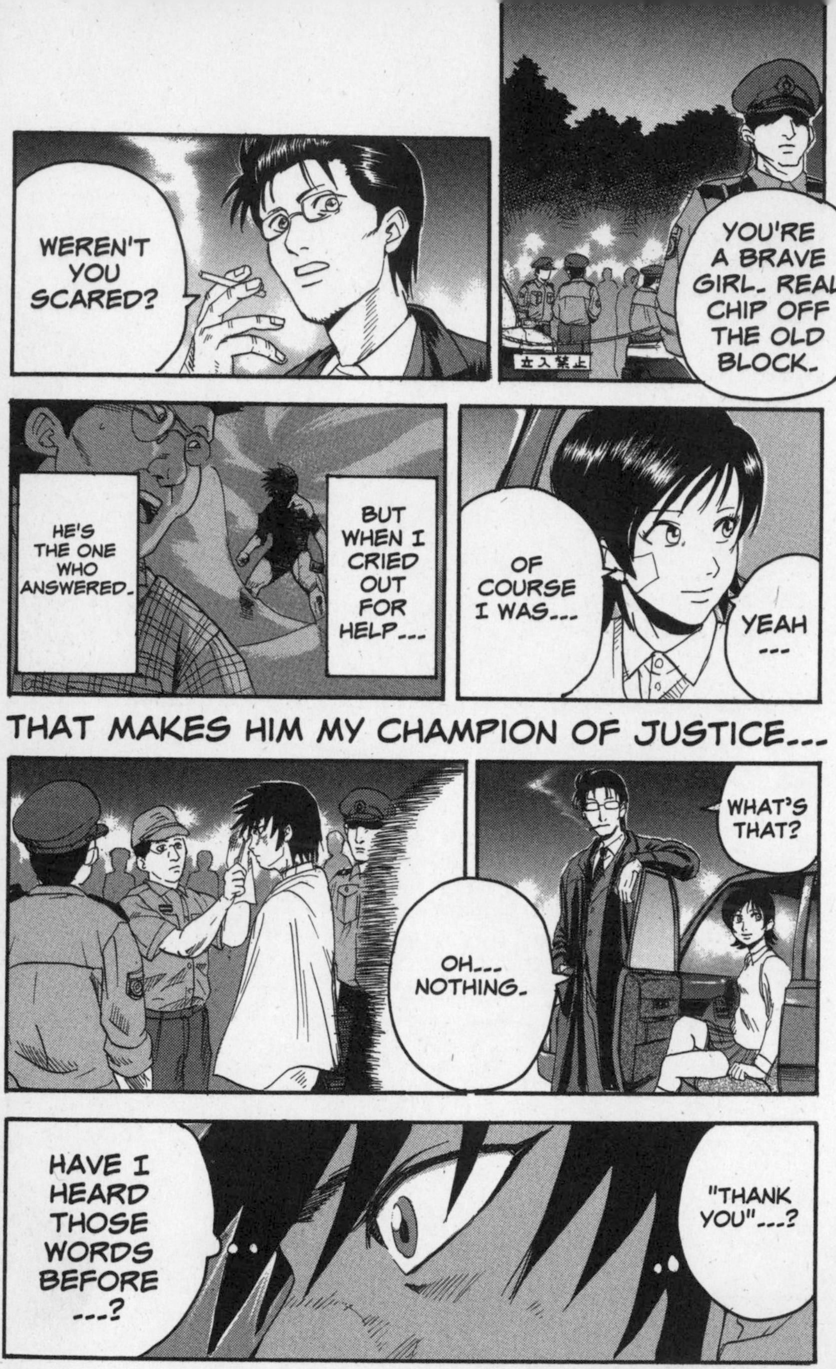
YOU'RE A BRAVE GIRL. REAL CHIP OFF THE OLD BLOCK.
立入禁止
WEREN'T YOU SCARED?
YEAH...
OF COURSE I WAS...
BUT WHEN I CRIED OUT FOR HELP...
HE'S THE ONE WHO ANSWERED.
THAT MAKES HIM MY CHAMPION OF JUSTICE...
WHAT'S THAT?
OH... NOTHING.
"THANK YOU"...?
HAVE I HEARD THOSE WORDS BEFORE...?

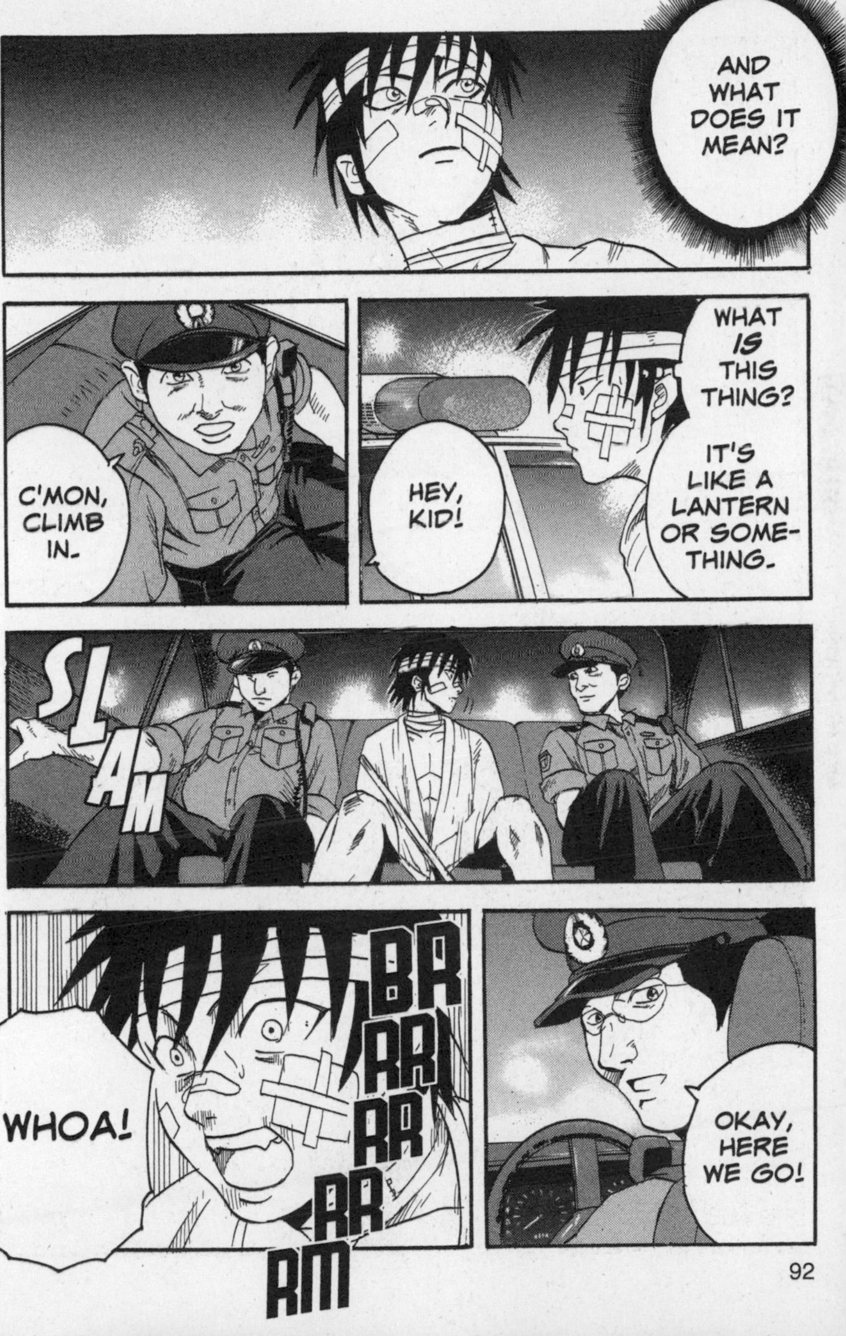
AND WHAT DOES IT MEAN?
WHAT *IS* THIS THING?
IT'S LIKE A LANTERN OR SOMETHING.
HEY, KID!
C'MON, CLIMB IN.
SLAM
OKAY, HERE WE GO!
BRRRRRRRRRM
WHOA!

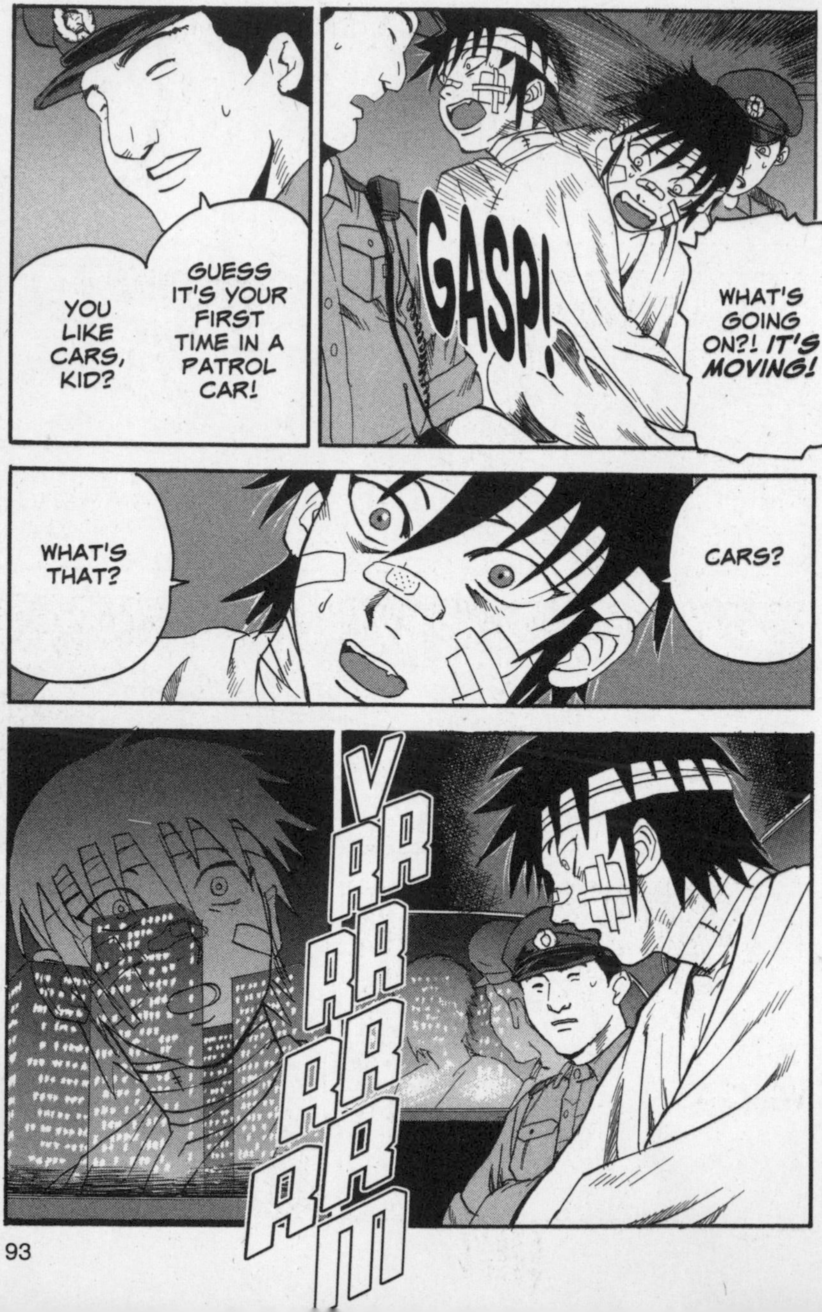
GASP!
WHAT'S GOING ON?! IT'S MOVING!
GUESS IT'S YOUR FIRST TIME IN A PATROL CAR!
YOU LIKE CARS, KID?
CARS?
WHAT'S THAT?
VRRRRRRRRRRRM

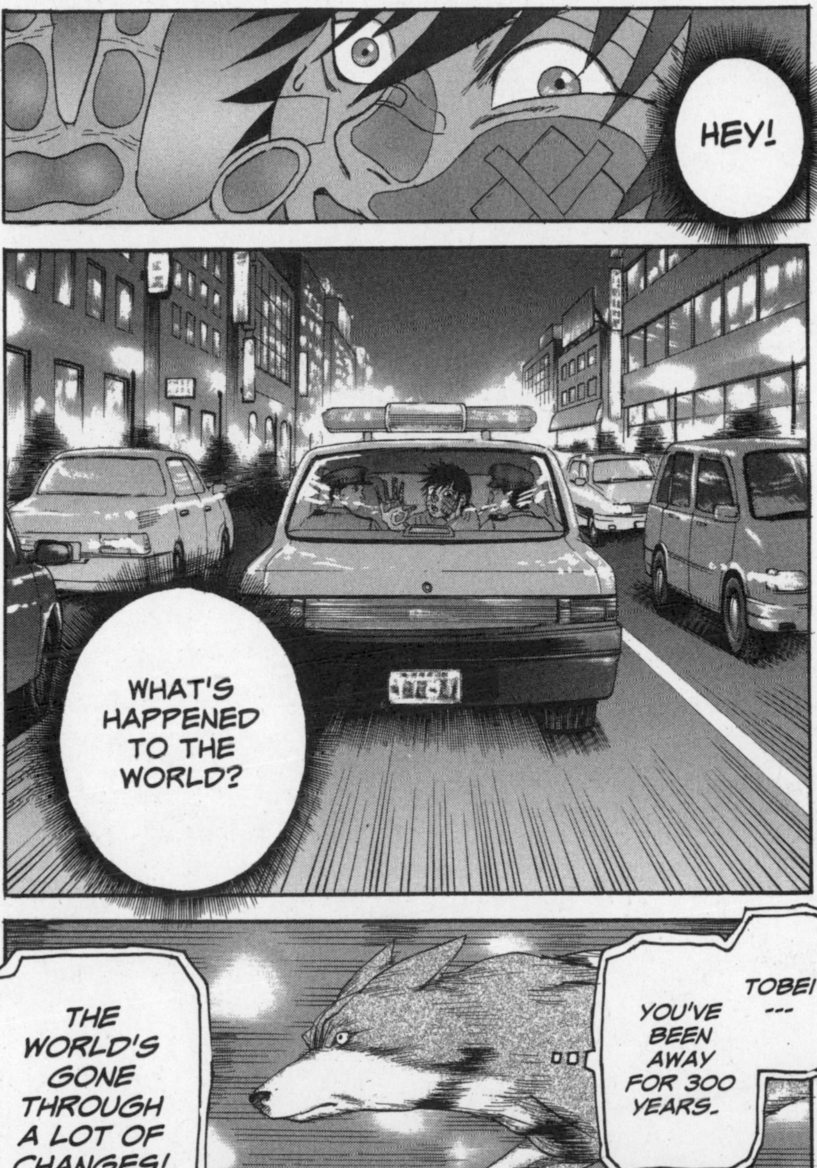
HEY!
WHAT'S HAPPENED TO THE WORLD?
TOBEI --- YOU'VE BEEN AWAY FOR 300 YEARS...
THE WORLD'S GONE THROUGH A LOT OF CHANGES!

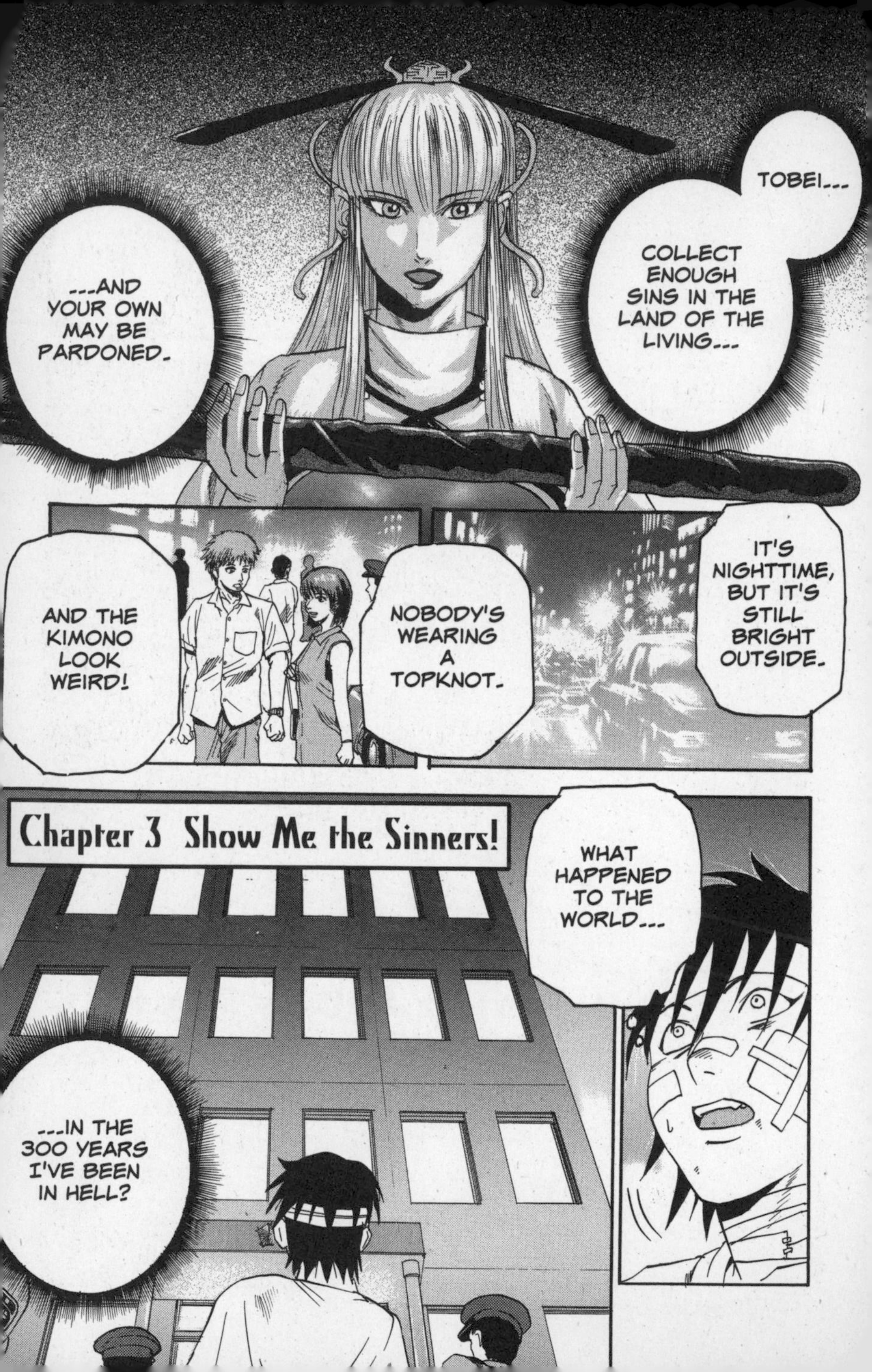
TOBEI...
COLLECT ENOUGH SINS IN THE LAND OF THE LIVING...
...AND YOUR OWN MAY BE PARDONED.
IT'S NIGHTTIME, BUT IT'S STILL BRIGHT OUTSIDE.
NOBODY'S WEARING A TOPKNOT.
AND THE KIMONO LOOK WEIRD!
WHAT HAPPENED TO THE WORLD...
Chapter 3 Show Me the Sinners!
...IN THE 300 YEARS I'VE BEEN IN HELL?

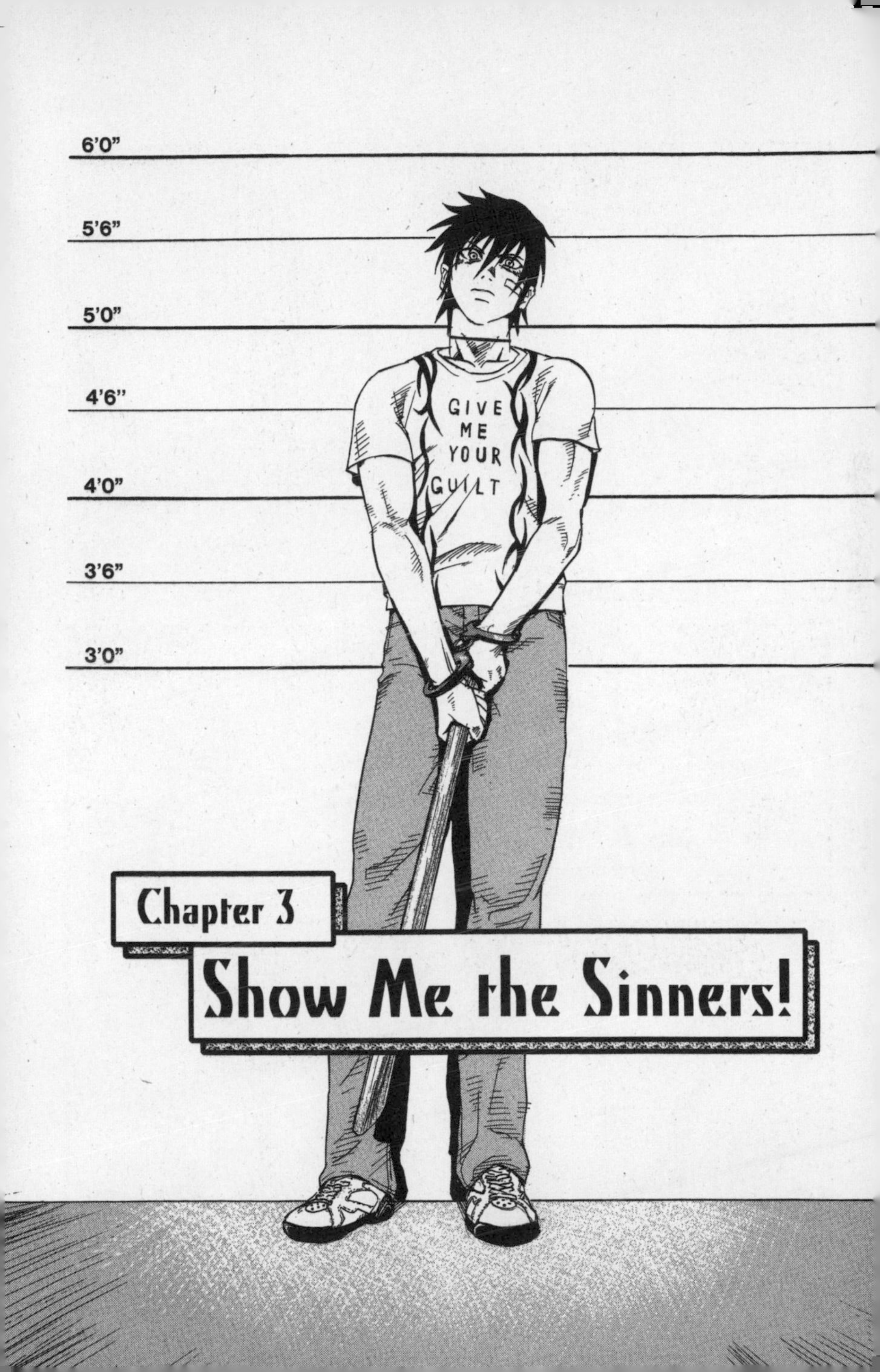
6'0"
5'6"
5'0"
4'6"
GIVE ME YOUR GUILT
4'0"
3'6"
3'0"

Chapter 3

Show Me the Sinners!

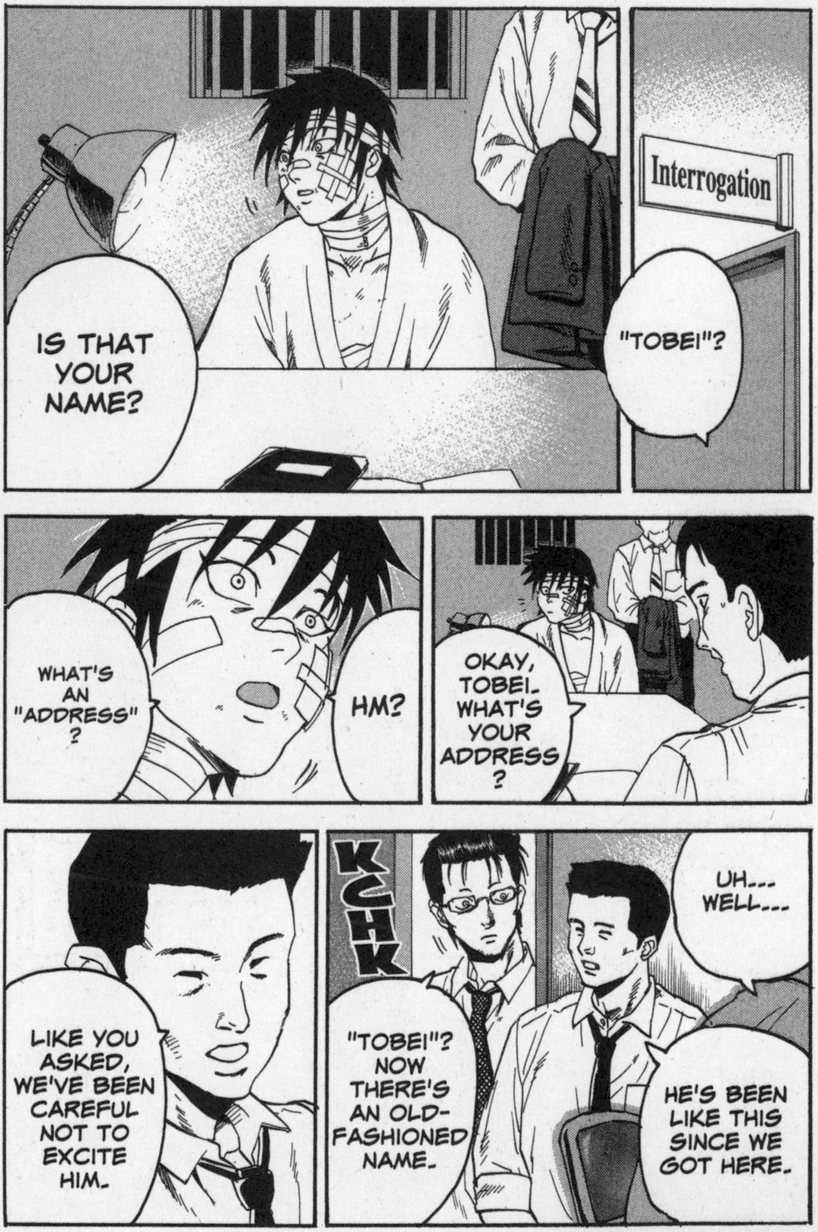
Interrogation
"TOBEI"?
IS THAT YOUR NAME?
OKAY, TOBEI. WHAT'S YOUR ADDRESS?
HM?
WHAT'S AN "ADDRESS"?
KCHK
"TOBEI"? NOW THERE'S AN OLD-FASHIONED NAME.
UH... WELL...
HE'S BEEN LIKE THIS SINCE WE GOT HERE.
LIKE YOU ASKED, WE'VE BEEN CAREFUL NOT TO EXCITE HIM.

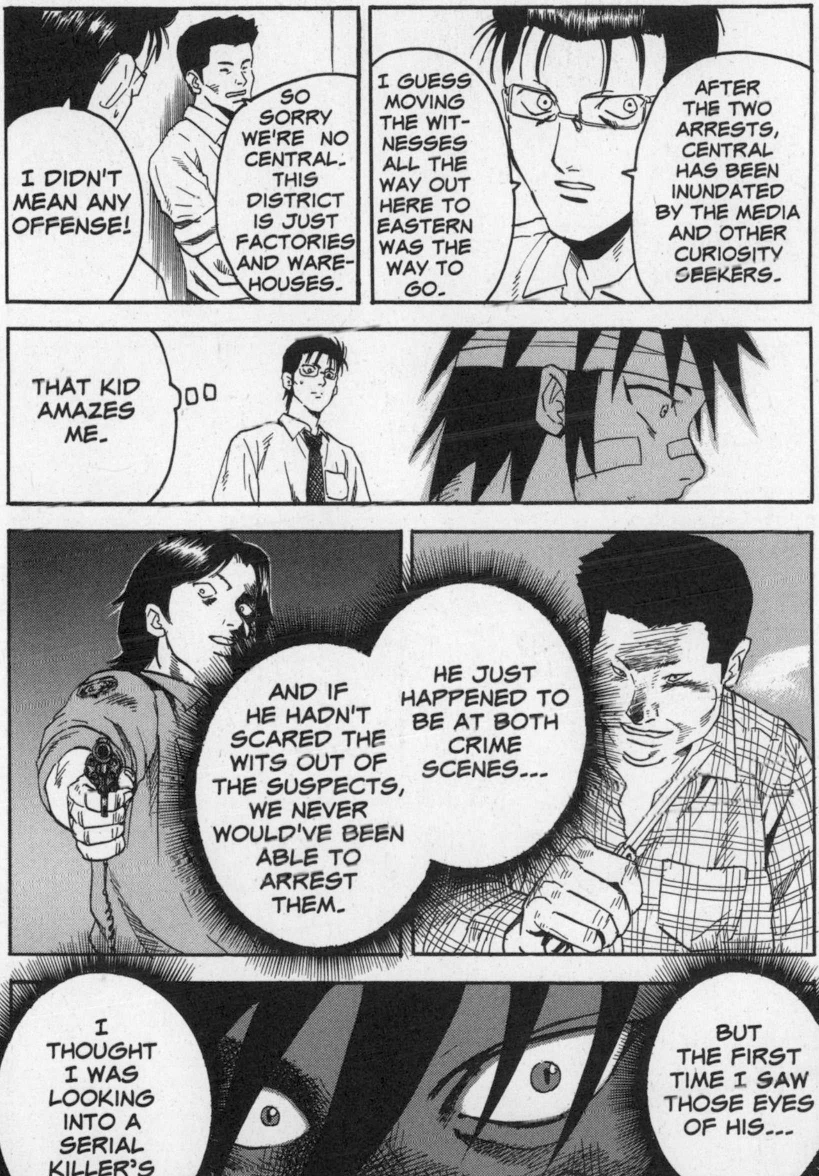
AFTER THE TWO ARRESTS, CENTRAL HAS BEEN INUNDATED BY THE MEDIA AND OTHER CURIOSITY SEEKERS.
I GUESS MOVING THE WITNESSES ALL THE WAY OUT HERE TO EASTERN WAS THE WAY TO GO.
SO SORRY WE'RE NO CENTRAL. THIS DISTRICT IS JUST FACTORIES AND WAREHOUSES.
I DIDN'T MEAN ANY OFFENSE!
THAT KID AMAZES ME.
HE JUST HAPPENED TO BE AT BOTH CRIME SCENES...
AND IF HE HADN'T SCARED THE WITS OUT OF THE SUSPECTS, WE NEVER WOULD'VE BEEN ABLE TO ARREST THEM.
BUT THE FIRST TIME I SAW THOSE EYES OF HIS...
I THOUGHT I WAS LOOKING INTO A SERIAL KILLER'S EYES.

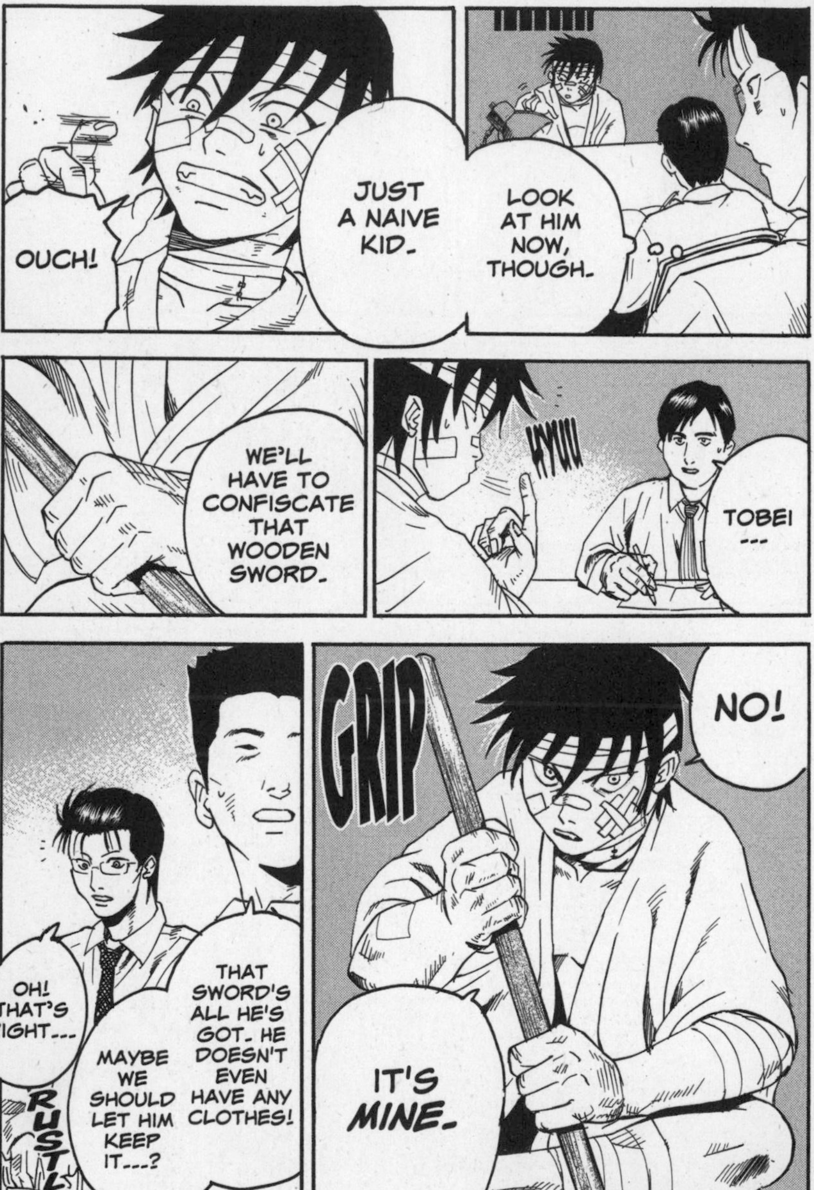
LOOK AT HIM NOW, THOUGH.
JUST A NAIVE KID.
OUCH!
TOBEI---
KYUU
WE'LL HAVE TO CONFISCATE THAT WOODEN SWORD.
NO!
GRIP
IT'S MINE.
THAT SWORD'S ALL HE'S GOT. HE DOESN'T EVEN HAVE ANY CLOTHES!
MAYBE WE SHOULD LET HIM KEEP IT---?
OH! THAT'S RIGHT---
RUSTLE

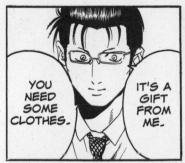

SLIDE
HERE YOU GO.
IT'S A GIFT FROM ME.
YOU NEED SOME CLOTHES.
A "GIFT"...?
FWP
GASP!
IT'S WRONG TO TAKE THINGS THAT DON'T BELONG TO YOU!
GASP
?
WHAT'S WRONG?
TELL ME.
IS IT A SIN TO STEAL THESE?
HUH?

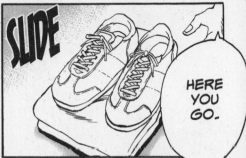

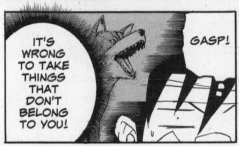

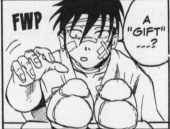

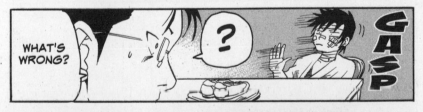

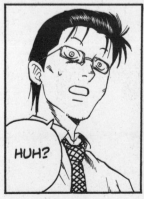

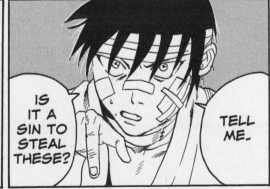

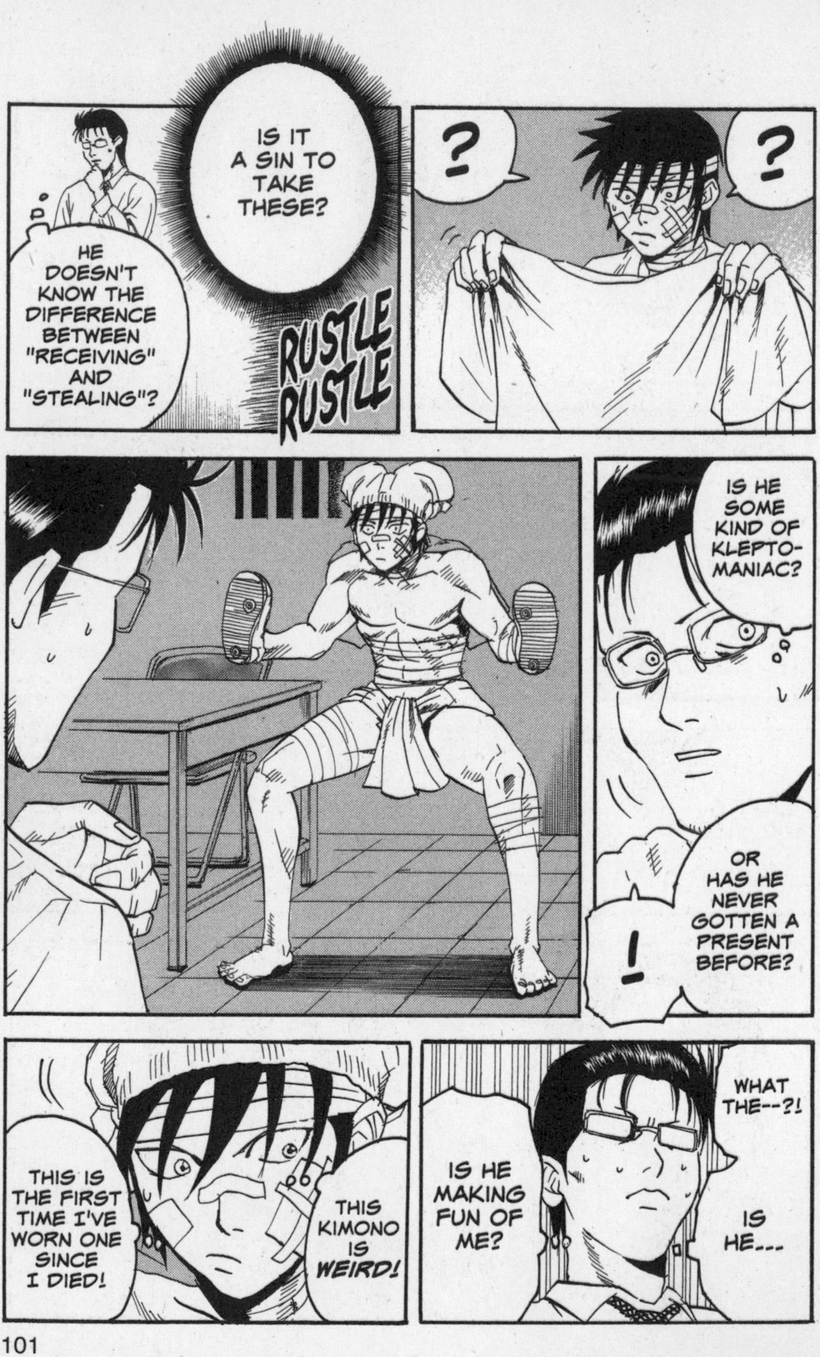
?
?
IS IT A SIN TO TAKE THESE?
RUSTLE RUSTLE
HE DOESN'T KNOW THE DIFFERENCE BETWEEN "RECEIVING" AND "STEALING"?
IS HE SOME KIND OF KLEPTO-MANIAC?
OR HAS HE NEVER GOTTEN A PRESENT BEFORE?
!
WHAT THE--?!
IS HE...
IS HE MAKING FUN OF ME?
THIS KIMONO IS *WEIRD!*
THIS IS THE FIRST TIME I'VE WORN ONE SINCE I DIED!

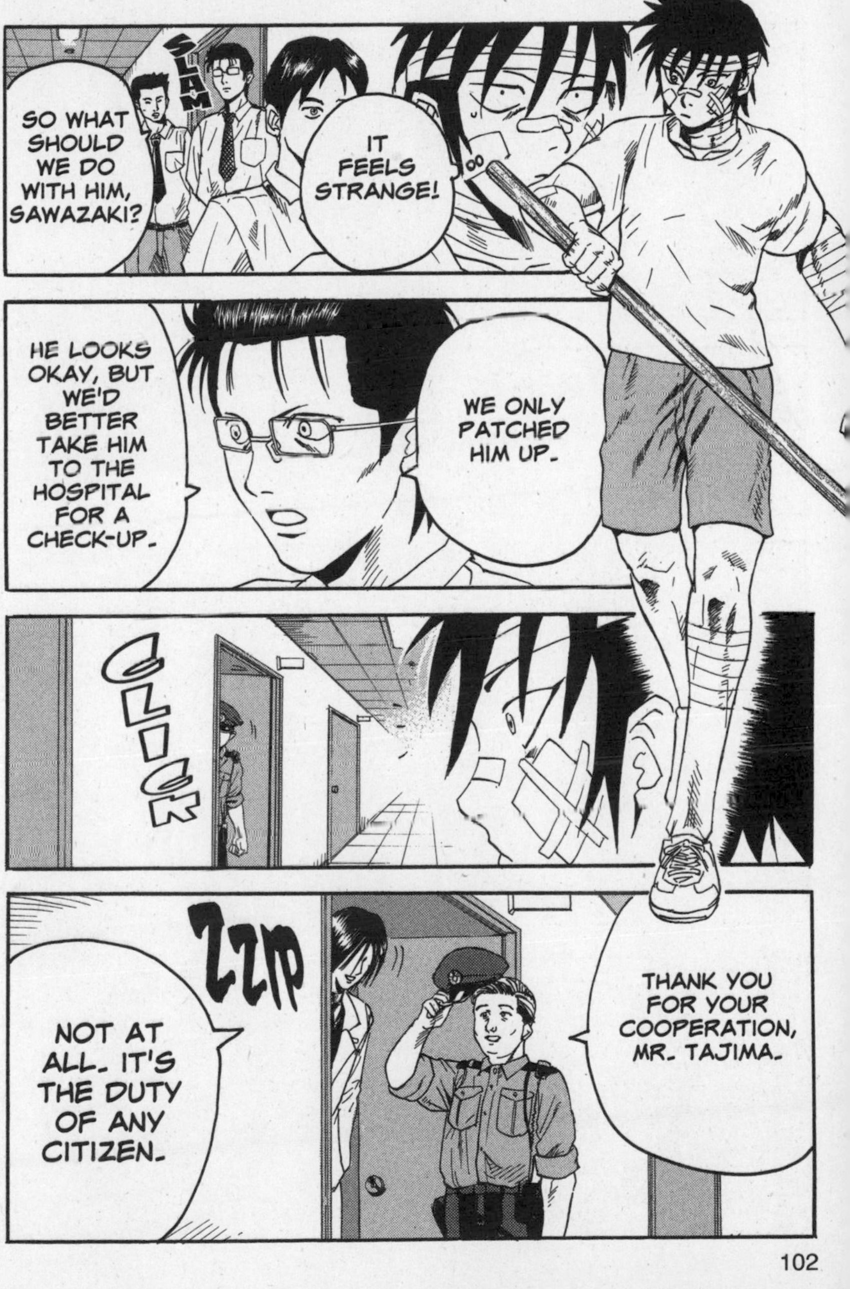
IT FEELS STRANGE!
SLAM
SO WHAT SHOULD WE DO WITH HIM, SAWAZAKI?
WE ONLY PATCHED HIM UP.
HE LOOKS OKAY, BUT WE'D BETTER TAKE HIM TO THE HOSPITAL FOR A CHECK-UP.
CLICK
THANK YOU FOR YOUR COOPERATION, MR. TAJIMA.
ZZIP
NOT AT ALL. IT'S THE DUTY OF ANY CITIZEN.

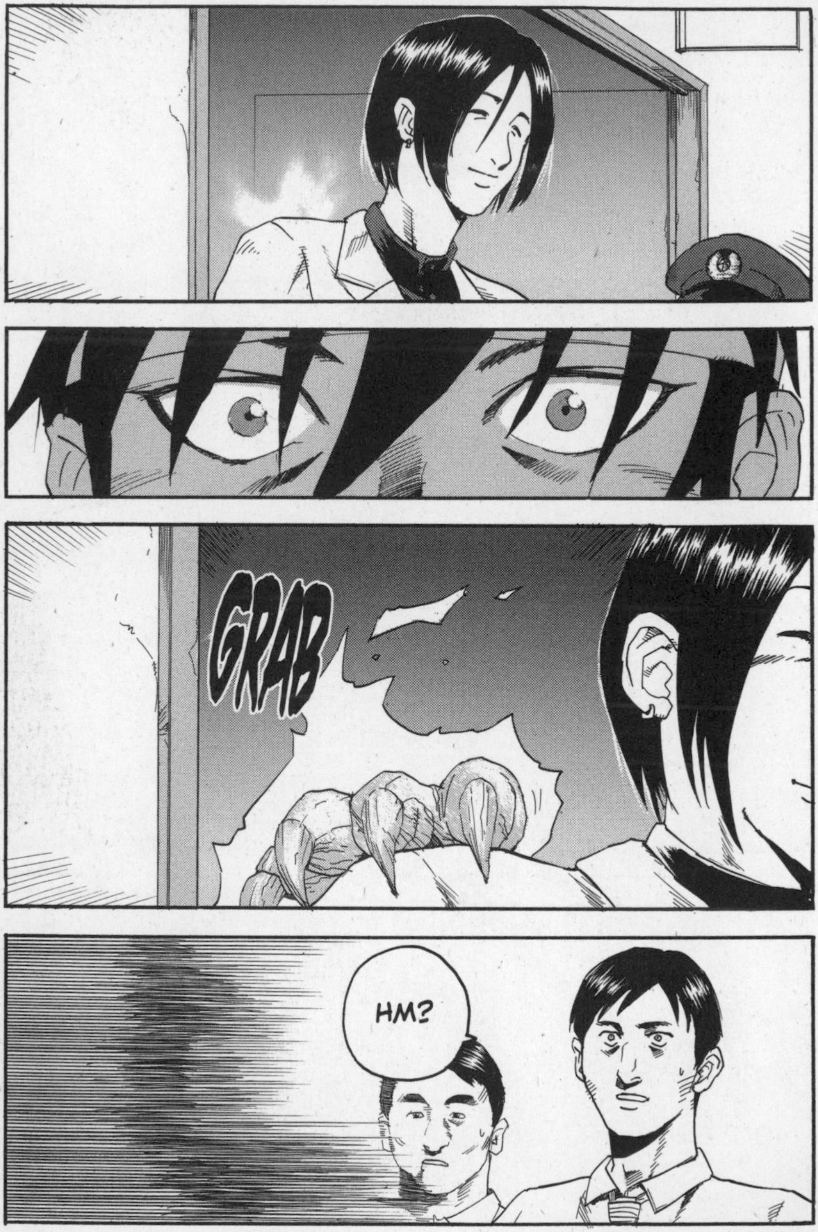
GRAB
HM?

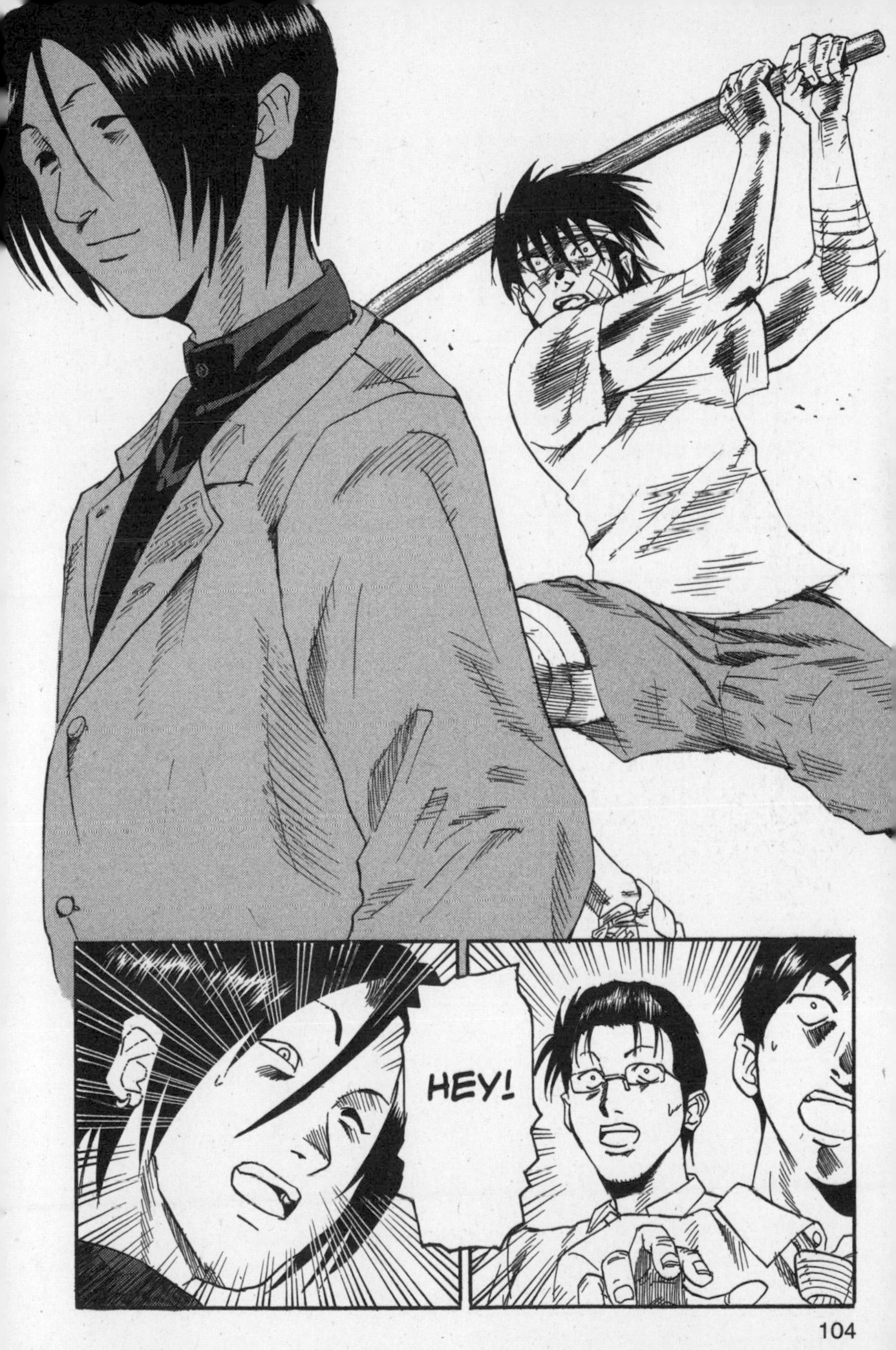
HEY!

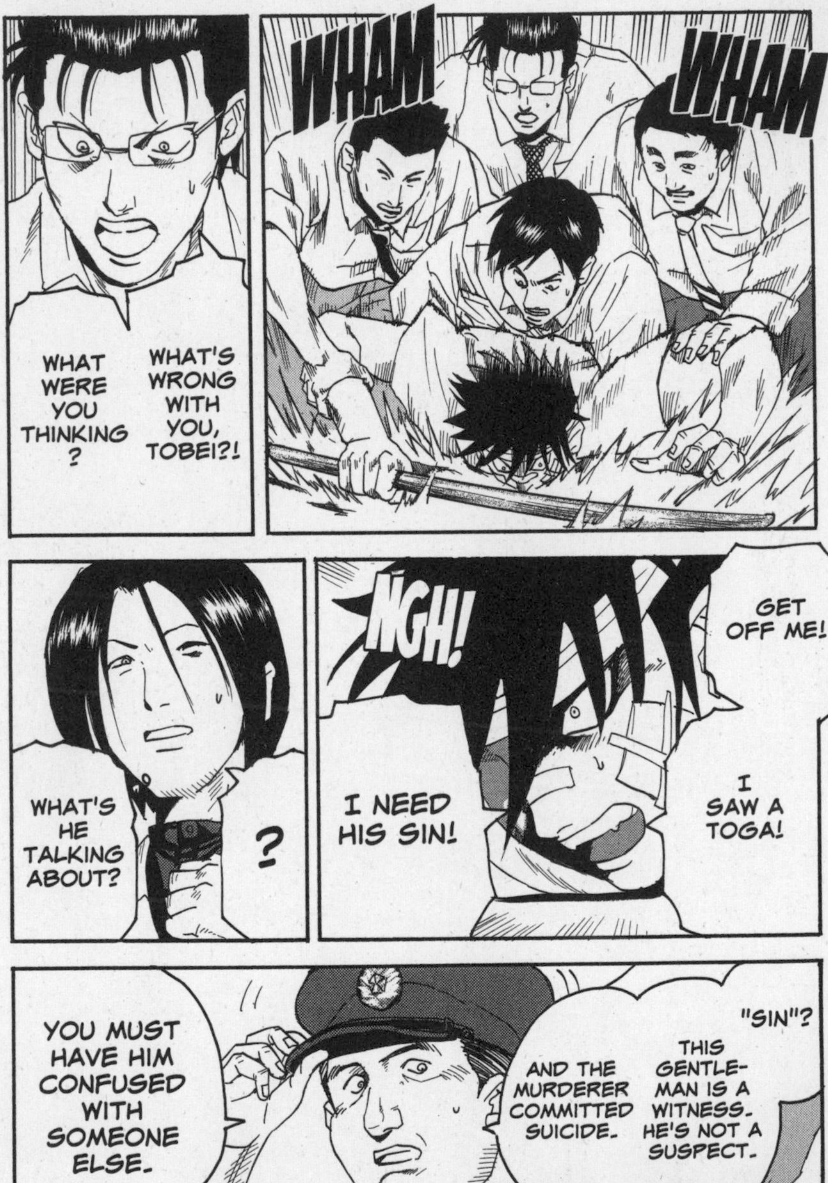
WHAM
WHAM
WHAT'S WRONG WITH YOU, TOBEI?!
WHAT WERE YOU THINKING?
GET OFF ME!
NGH!
I SAW A TOGA!
I NEED HIS SIN!
?
WHAT'S HE TALKING ABOUT?
"SIN"?
THIS GENTLE-MAN IS A WITNESS. HE'S NOT A SUSPECT.
AND THE MURDERER COMMITTED SUICIDE.
YOU MUST HAVE HIM CONFUSED WITH SOMEONE ELSE.

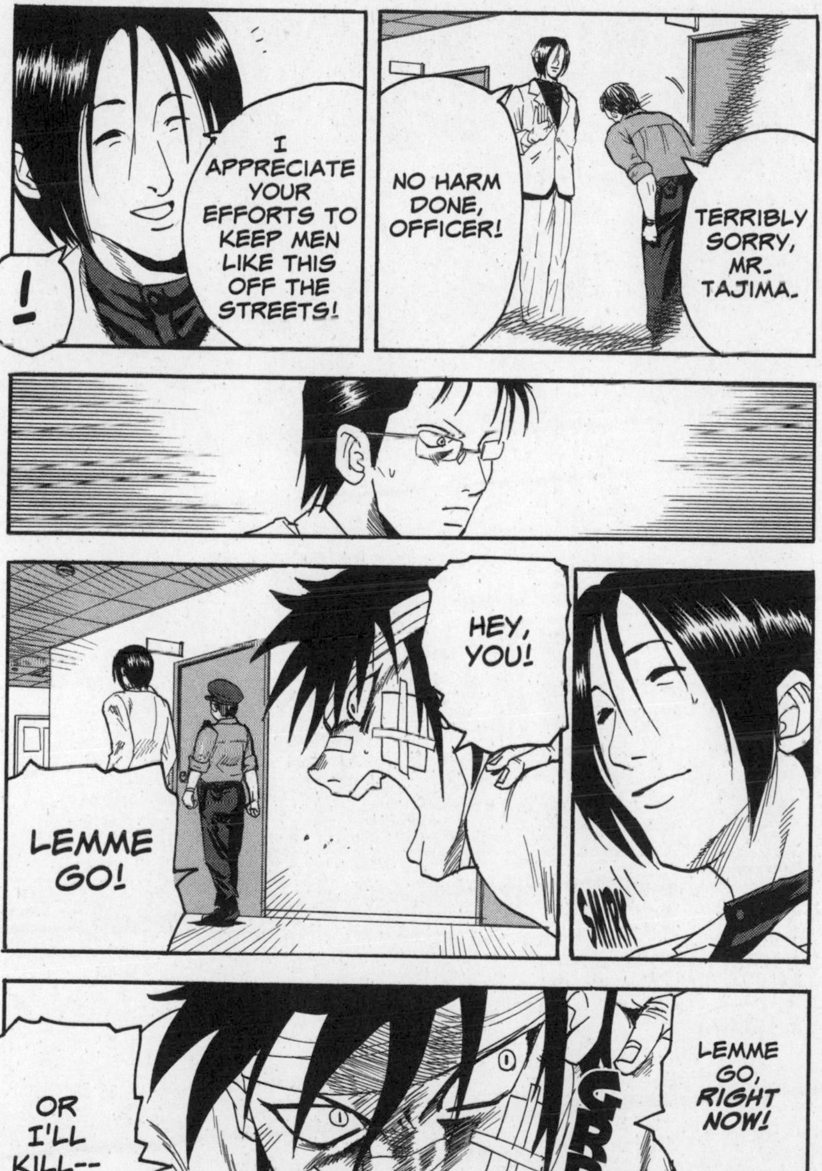
TERRIBLY SORRY, MR. TAJIMA.
NO HARM DONE, OFFICER!
I APPRECIATE YOUR EFFORTS TO KEEP MEN LIKE THIS OFF THE STREETS!
!
SMIRK
HEY, YOU!
LEMME GO!
LEMME GO, RIGHT NOW!
GRRRR
OR I'LL KILL--

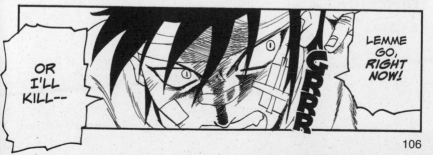

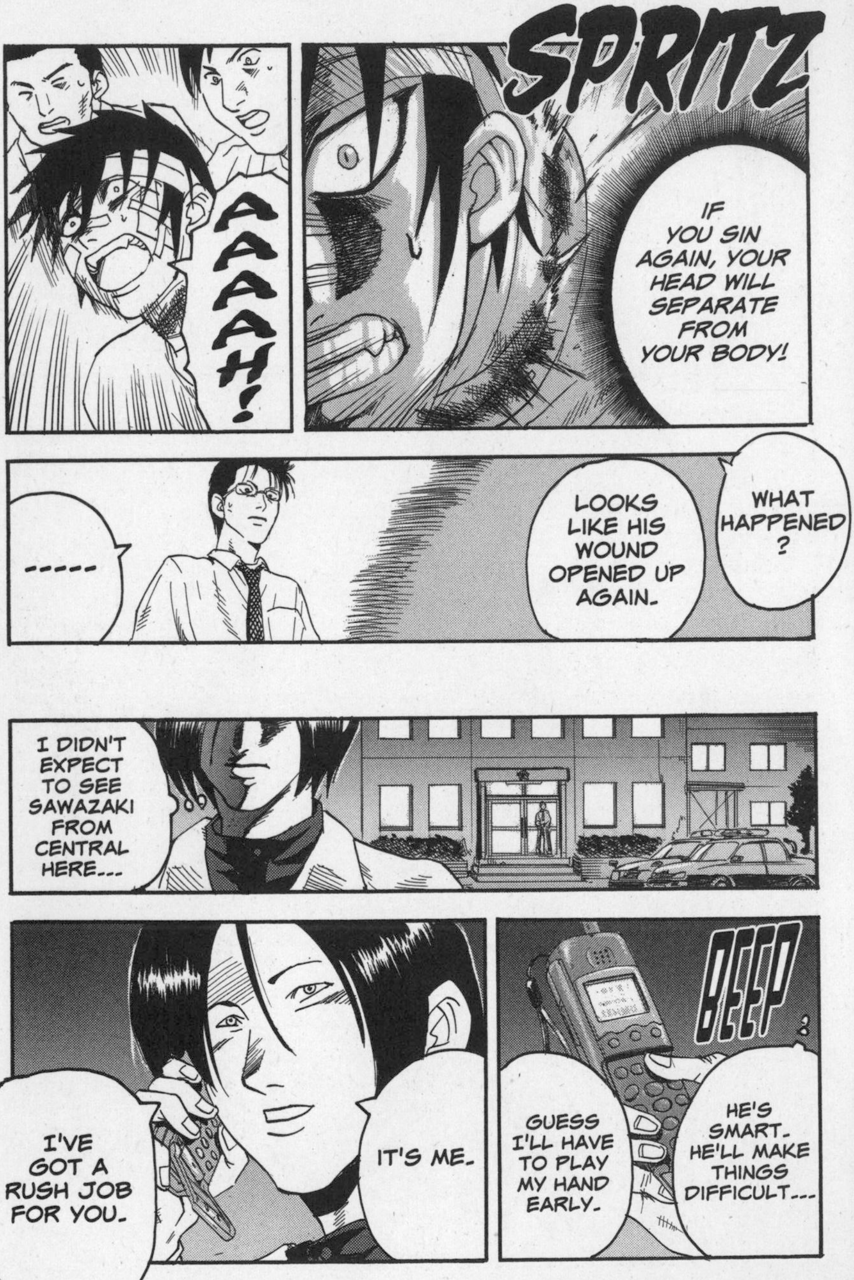
SPRITZ
IF YOU SIN AGAIN, YOUR HEAD WILL SEPARATE FROM YOUR BODY!
AAAAAH!
WHAT HAPPENED?
LOOKS LIKE HIS WOUND OPENED UP AGAIN.

I DIDN'T EXPECT TO SEE SAWAZAKI FROM CENTRAL HERE...
BEEP
HE'S SMART. HE'LL MAKE THINGS DIFFICULT...
GUESS I'LL HAVE TO PLAY MY HAND EARLY.
IT'S ME.
I'VE GOT A RUSH JOB FOR YOU.

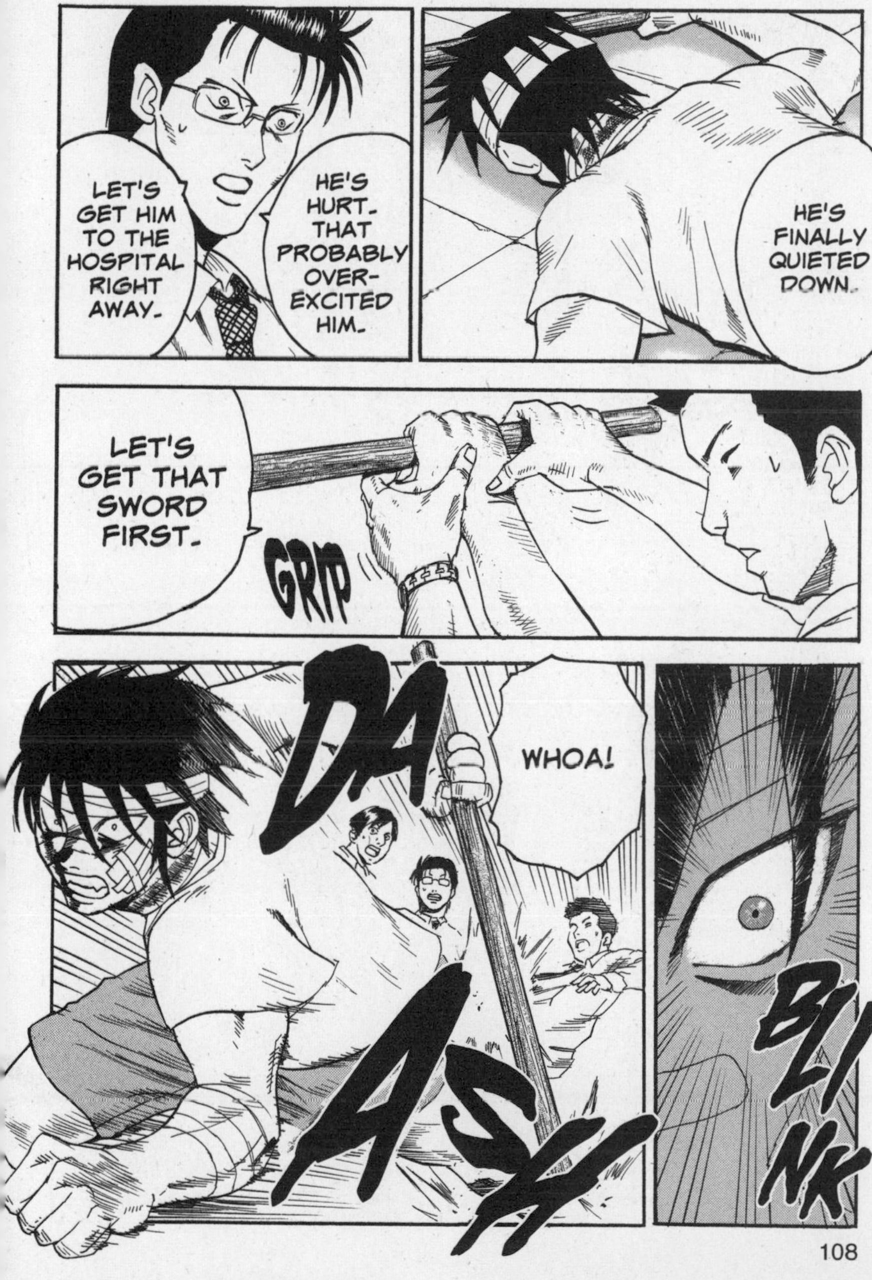
HE'S FINALLY QUIETED DOWN.
HE'S HURT. THAT PROBABLY OVER-EXCITED HIM.
LET'S GET HIM TO THE HOSPITAL RIGHT AWAY.
LET'S GET THAT SWORD FIRST.
GRIP
BLINK
WHOA!
DAASH

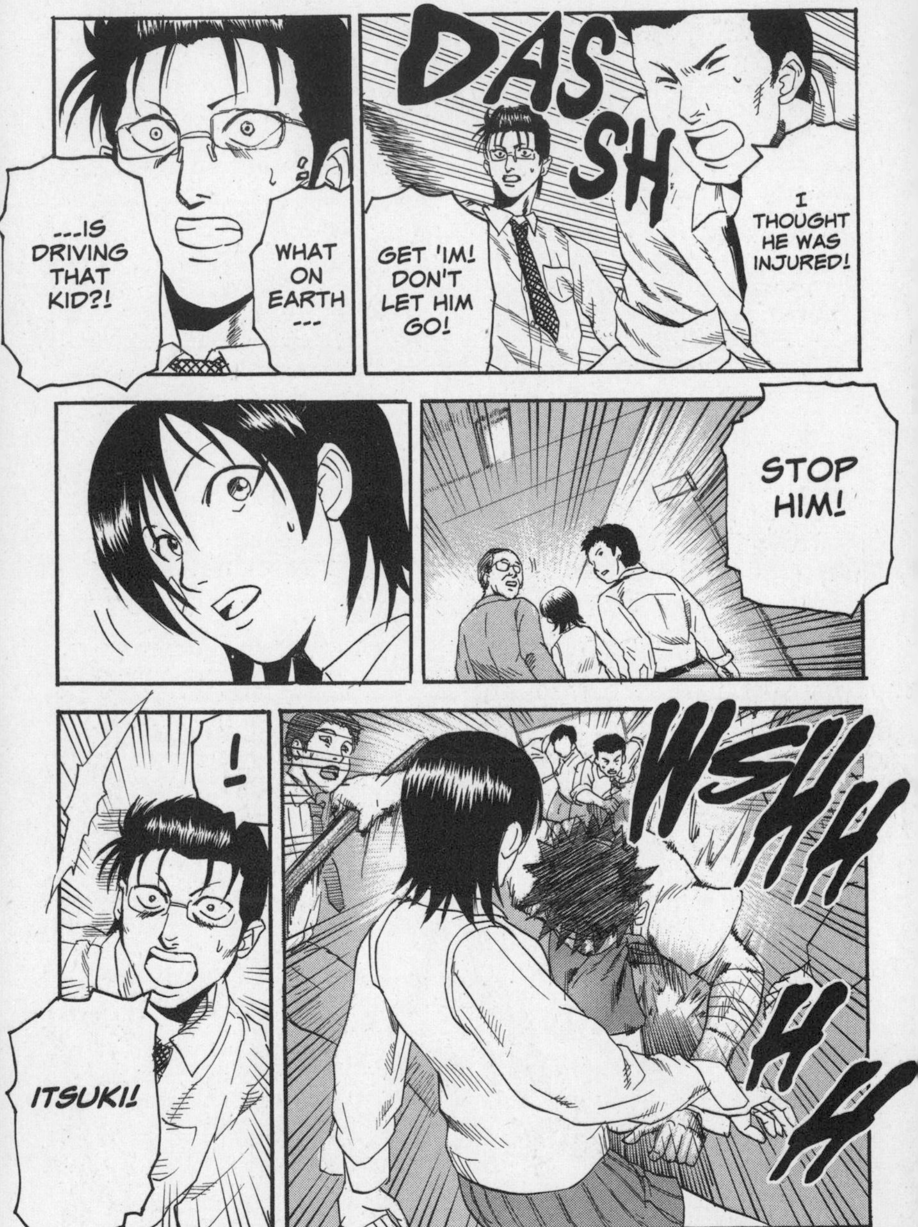
DAS
SH
I THOUGHT HE WAS INJURED!
GET 'IM! DON'T LET HIM GO!
WHAT ON EARTH ---
---IS DRIVING THAT KID?!
STOP HIM!
WSHHHHH
!
ITSUKI!

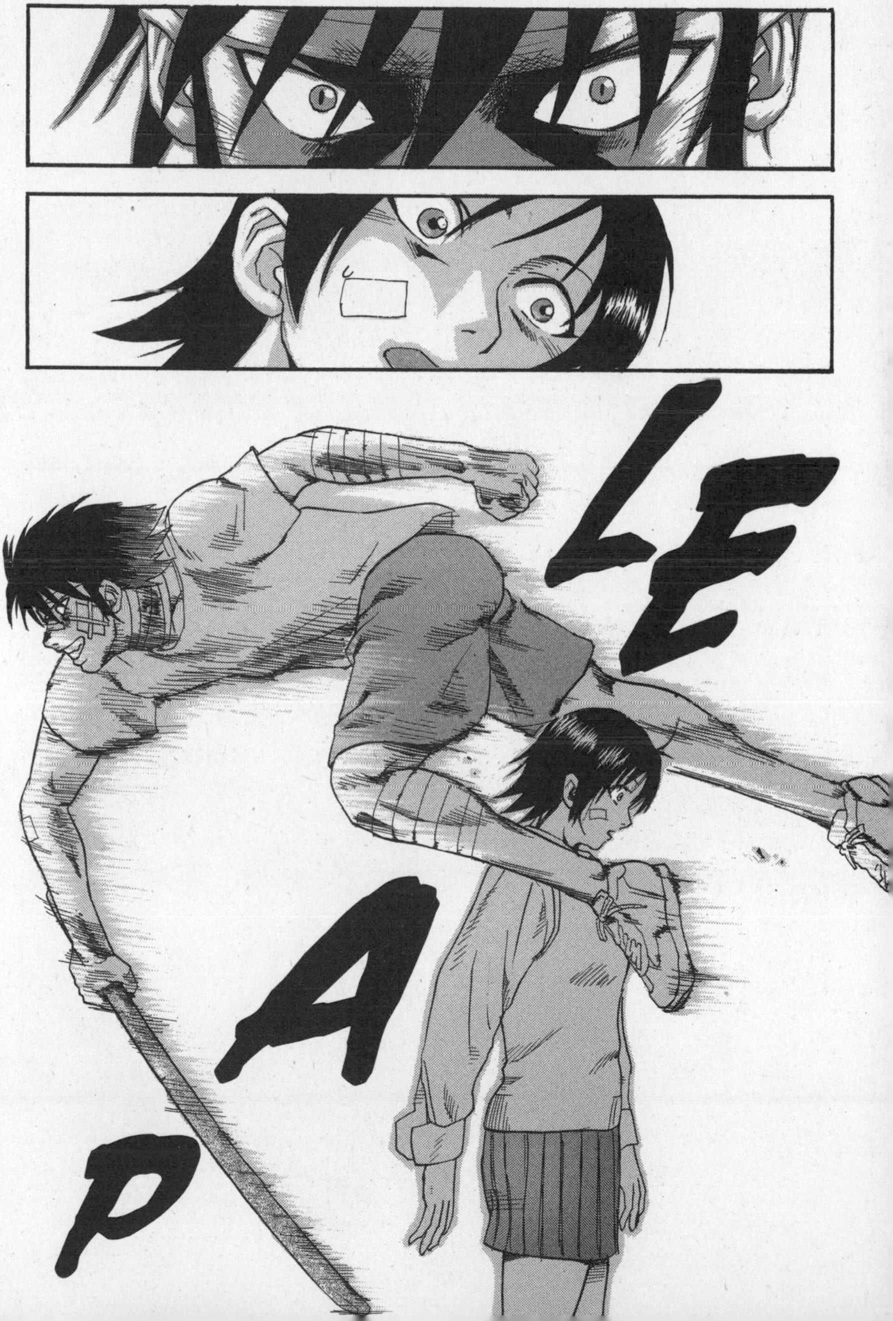
LEE
PA

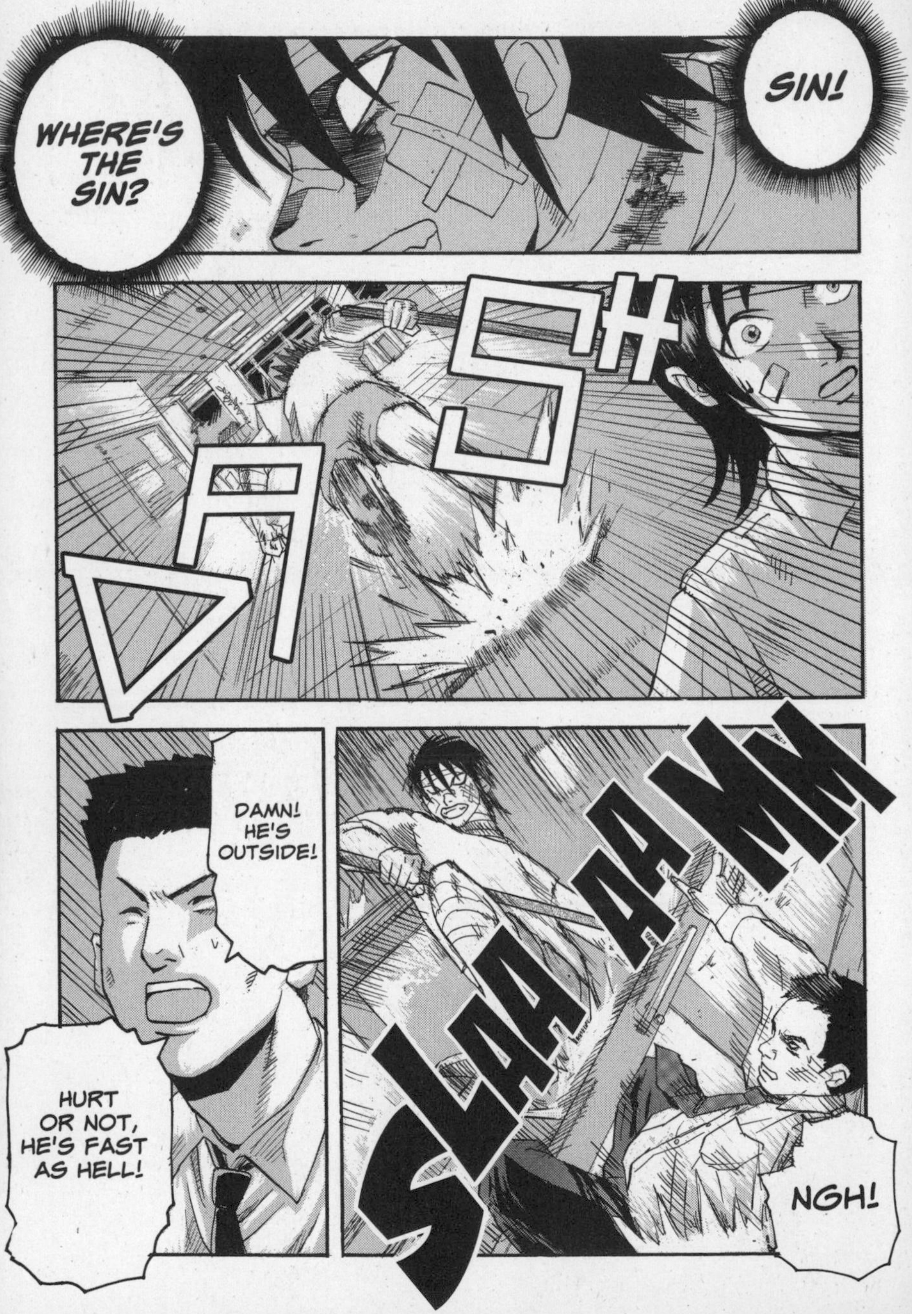
SIN!
WHERE'S THE SIN?
DASH
SLAAAAMM
NGH!
DAMN! HE'S OUTSIDE!
HURT OR NOT, HE'S FAST AS HELL!

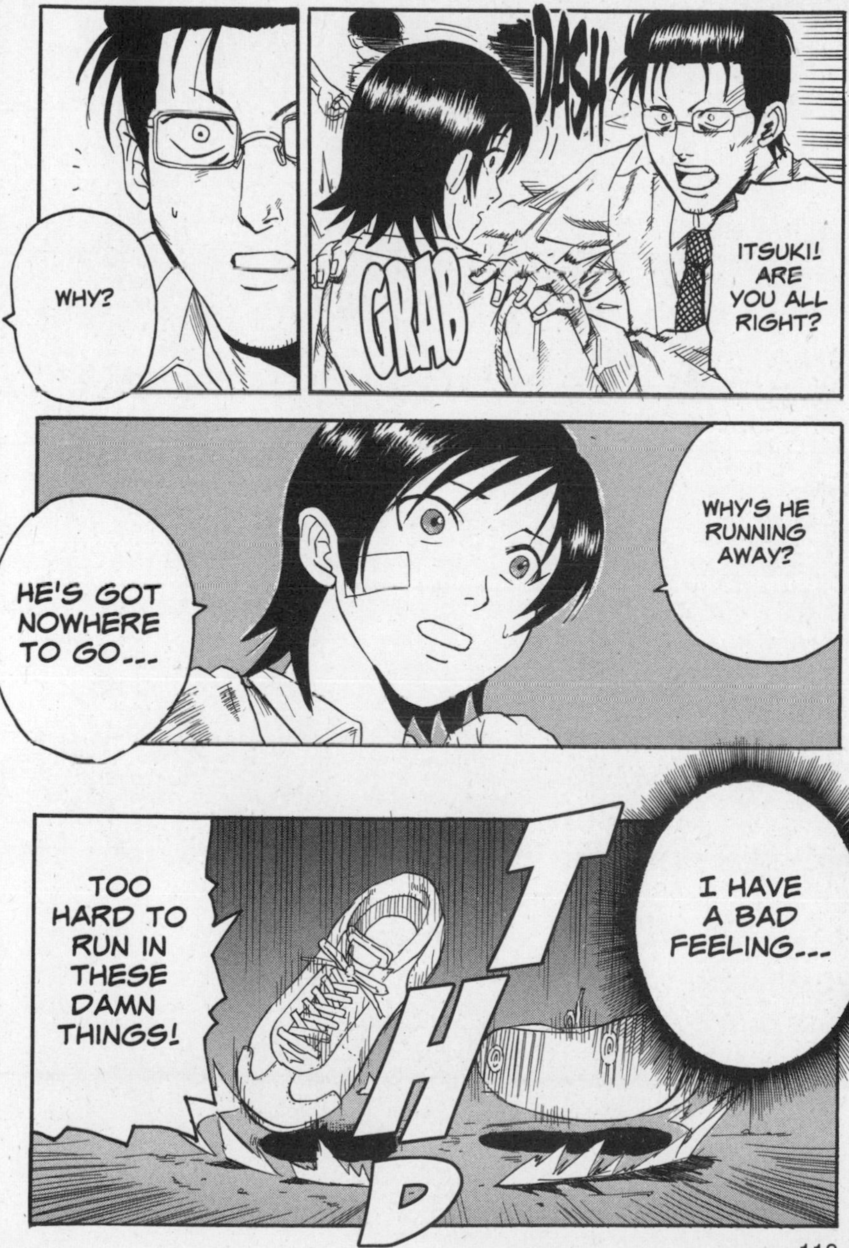
DASH
ITSUKI! ARE YOU ALL RIGHT?
GRAB
WHY?
WHY'S HE RUNNING AWAY?
HE'S GOT NOWHERE TO GO...
I HAVE A BAD FEELING...
THUD
TOO HARD TO RUN IN THESE DAMN THINGS!

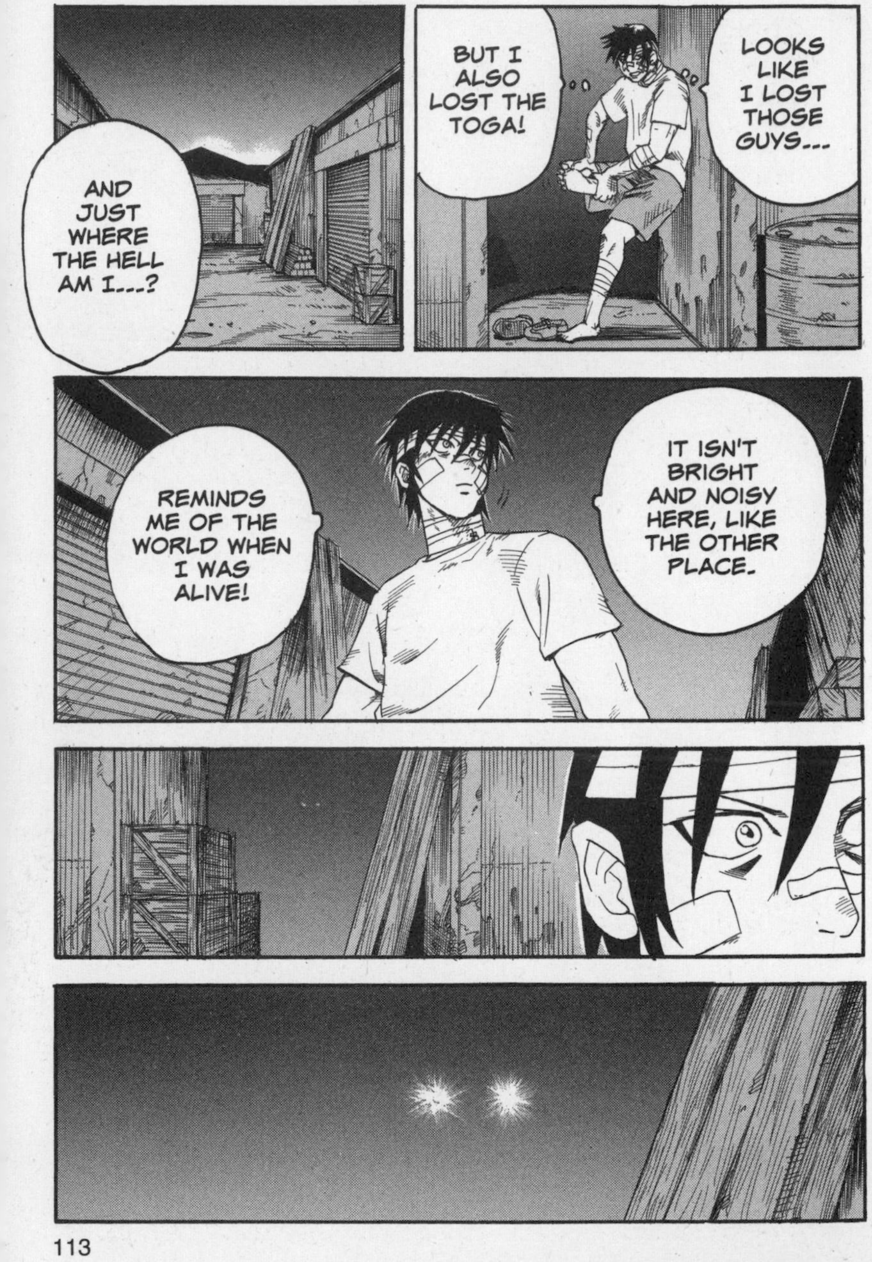
LOOKS LIKE I LOST THOSE GUYS...
BUT I ALSO LOST THE TOGA!
AND JUST WHERE THE HELL AM I...?
IT ISN'T BRIGHT AND NOISY HERE, LIKE THE OTHER PLACE.
REMINDS ME OF THE WORLD WHEN I WAS ALIVE!

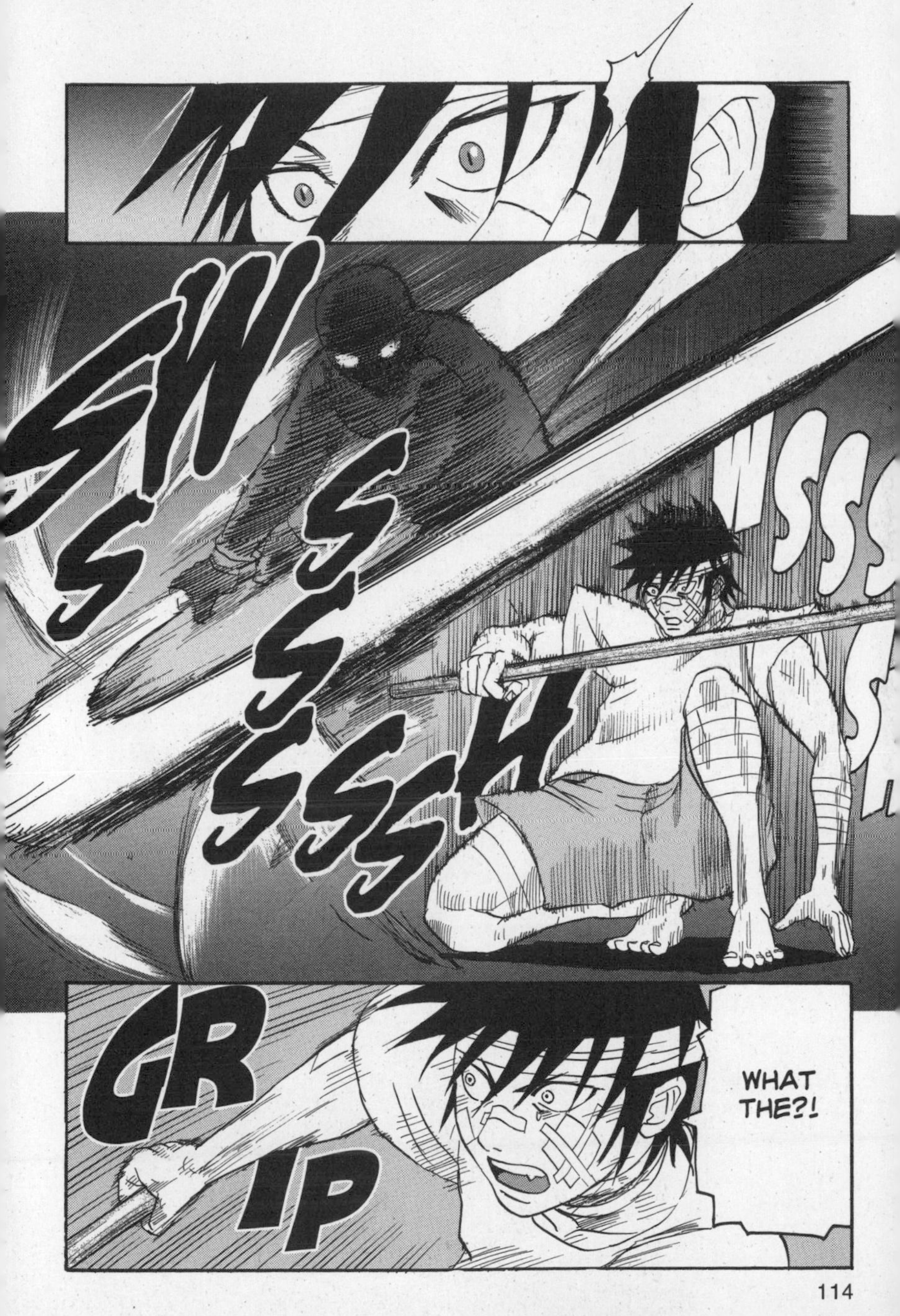
WHAT THE?!
GRIP

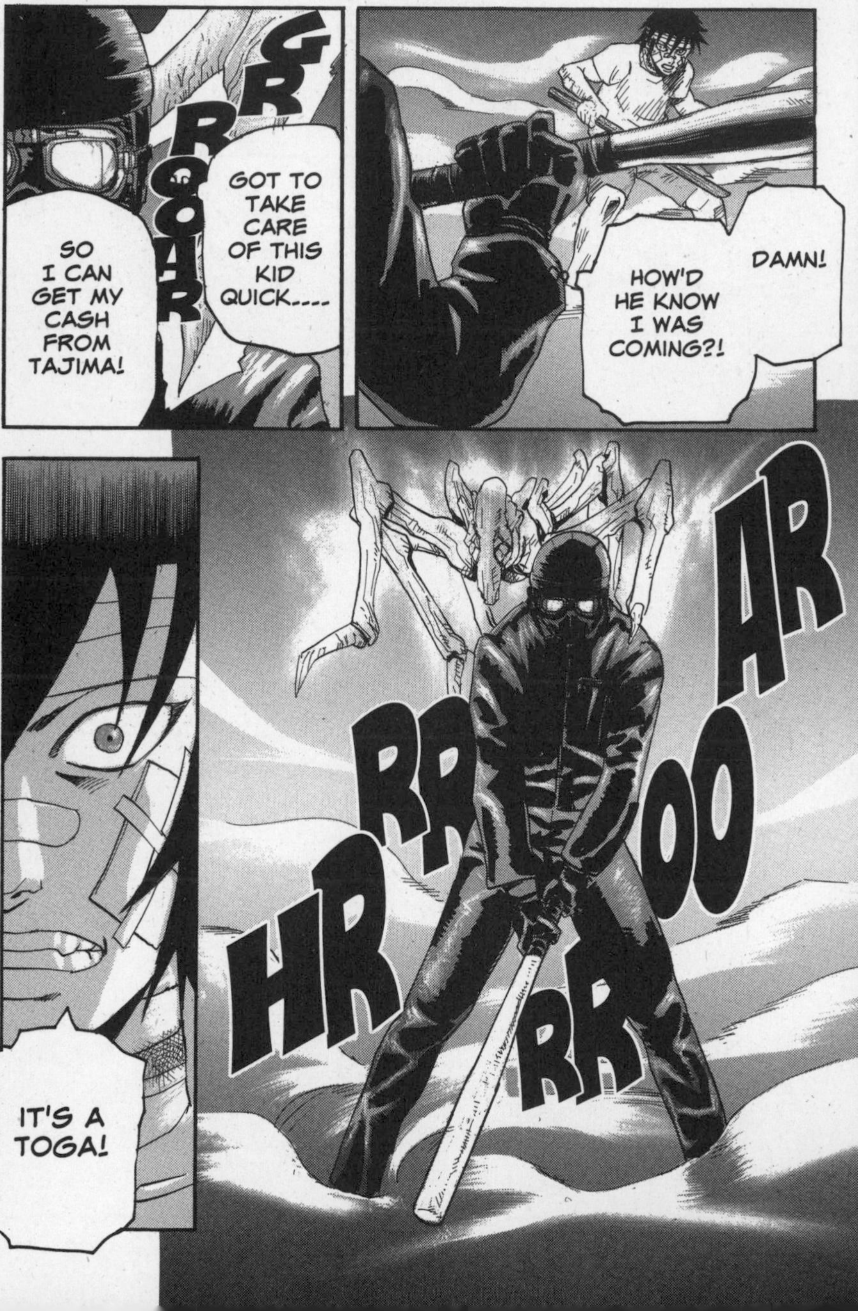
DAMN!
HOW'D HE KNOW I WAS COMING?!
GOT TO TAKE CARE OF THIS KID QUICK....
SO I CAN GET MY CASH FROM TAJIMA!
IT'S A TOGA!

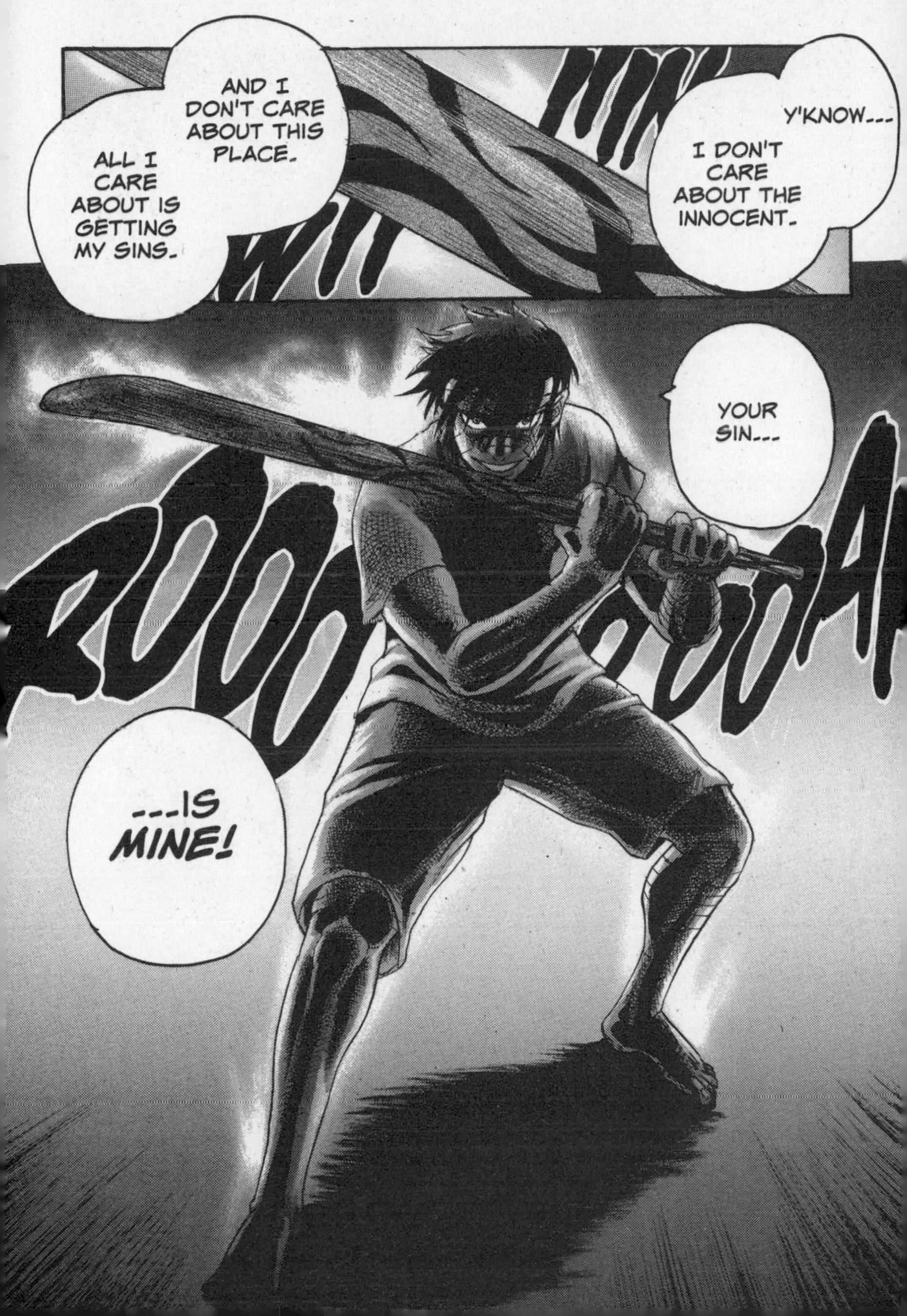
Y'KNOW...
I DON'T CARE ABOUT THE INNOCENT.
AND I DON'T CARE ABOUT THIS PLACE.
ALL I CARE ABOUT IS GETTING MY SINS.
YOUR SIN...
...IS MINE!

Chapter 4 Is This How It's Supposed to Be?

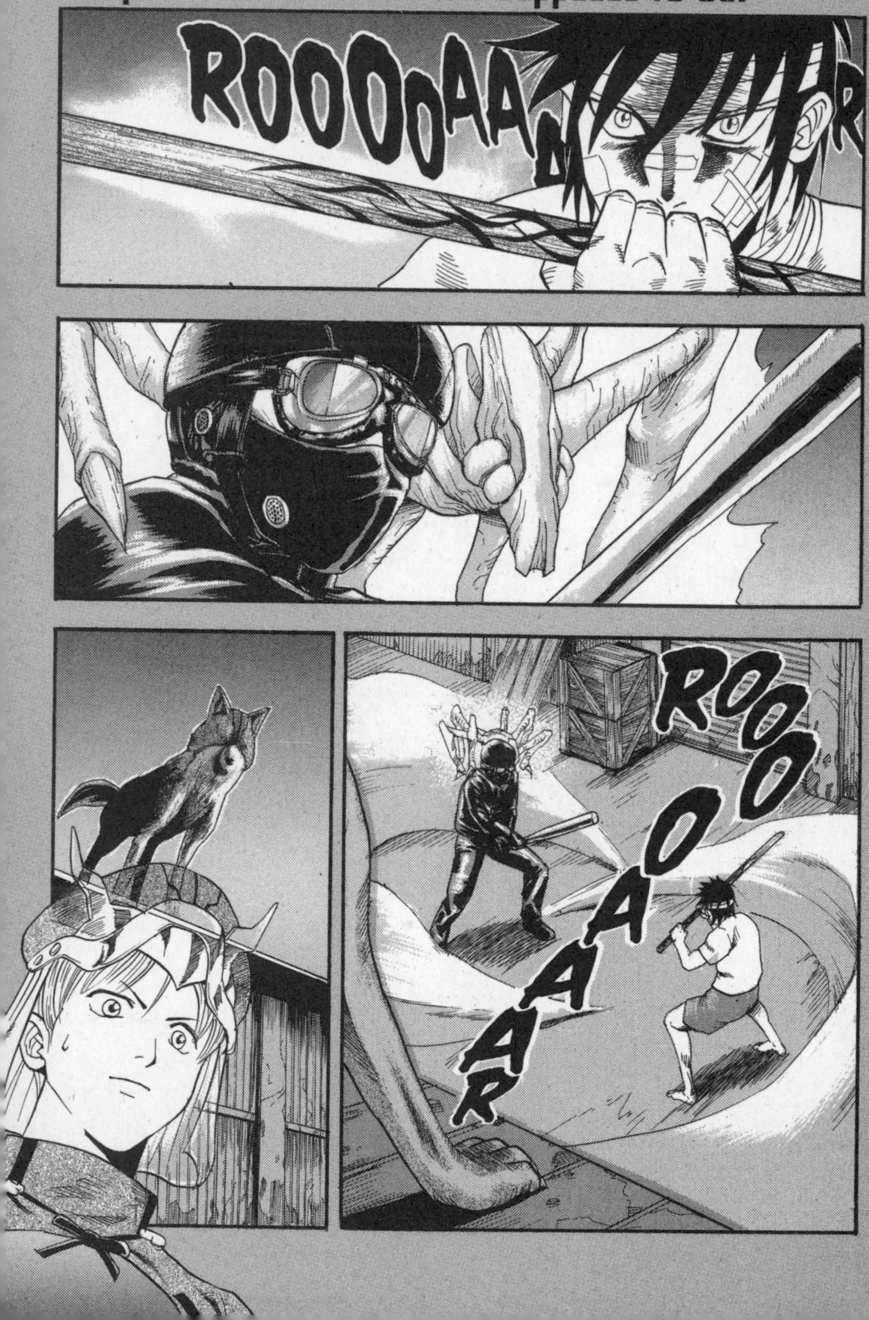
ROOOOAAAR
ROOOOOAAAAR

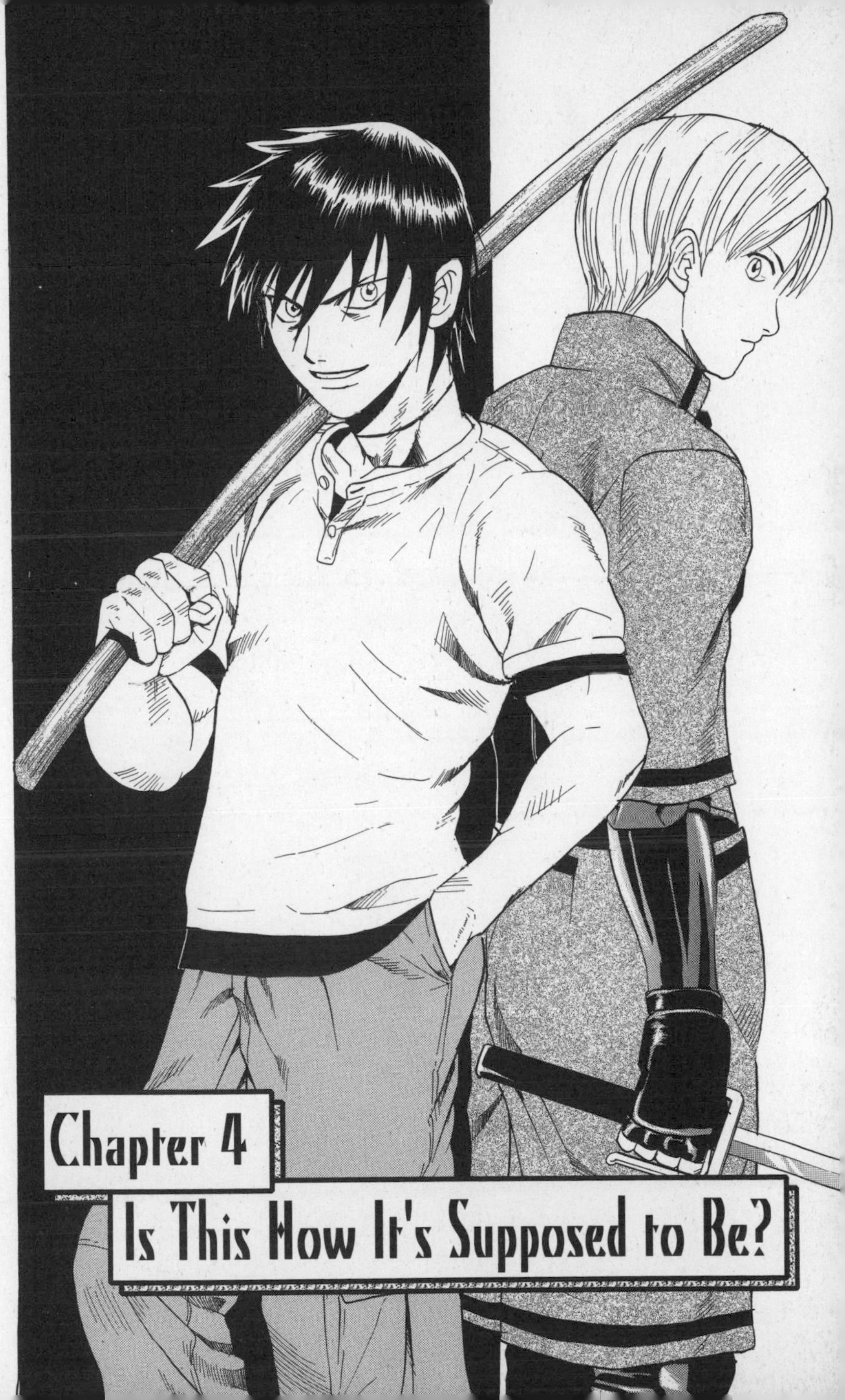
Chapter 4
Is This How It's Supposed to Be?

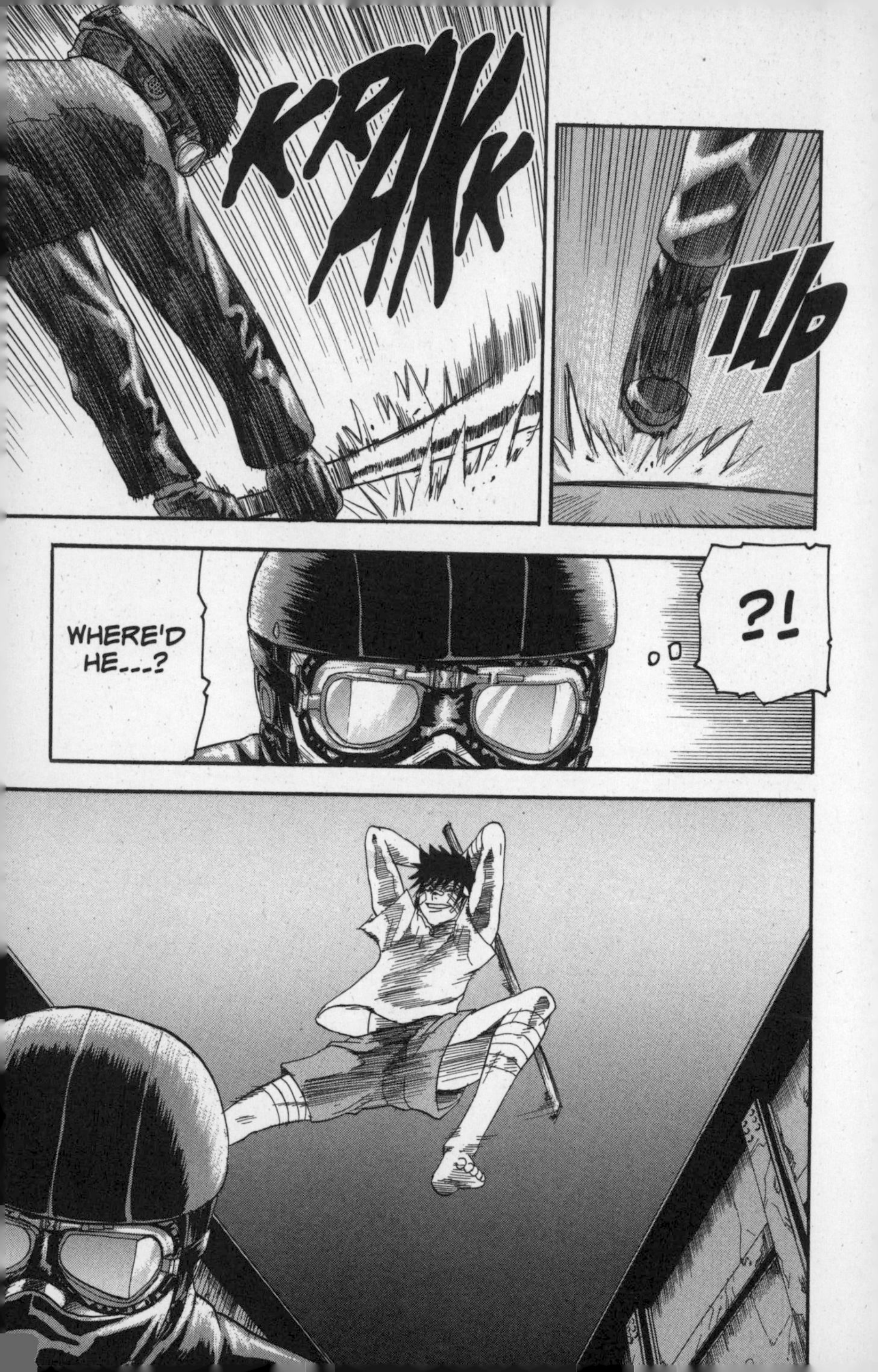
TUP
?!
WHERE'D HE...?

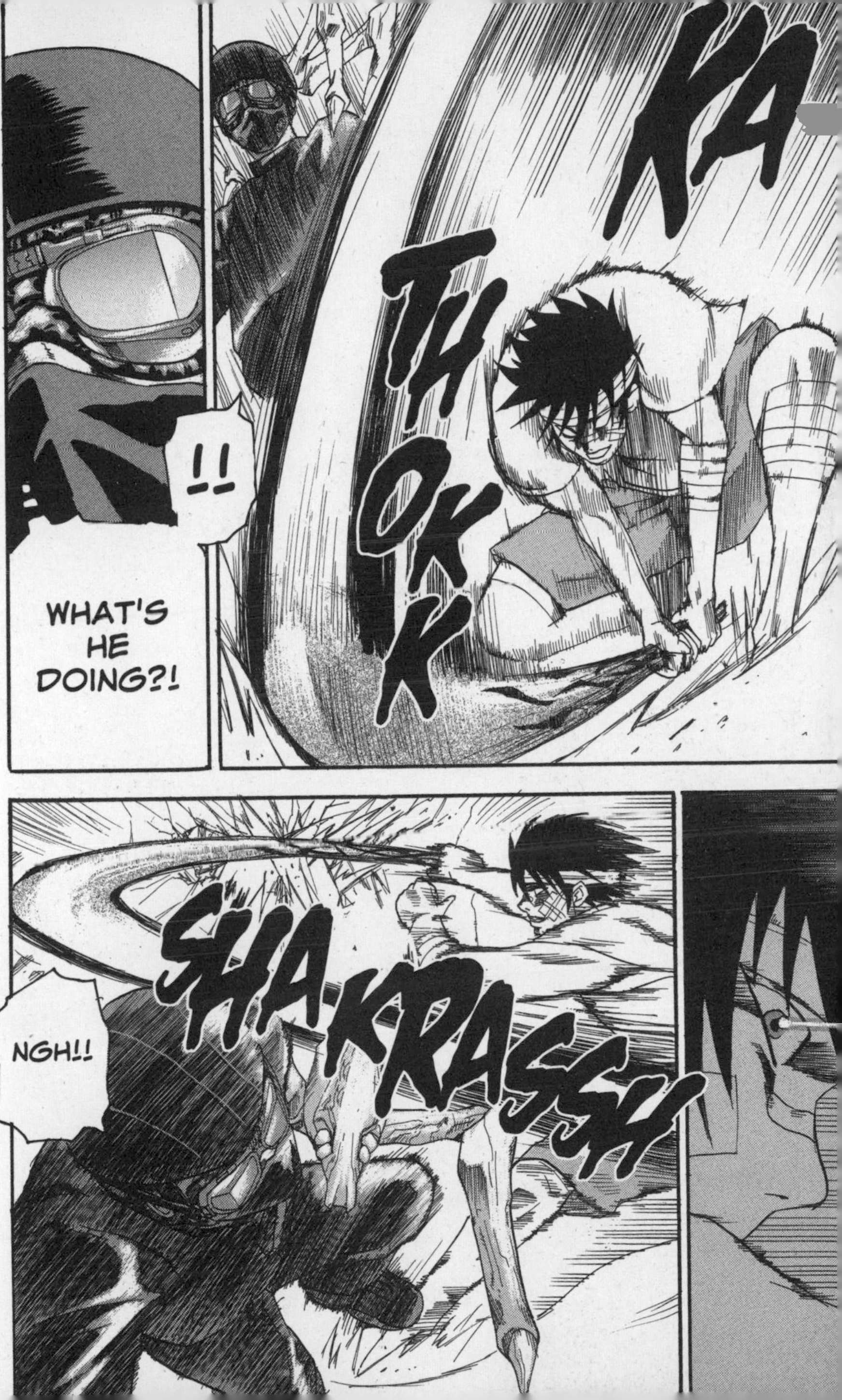
KA
THOKK
!!
WHAT'S HE DOING?!
SHA-KRASSH
NGH!!

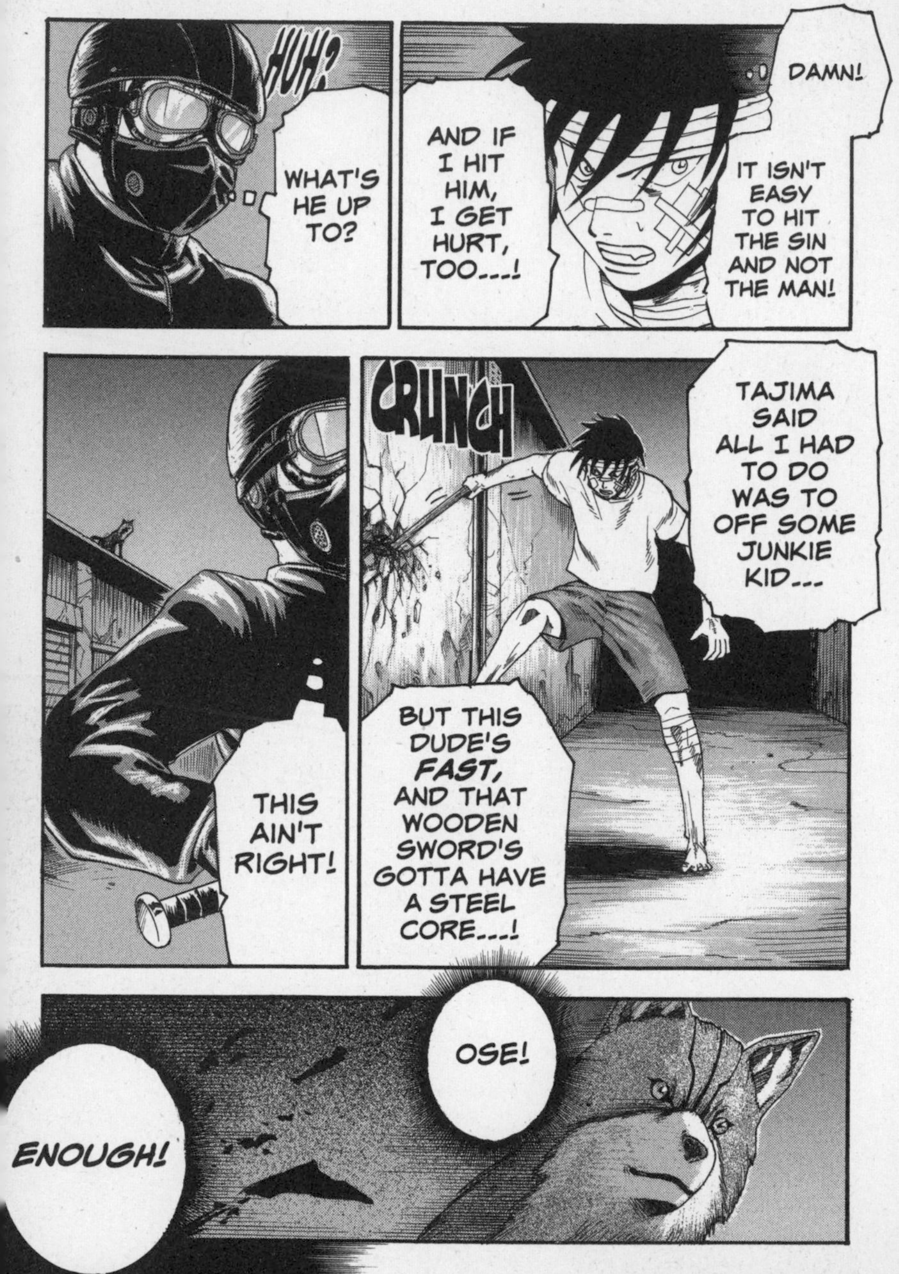
DAMN!
IT ISN'T EASY TO HIT THE SIN AND NOT THE MAN!
AND IF I HIT HIM, I GET HURT, TOO...!
HUH?
WHAT'S HE UP TO?
CRUNCH
TAJIMA SAID ALL I HAD TO DO WAS TO OFF SOME JUNKIE KID...
BUT THIS DUDE'S *FAST,* AND THAT WOODEN SWORD'S GOTTA HAVE A STEEL CORE...!
THIS AIN'T RIGHT!
OSE!
ENOUGH!

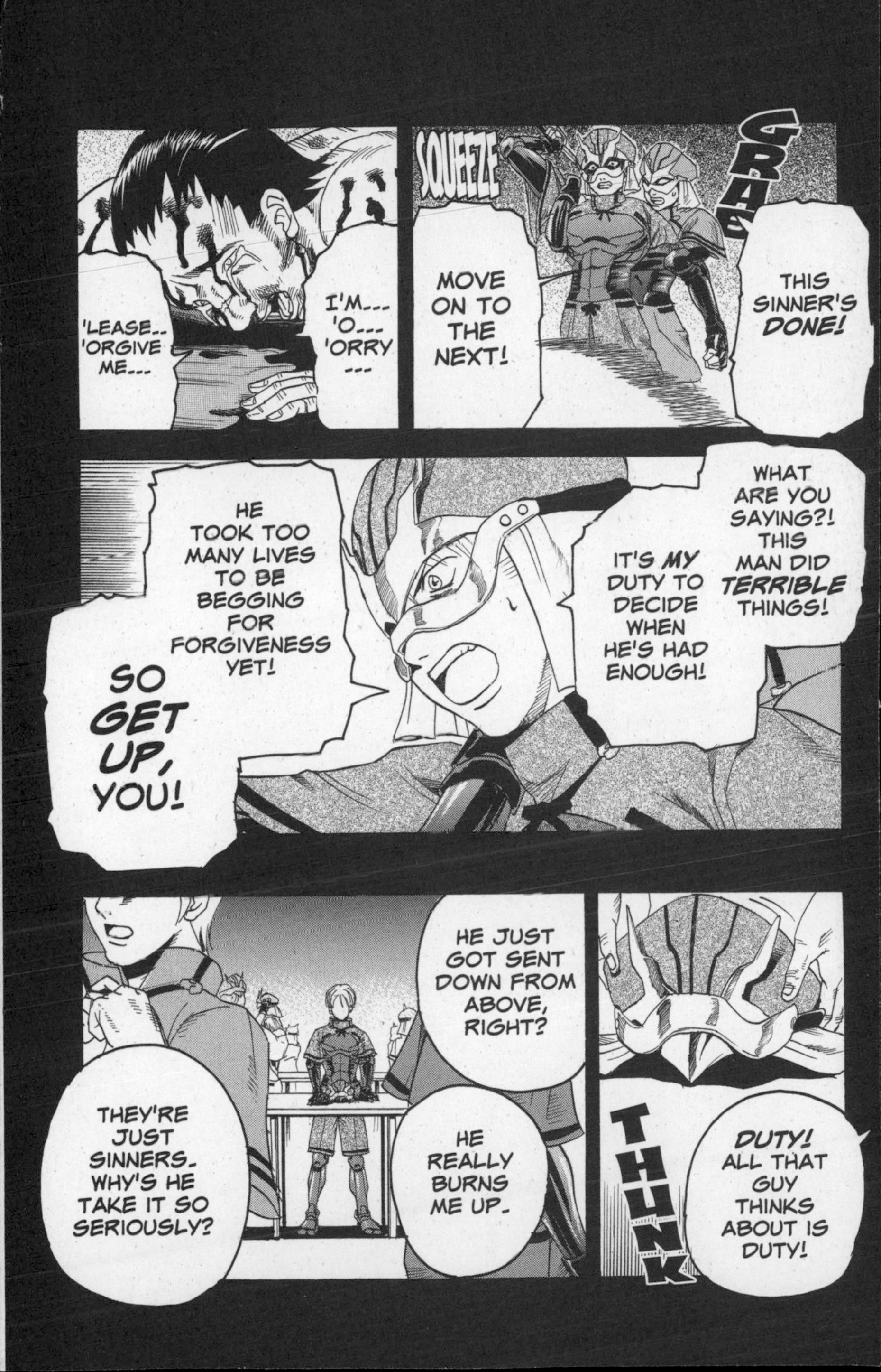
GRAB
THIS SINNER'S DONE!
SQUEEZE
MOVE ON TO THE NEXT!
I'M... 'O... 'ORRY ...
'LEASE.. 'ORGIVE ME...
WHAT ARE YOU SAYING?! THIS MAN DID TERRIBLE THINGS!
IT'S MY DUTY TO DECIDE WHEN HE'S HAD ENOUGH!
HE TOOK TOO MANY LIVES TO BE BEGGING FOR FORGIVENESS YET!
SO GET UP, YOU!
DUTY! ALL THAT GUY THINKS ABOUT IS DUTY!
THUNK
HE JUST GOT SENT DOWN FROM ABOVE, RIGHT?
HE REALLY BURNS ME UP.
THEY'RE JUST SINNERS. WHY'S HE TAKE IT SO SERIOUSLY?

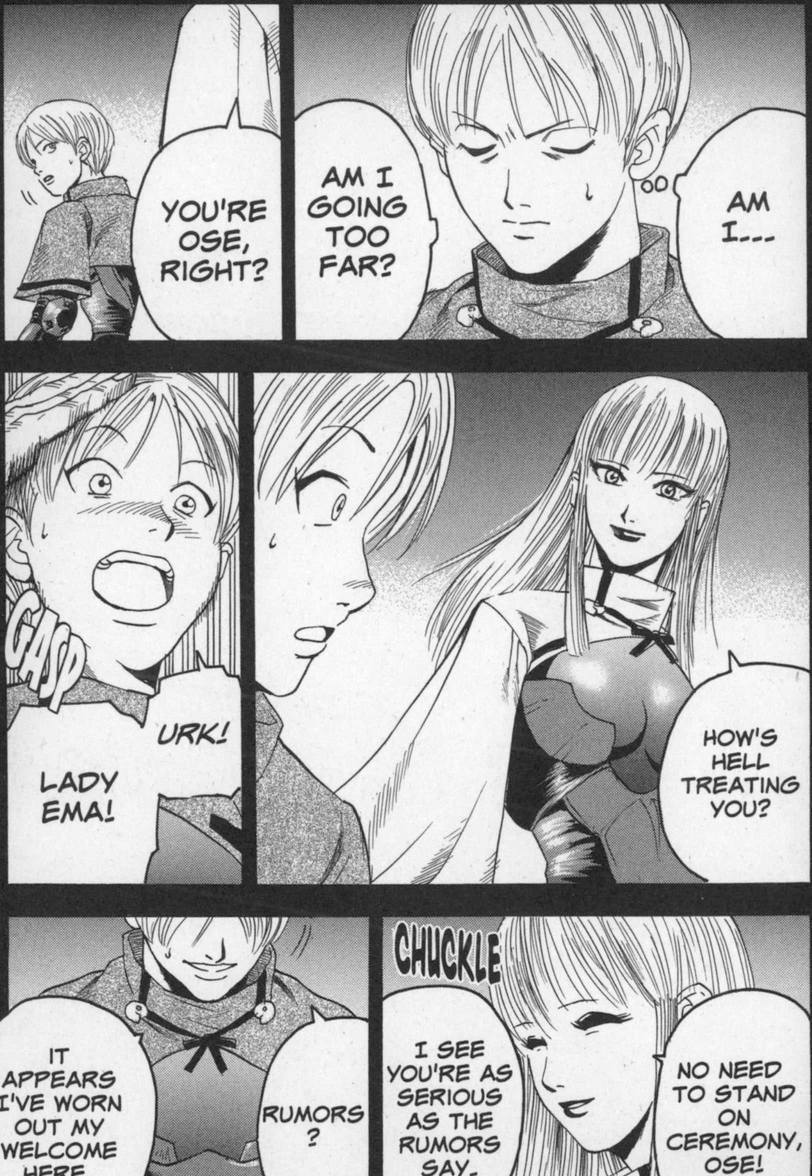
AM I...
AM I GOING TOO FAR?
YOU'RE OSE, RIGHT?
HOW'S HELL TREATING YOU?
GASP
URK!
LADY EMA!
CHUCKLE
NO NEED TO STAND ON CEREMONY, OSE!
I SEE YOU'RE AS SERIOUS AS THE RUMORS SAY.
RUMORS?
IT APPEARS I'VE WORN OUT MY WELCOME HERE.

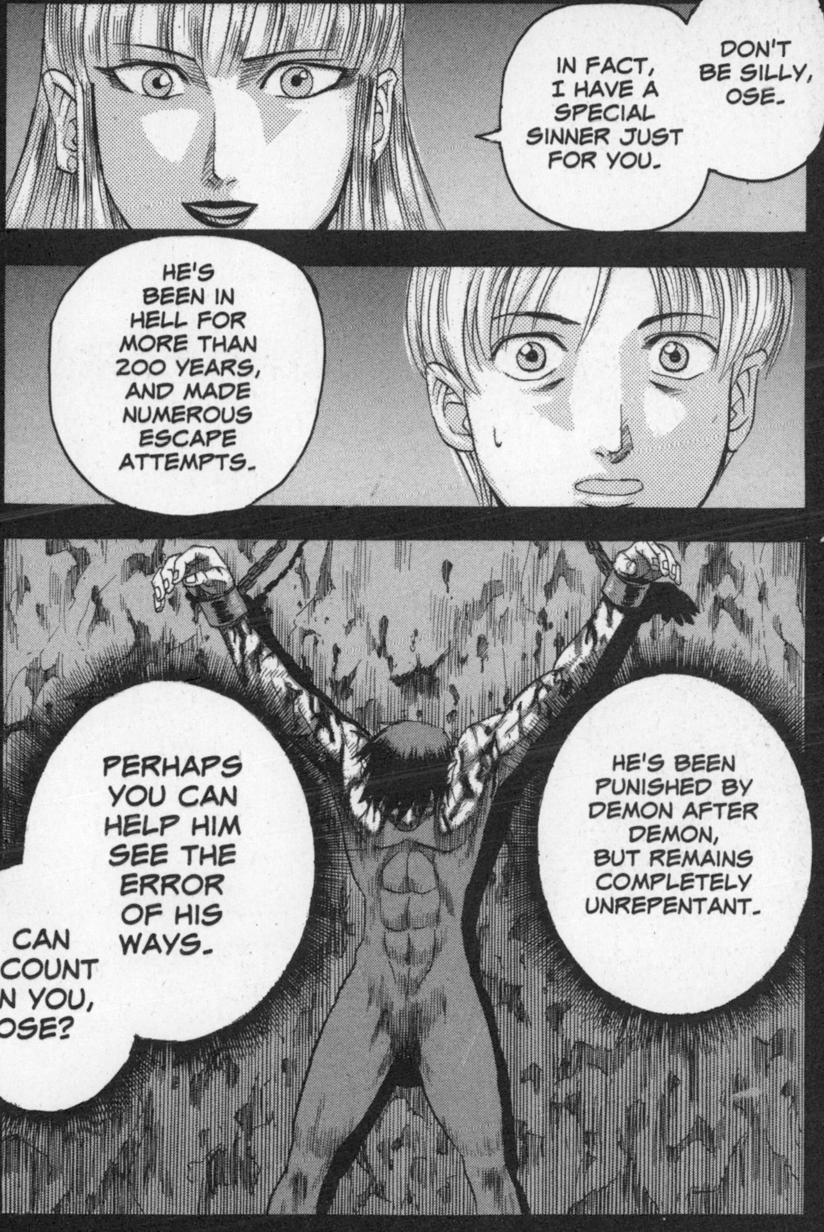
DON'T BE SILLY, OSE.
IN FACT, I HAVE A SPECIAL SINNER JUST FOR YOU.
HE'S BEEN IN HELL FOR MORE THAN 200 YEARS, AND MADE NUMEROUS ESCAPE ATTEMPTS.
HE'S BEEN PUNISHED BY DEMON AFTER DEMON, BUT REMAINS COMPLETELY UNREPENTANT.
PERHAPS YOU CAN HELP HIM SEE THE ERROR OF HIS WAYS.
CAN I COUNT ON YOU, OSE?

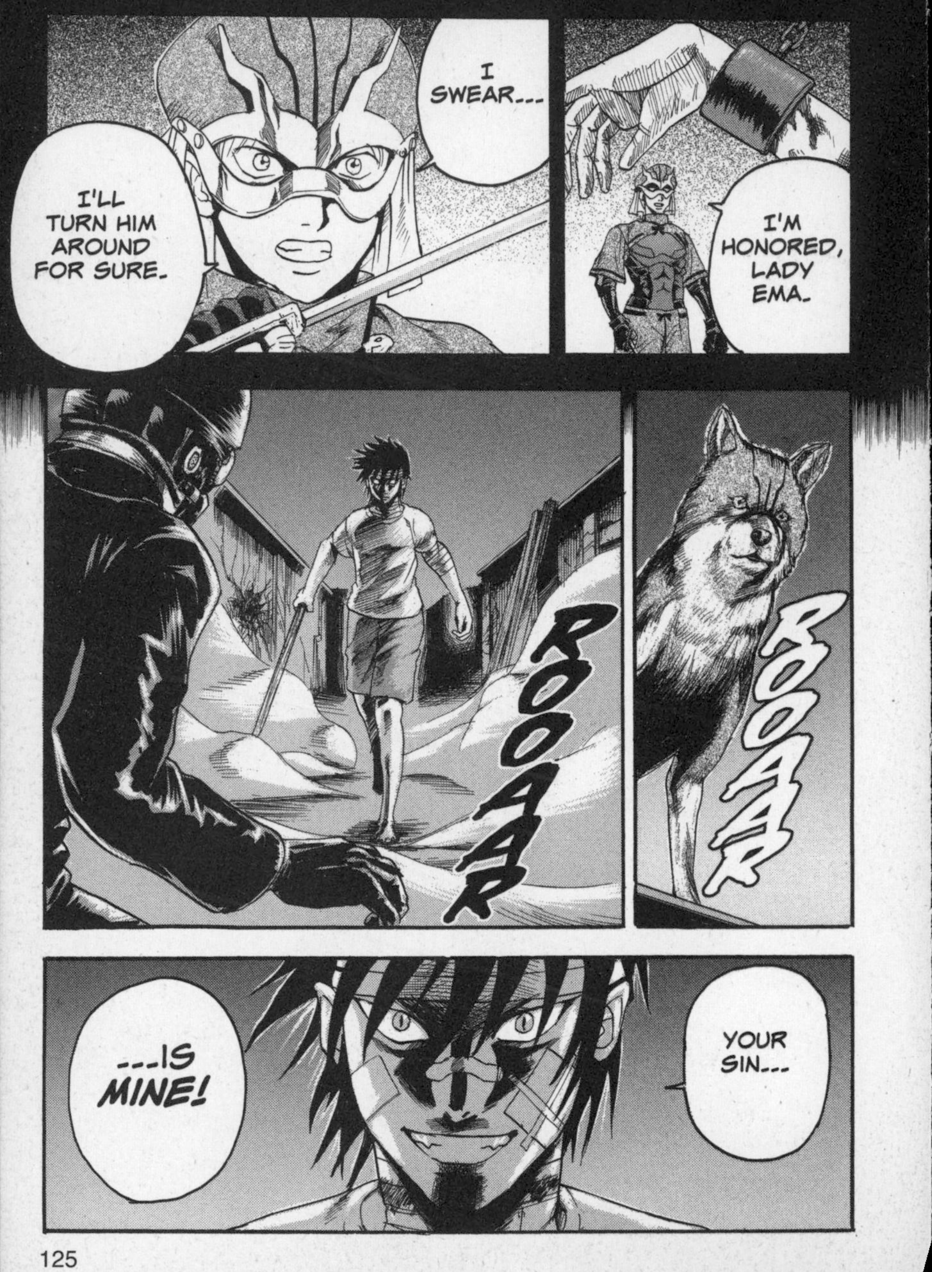
I'M HONORED, LADY EMA.
I SWEAR...
I'LL TURN HIM AROUND FOR SURE.
ROOOAAR
ROOOAAR
YOUR SIN...
...IS MINE!

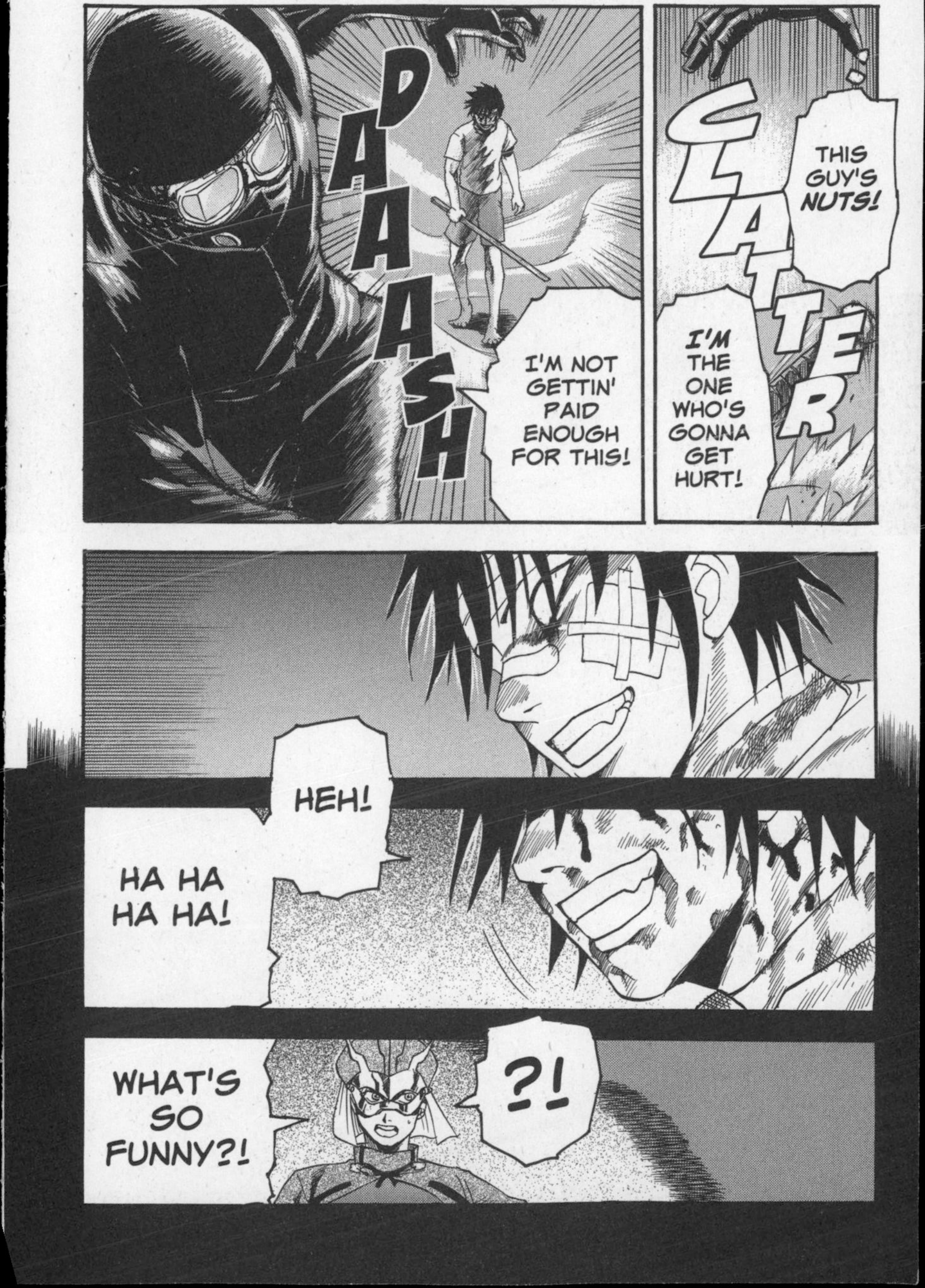
CLATTER
THIS GUY'S NUTS!
I'M THE ONE WHO'S GONNA GET HURT!
DAAAASH
I'M NOT GETTIN' PAID ENOUGH FOR THIS!
HEH!
HA HA HA HA!
?!
WHAT'S SO FUNNY?!

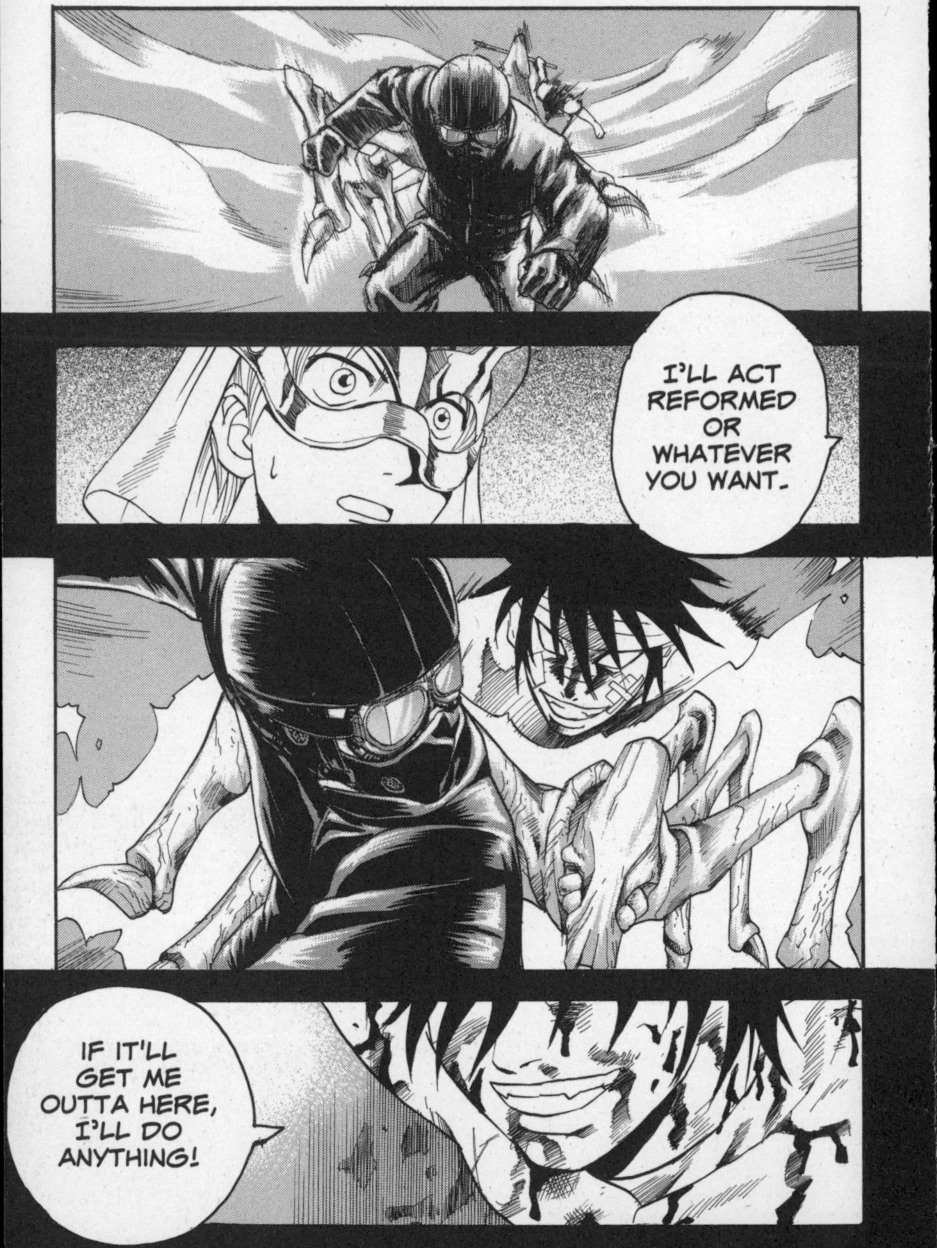
I'LL ACT REFORMED OR WHATEVER YOU WANT...
IF IT'LL GET ME OUTTA HERE, I'LL DO ANYTHING!

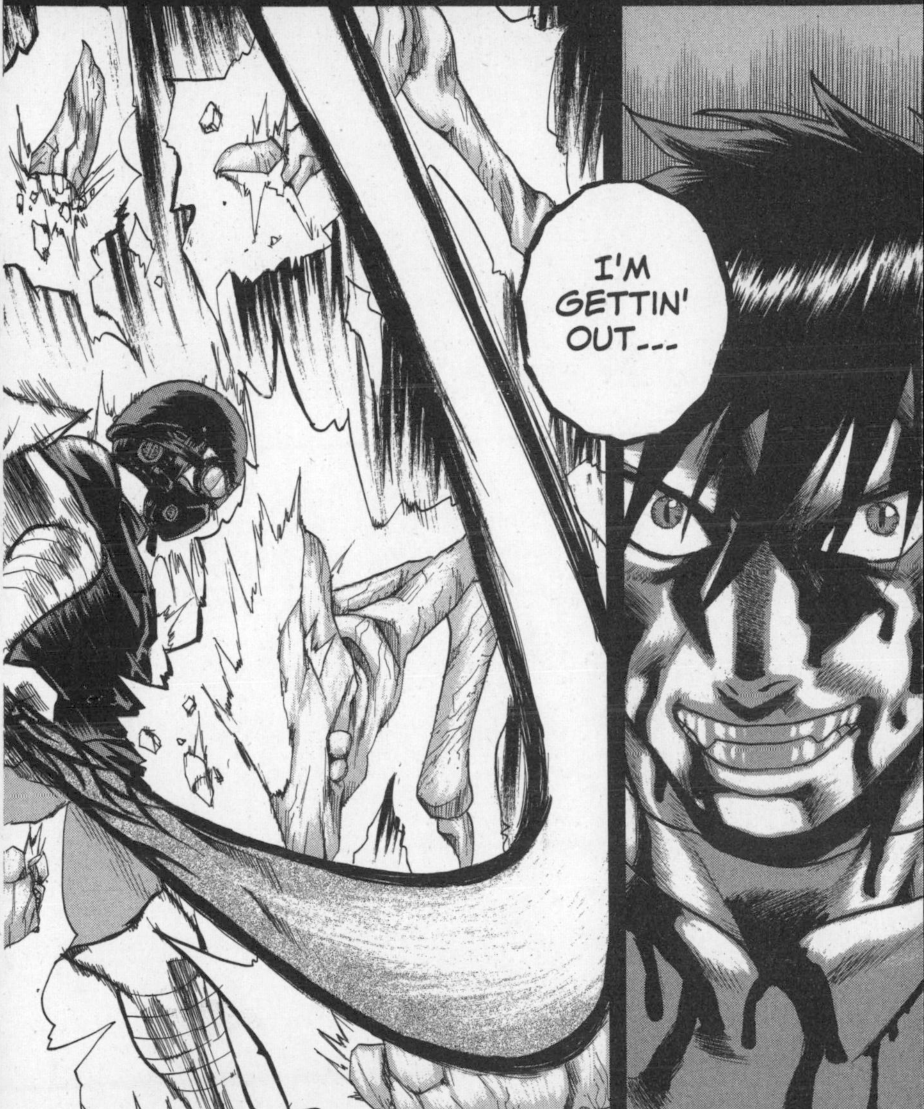
I'M GETTIN' OUT---

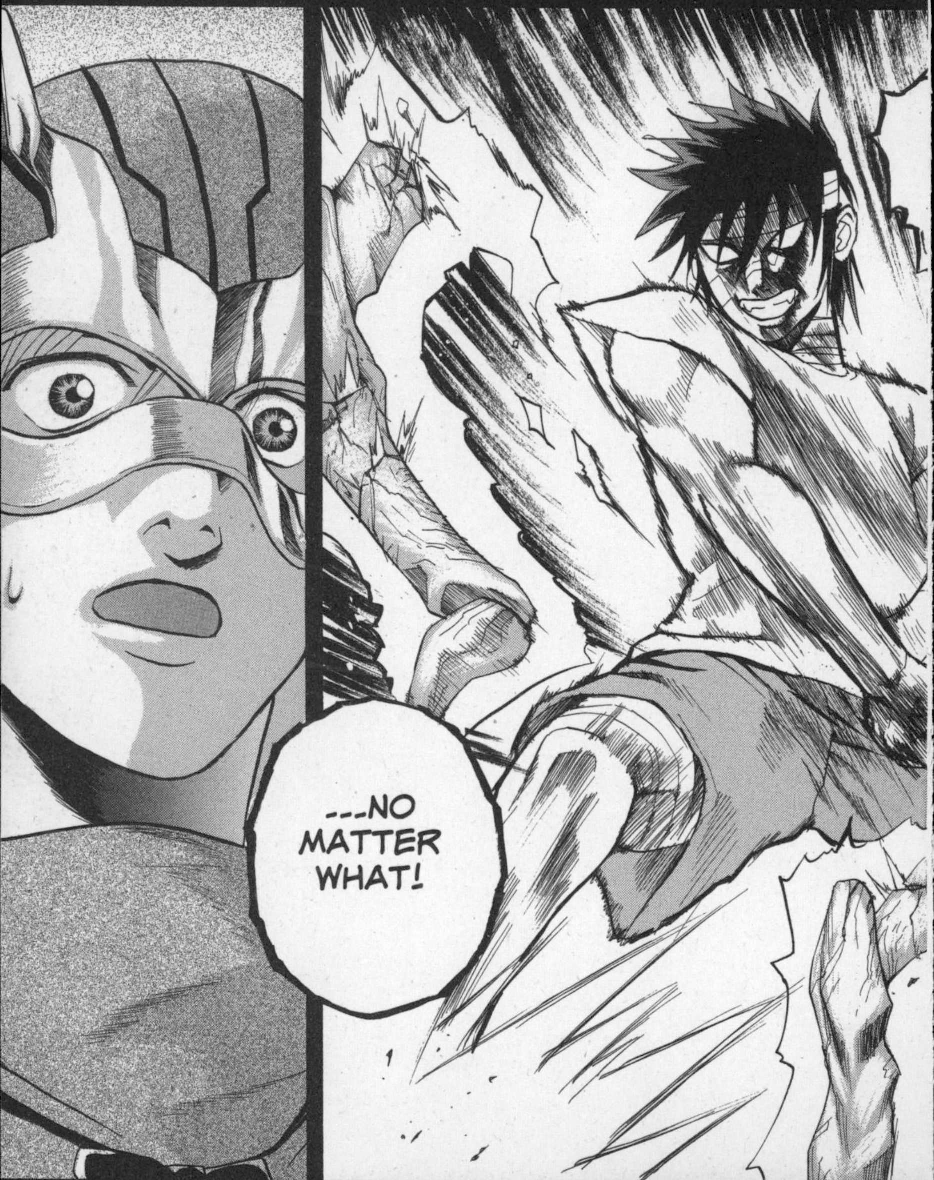
---NO MATTER WHAT!

THUDD
THAT WAS ONE WEAK TOGA.
BUT I DON'T CARE.

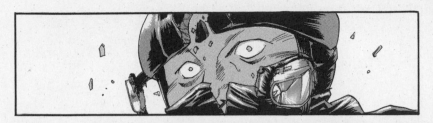

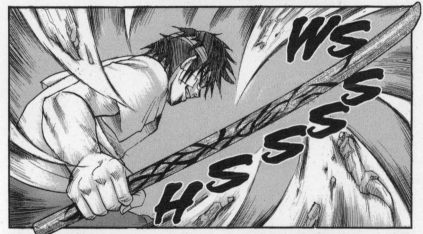

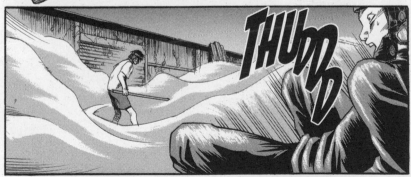

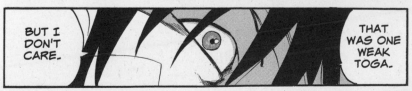

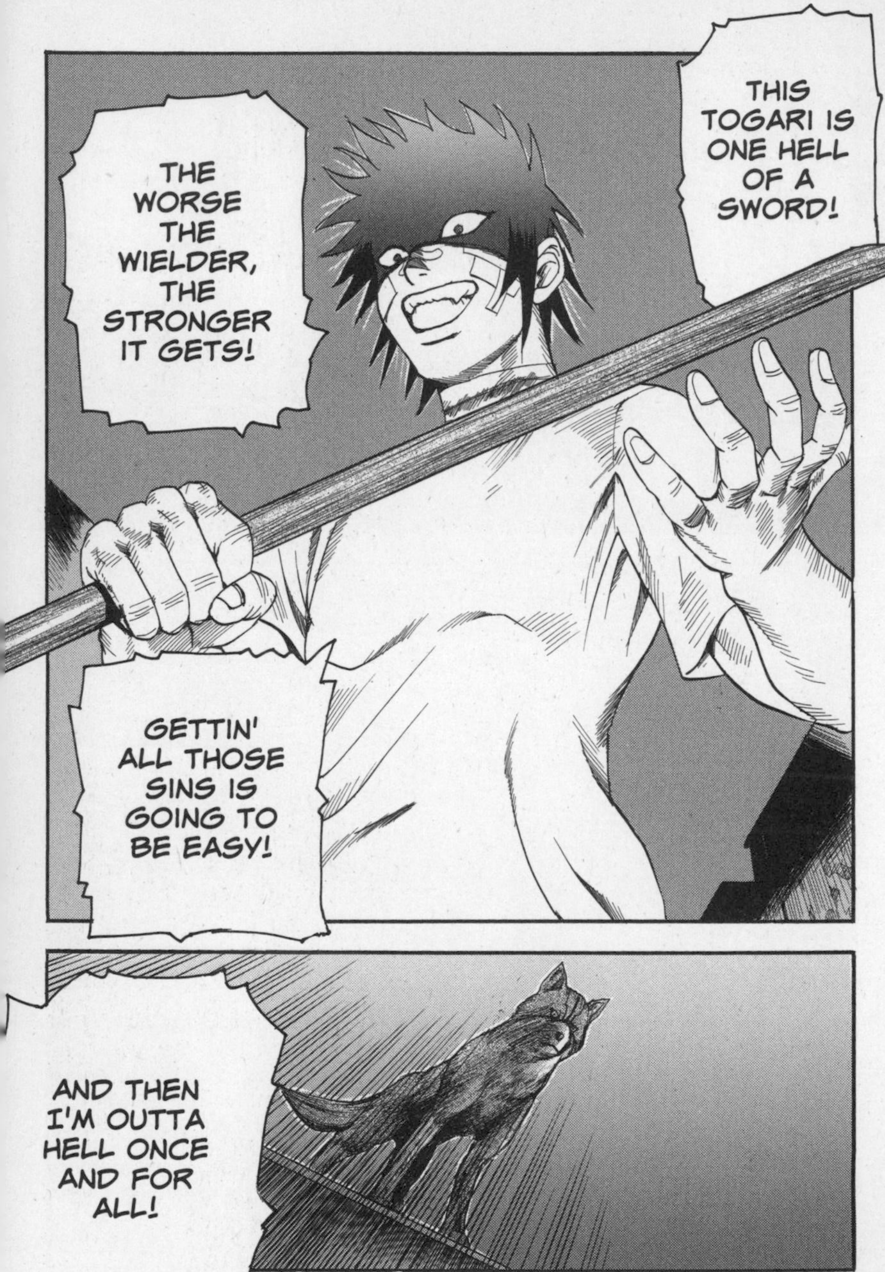
THIS TOGARI IS ONE HELL OF A SWORD!
THE WORSE THE WIELDER, THE STRONGER IT GETS!
GETTIN' ALL THOSE SINS IS GOING TO BE EASY!
AND THEN I'M OUTTA HELL ONCE AND FOR ALL!

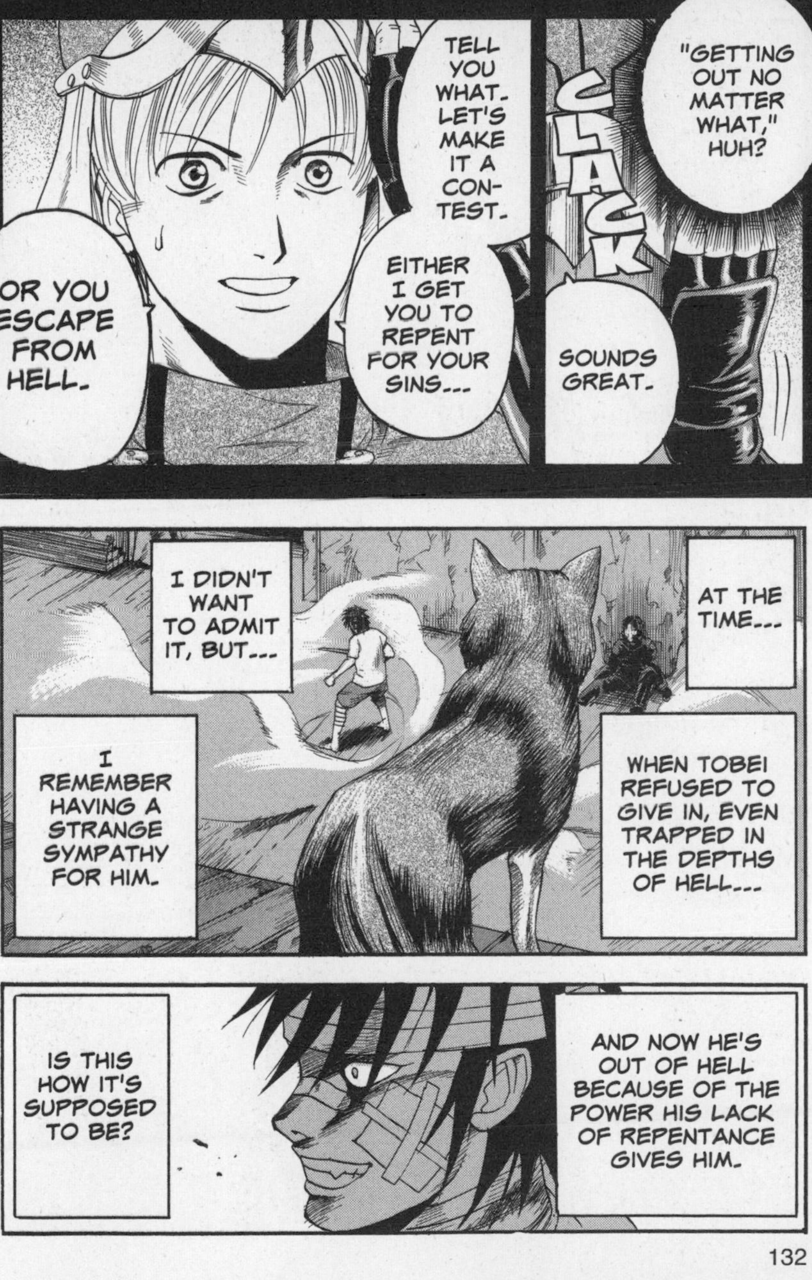
"GETTING OUT NO MATTER WHAT," HUH?
CLACK
SOUNDS GREAT.
TELL YOU WHAT. LET'S MAKE IT A CON-TEST.
EITHER I GET YOU TO REPENT FOR YOUR SINS...
OR YOU ESCAPE FROM HELL.
AT THE TIME...
WHEN TOBEI REFUSED TO GIVE IN, EVEN TRAPPED IN THE DEPTHS OF HELL...
I DIDN'T WANT TO ADMIT IT, BUT...
I REMEMBER HAVING A STRANGE SYMPATHY FOR HIM.
AND NOW HE'S OUT OF HELL BECAUSE OF THE POWER HIS LACK OF REPENTANCE GIVES HIM.
IS THIS HOW IT'S SUPPOSED TO BE?

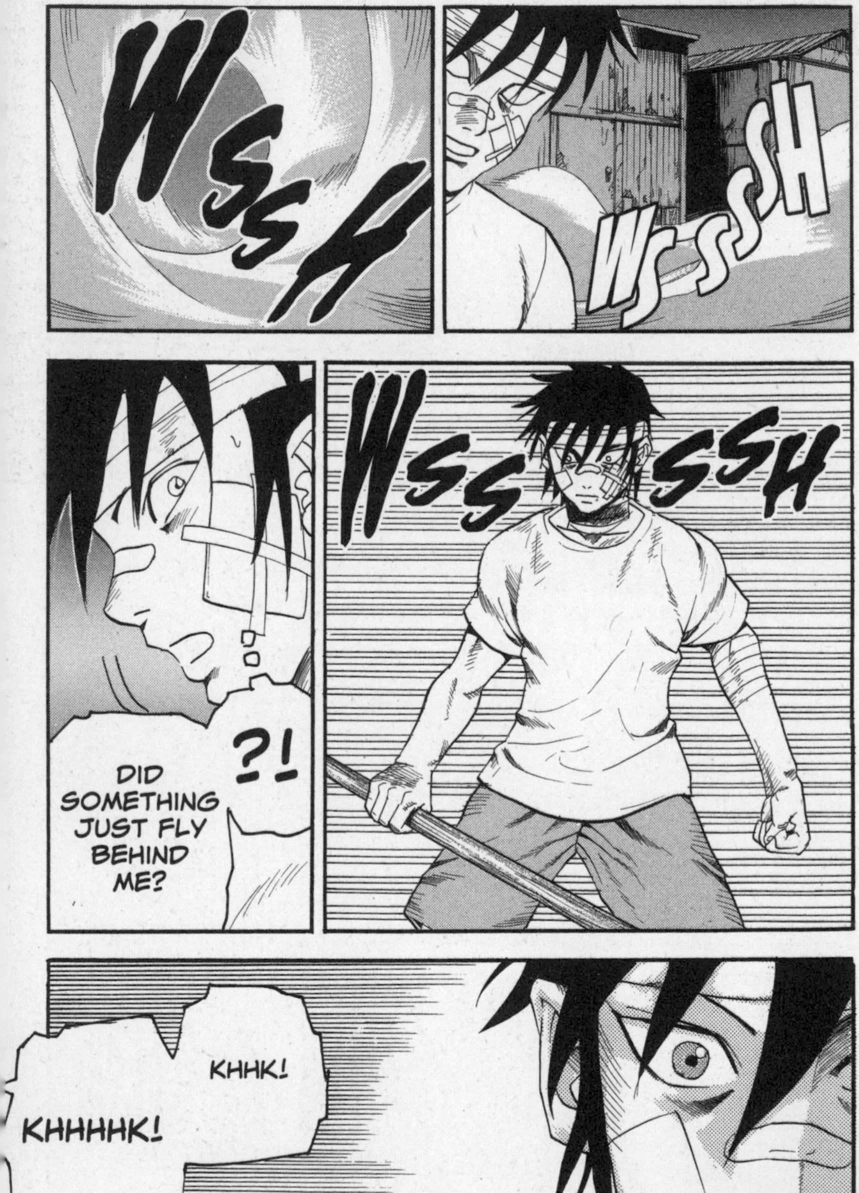
WSSSSH
WSSH
WSSSSH
?!
DID SOMETHING JUST FLY BEHIND ME?
KHHK!
KHHHHK!

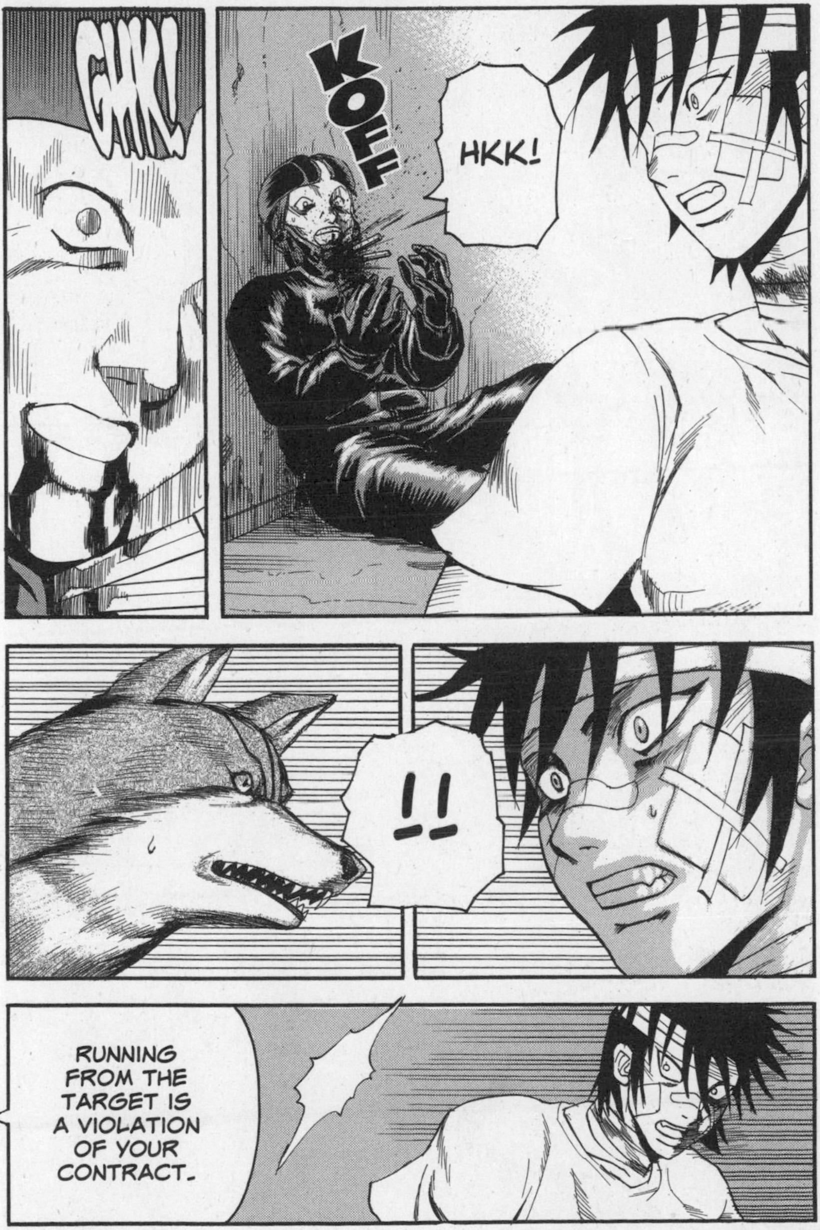
HKK!
KOFF
GHK!
!!
RUNNING FROM THE TARGET IS A VIOLATION OF YOUR CONTRACT.

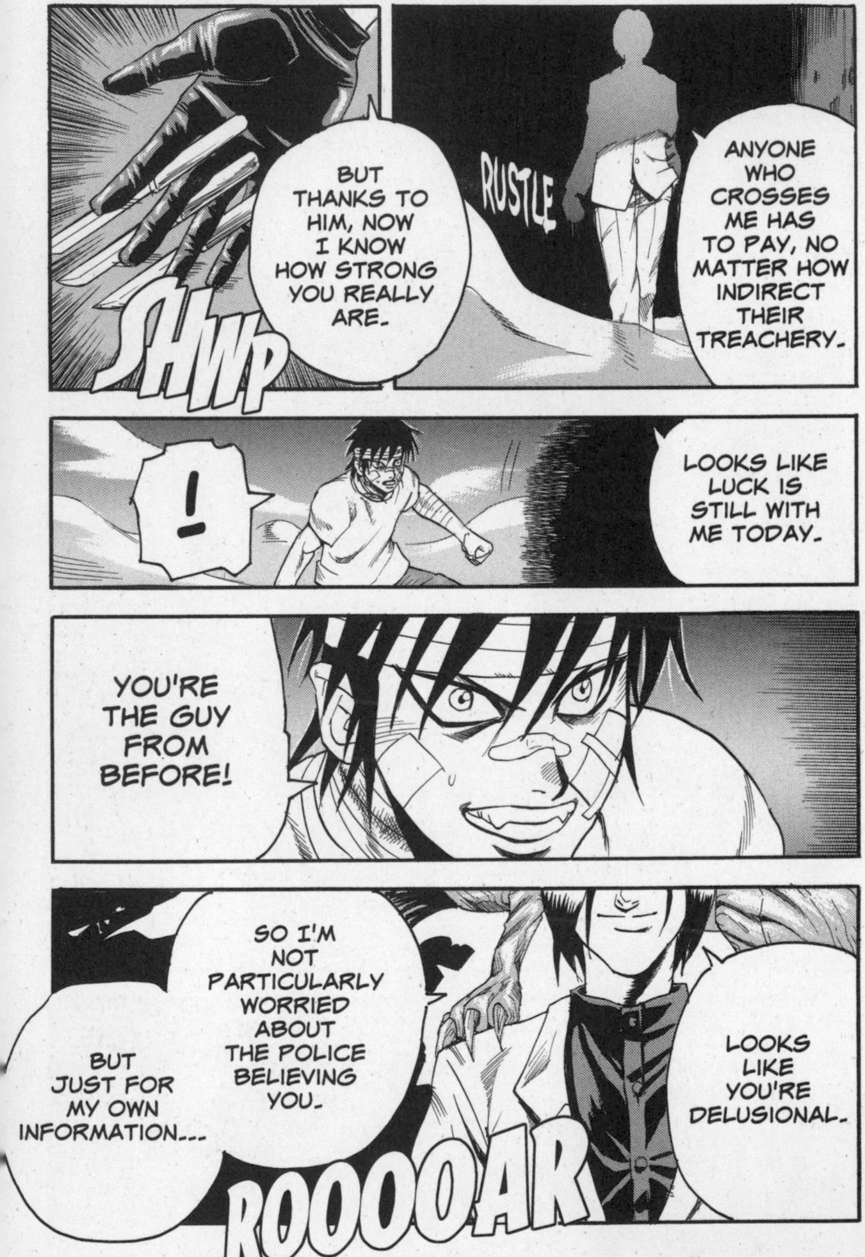
ANYONE WHO CROSSES ME HAS TO PAY, NO MATTER HOW INDIRECT THEIR TREACHERY.
RUSTLE
BUT THANKS TO HIM, NOW I KNOW HOW STRONG YOU REALLY ARE.
SHWP
LOOKS LIKE LUCK IS STILL WITH ME TODAY.
!
YOU'RE THE GUY FROM BEFORE!
LOOKS LIKE YOU'RE DELUSIONAL.
SO I'M NOT PARTICULARLY WORRIED ABOUT THE POLICE BELIEVING YOU.
BUT JUST FOR MY OWN INFORMATION...
ROOOOAR

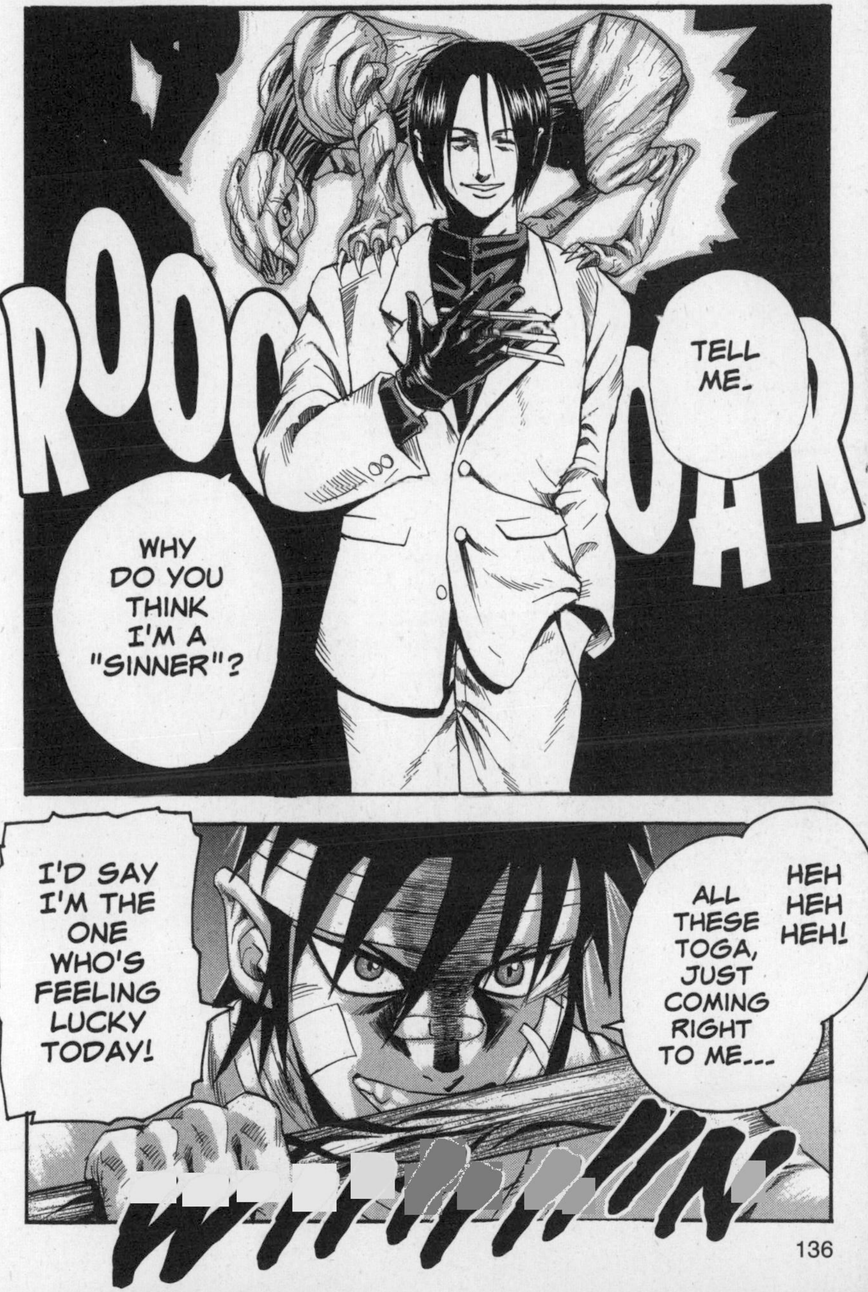
TELL ME...
WHY DO YOU THINK I'M A "SINNER"?
ROOOOAR
HEH HEH HEH!
ALL THESE TOGA, JUST COMING RIGHT TO ME...
I'D SAY I'M THE ONE WHO'S FEELING LUCKY TODAY!

Chapter 5 The Power of Togari

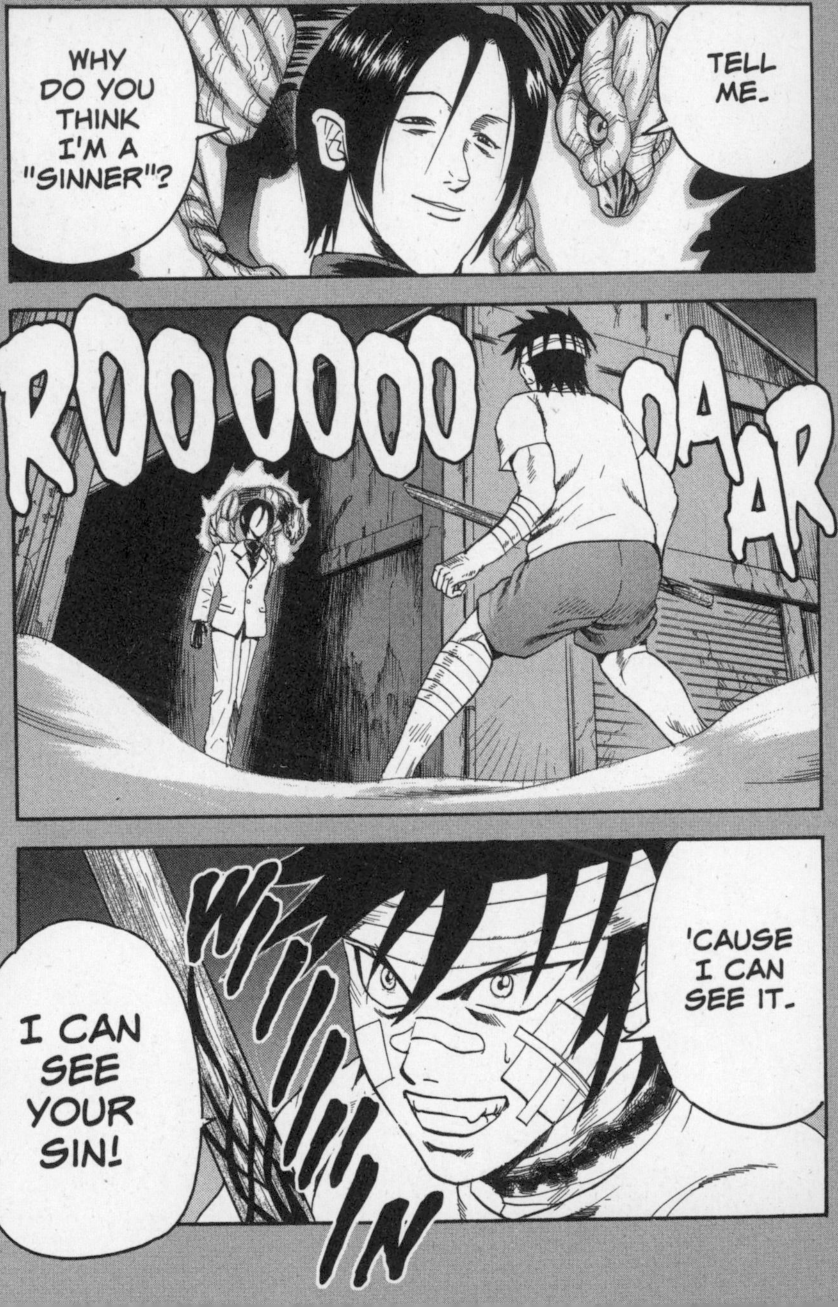
TELL ME…
WHY DO YOU THINK I'M A "SINNER"?
ROOOOOOOAAR
'CAUSE I CAN SEE IT…
I CAN SEE YOUR SIN!
WIIIIIIIN

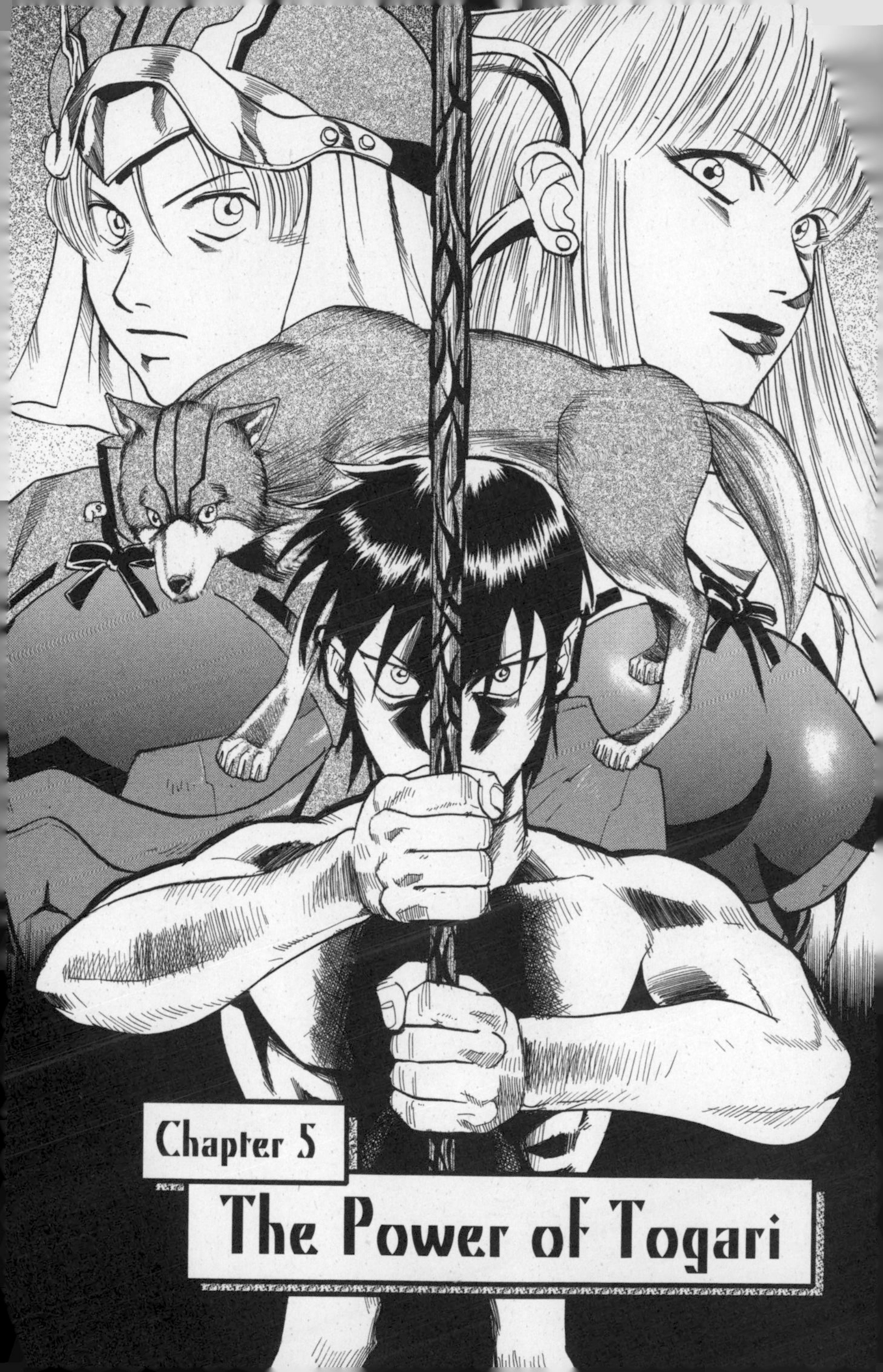
Chapter 5
The Power of Togari

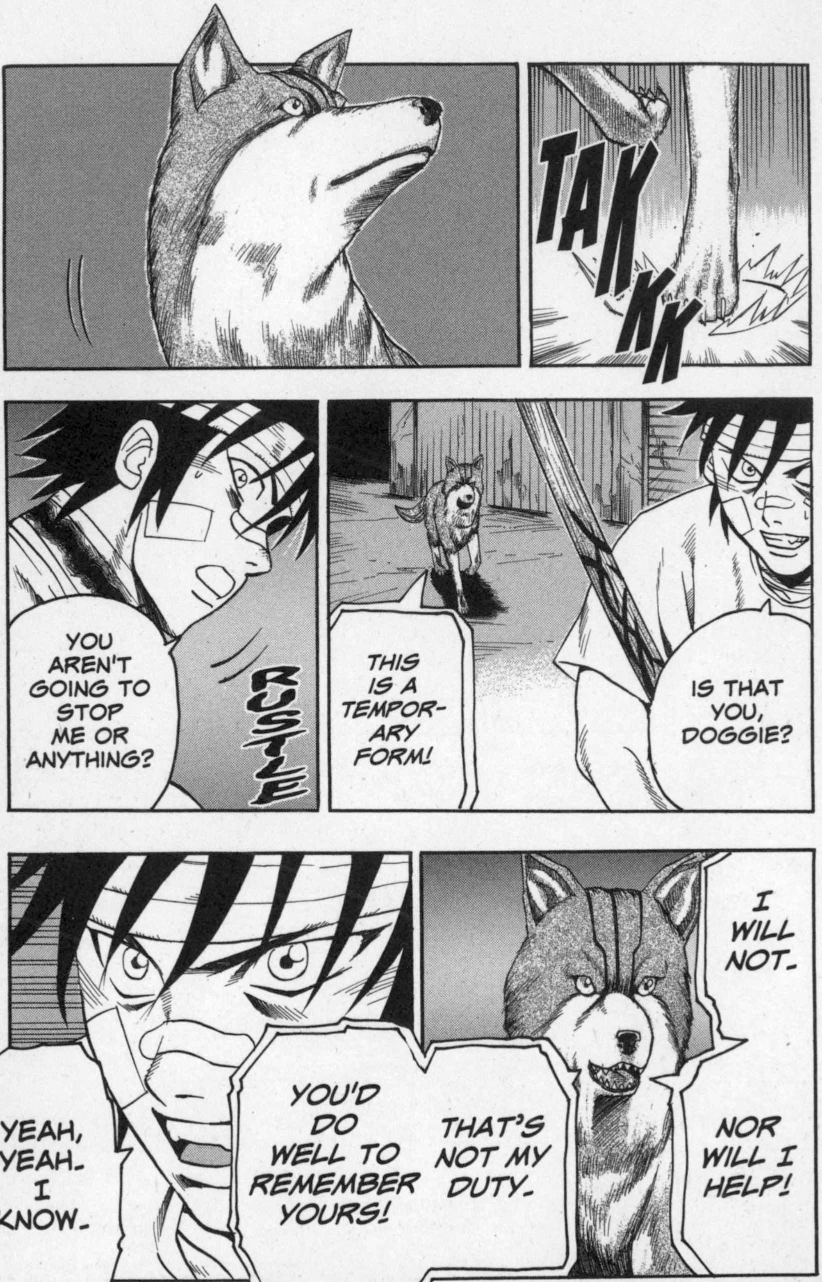
TAKKK
IS THAT YOU, DOGGIE?
THIS IS A TEMPORARY FORM!
RUSTLE
YOU AREN'T GOING TO STOP ME OR ANYTHING?
I WILL NOT...
NOR WILL I HELP!
THAT'S NOT MY DUTY...
YOU'D DO WELL TO REMEMBER YOURS!
YEAH, YEAH... I KNOW...

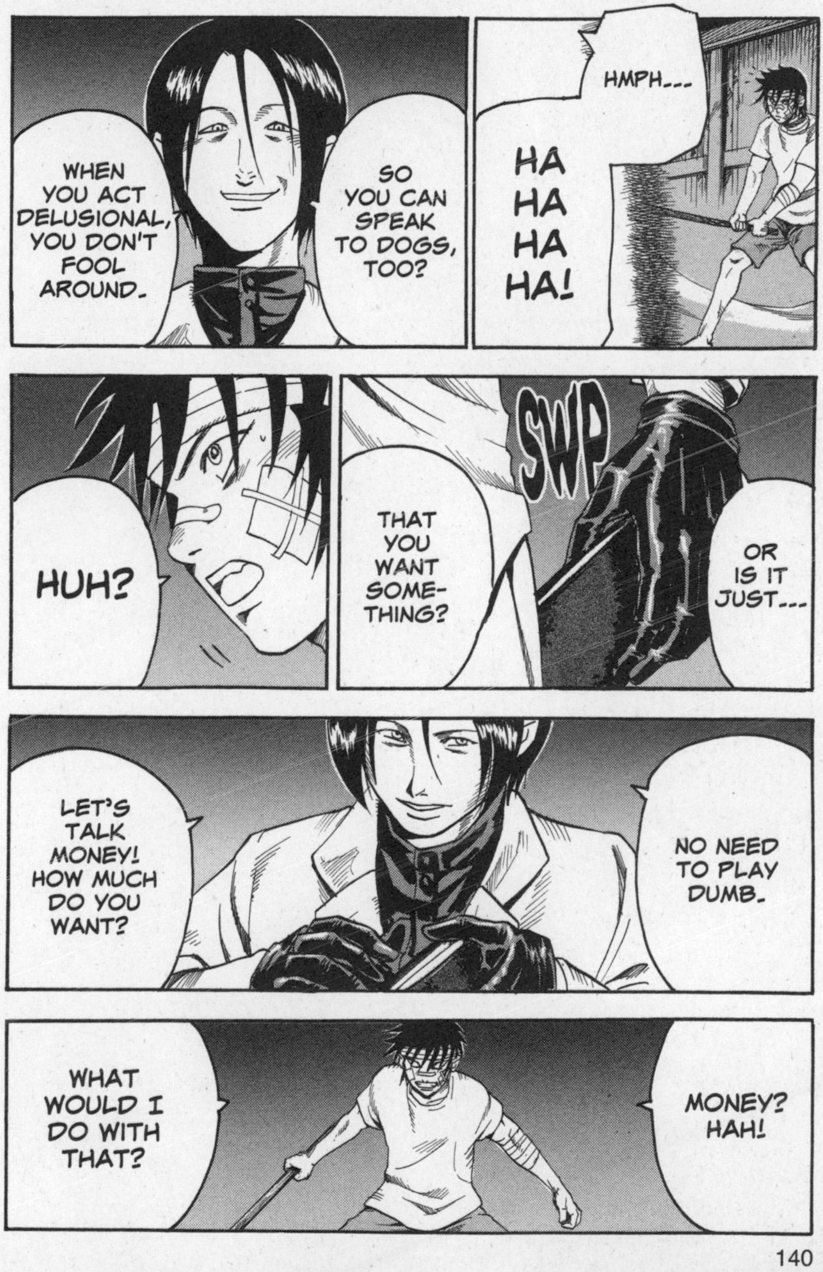
HMPH...
HA HA HA HA!
SO YOU CAN SPEAK TO DOGS, TOO?
WHEN YOU ACT DELUSIONAL, YOU DON'T FOOL AROUND.
SWP
OR IS IT JUST...
THAT YOU WANT SOME-THING?
HUH?
NO NEED TO PLAY DUMB.
LET'S TALK MONEY! HOW MUCH DO YOU WANT?
MONEY? HAH!
WHAT WOULD I DO WITH THAT?

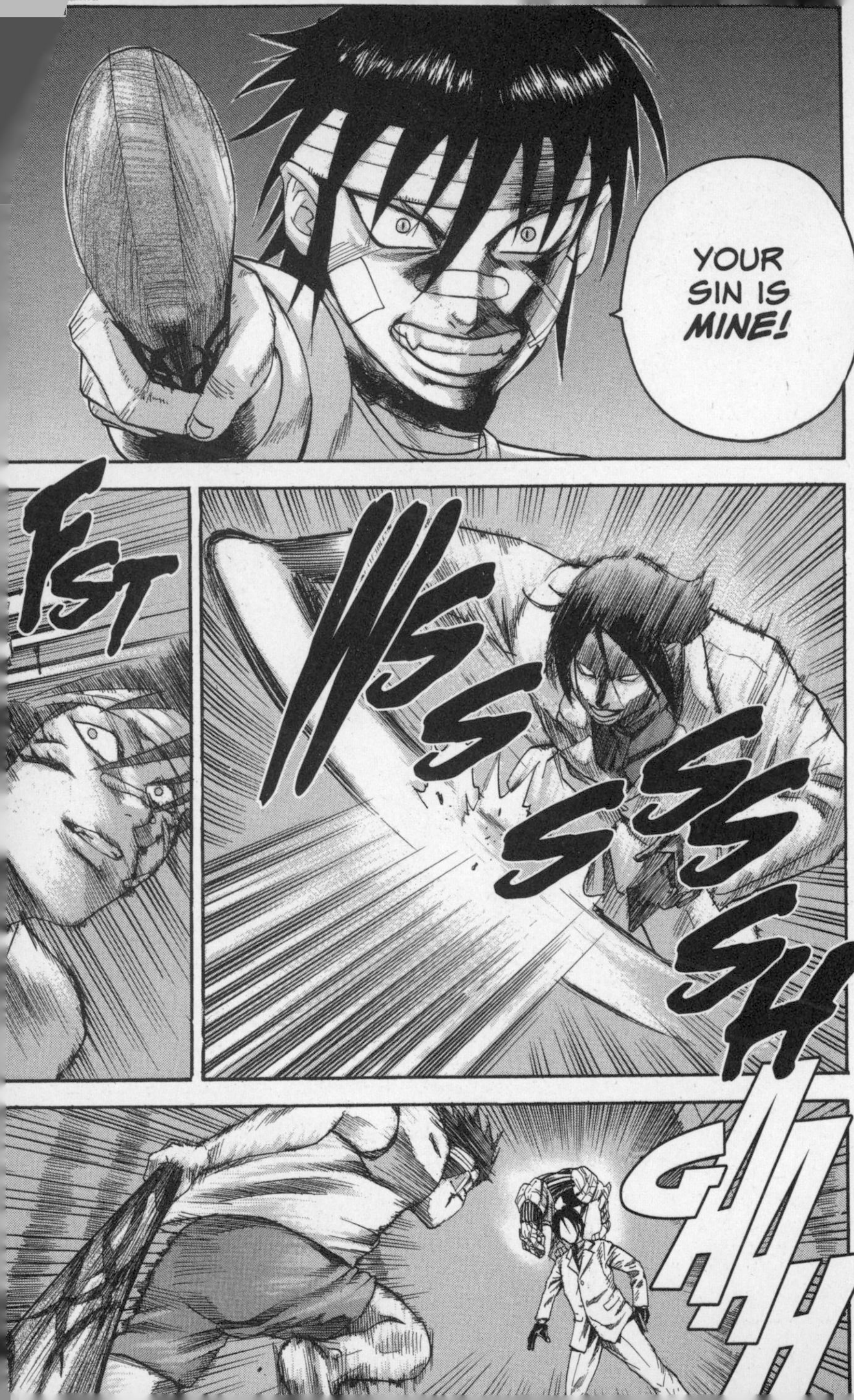
YOUR SIN IS MINE!
WSSSSSSSH
FST
GAAH

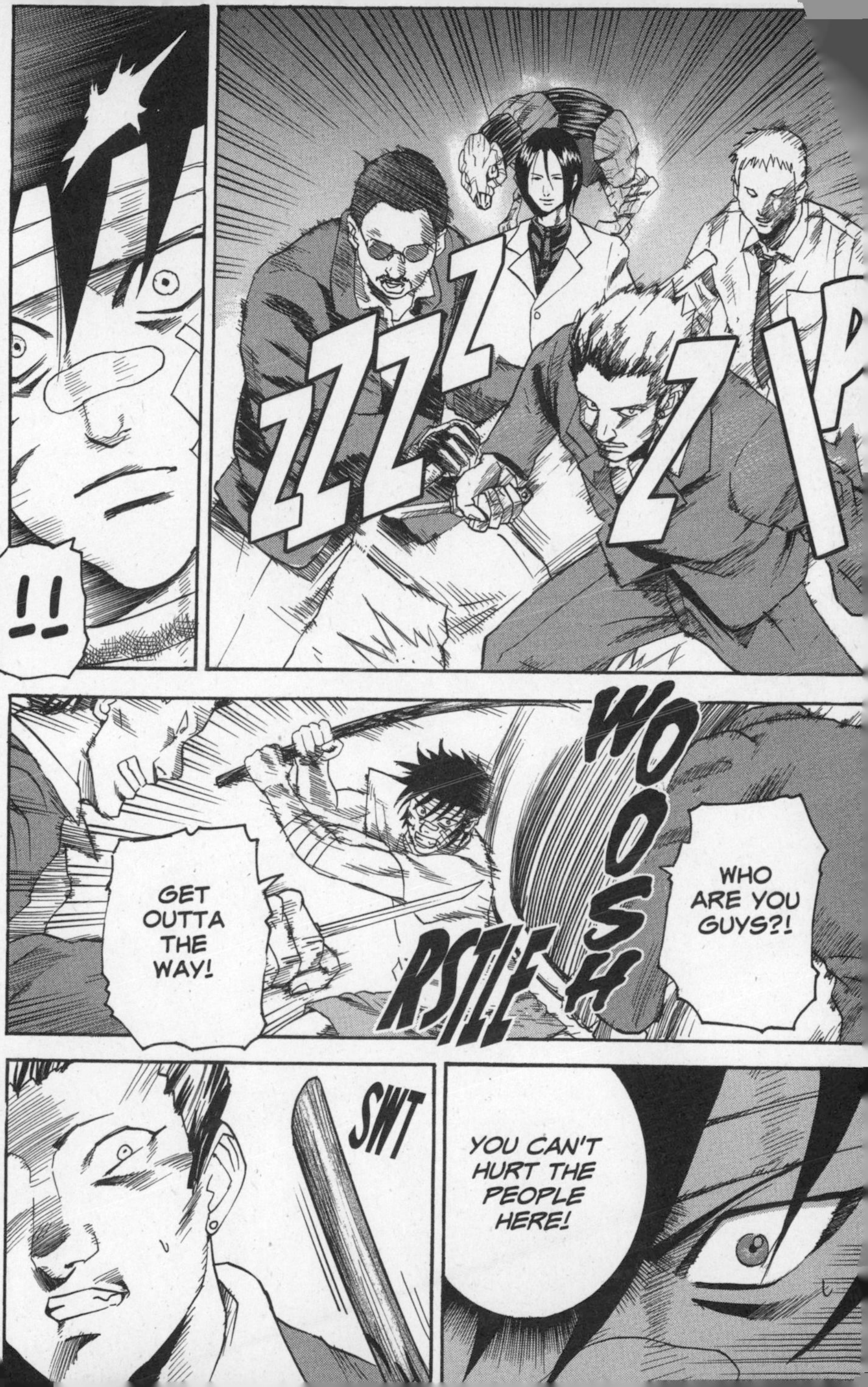
ZZZZ
ZIP
!!
WHO ARE YOU GUYS?!
WOOSH
RSTLE
GET OUTTA THE WAY!
YOU CAN'T HURT THE PEOPLE HERE!
SWT

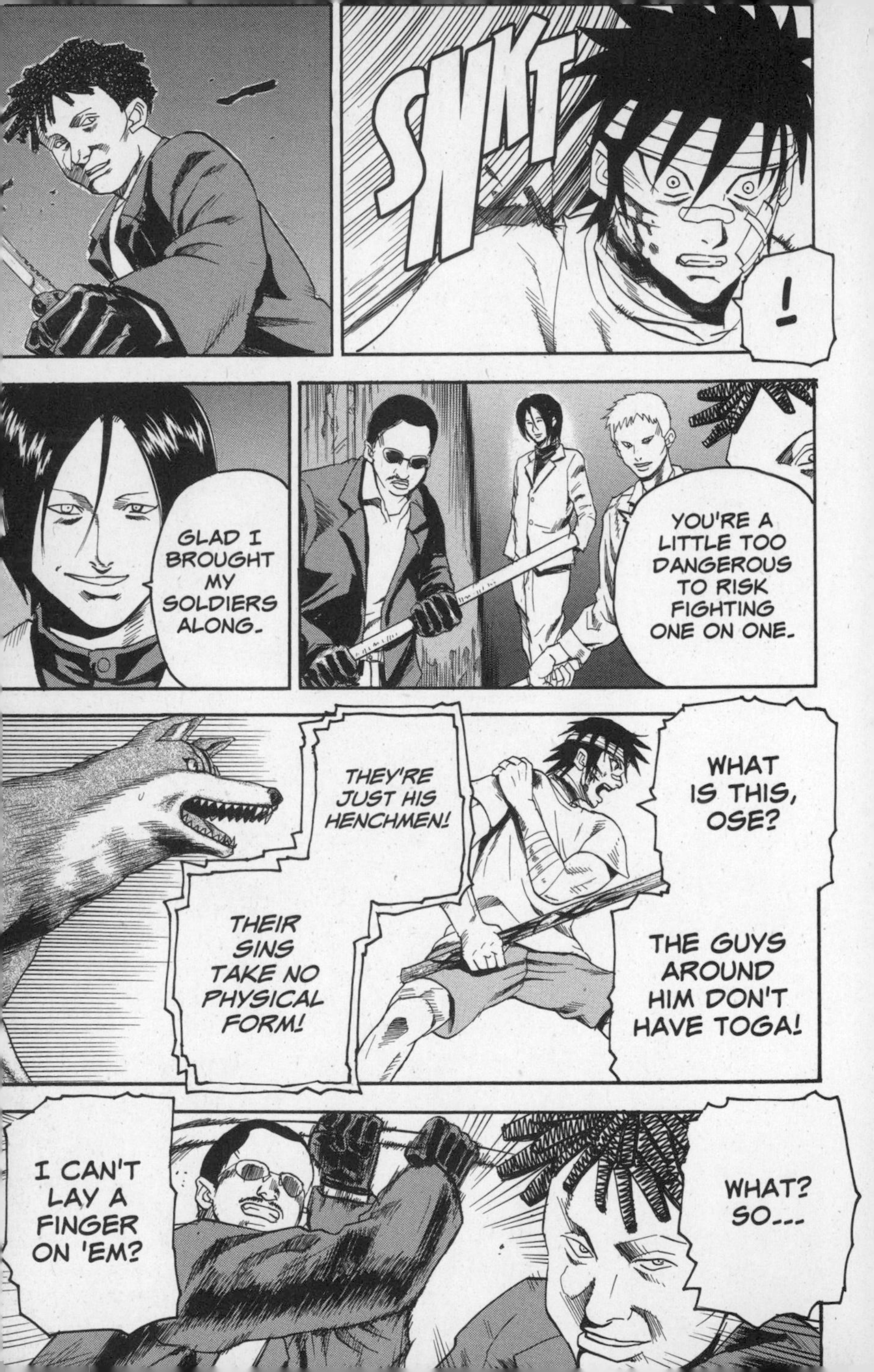
SNKT
!
YOU'RE A LITTLE TOO DANGEROUS TO RISK FIGHTING ONE ON ONE.
GLAD I BROUGHT MY SOLDIERS ALONG.
WHAT IS THIS, OSE?
THE GUYS AROUND HIM DON'T HAVE TOGA!
THEY'RE JUST HIS HENCHMEN!
THEIR SINS TAKE NO PHYSICAL FORM!
WHAT? SO...
I CAN'T LAY A FINGER ON 'EM?

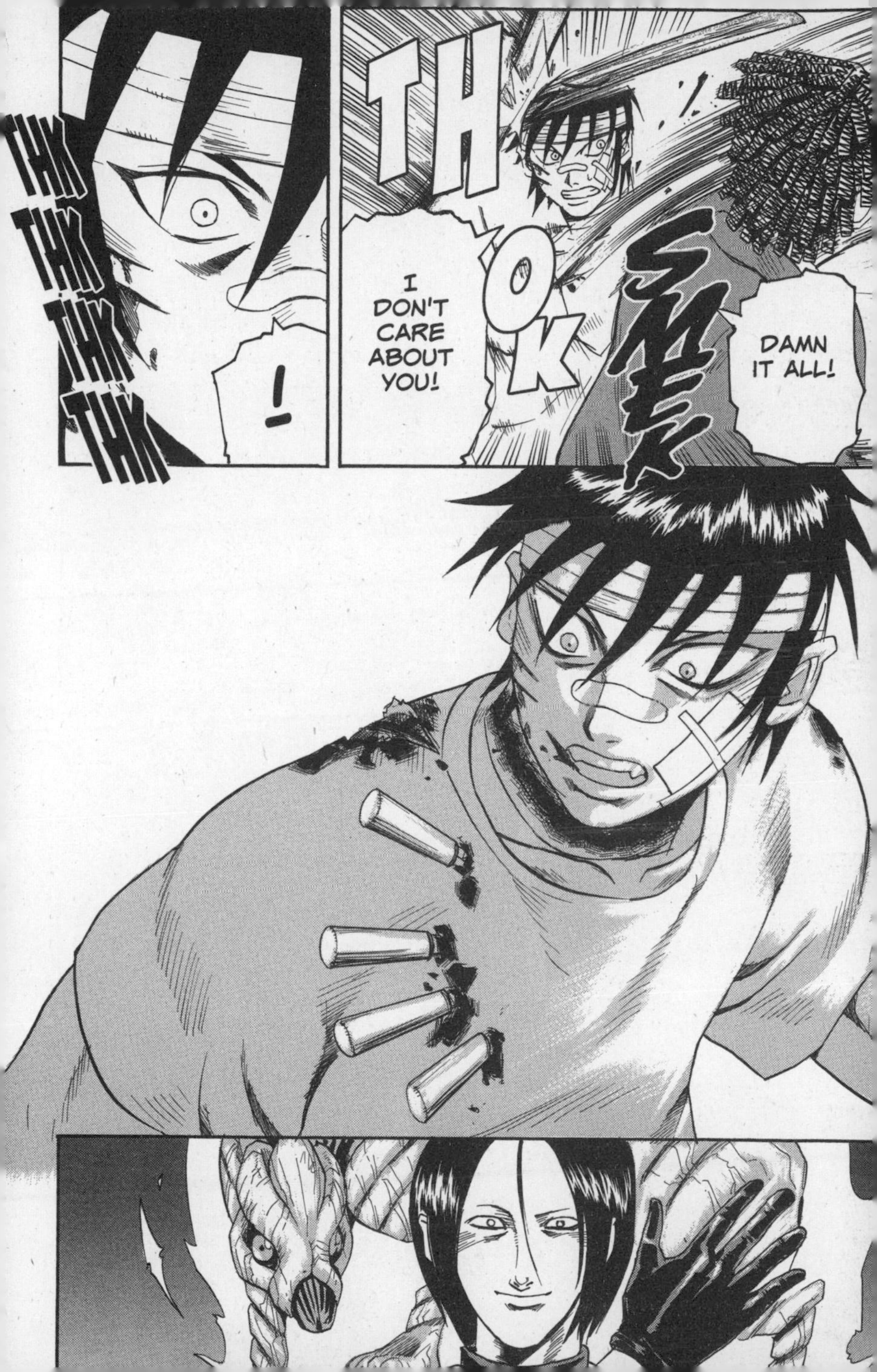
THOK
DAMN IT ALL!
I DON'T CARE ABOUT YOU!
THK THK THK THK THK
!

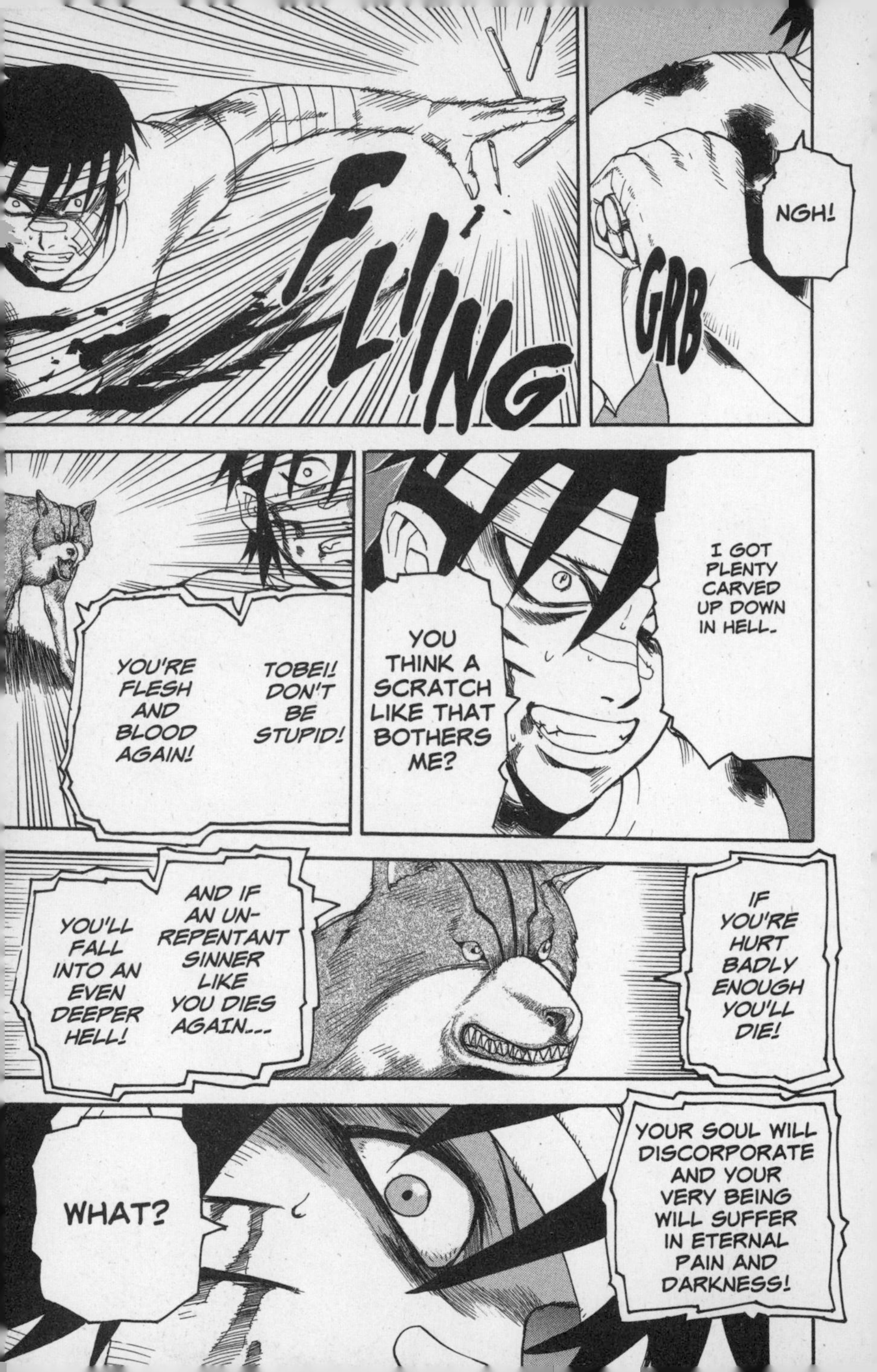
NGH!
GRB
FLING
I GOT PLENTY CARVED UP DOWN IN HELL.
YOU THINK A SCRATCH LIKE THAT BOTHERS ME?
TOBEI! DON'T BE STUPID!
YOU'RE FLESH AND BLOOD AGAIN!
IF YOU'RE HURT BADLY ENOUGH YOU'LL DIE!
AND IF AN UN-REPENTANT SINNER LIKE YOU DIES AGAIN...
YOU'LL FALL INTO AN EVEN DEEPER HELL!
YOUR SOUL WILL DISCORPORATE AND YOUR VERY BEING WILL SUFFER IN ETERNAL PAIN AND DARKNESS!
WHAT?

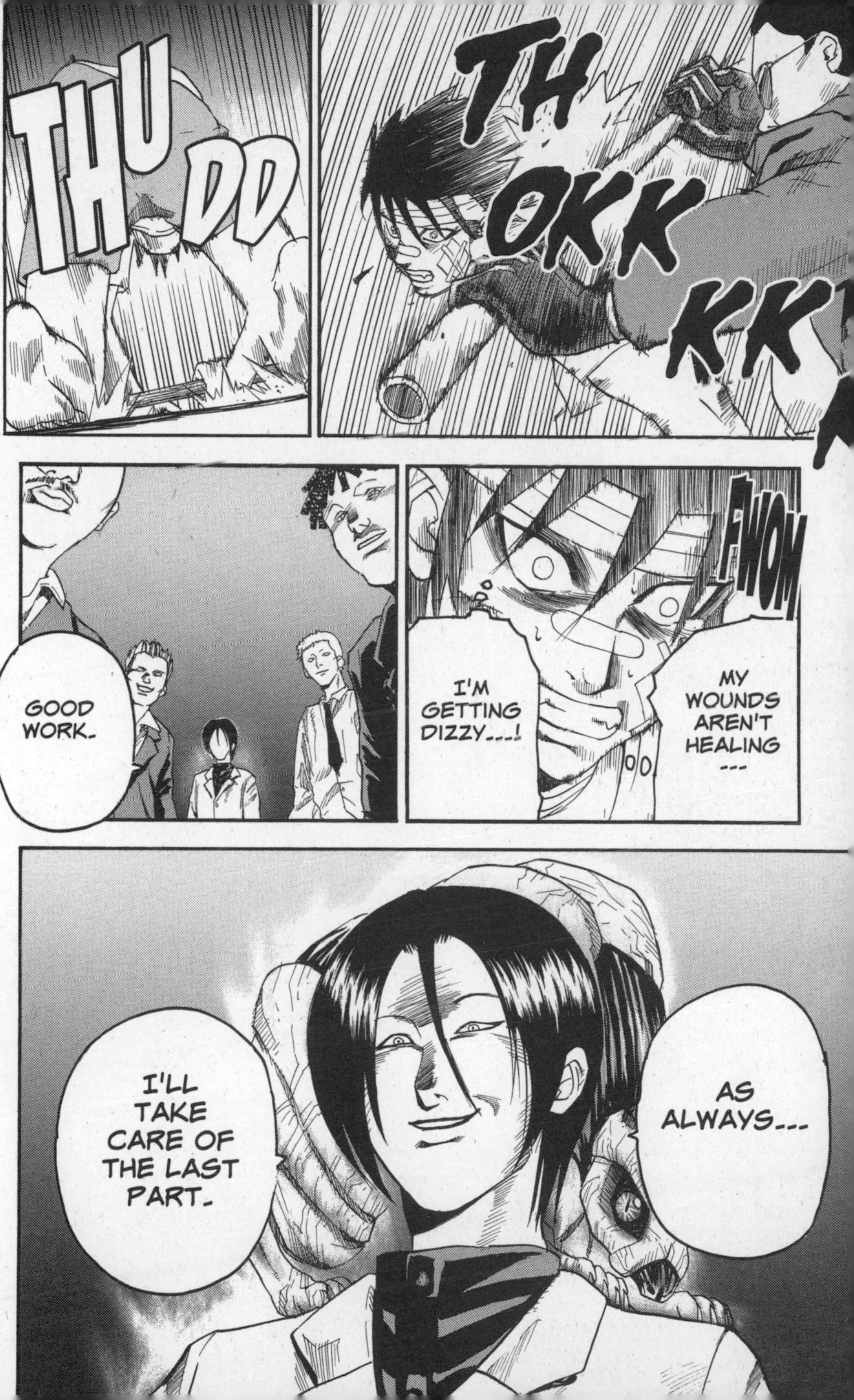
THOKKKK
THUDD
FWOM
MY WOUNDS AREN'T HEALING...
I'M GETTING DIZZY...!
GOOD WORK.
AS ALWAYS...
I'LL TAKE CARE OF THE LAST PART.

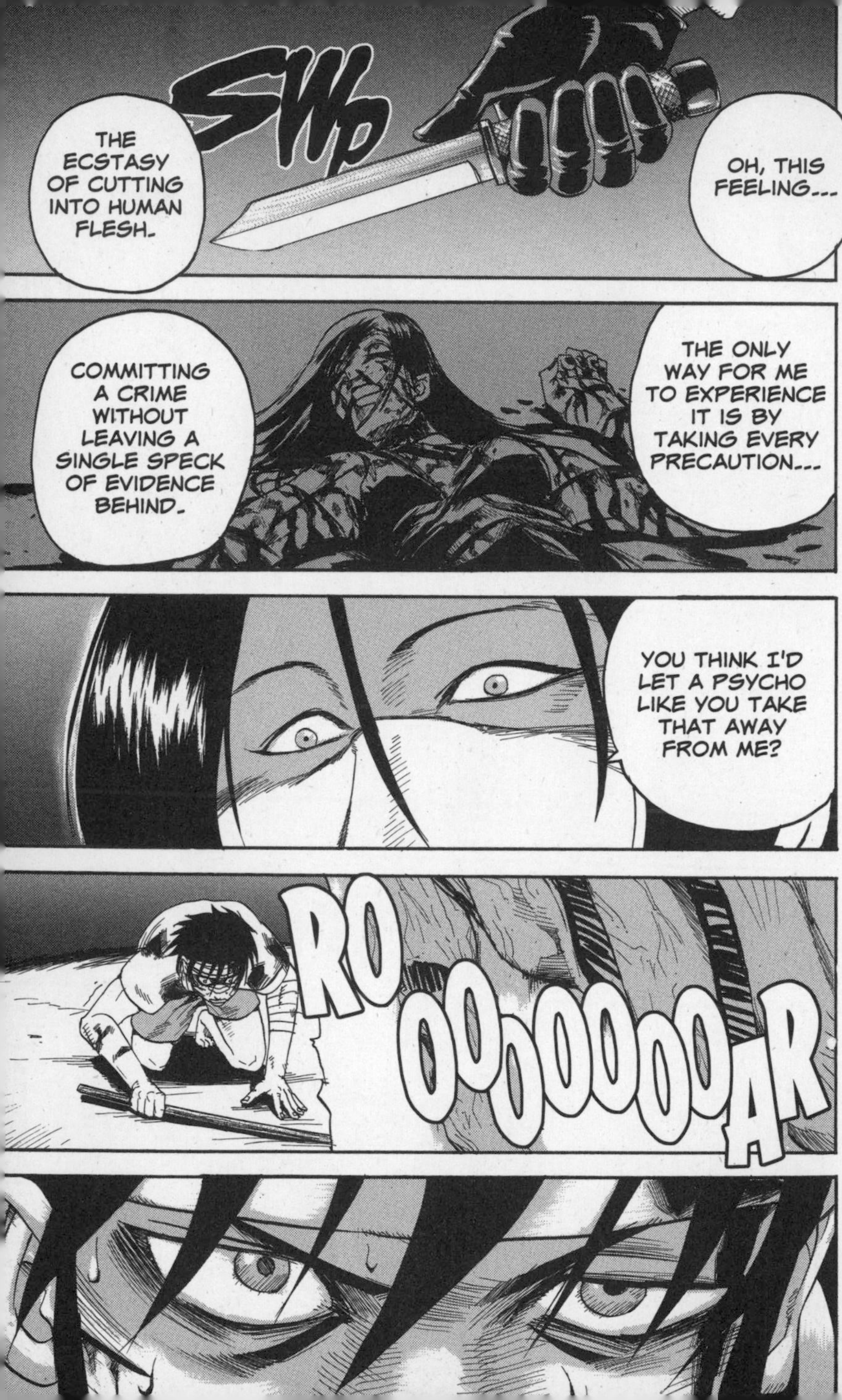

OH, THIS FEELING...
SWP
THE ECSTASY OF CUTTING INTO HUMAN FLESH.
THE ONLY WAY FOR ME TO EXPERIENCE IT IS BY TAKING EVERY PRECAUTION...
COMMITTING A CRIME WITHOUT LEAVING A SINGLE SPECK OF EVIDENCE BEHIND.
YOU THINK I'D LET A PSYCHO LIKE YOU TAKE THAT AWAY FROM ME?
ROOOOOOOOOAR

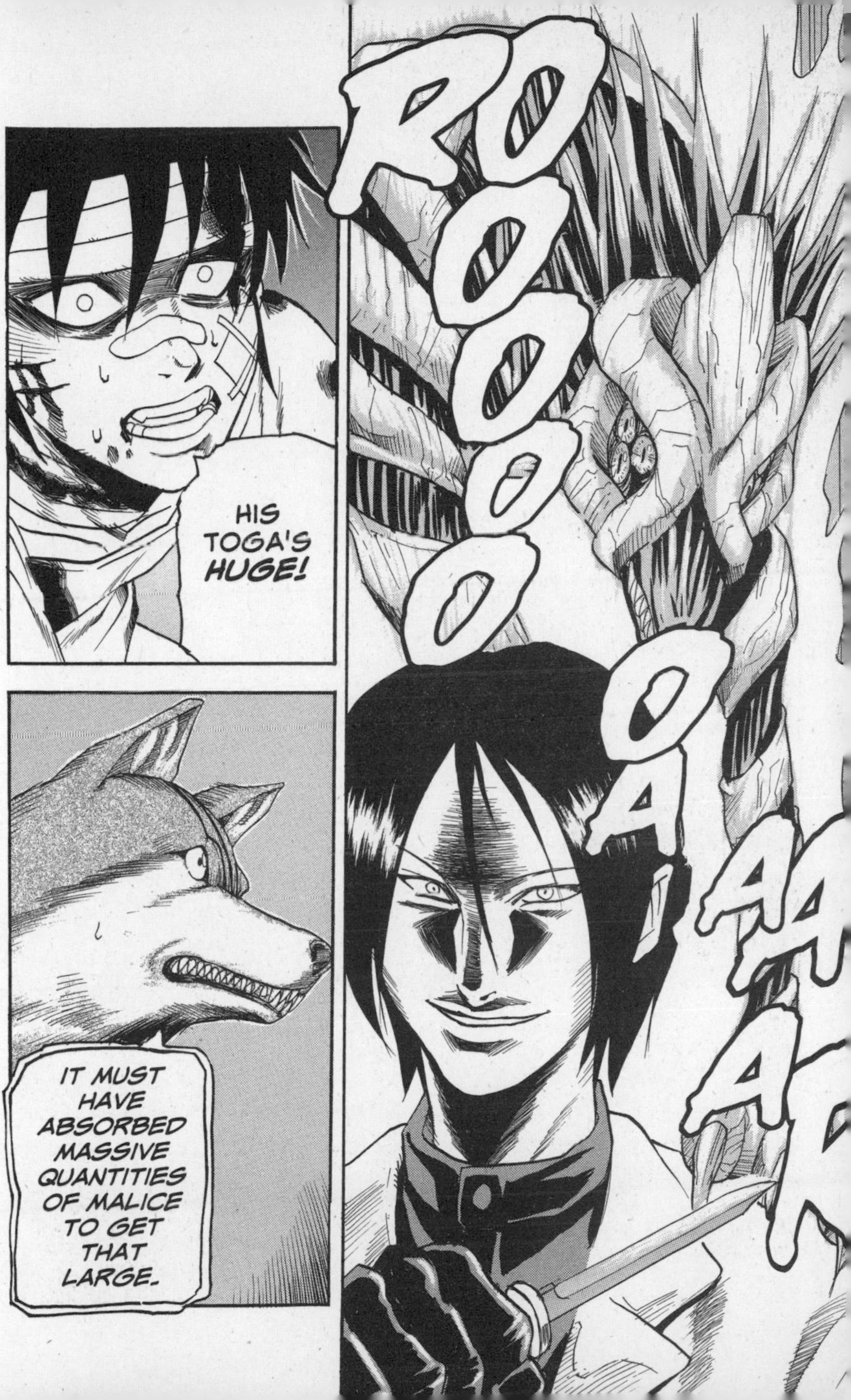
ROOOOOOAAAA
HIS TOGA'S HUGE!
IT MUST HAVE ABSORBED MASSIVE QUANTITIES OF MALICE TO GET THAT LARGE.

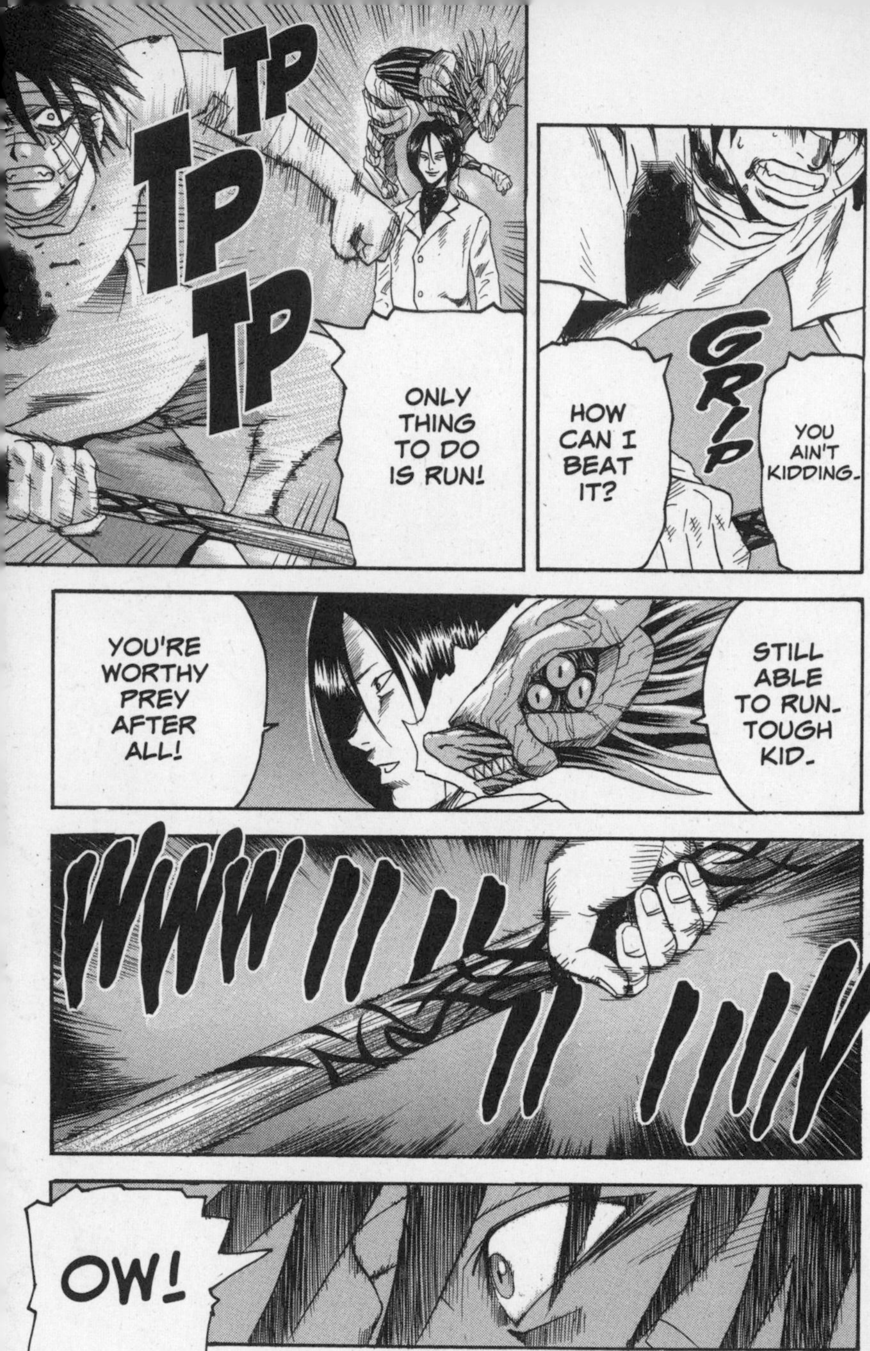
YOU AIN'T KIDDING.
GRIP
HOW CAN I BEAT IT?
TP TP TP TP
ONLY THING TO DO IS RUN!
STILL ABLE TO RUN. TOUGH KID.
YOU'RE WORTHY PREY AFTER ALL!
OW!

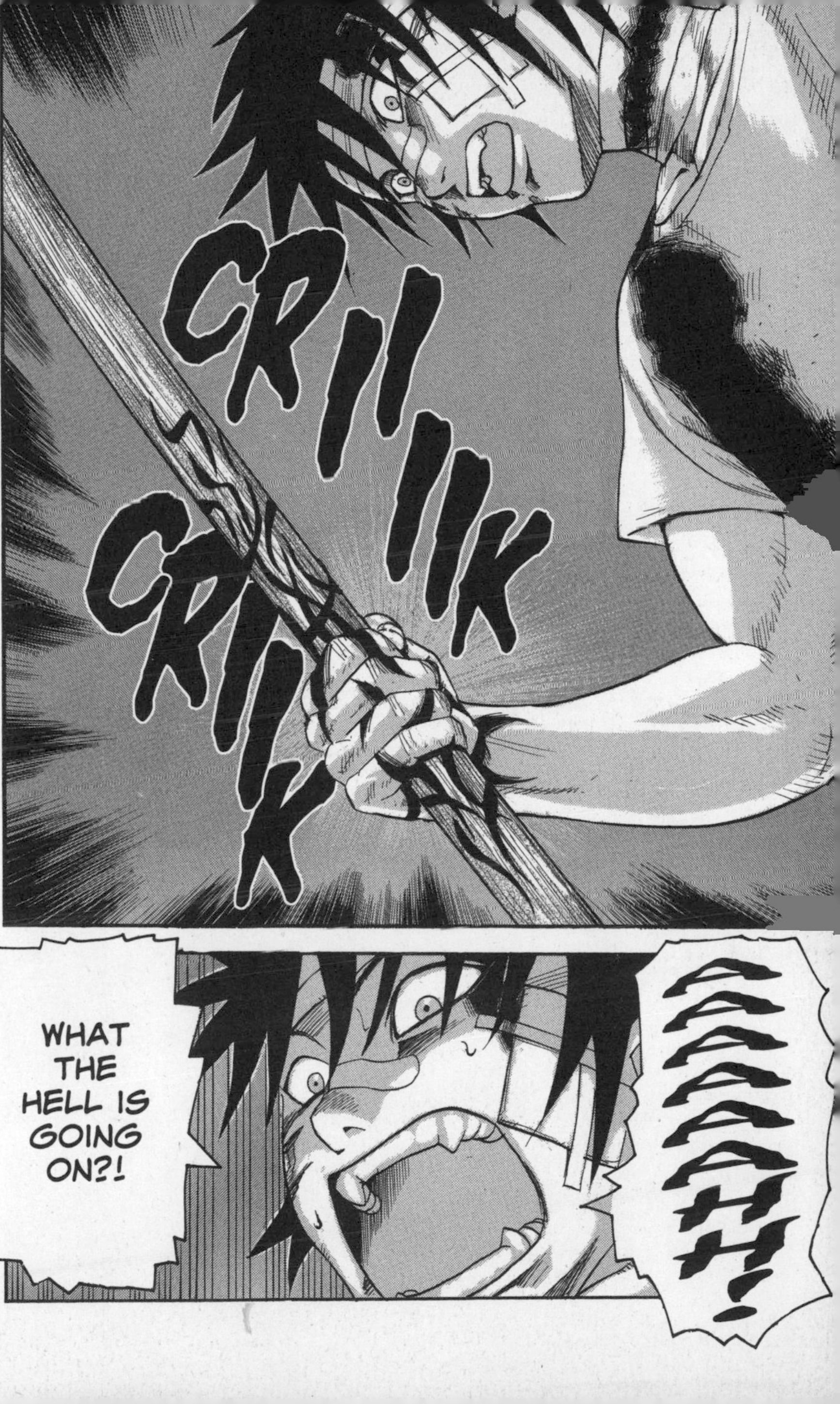
CRIIIIK
CRIIIK
AAAAAH?!
WHAT THE HELL IS GOING ON?!

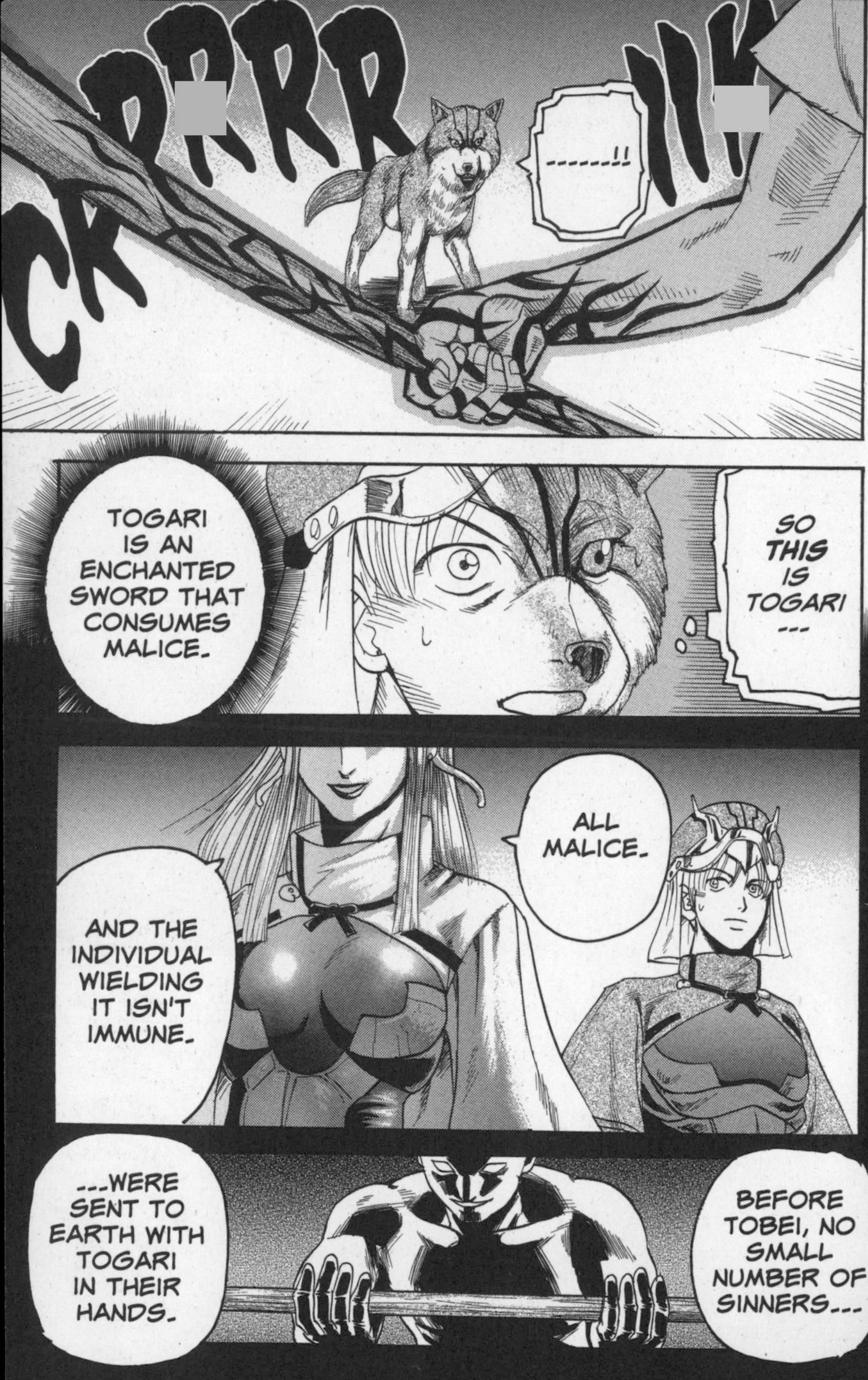

CRRRR
IIK
------!!
SO THIS IS TOGARI ---
TOGARI IS AN ENCHANTED SWORD THAT CONSUMES MALICE.
ALL MALICE.
AND THE INDIVIDUAL WIELDING IT ISN'T IMMUNE.
BEFORE TOBEI, NO SMALL NUMBER OF SINNERS---
---WERE SENT TO EARTH WITH TOGARI IN THEIR HANDS.

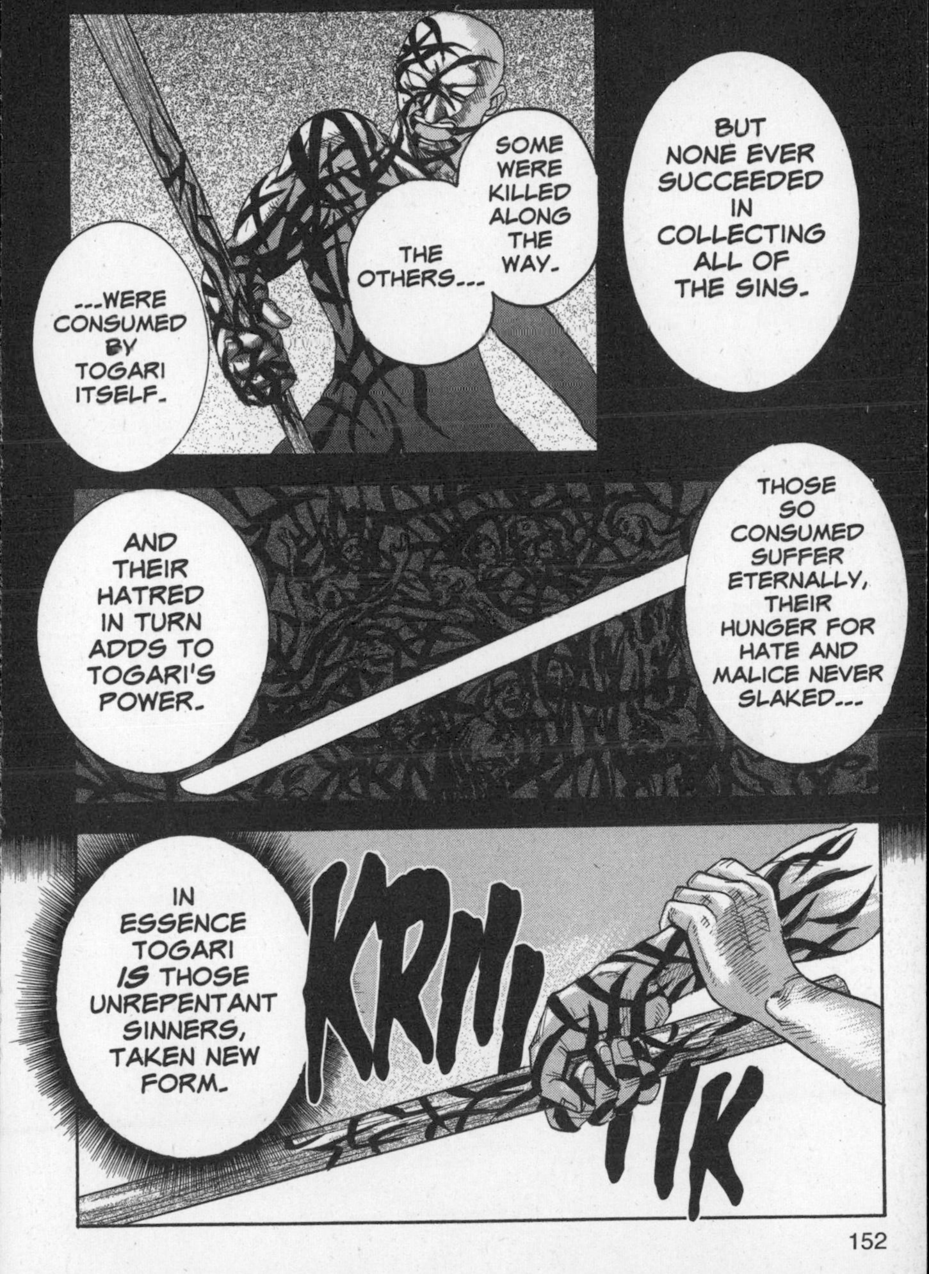
BUT NONE EVER SUCCEEDED IN COLLECTING ALL OF THE SINS.
SOME WERE KILLED ALONG THE WAY.
THE OTHERS...
...WERE CONSUMED BY TOGARI ITSELF.
THOSE SO CONSUMED SUFFER ETERNALLY, THEIR HUNGER FOR HATE AND MALICE NEVER SLAKED...
AND THEIR HATRED IN TURN ADDS TO TOGARI'S POWER.
KRIIIIK
IN ESSENCE TOGARI *IS* THOSE UNREPENTANT SINNERS, TAKEN NEW FORM.

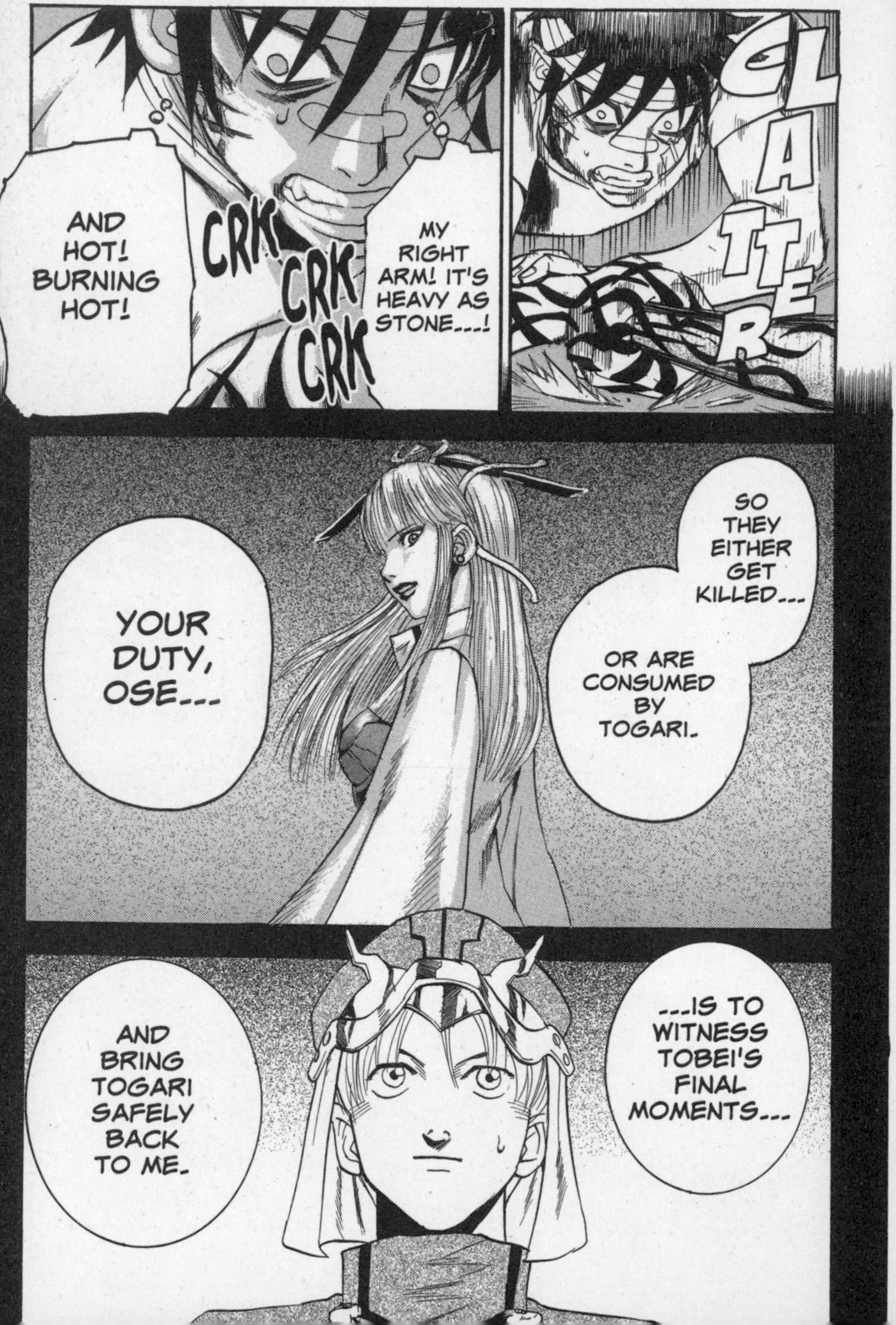
CLATTER
MY RIGHT ARM! IT'S HEAVY AS STONE...!
CRK CRK CRK
AND HOT! BURNING HOT!
SO THEY EITHER GET KILLED...
OR ARE CONSUMED BY TOGARI.
YOUR DUTY, OSE...
...IS TO WITNESS TOBEI'S FINAL MOMENTS...
AND BRING TOGARI SAFELY BACK TO ME.

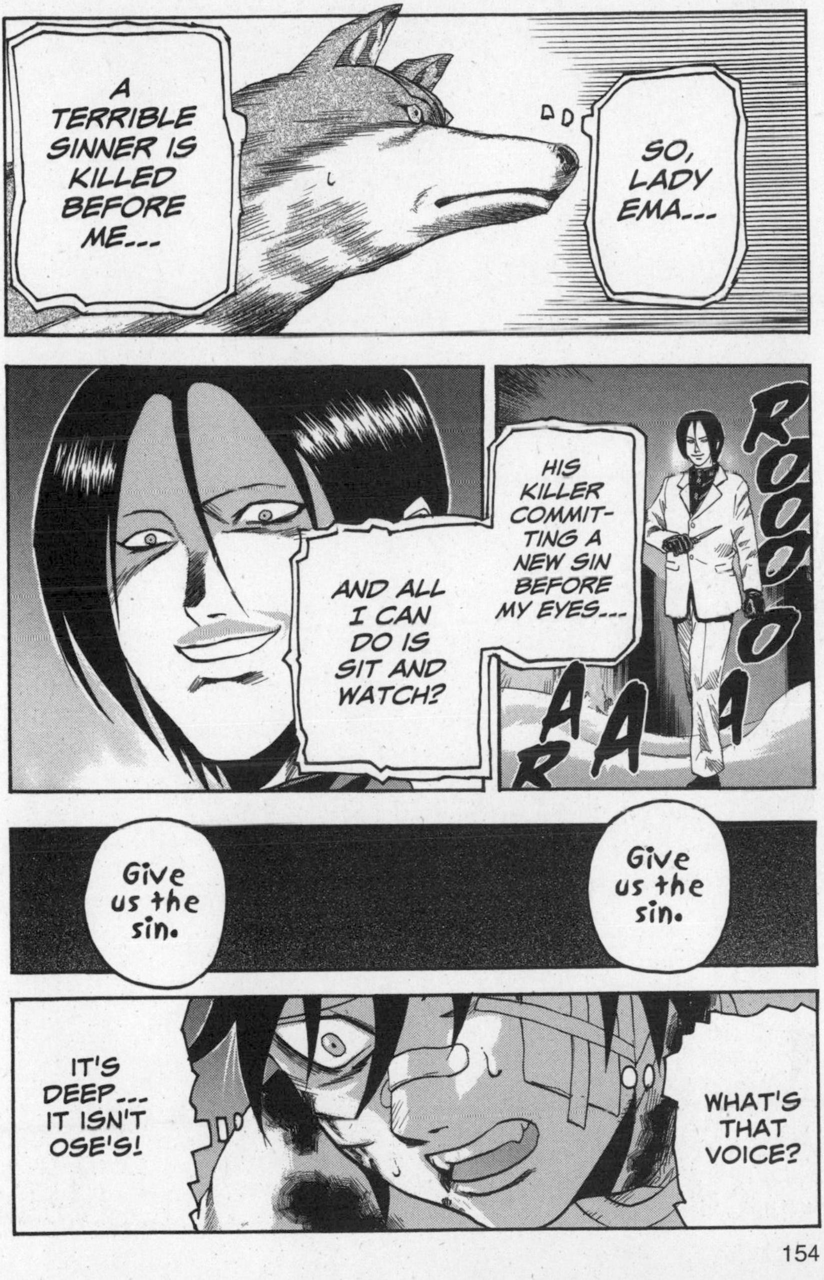
SO, LADY EMA...
A TERRIBLE SINNER IS KILLED BEFORE ME...
ROOOOOAAAR
HIS KILLER COMMITTING A NEW SIN BEFORE MY EYES...
AND ALL I CAN DO IS SIT AND WATCH?
Give us the sin.
Give us the sin.
WHAT'S THAT VOICE?
IT'S DEEP... IT ISN'T OSE'S!

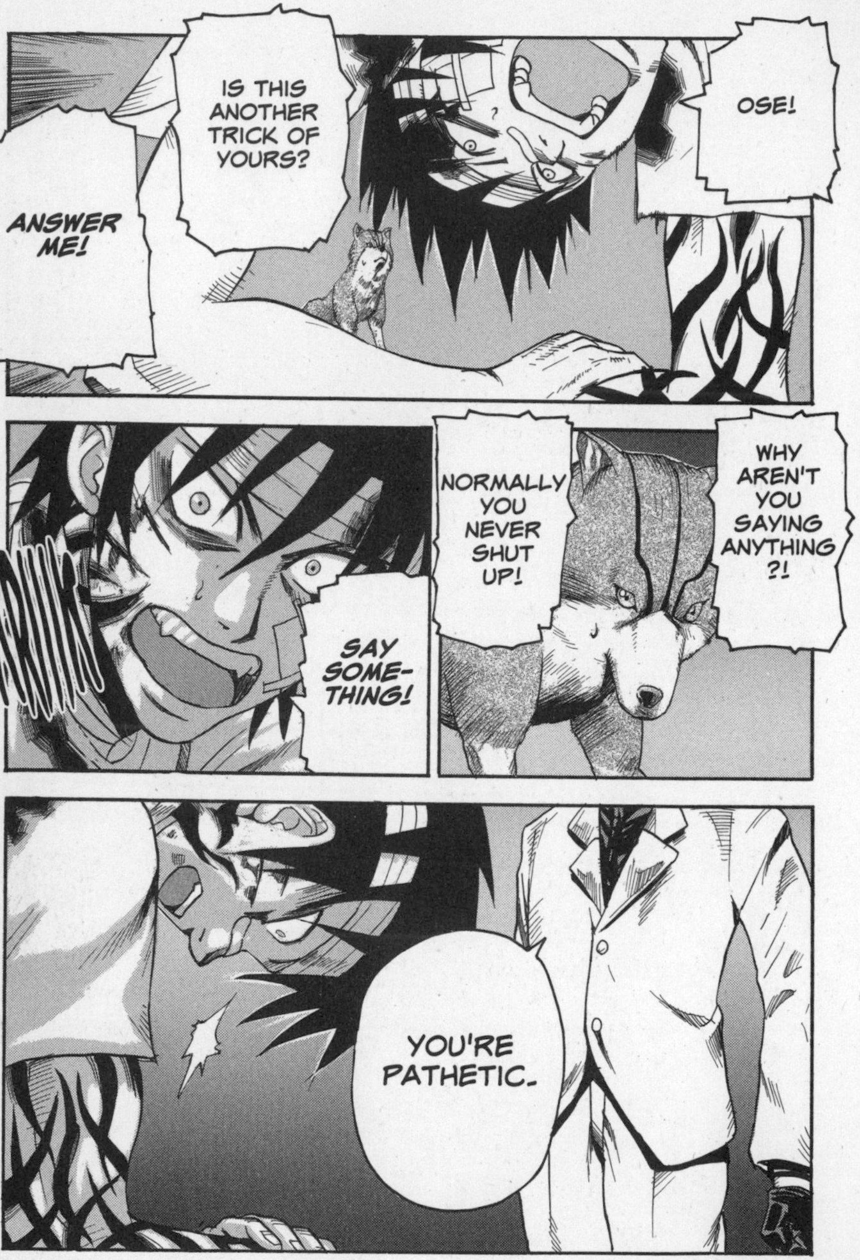
OSE!
IS THIS ANOTHER TRICK OF YOURS?
ANSWER ME!
WHY AREN'T YOU SAYING ANYTHING ?!
NORMALLY YOU NEVER SHUT UP!
SAY SOME-THING!
YOU'RE PATHETIC.

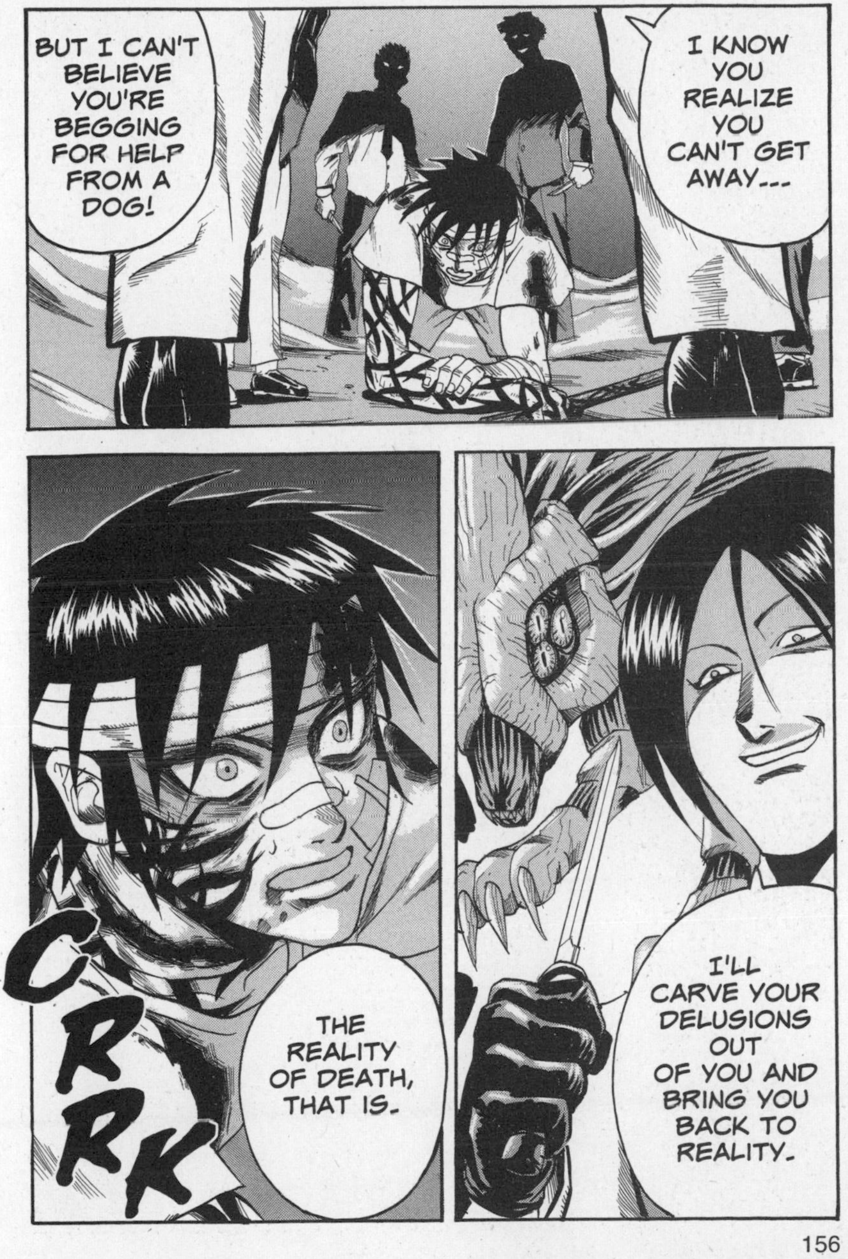
I KNOW YOU REALIZE YOU CAN'T GET AWAY...
BUT I CAN'T BELIEVE YOU'RE BEGGING FOR HELP FROM A DOG!
I'LL CARVE YOUR DELUSIONS OUT OF YOU AND BRING YOU BACK TO REALITY.
THE REALITY OF DEATH, THAT IS.
CRRK

Chapter 6 Hate Everything

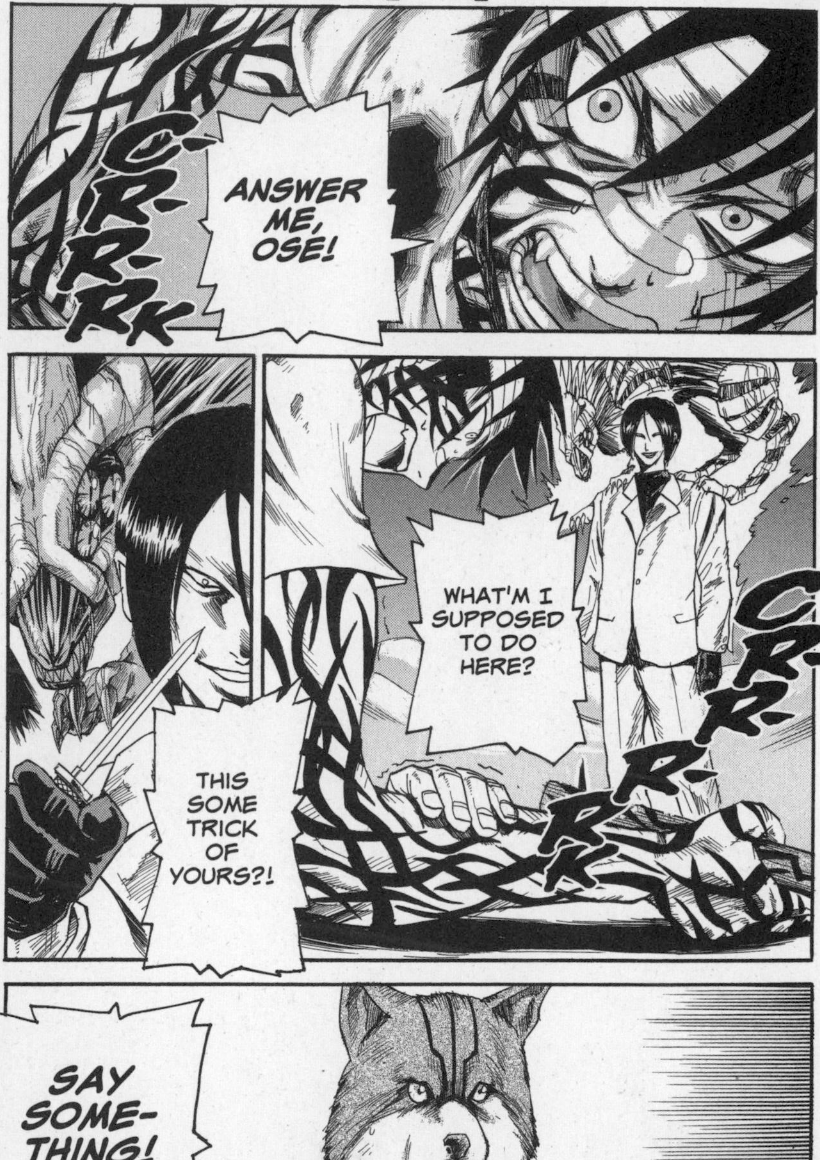
C-R-R-R-RK
ANSWER ME, OSÉ!
WHAT'M I SUPPOSED TO DO HERE?
C-R-R-R-R-RK
THIS SOME TRICK OF YOURS?!
SAY SOME-THING!

Chapter 6

Hate Everything

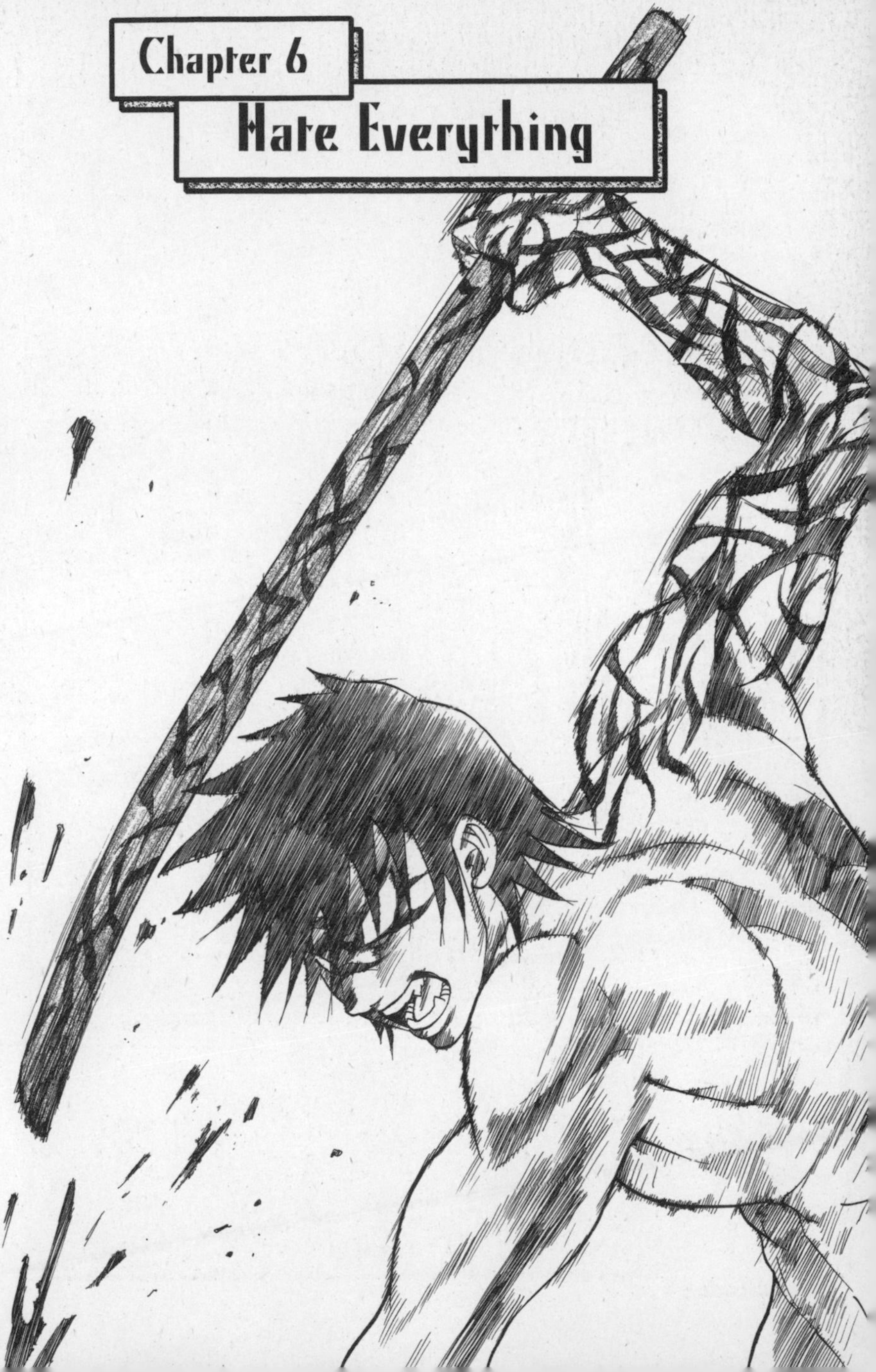

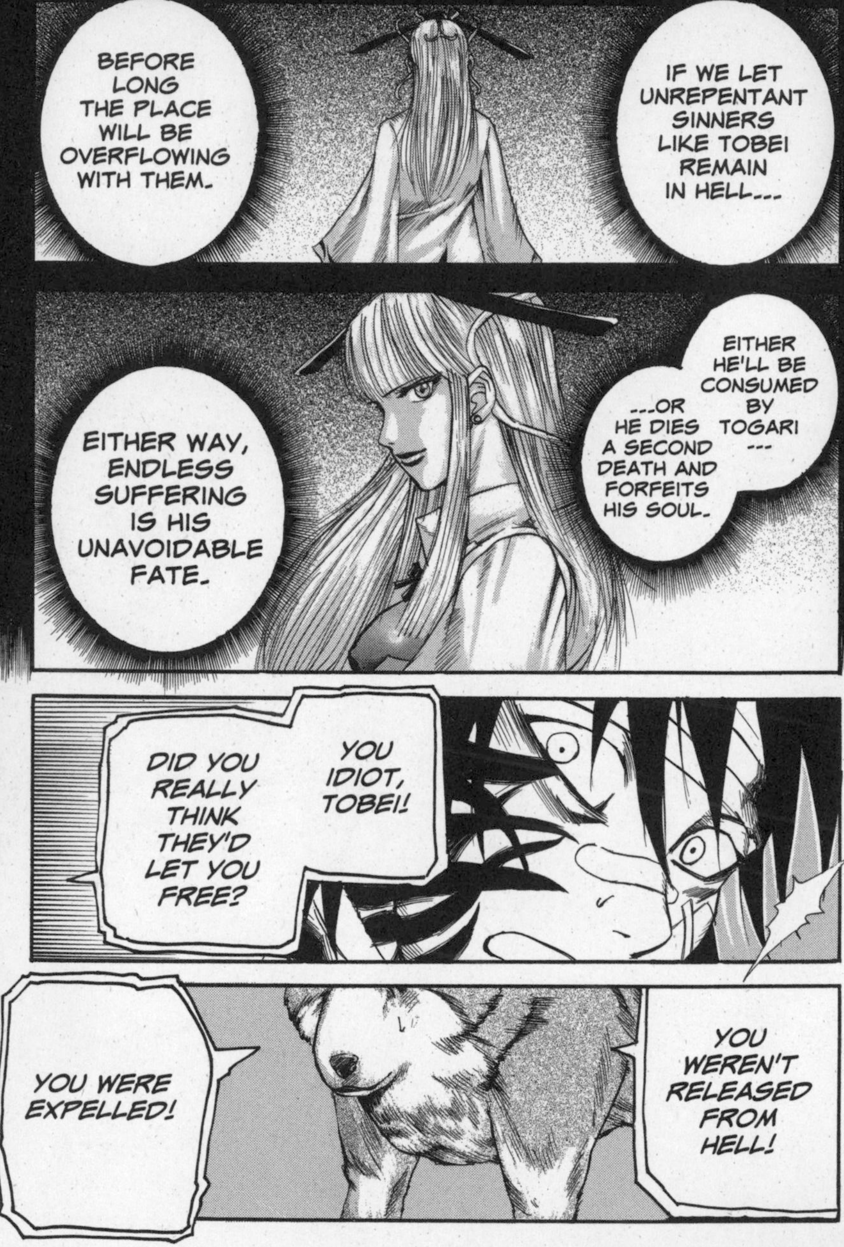
IF WE LET UNREPENTANT SINNERS LIKE TOBEI REMAIN IN HELL...
BEFORE LONG THE PLACE WILL BE OVERFLOWING WITH THEM.
EITHER HE'LL BE CONSUMED BY TOGARI---
...OR HE DIES A SECOND DEATH AND FORFEITS HIS SOUL.
EITHER WAY, ENDLESS SUFFERING IS HIS UNAVOIDABLE FATE.
YOU IDIOT, TOBEI!
DID YOU REALLY THINK THEY'D LET YOU FREE?
YOU WEREN'T RELEASED FROM HELL!
YOU WERE EXPELLED!

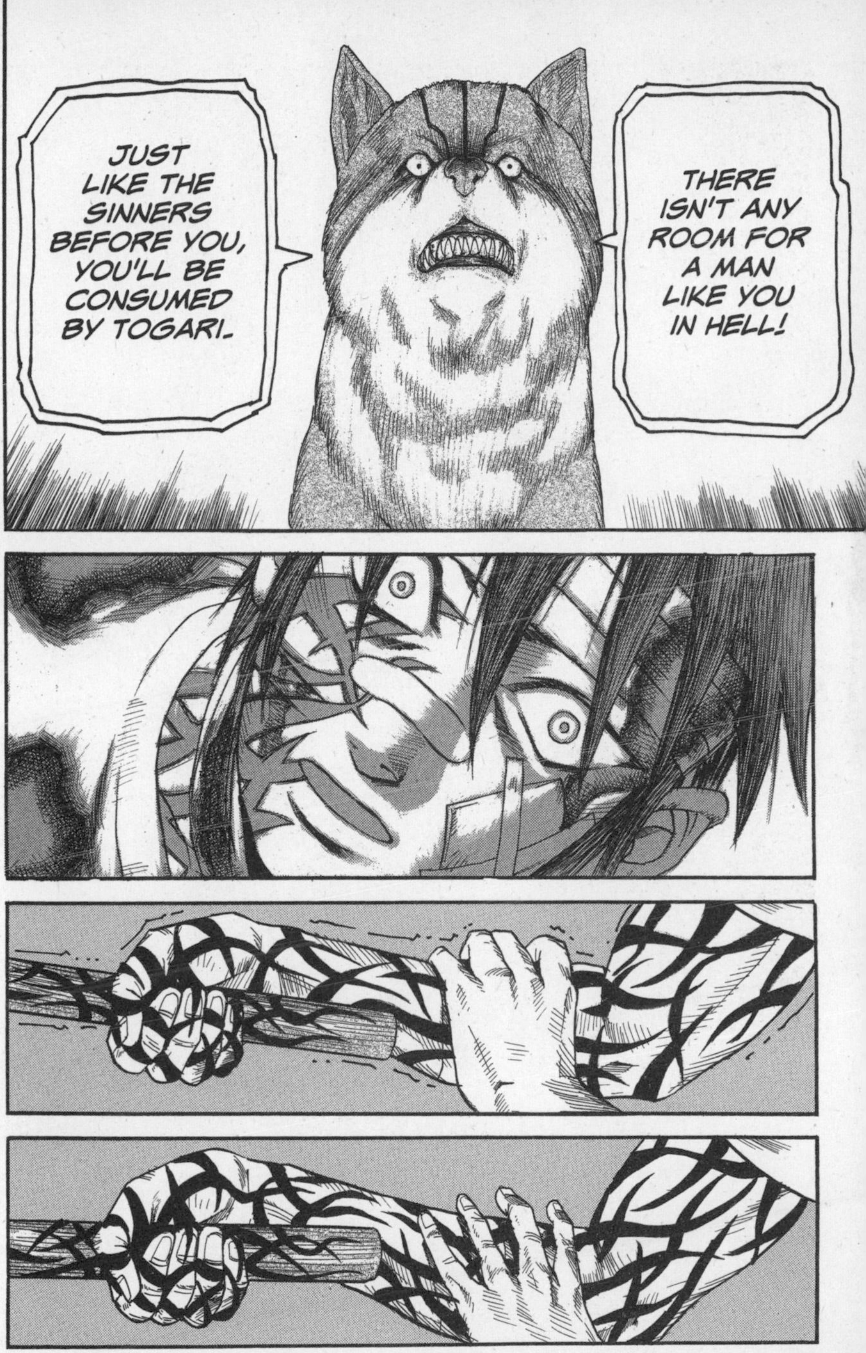
THERE ISN'T ANY ROOM FOR A MAN LIKE YOU IN HELL!
JUST LIKE THE SINNERS BEFORE YOU, YOU'LL BE CONSUMED BY TOGARI...

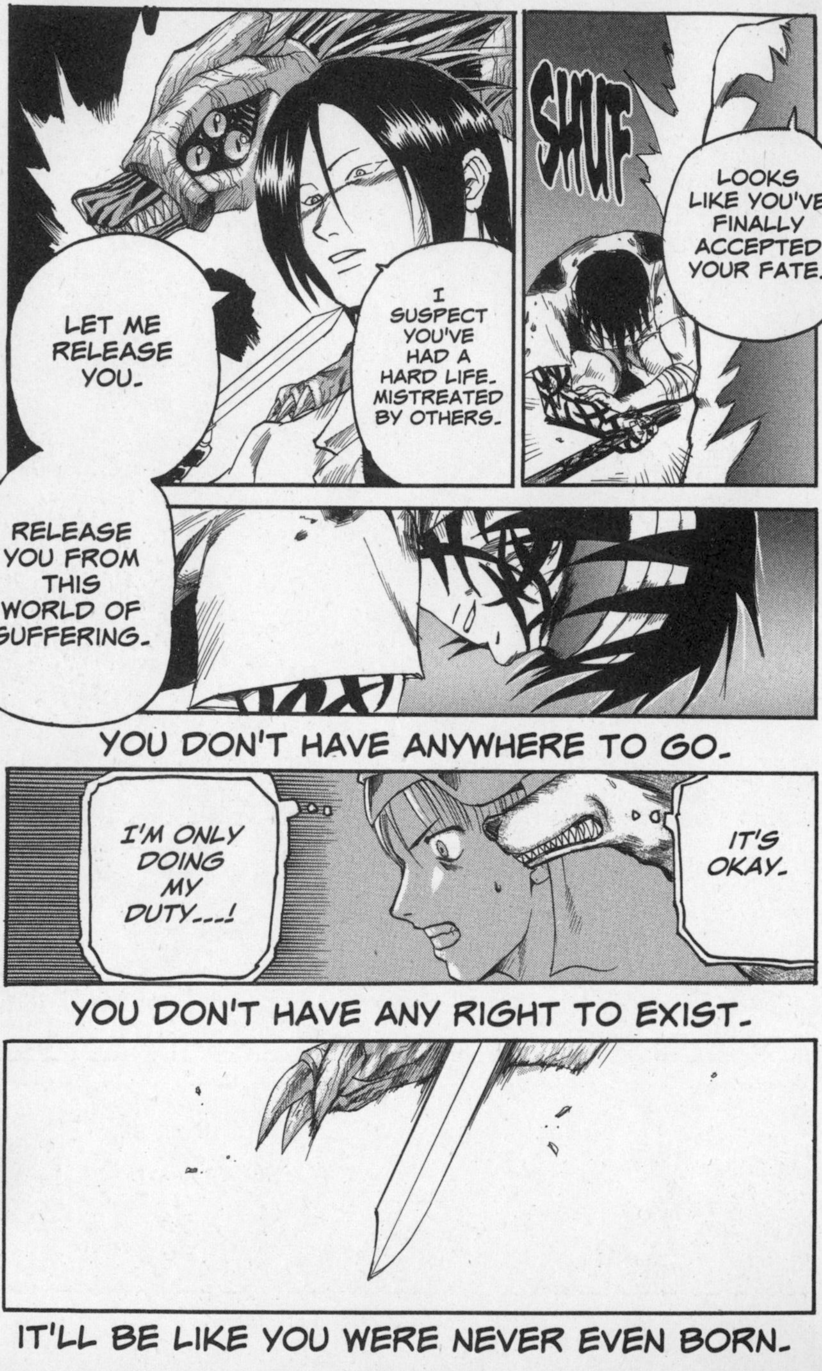
SHUF
LOOKS LIKE YOU'VE FINALLY ACCEPTED YOUR FATE.
I SUSPECT YOU'VE HAD A HARD LIFE. MISTREATED BY OTHERS.
LET ME RELEASE YOU.
RELEASE YOU FROM THIS WORLD OF SUFFERING.
YOU DON'T HAVE ANYWHERE TO GO.
IT'S OKAY.
I'M ONLY DOING MY DUTY...!
YOU DON'T HAVE ANY RIGHT TO EXIST.
IT'LL BE LIKE YOU WERE NEVER EVEN BORN.

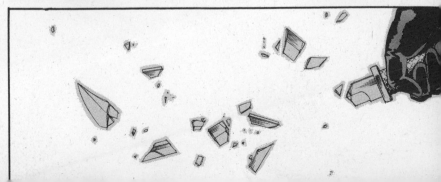

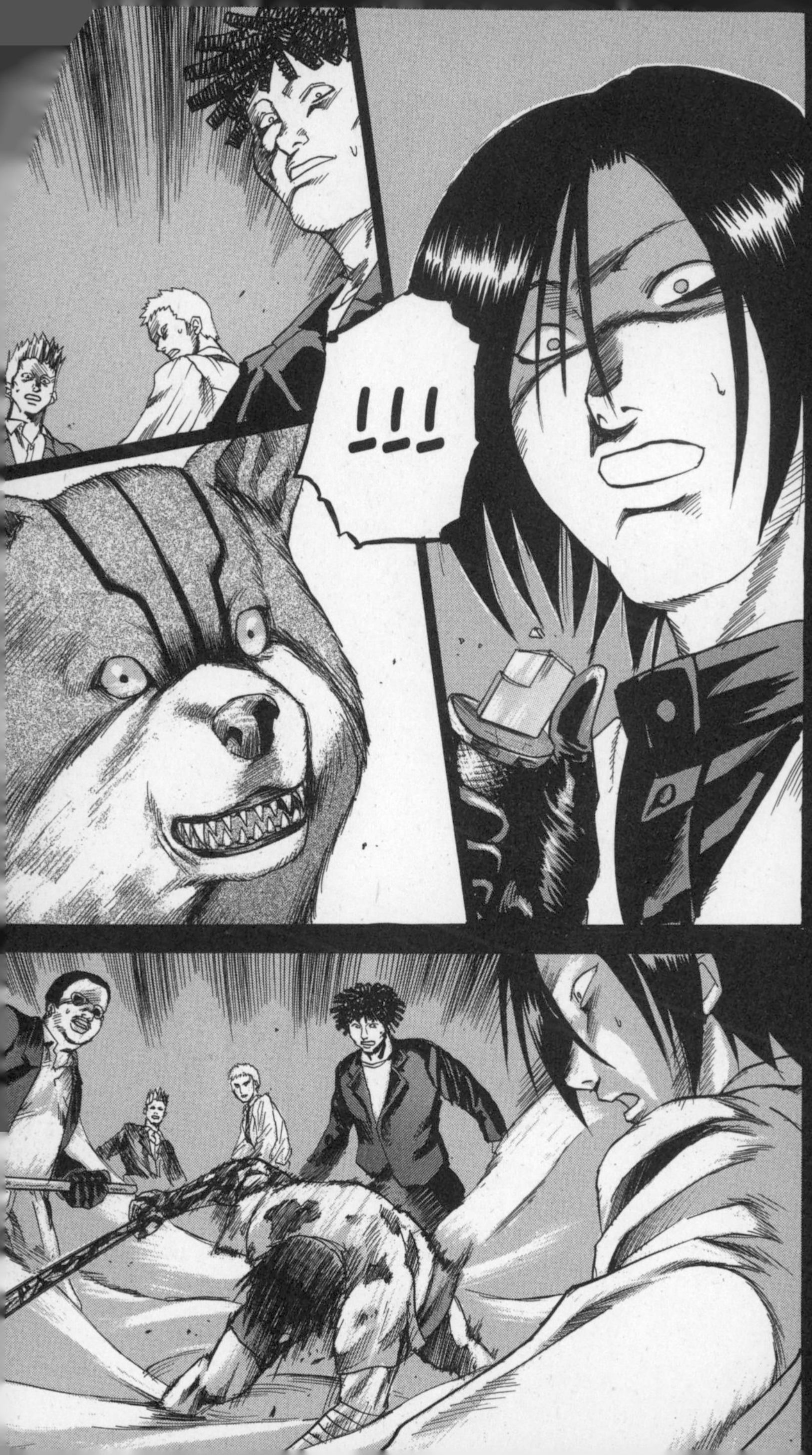
!!!

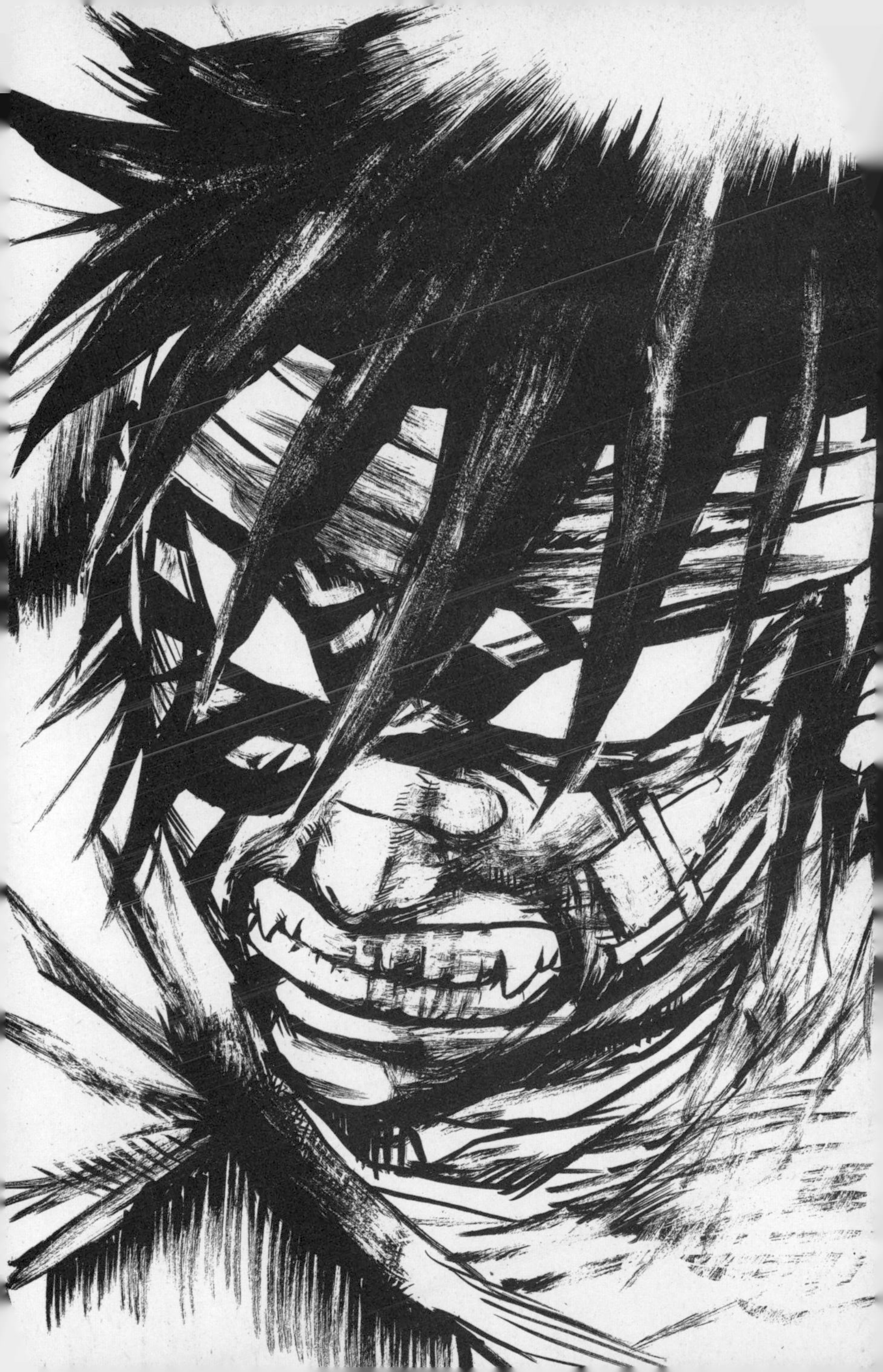

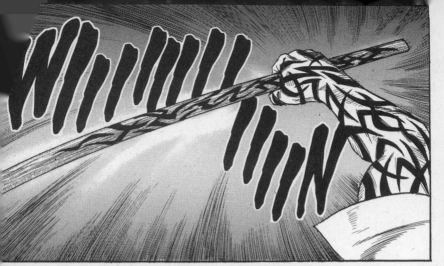

WHAT?!

HAS
TOGARI...

HAS
TOGARI
TAKEN
CONTROL
OF HIM?!

ROA

AAAR

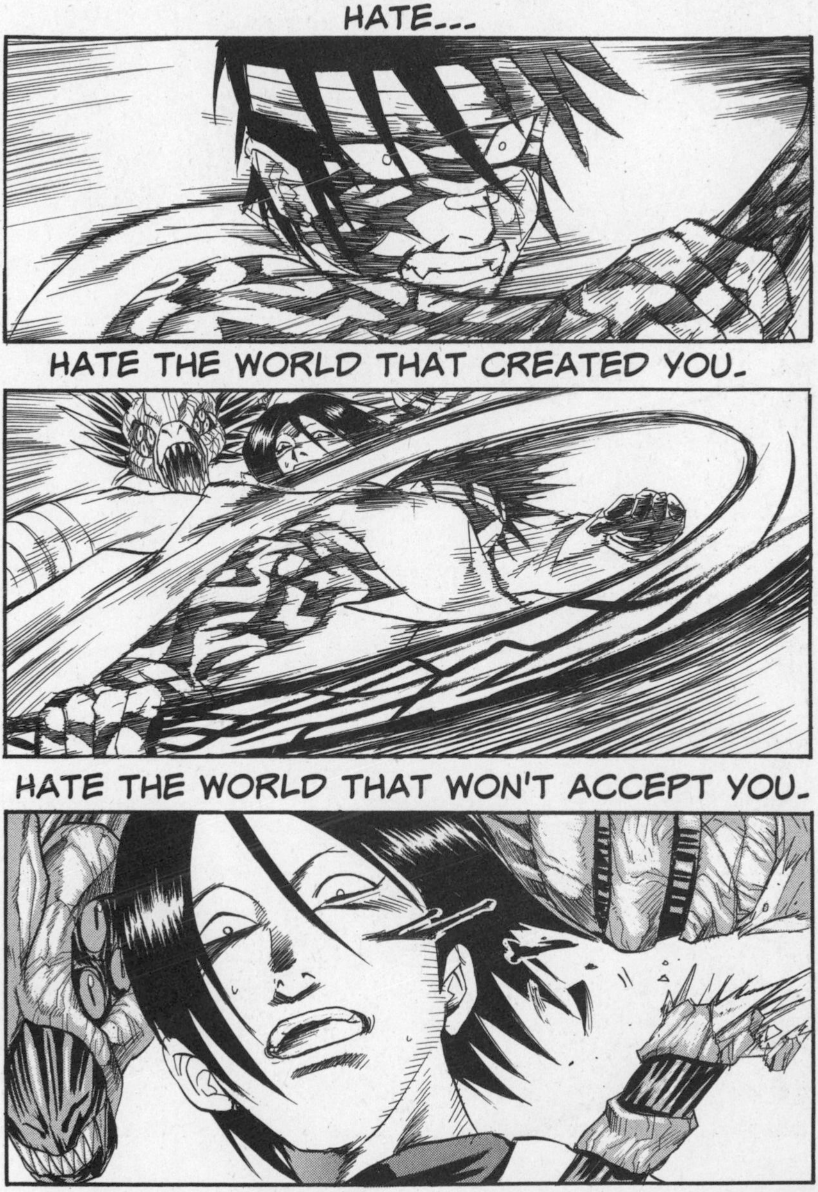
HATE...
HATE THE WORLD THAT CREATED YOU.
HATE THE WORLD THAT WON'T ACCEPT YOU.

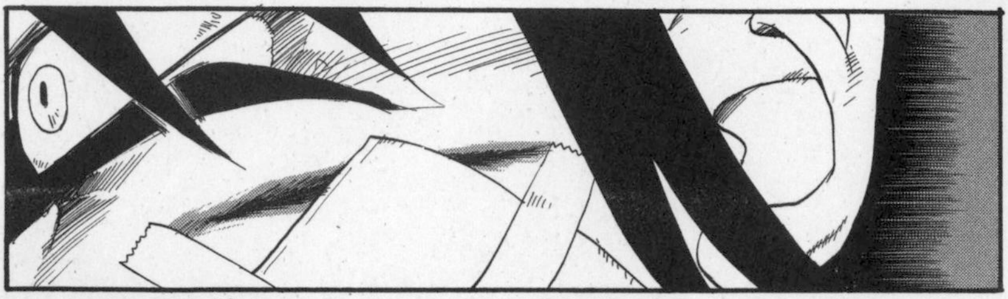

THERE'S NO PLACE FOR YOU TO GO.

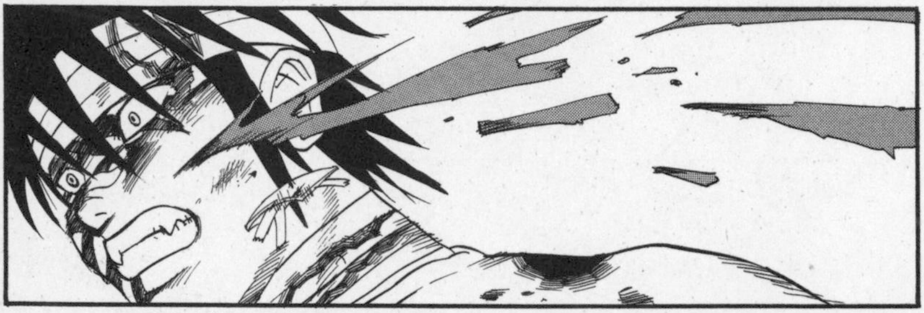

THERE'S NO PLACE FOR YOU TO BE.

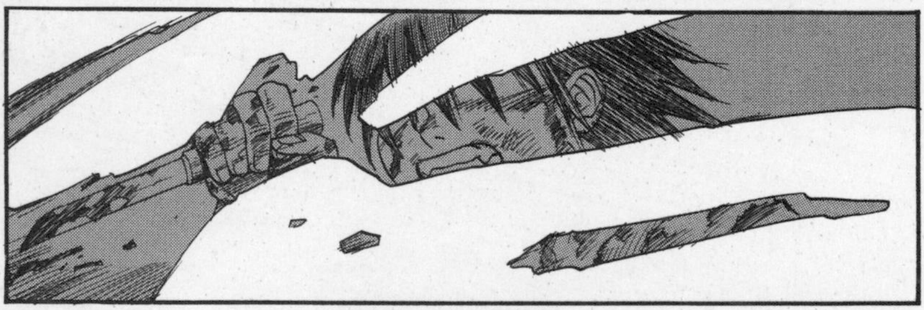

SO TAKE IT.

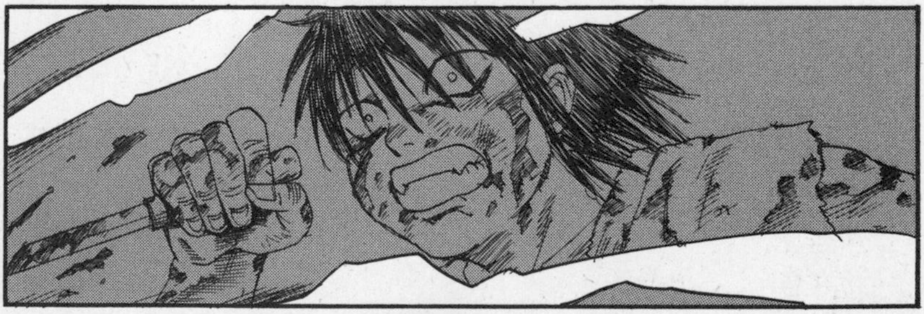

TAKE IT...

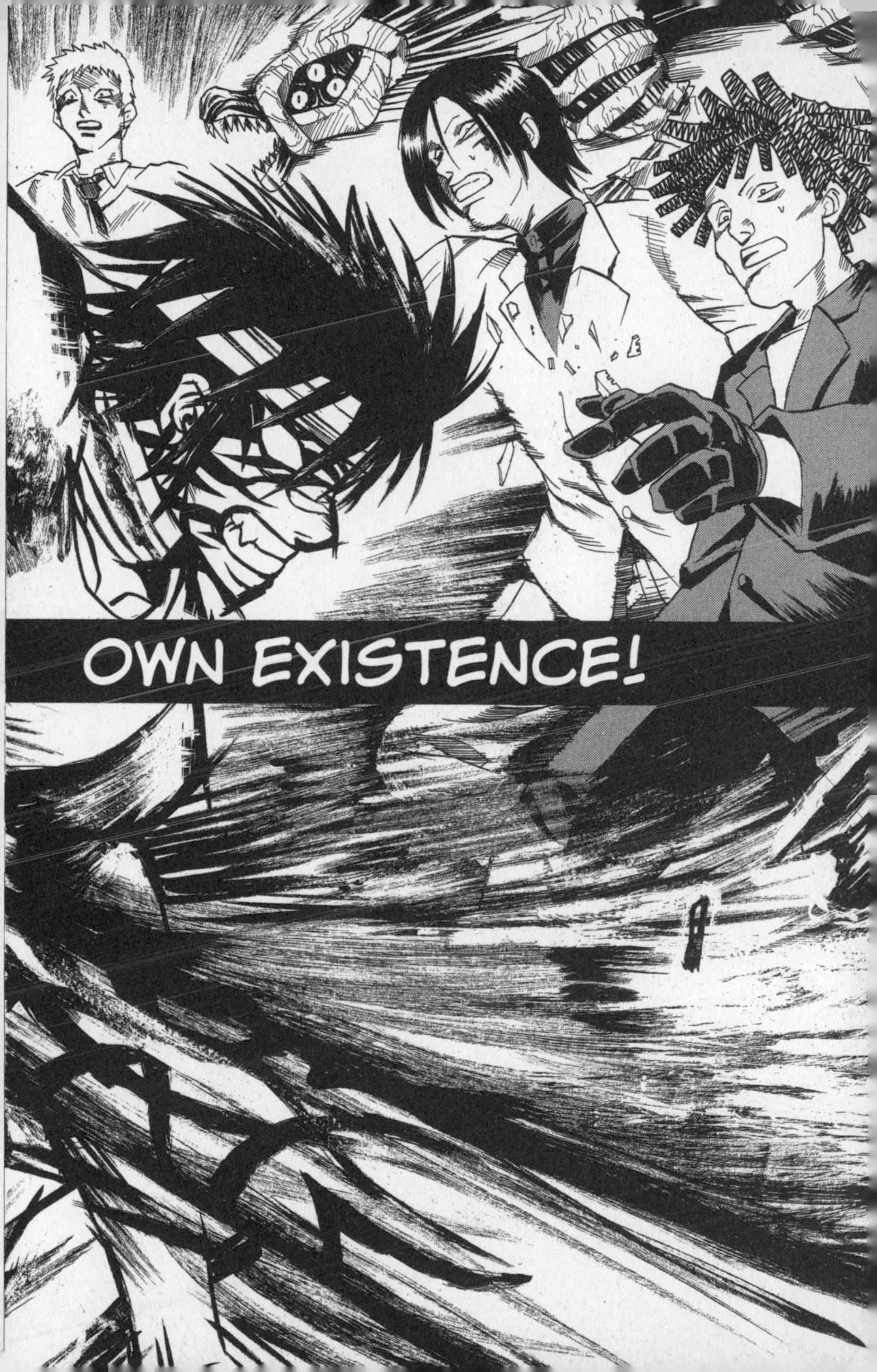
OWN EXISTENCE!

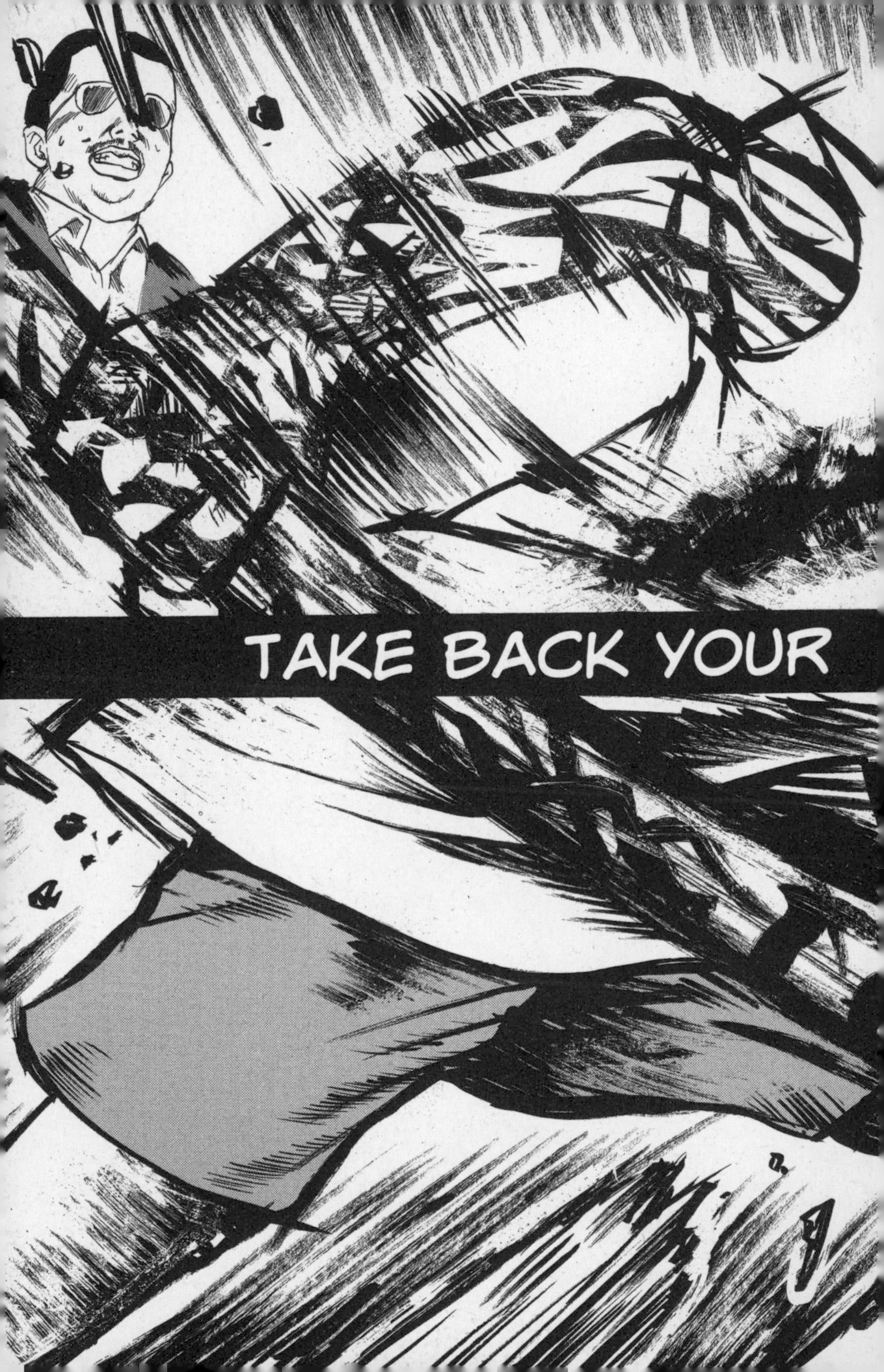
TAKE BACK YOUR

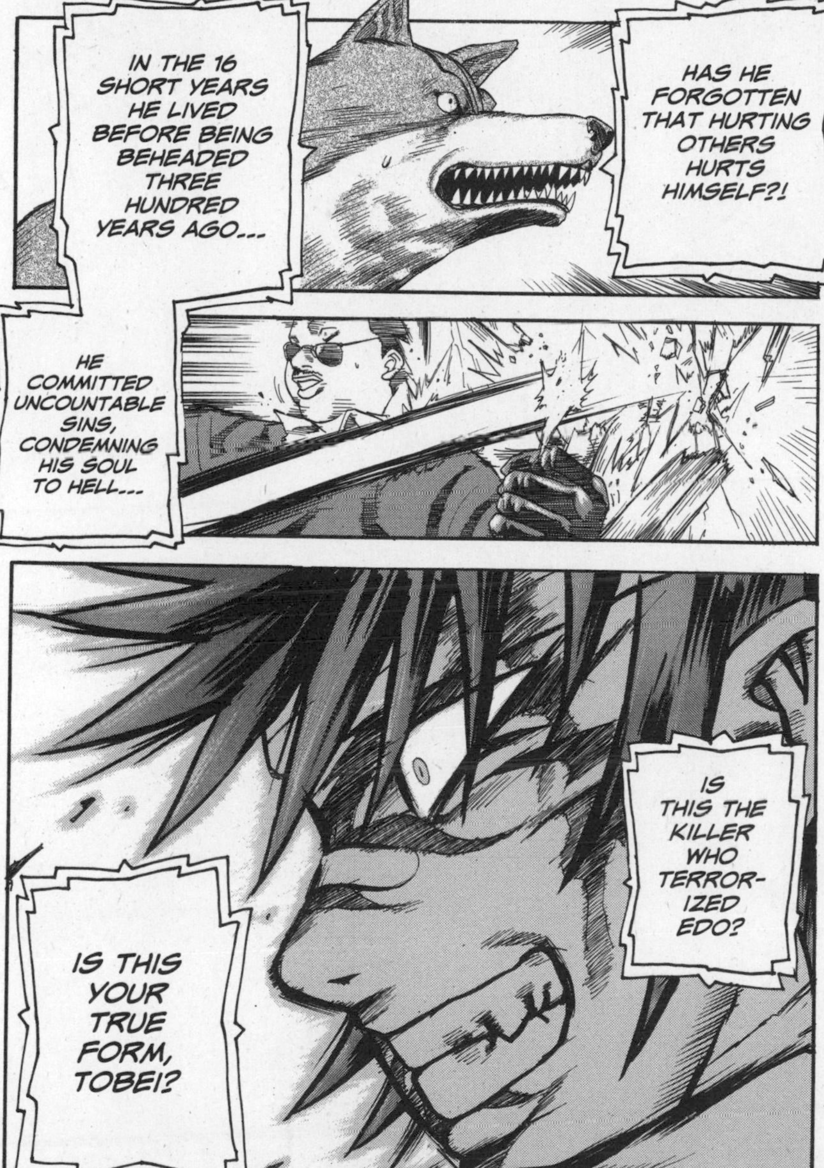
HAS HE FORGOTTEN THAT HURTING OTHERS HURTS HIMSELF?!
IN THE 16 SHORT YEARS HE LIVED BEFORE BEING BEHEADED THREE HUNDRED YEARS AGO...
HE COMMITTED UNCOUNTABLE SINS, CONDEMNING HIS SOUL TO HELL...
IS THIS THE KILLER WHO TERROR-IZED EDO?
IS THIS YOUR TRUE FORM, TOBEI?

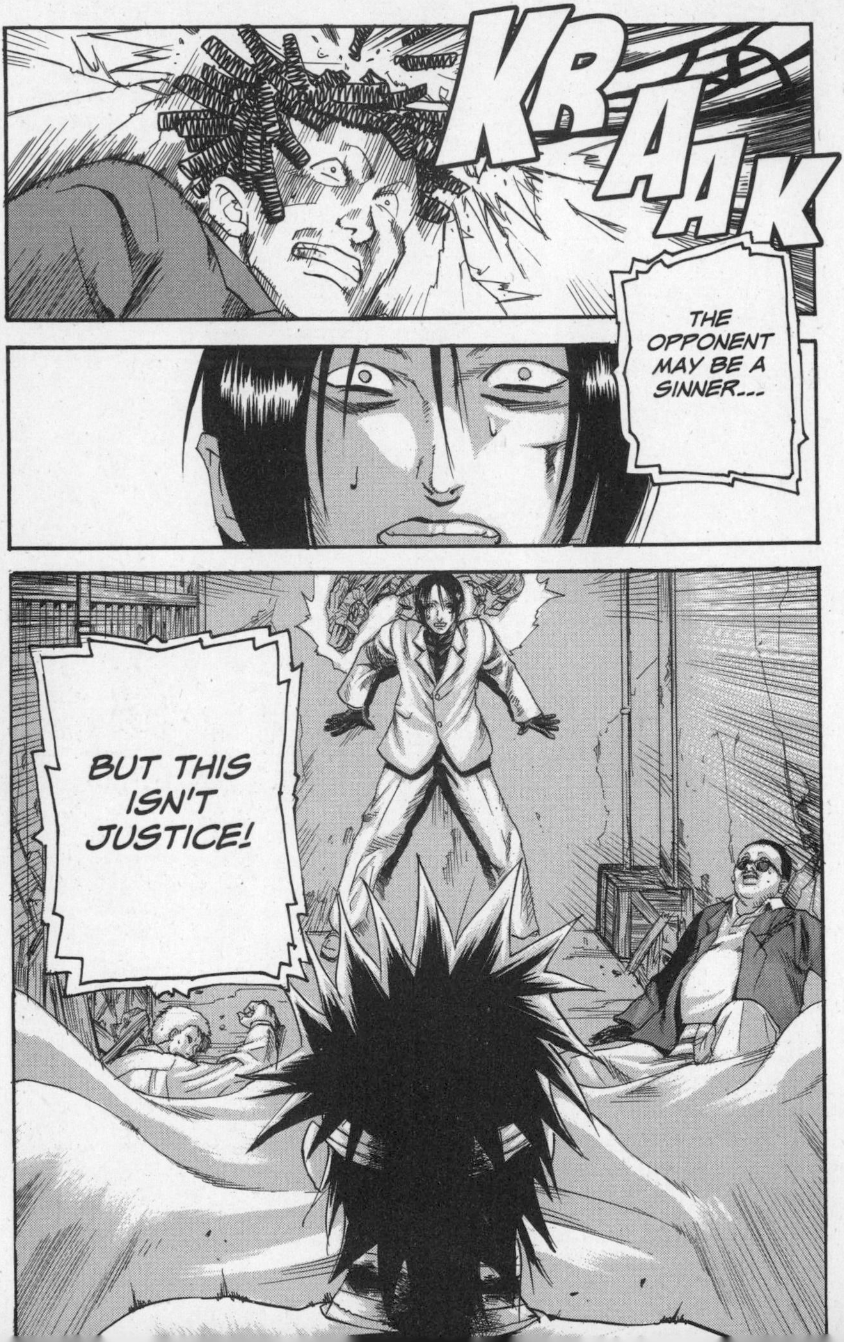
KRAAK
THE OPPONENT MAY BE A SINNER...
BUT THIS ISN'T JUSTICE!

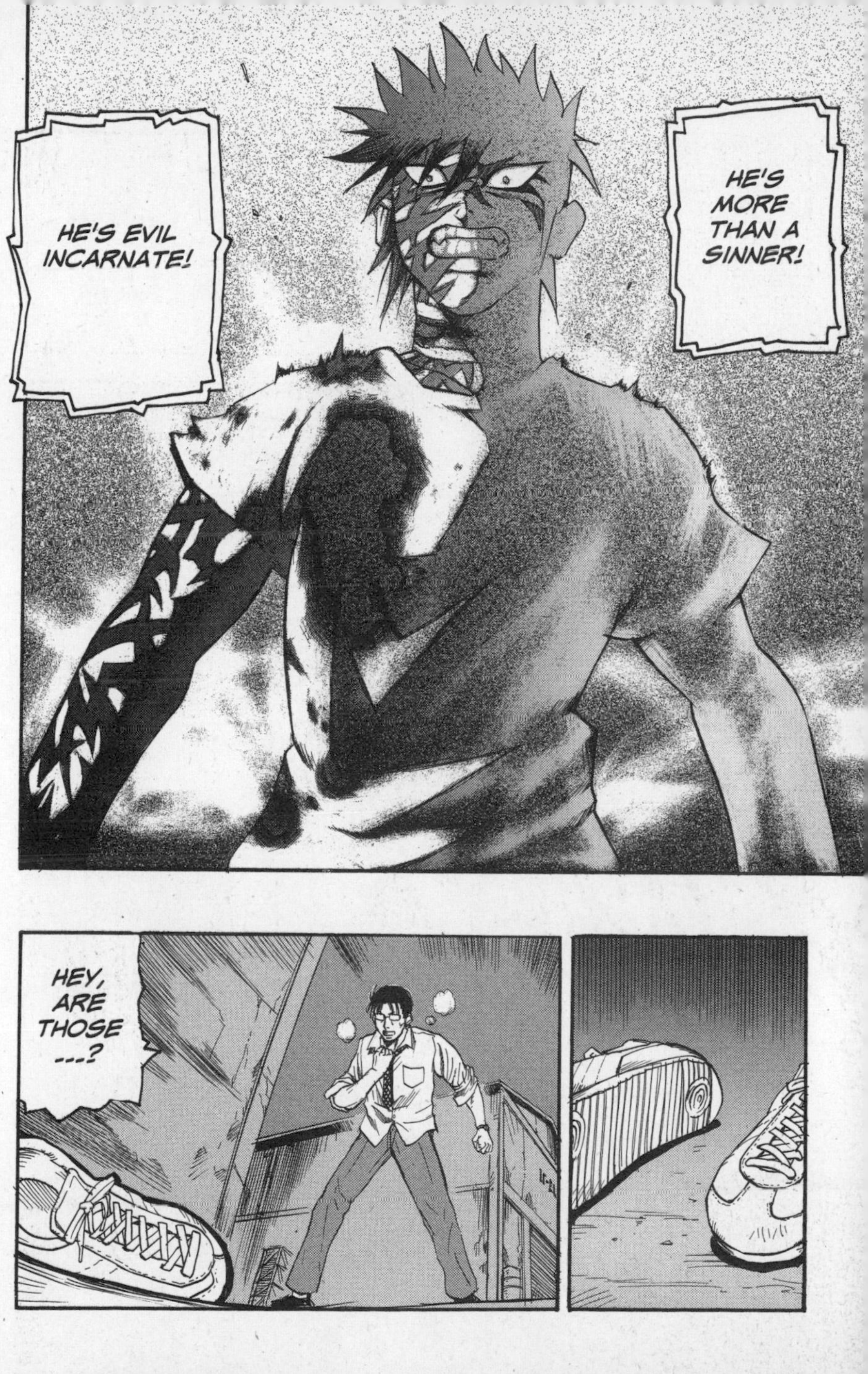
HE'S MORE THAN A SINNER!
HE'S EVIL INCARNATE!
HEY, ARE THOSE---?

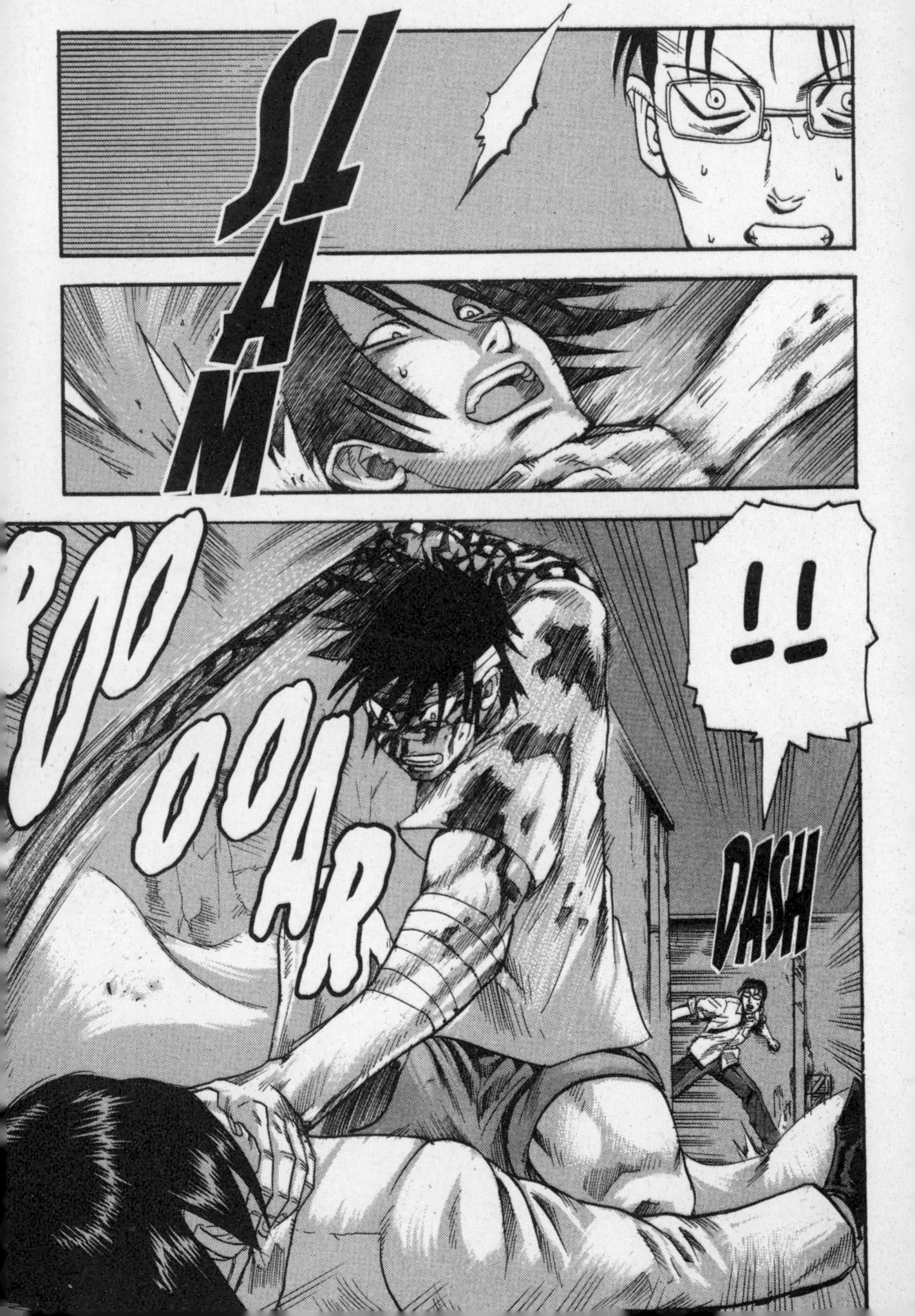
SLAM
!!
DASH
ROOOOAR

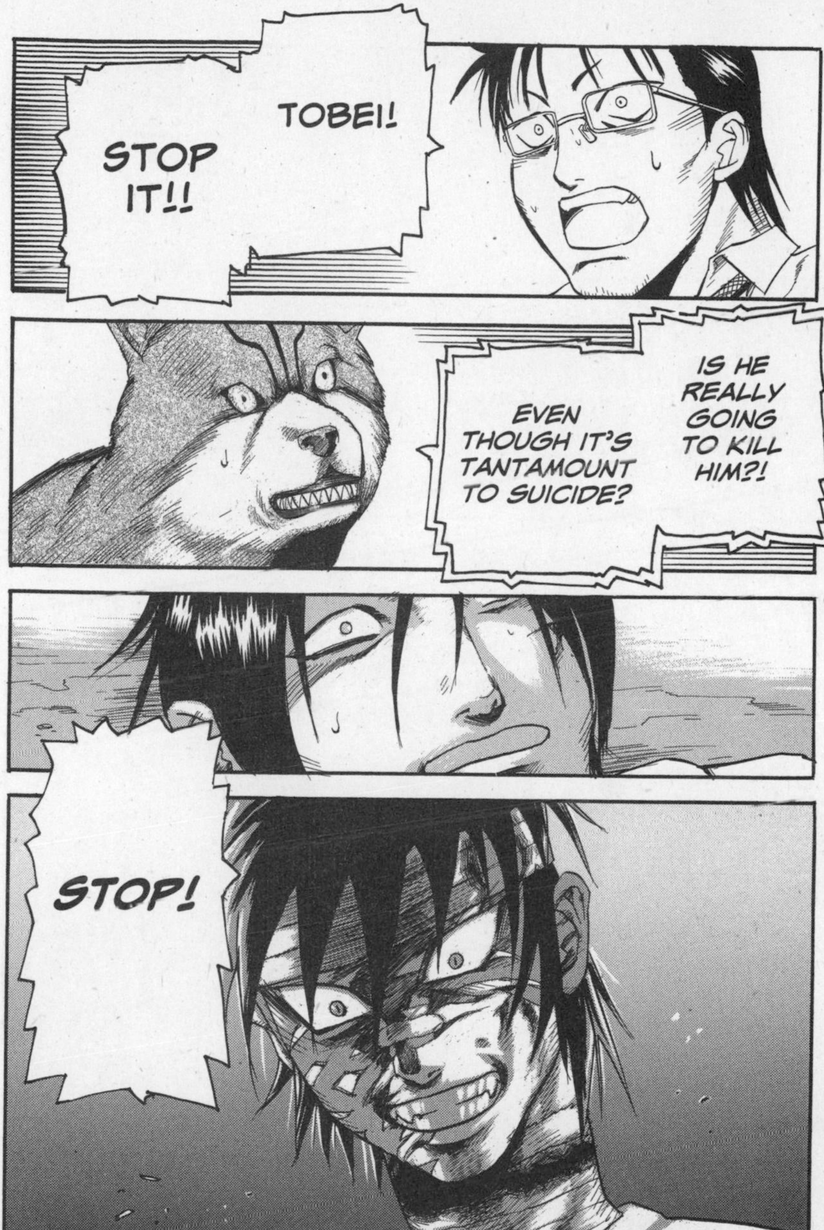
TOBEI!
STOP IT!!
IS HE REALLY GOING TO KILL HIM?!
EVEN THOUGH IT'S TANTAMOUNT TO SUICIDE?
STOP!

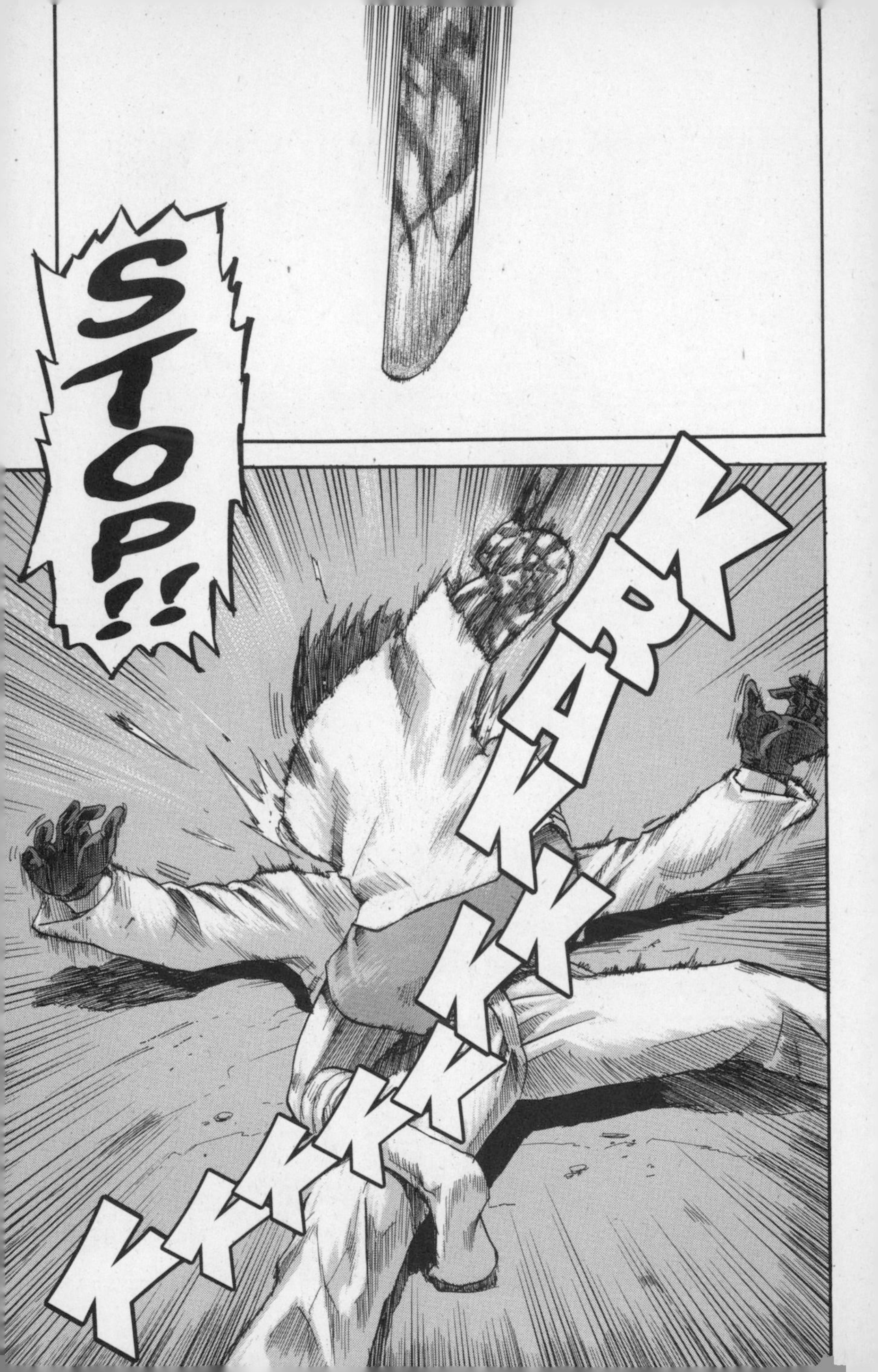

STOP!!
KRAKKKKKKK

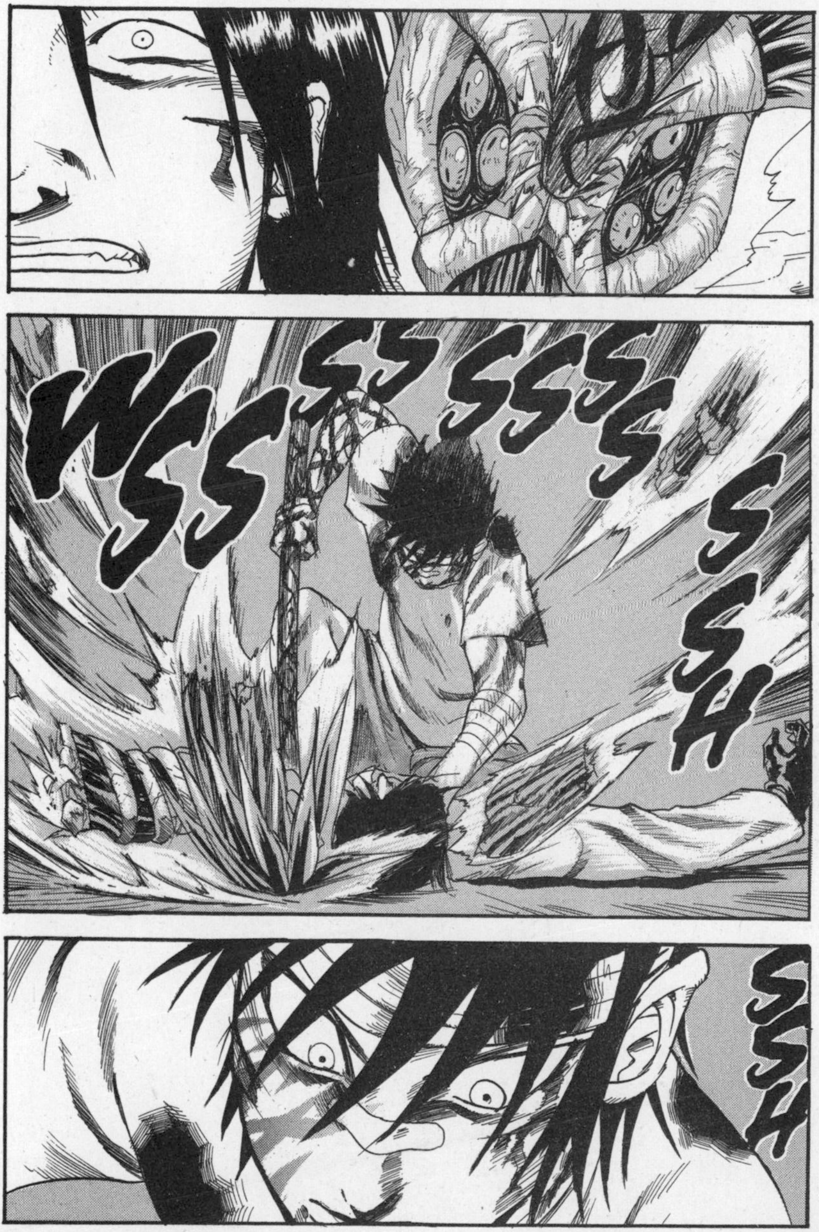
WSSSSSSSSSSH
SSSH

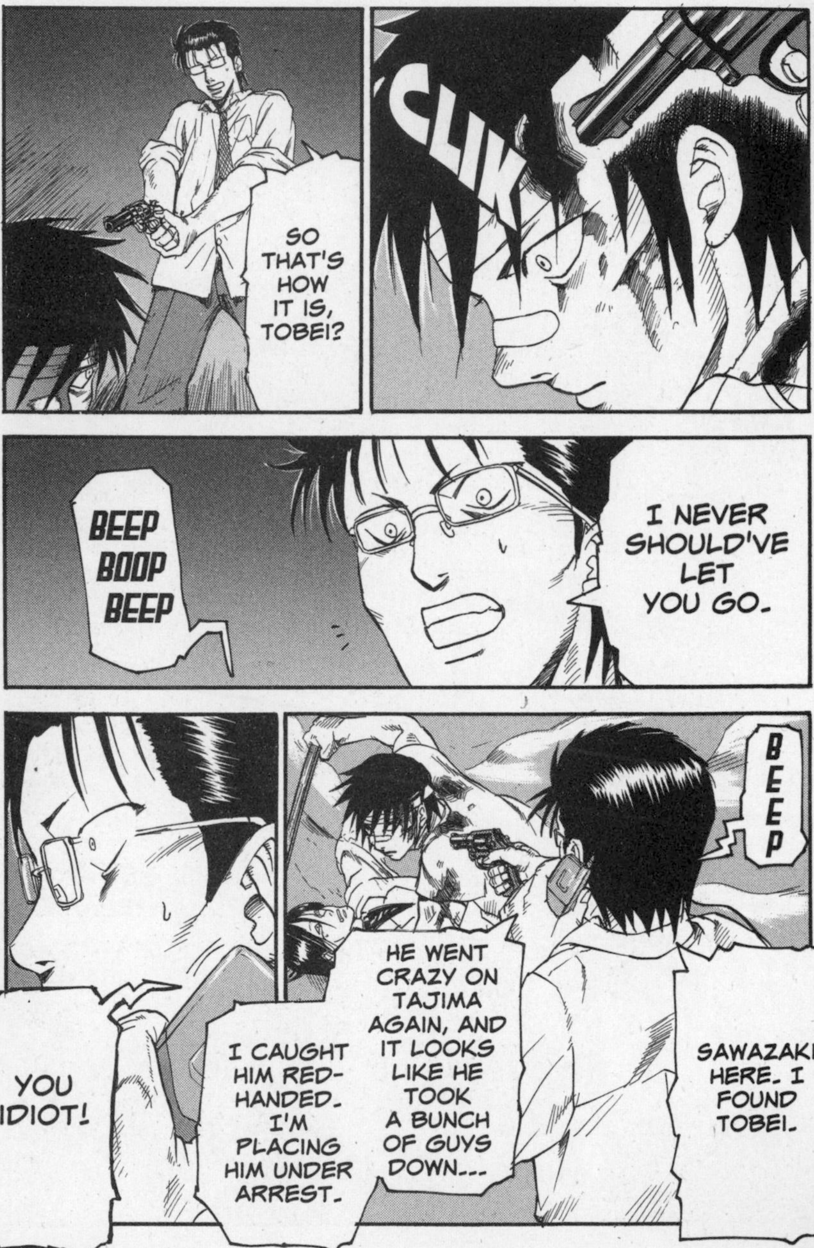
CLIK
SO THAT'S HOW IT IS, TOBEI?
I NEVER SHOULD'VE LET YOU GO.
BEEP BOOP BEEP
BEEP
SAWAZAKI HERE. I FOUND TOBEI.
HE WENT CRAZY ON TAJIMA AGAIN, AND IT LOOKS LIKE HE TOOK A BUNCH OF GUYS DOWN...
I CAUGHT HIM RED-HANDED. I'M PLACING HIM UNDER ARREST.
YOU IDIOT!

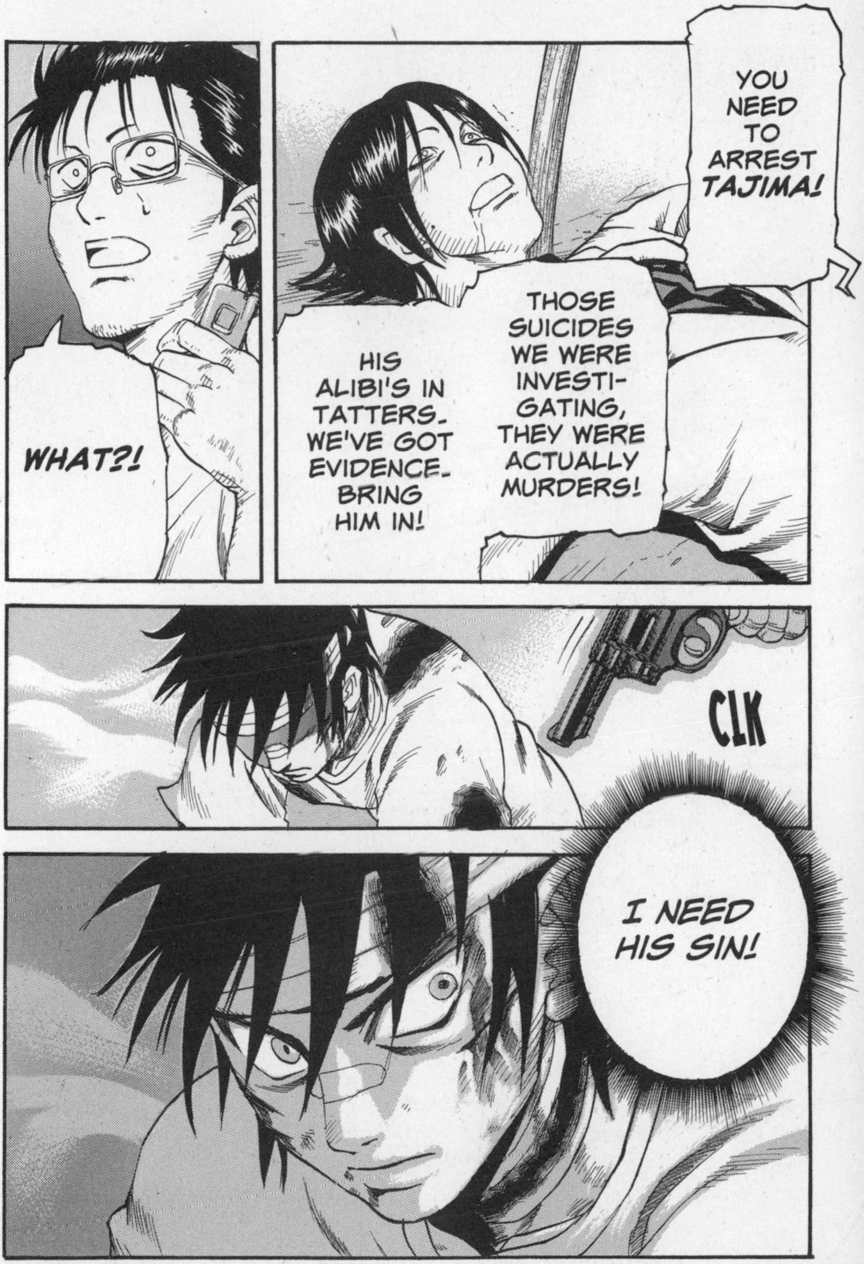
YOU NEED TO ARREST TAJIMA!
THOSE SUICIDES WE WERE INVESTIGATING, THEY WERE ACTUALLY MURDERS!
HIS ALIBI'S IN TATTERS. WE'VE GOT EVIDENCE. BRING HIM IN!
WHAT?!
CLK
I NEED HIS SIN!

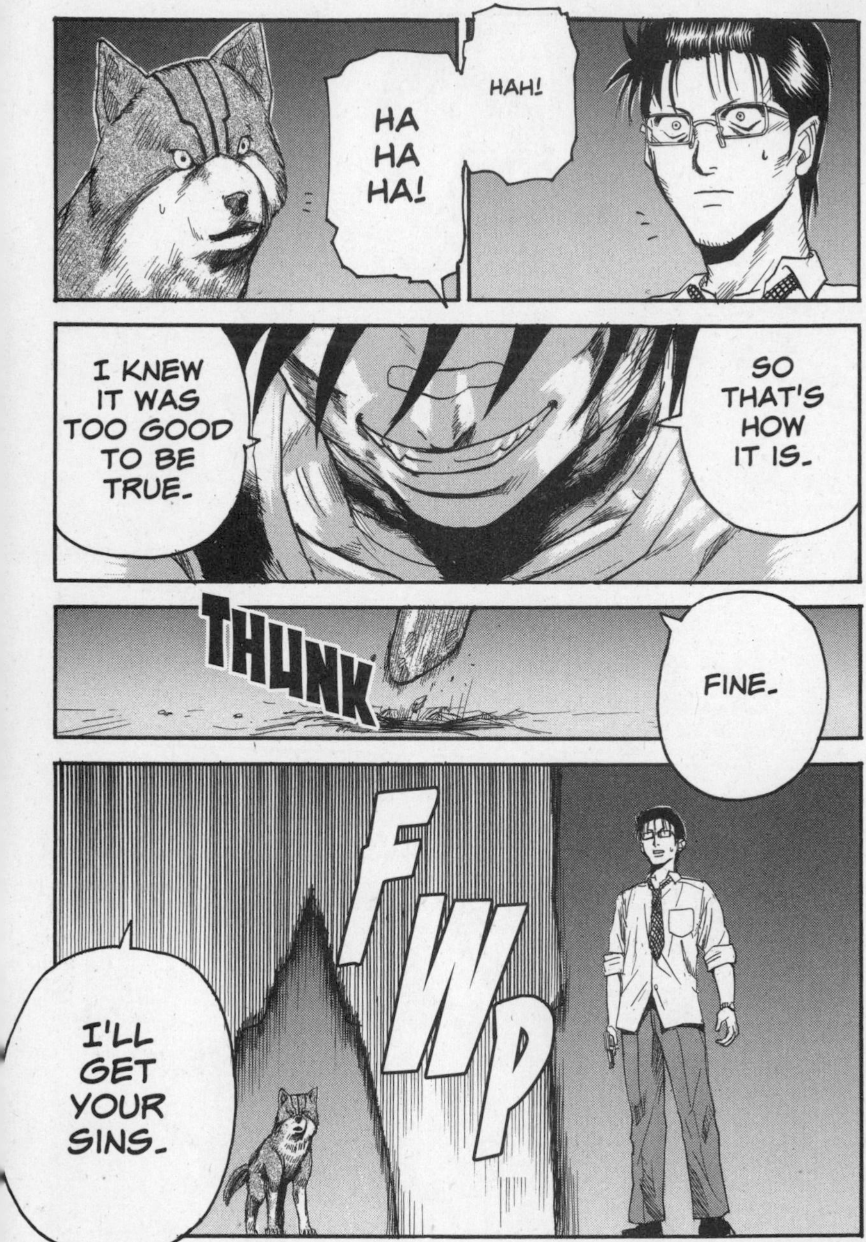
HAH! HA HA HA!
SO THAT'S HOW IT IS.
I KNEW IT WAS TOO GOOD TO BE TRUE.
FINE.
THUNK
FWP
I'LL GET YOUR SINS.

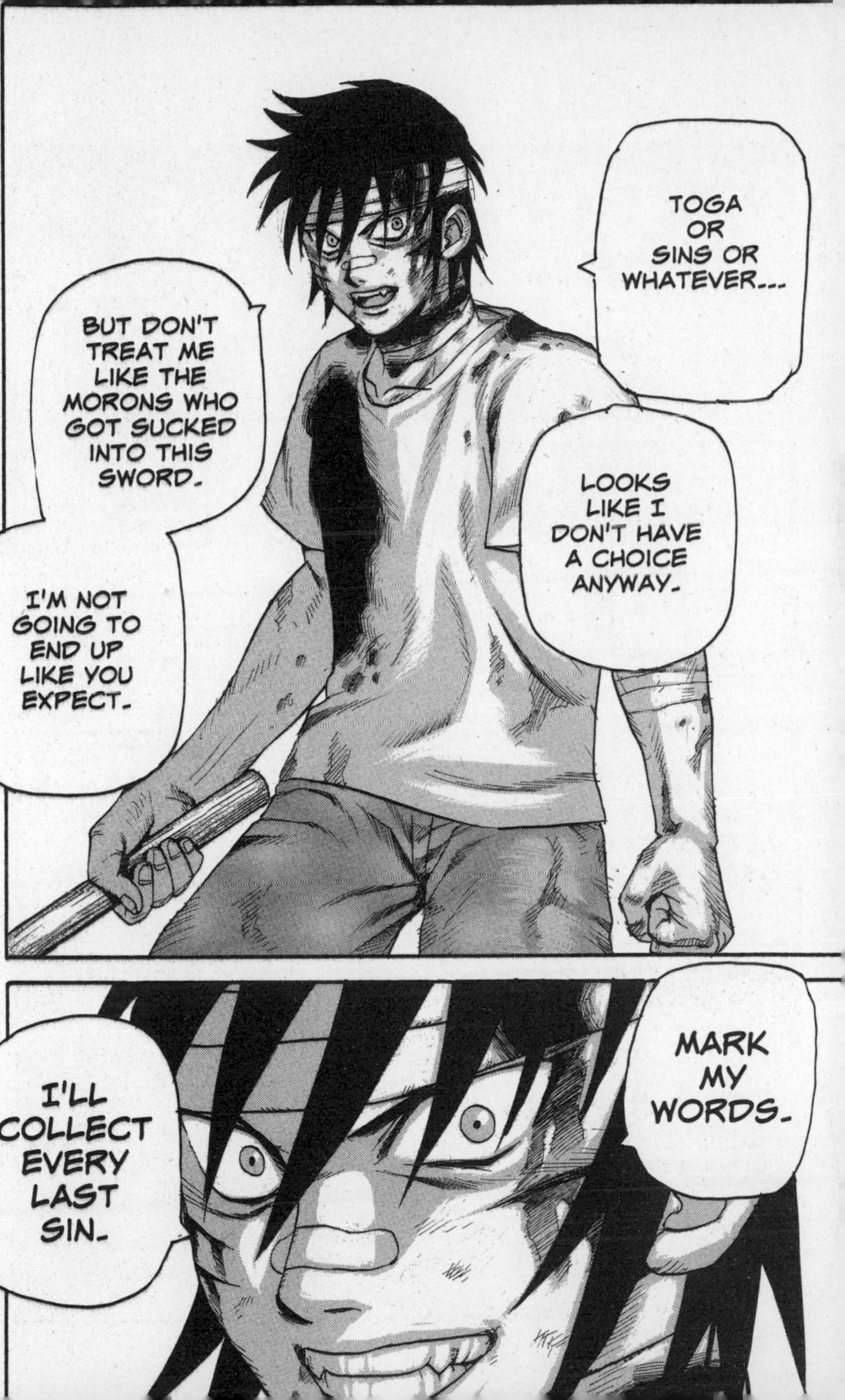
TOGA OR SINS OR WHATEVER...
LOOKS LIKE I DON'T HAVE A CHOICE ANYWAY.
BUT DON'T TREAT ME LIKE THE MORONS WHO GOT SUCKED INTO THIS SWORD.
I'M NOT GOING TO END UP LIKE YOU EXPECT.
MARK MY WORDS.
I'LL COLLECT EVERY LAST SIN.

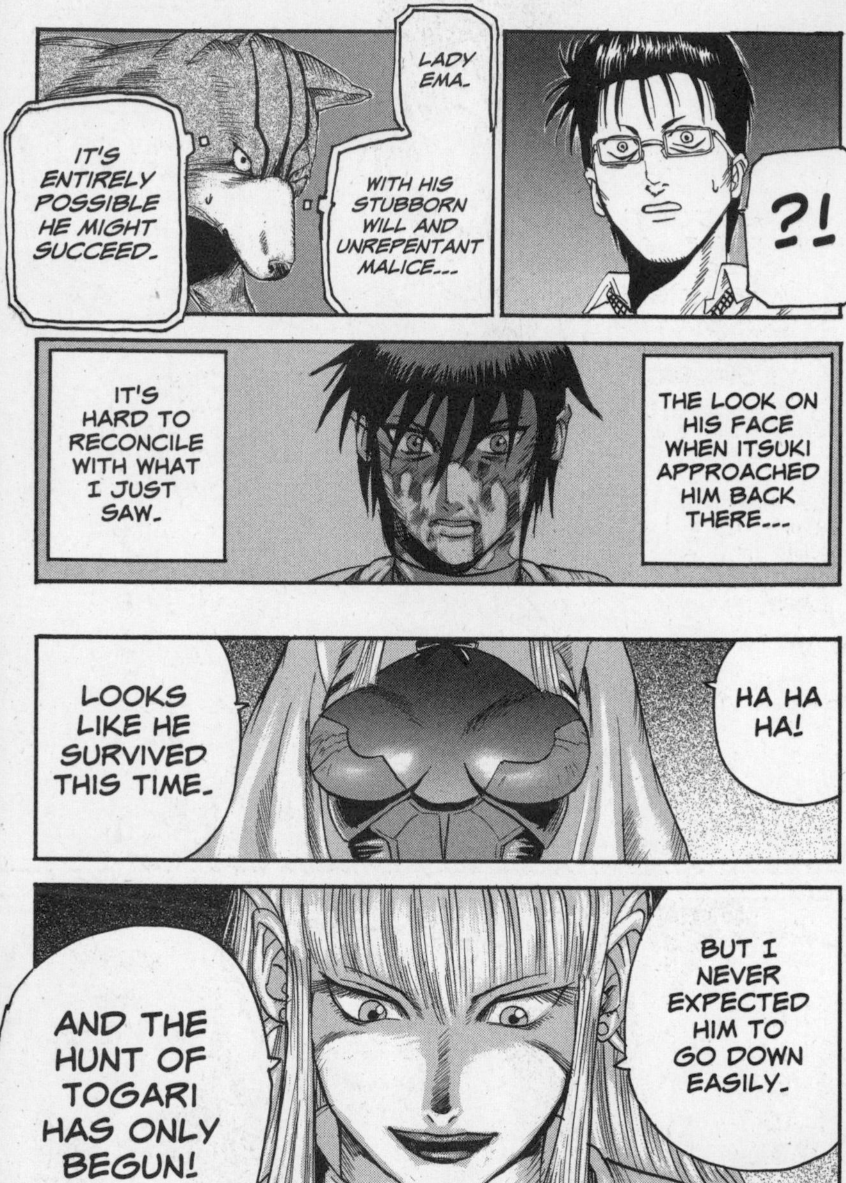
?!
LADY EMA.
WITH HIS STUBBORN WILL AND UNREPENTANT MALICE...
IT'S ENTIRELY POSSIBLE HE MIGHT SUCCEED.
THE LOOK ON HIS FACE WHEN ITSUKI APPROACHED HIM BACK THERE...
IT'S HARD TO RECONCILE WITH WHAT I JUST SAW.
HA HA HA!
LOOKS LIKE HE SURVIVED THIS TIME.
BUT I NEVER EXPECTED HIM TO GO DOWN EASILY.
AND THE HUNT OF TOGARI HAS ONLY BEGUN!

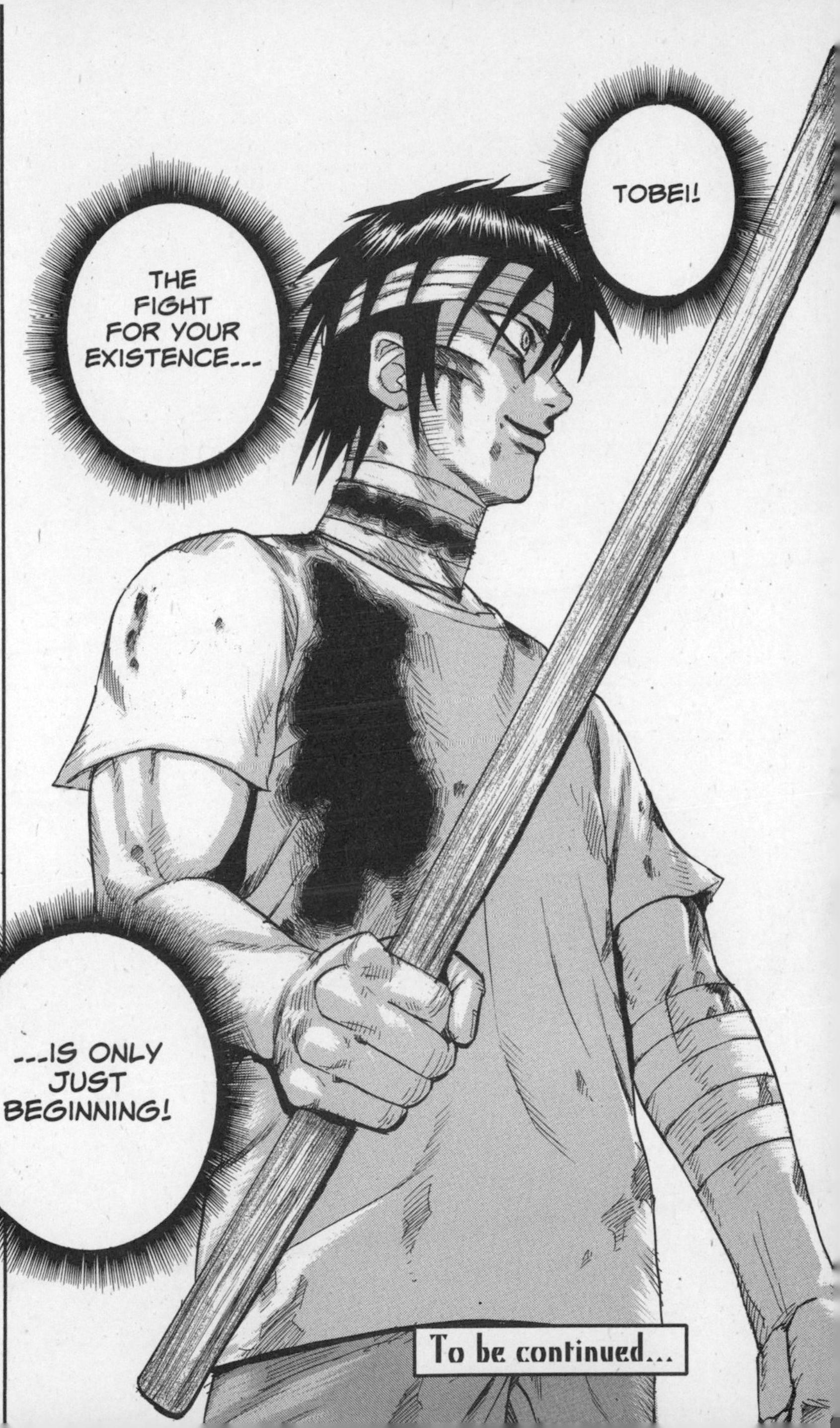
TOBEI!
THE FIGHT FOR YOUR EXISTENCE...
...IS ONLY JUST BEGINNING!
To be continued...

✦✦T⌐O G✦A R⁀I

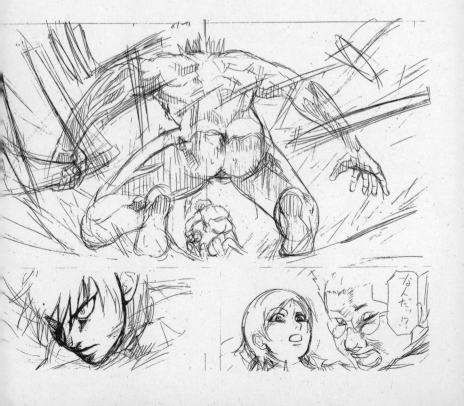

Bonus

The Road to Togari

Thank you for buying this issue of *Togari*. As a sort of present to those of you reading, I thought I'd share some of the drawings I made along the way. When it comes to drawing manga, there aren't any hard and fast rules about style, so what I want readers to take away from these pages is something like, "Ah, that's how he did it." And besides, I had a ton of these drawings lying around anyway!

2000.11.20 Yoshinori Natsume

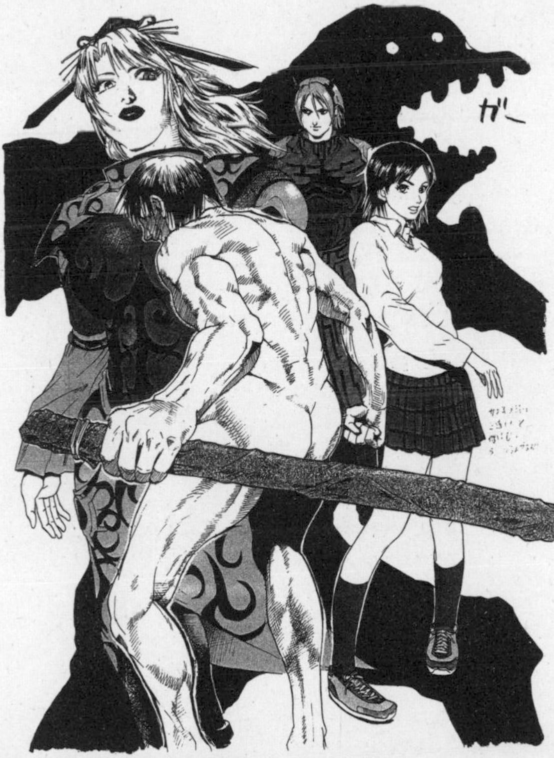
ガー

A rough illustration I did as a joke for a proposed comic short serial. It had been a while since I'd picked up the pen, so if you look closely it's actually pretty off-balance. The designs are all subtly different from how they ended up, too.

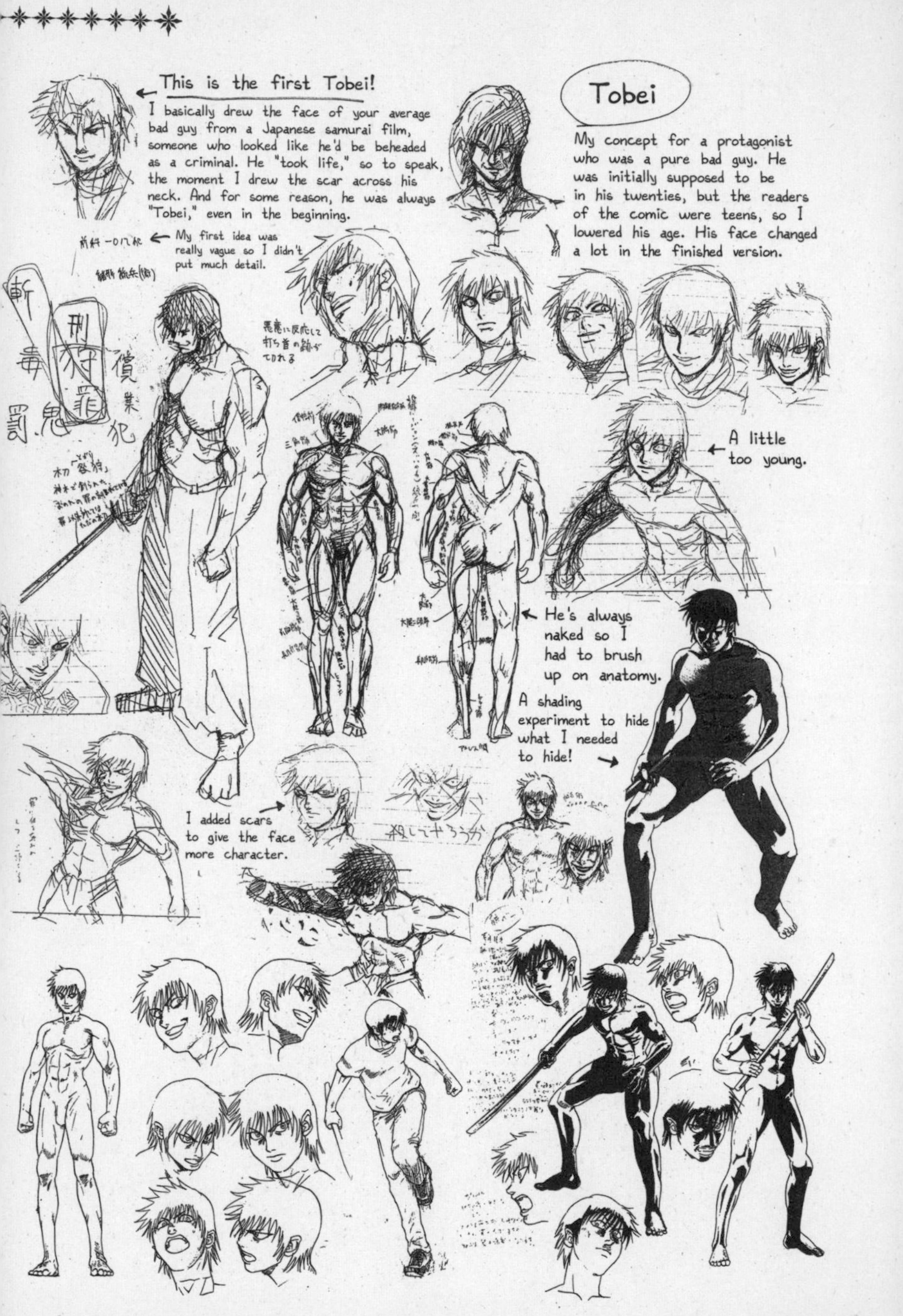
This is the first Tobei!
I basically drew the face of your average bad guy from a Japanese samurai film, someone who looked like he'd be beheaded as a criminal. He "took life," so to speak, the moment I drew the scar across his neck. And for some reason, he was always "Tobei," even in the beginning.
My first idea was really vague so I didn't put much detail.
Tobei
My concept for a protagonist who was a pure bad guy. He was initially supposed to be in his twenties, but the readers of the comic were teens, so I lowered his age. His face changed a lot in the finished version.
A little too young.
He's always naked so I had to brush up on anatomy.
A shading experiment to hide what I needed to hide!
I added scars to give the face more character.

Itsuki

The heroine. Fairly undefined until the very end. I'm notoriously bad at drawing girls, so I did a lot of research reading magazines and stuff. She's my first really feminine girl character.

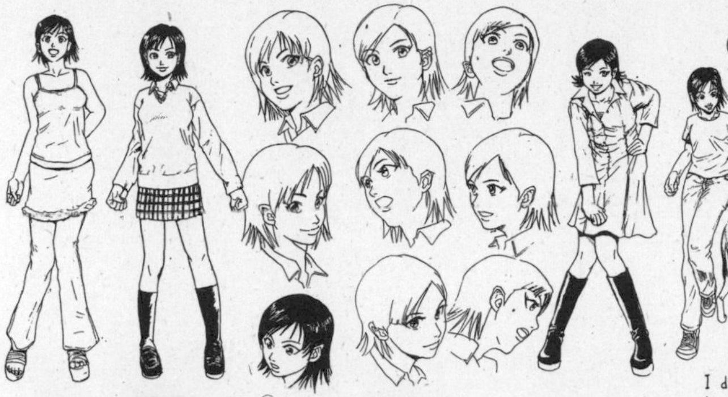

Her hairstyle kept changing right up to the end. I finally settled on this one, a sort of Ai Kato look (an early one). I made the face resemble hers too, but then someone told me it looked too close to Tobei's and I changed it.

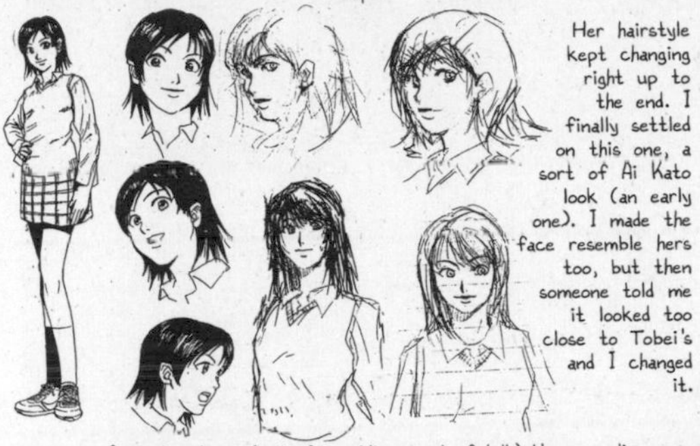

I didn't want to make her someone who needed to be protected, so I gave her a cool and modern look, someone who the readers would be able to sympathize with as she interacted with Tobei.

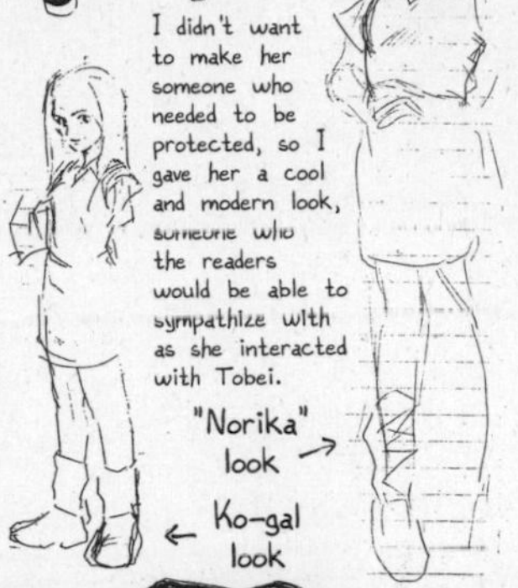

"Norika" look
Ko-gal look

Ose

A guardian demon (sort of a public servant of hell.) He came alive after I decided to make him transform into a dog. Why a dog? Because there was a stone "koma-inu" gargoyle dog at the shrine he first appeared in, but that scene was dropped from the actual comic. His name comes from one of the fallen angels that came to Earth with Lucifer.

This was my first Ose! He was originally intended to be a stereotypical demon but I ended up making him a serious type as a foil to Tobei.

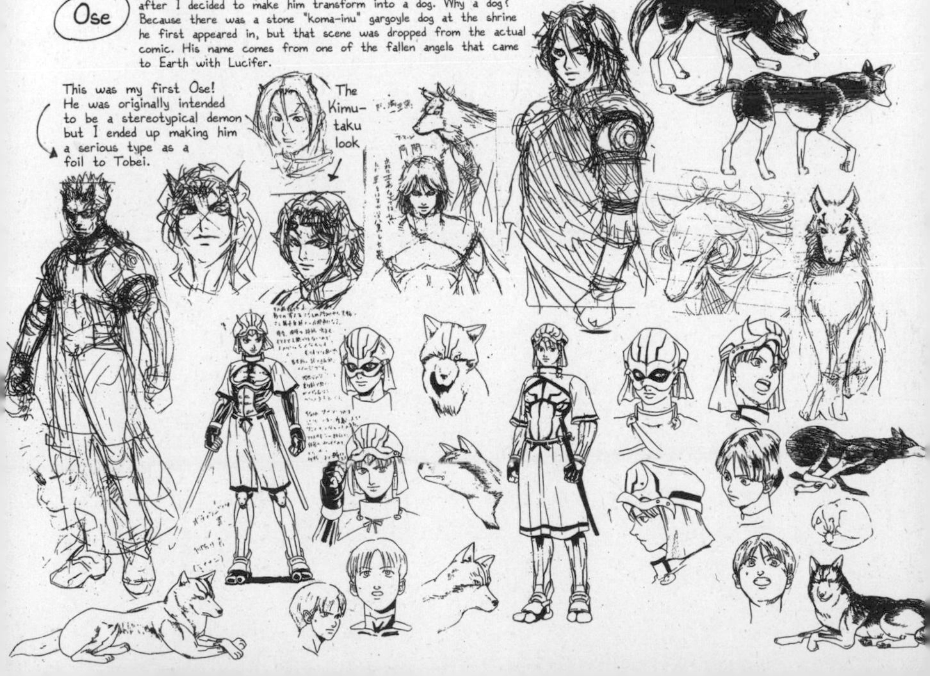

The Kimu-taku look

Lady Ema

I had the image of the Buddhist deity "Enma Daio" in my head, but she ended up turning into a sexy bombshell. At first I was thinking to give her curly hair, but her outfit's kind of Japanese so I made it straight. I didn't want to portray hell as unnecessarily dark so I decided to go as silly as possible.

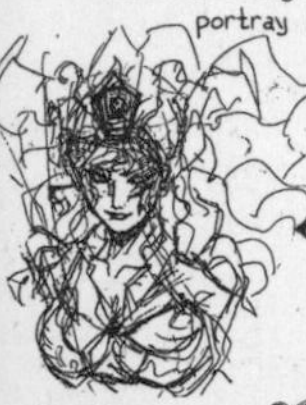

←The first Ema! But she didn't change much.

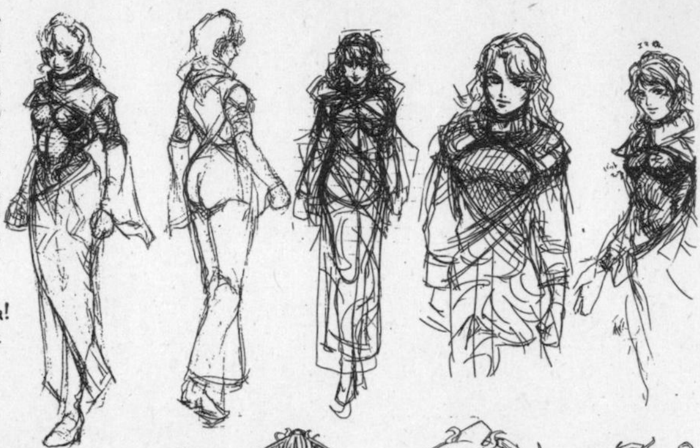

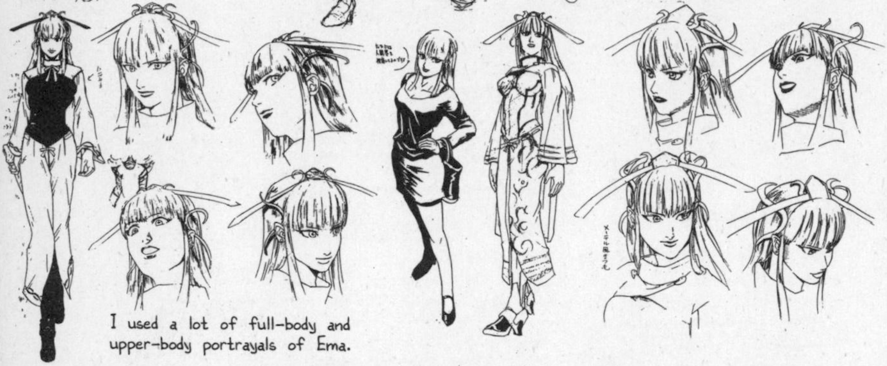

I used a lot of full-body and upper-body portrayals of Ema.

Sawazaki

He never really changed from my first rough drawing. I like drawing angled faces like his, maybe because they resemble my own!

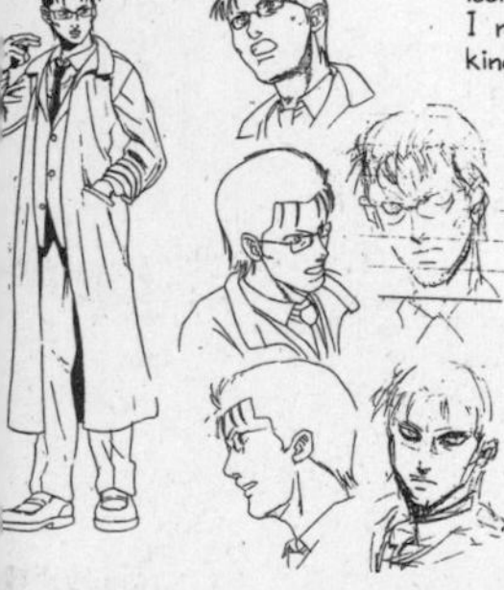

Toga

At first I called them "Sins," but as I kept working the word got on my nerves and so I changed it to Toga. Also, because they're attached to criminals, I tried not to make them look cool. In fact I made them kind of silly.

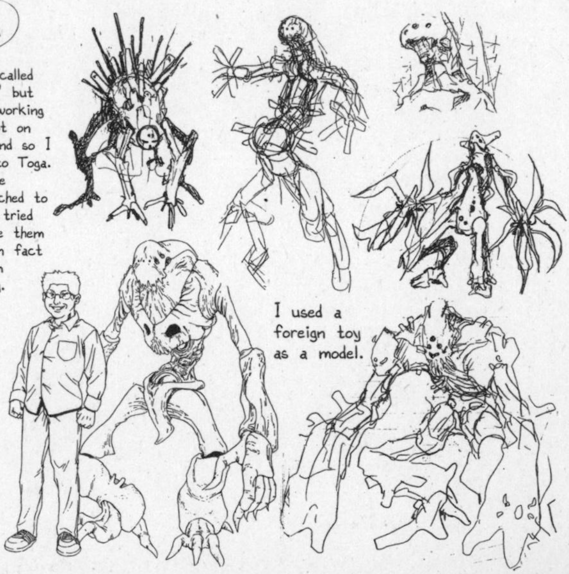

I used a foreign toy as a model.

○ The Mysterious Self-Contained First Story (Layout Only)

The first draft of the story had Tobei fighting not the Toga but rather his OWN sin taken physical form, but I dropped the idea because I realized that wouldn't give him much connection to society. So I decided to have him collect the sins of others instead. It's pretty much summarized by the final line: "This sure beats being in hell!"

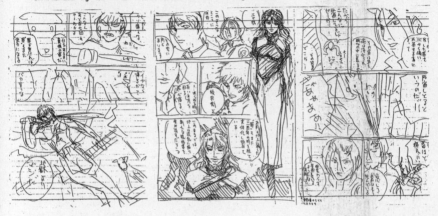

○ Rough Story Drafts (Before the Layout Stage)

When I write stories, I write down the key plot points and characters and arrange them in rough order. Manga have pages, of course, and this is where what unfolds on how many pages is roughly decided. Rather than a "story" per se it's more like a list of scenes and lines. If the plot isn't smoothed out here, the finished product won't be smooth either, and readers will get confused and in the worst case even skip over pages. I use a lot of pages for scenes I really like, then add bridge pages, and try to make it a smooth read.

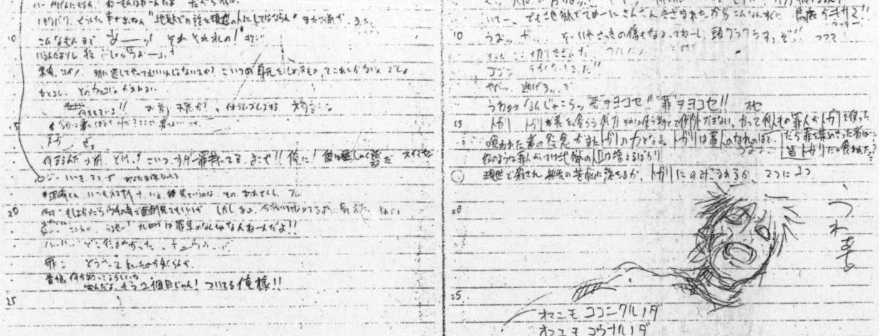

✴ ✴ ✴ ✴ ✴ ✴ ✴ ✴

This caused a lot of hilarity when I showed it to my mentor. It's the legendary 32 panels on one page layout! I split the very first draft into panels, deciding all the drawings, two-page spreads, scene changes, and page changes. Most of the drawings and text are indecipherable except by me. Manga are different from film in that you have to match the pacing to the reader's turning of the page, and even the same drawings will have totally different meanings depending on where on the page they appear, so there's a unique "idiom" to it. This isn't the standard way of paneling a story. It's completely my own thing. I think it's important to come up with methods that suit your own personality. This is mine.

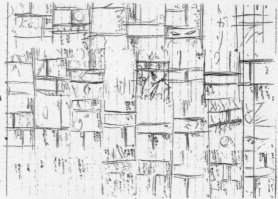

Even after I've sketched out the basic story in my notebook, there can be major changes. So maybe you're thinking, "what's the point of what you did up to now?" Manga is very character-driven, so when you draw in actual gestures and expressions, sometimes you see new story directions and things. Here I'd like to show you some scenes that didn't make it into the comic. I drew way more rough layout pages than made it into the actual comic, so maybe you could say I created a lot of layers to filter the story through before arriving at the rough draft. And even after that I made a lot of changes.

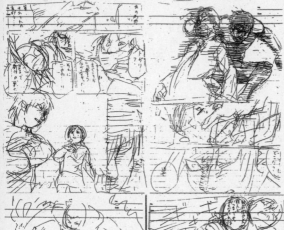

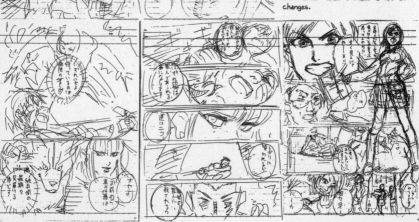

Recently, I don't do this much drawing, I use a really simplified style instead. Drawing this much takes about half a day. Then the layouts go to the editor, I finalize the drawings, and ink them. Then they're done!

SPECIAL THANKS

The serialized chapters (1-6) contained in this first collection were produced in a studio with next to no equipment, and since I didn't even have the resources to hire an assistant, I relied heavily on my friends to get the job done. It's thanks to them that the collection you're holding was completed, and I'd like to use this opportunity to thank them!

I asked way too much of you!

(In no particular order)
Shinya Itagaki
Hisao Inomata
Chiaki Imai
Koichi Kato
Daigo Kato
Akihiro Seki
Haruko Tomitani
Jun Nakayama
Hiroshi Hanawa
Takuya Araki
Yuusuke Watanabe
Masahide Akita
Takuya Morikawa
Nozomi Aoyama
Ichiro Kawano
Miya Kijishima
Akira Yoshimura

(Continuation of series)
Shintaro Kayou
Akihiro Nakamura

Okashira
Seika Hinata

And to everyone who sent fan mail and letters...
THANK YOU VERY MUCH!

Thanks also to all of Togari's readers.
Please keep reading!

YOSHINORI NATSUME

A HERO CAN FIGHT FOR JUSTICE, FIGHT TO PROTECT HIS FAMILY OR A LOVE INTEREST, OR HE CAN EVEN FIGHT FOR WORLD PEACE. BUT TOBEI, THE MAIN CHARACTER OF **TOGARI**, ISN'T THAT TYPE OF CHARACTER. HE'S A RUTHLESS YOUNG MAN WHO'S ONLY LOOKING OUT FOR HIMSELF. AN IMPERFECT HERO, TOBEI IS THROWN INTO THE MODERN WORLD AND ENCOUNTERS STRANGE SITUATIONS AND MEETS NEW PEOPLE. ALL OF YOU READERS AND I WILL WATCH OVER TOBEI ON HIS JOURNEY. WE'LL SEE HOW HE CHANGES AND GROWS. JUST LIKE TOBEI, I'M AN IMPERFECT MANGA ARTIST, BUT THIS IS THE ONLY PATH FOR ME. CREATING MANGA IS ALL I HAVE. **TOGARI** HAS ONLY JUST STARTED—THIS IS WHERE THE REAL BATTLE BEGINS!

ITSUKI ASAGI

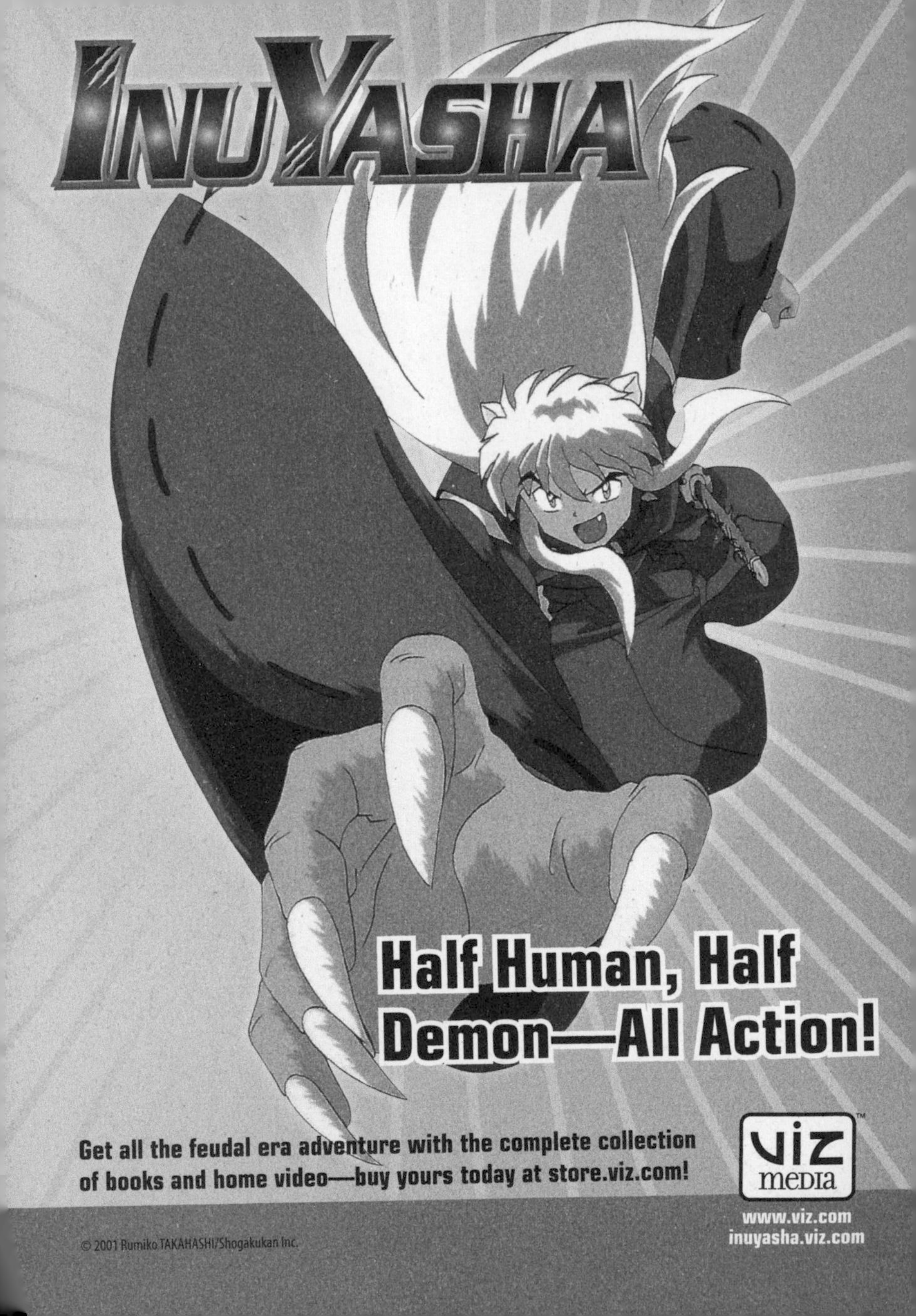
InuYasha
Half Human, Half Demon—All Action!
Get all the feudal era adventure with the complete collection of books and home video—buy yours today at store.viz.com!
viz media
www.viz.com
inuyasha.viz.com
© 2001 Rumiko TAKAHASHI/Shogakukan Inc.

INUYASHA

Read the action from the start with the original manga series

Full color adaptation of the popular TV series

Art book with cel art, paintings, character profiles and more

TV SERIES & MOVIES ON DVD!

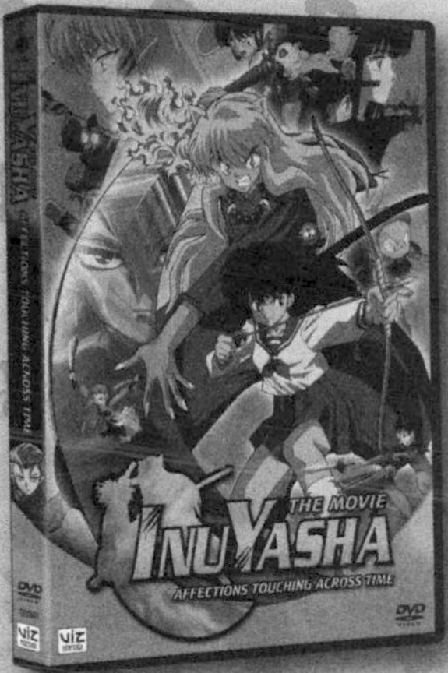
INUYASHA THE MOVIE
AFFECTIONS TOUCHING ACROSS TIME

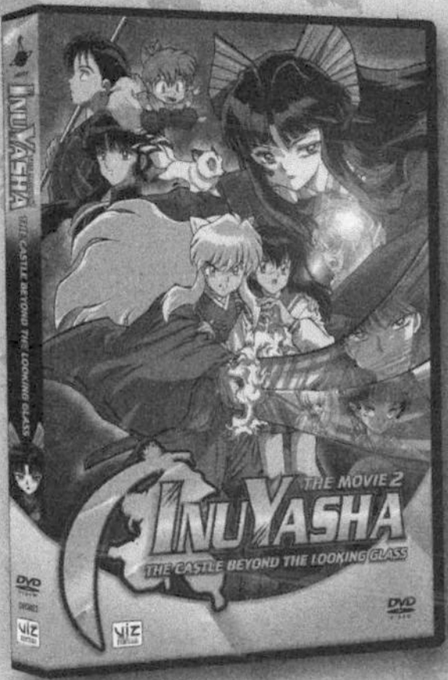
INUYASHA THE MOVIE 2
THE CASTLE BEYOND THE LOOKING GLASS

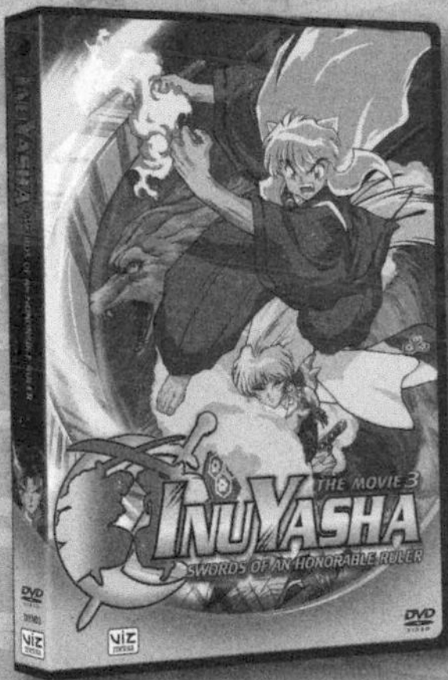
INUYASHA THE MOVIE 3
SWORDS OF AN HONORABLE RULER

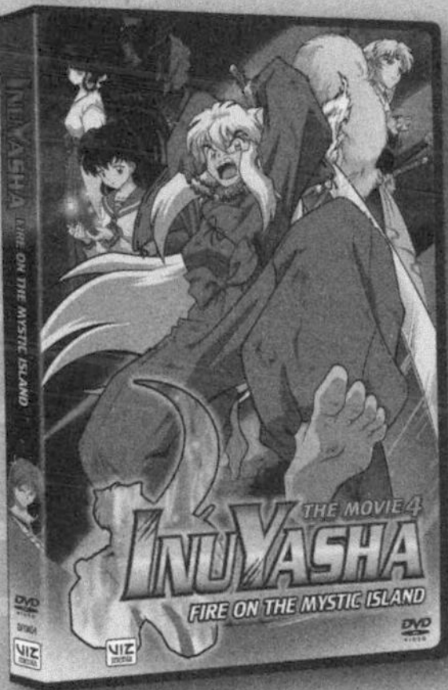
INUYASHA THE MOVIE 4
FIRE ON THE MYSTIC ISLAND

See more of the action in Inuyasha full-length movies

viz media

www.viz.com
inuyasha.viz.com

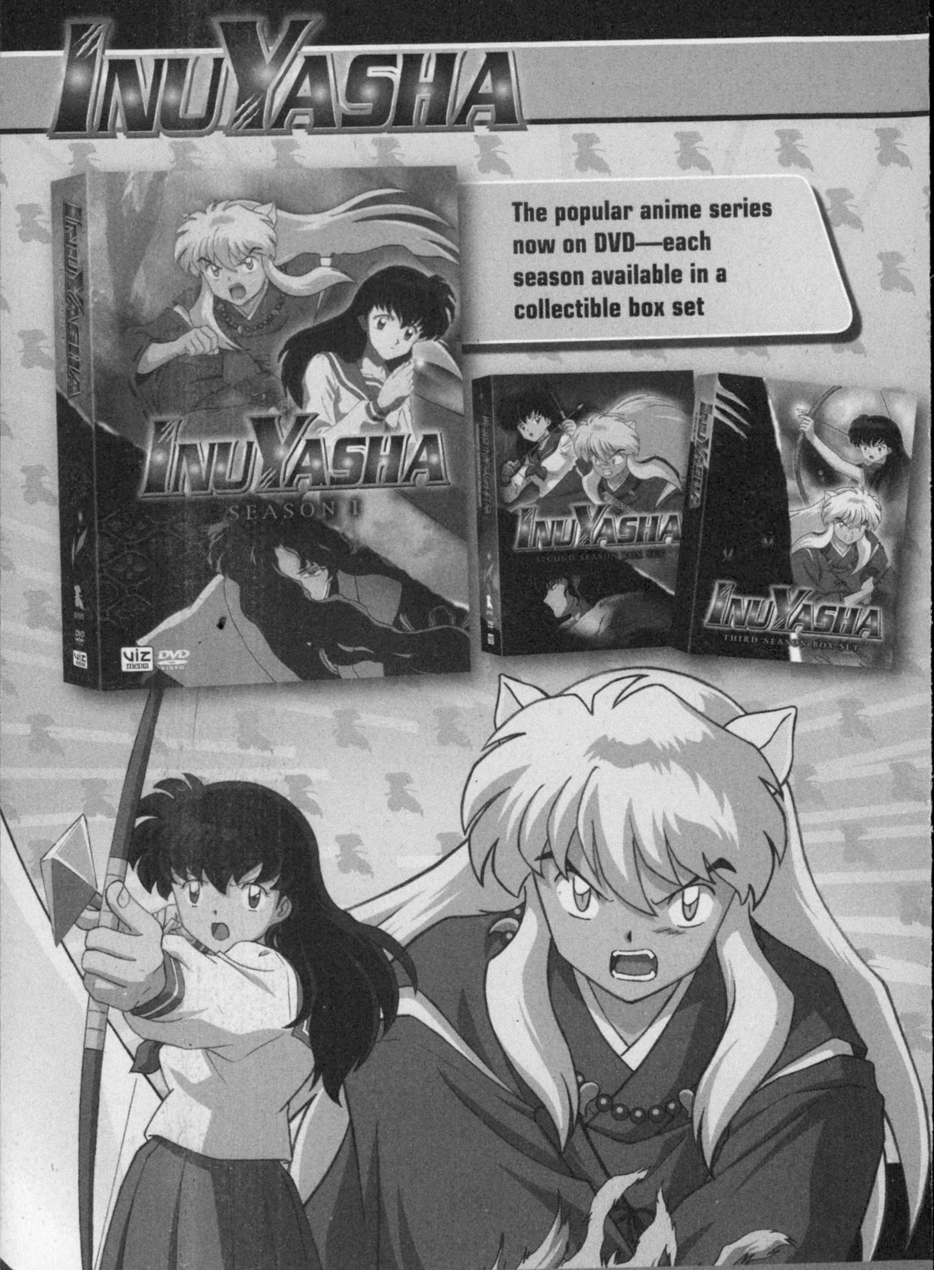
InuYasha
The popular anime series now on DVD—each season available in a collectible box set
InuYasha
SEASON 1
InuYasha
InuYasha
THIRD SEASON BOX SET

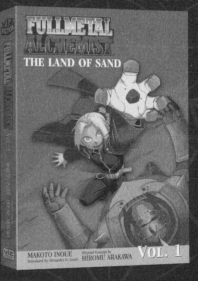

LOVE MANGA?
LET US KNOW WHAT YOU THINK!

OUR MANGA SURVEY IS NOW
AVAILABLE ONLINE. PLEASE VISIT:
VIZ.COM/MANGASURVEY

HELP US MAKE THE MANGA
YOU LOVE BETTER!

VIZ
media